THE HISTORY OF ROANE COUNTY, TENNESSEE 1801-1870

By
EMMA MIDDLETON WELLS

REPRINTED WITH A NEW INDEX
By
Jessica Budick
and
Anita Comtois

CLEARFIELD

Originally Published
Chattanooga, Tennessee
1927

Reprinted with a New Index
Regional Publishing Company
Baltimore, 1975

Reprinted for
Clearfield Company, Inc. by
Genealogical Publishing Co., Inc.
Baltimore, Maryland
1994, 1997

Library of Congress Catalogue Card Number 75-7959
International Standard Book Number 0-8063-8003-9

Copyright © 1975
Regional Publishing Company
Baltimore, Maryland
All rights reserved

Made in the United States of America

PREFACE

This book has been compiled not to exploit the deeds and virtues of a few but to print important records of pioneers of Roane County, Tennessee.

The records show that many of the men who came into the county before the county was organized were Revolutionary soldiers and that their wives in many cases were daughters of soldiers of that War. Many were given land grants for service rendered their country. Some brought their slaves from as far east as Massachusetts. Their wills show that besides land, slaves and stock, they possessed furniture of the best make. Many pieces now in possession of their descendants are of beautiful design. They were mostly people of education as their letters and signatures testify. There have gone out from the county men who have become leaders in the professional and commercial world, Governors of States, Judges of the Supreme Court, Generals in the Army, Presidents of Colleges and leaders in many other walks of life.

The original spelling has been followed in copying the records.

EMMA MIDDLETON WELLS

CONTENTS

PART I.
KINGSTON AND THE COUNTY 9
    Tax List 1802, 1808
    First Licensed Merchants and Hotels
    List of Voters 1809
    Summons for Jury 1809
    Members of Militia Companies 1855
    Justices 1819

PART II.
MILITARY RECORD 27
    Revolutionary Soldiers
    Graves of Revolutionary Soldiers
    Soldiers of War of 1812
    List of First Volunteers of 1812
    Soldiers of Mexican War
    War Between The States
    World War Records
    Gold Star List
    Distinguished Service Crosses

PART III.
CHURCHES, ACADEMY AND LODGE 41
    Post Oak
    Bethel Church
    Rittenhouse Academy
    Kingston Grave Yard
    Masonic Lodge

PART IV.
    MARRIAGE RECORDS 71

PART V.
RECORDS OF EARLY FAMILIES 133

INDEX 309

PART ONE

KINGSTON AND THE COUNTY

A Fort at South West Point was established in 1792 and Gen. John Sevier was stationed there in November by William Blount, Governor of the Territory of the United States South of the Ohio. Gen. John Sevier gave the station its name, South West Point. United States Troops were quartered there until 1817 to prevent incursions from Cherokee Indians into the settlement, when the garrison was moved to a point on the right bank of the Tennessee River, near Washington, Tenn.

October 23, 1799, the Tennessee Legislature passed an act for the establishment of a town, to be known as Kingston, on lands owned by Major Robert King. David Miller, Alexander Carmichael, George Preston, John Smith T., William Lovely, Meriwether Smith and Thomas N. Clark, were appointed commissioners. The act of the Legislature establishing Roane County was passed November 1, 1801. The county at that time extended from Anderson and Knox Counties to the southern boundary of the State, but did not include any territory south of the Holston and Tennessee Rivers.

For Military and Civil purposes the County was divided into six companies commanded by: Thomas Coulter, Richard Oliver, Gray Sims, George Ingram, John Walker, and Hugh Francis.

It is believed that all of these men served in the Revolution. Service of most of them is proved.

In 1802 the population of the county included 275 whites and 137 blacks. Only eight of the whites were unable to write.

Hugh Beatty and John Stone operated Cotton Gins. Mathew Nelson opened a Tavern in 1808. Henry Liggett was a hatter and lived where the Dixie Hotel is now.

Sam Houston, afterwards Governor of Tennessee and Texas, was a clerk in a store in Kingston when he enlisted in the Creek War.

The Court of Pleas and Quarter Sessions was organized December 20, 1801, at the home of Hugh Beatty and the following qualified as magistrates: William White, Samuel Miller, Hugh Nelson, Paul Harelson, Zacheus Ayers, George Preston,

THE HISTORY OF ROANE COUNTY

William Campbell, James Preston, Isham Cox, William Barnett, George McPherson, and Abraham McClelland.

Zacheus Ayers was appointed Entry Taker; Jacob Jones, Surveyor; George McPherson, Ranger, the constables were: Francis Lea, Robert Kirkpatrick, and Patrick Burrus; Thomas Brown was collector of the District Tax.

The Circuit Court was organized on the first Monday in March 1811, by James Trimble, Judge of the Second Judicial Court.

The first Grand Jury was composed of John Givens, James Todd, Jesse White, William Waller, Samuel Hays, Thomas Rayburn, Jacob Warren, Jacob (or James) Robinson, Nicholas Nail, John McKinney, Thomas Ogden, Asa Cobb, John Rector, Henry McPherson and George Cross.

Chancery Court was organized at Kingston, October 21, 1824, for the District including the counties of Knox, Anderson, Morgan, Rhea, Roane, Hamilton, Campbell, McMinn, Monroe, and Blount, by John Catron, Judge of the Supreme Court of Tennessee.

The Legislature appointe Hugh Nelson, John Smith T, Alexander Carmichael, William Barnett, Paul Harelson, and Zacheus Ayers, commissioners to erect the Court House which was finished in 1803. The present Court House was built in 1853.

The General Assembly of Tennessee was held in Kingston, September 21, 1807 and adjourned to meet in Knoxville September 23, 1807.

In a treaty made with the Indians they had reserved a mile square in the fork of the rivers. Kingston had been laid out and houses were being erected around the reservation and there were hopes that the capitol of the state would be erected here. The whites wanted the mile square reservation. The Indians agreed to the sale, but had the cause thereof stated in the deed. The commissioners said they had no right to contract that the capitol should be built here, but assured the Indian Chief, Tullentuskie, that the legislature should be convened there. It was for this reason that the legislature met here, but adjourned next day to Knoxville, alleging it was for want of a suitable hall and room. This was not the truth, as a matter of course, because the courthouse was finished the year before. The truth is, it was merely a trick played upon the Indians in order to negotiate the purchase of the reservation.

THE HISTORY OF ROANE COUNTY

Kingston was an important point as early as 1800, with a Military Post at South West Point within a mile of the town and the stage route from Nashville to Washington passing through. It was the stopping place for Andrew Jackson, John Sevier and other men of importance. Bishop Asbury tells of stopping in 1801 at the home of Thomas N. Clark "which was a comfortable home with open fires in the upstairs bed rooms."

General Sevier always stopped at the home of Thomas N. Clark which stood near the big spring. His house was part of the block house built by General Sevier in 1792.

There were two taverns in the town, Alexander's occupied the site of the present Exchange Hotel and stood back from the street in the brick ell. Dr. John W. Wester remodeled the building in 1850 making it as it stands today. It was here that General Andrew Jackson always stopped. The other tavern stood a block and a half up the street from the Alexander Tavern and was the place of meeting of the Legislature in September 1807.

The County today has a fine system of highways, with flourishing towns supplied with good churches, schools, banks, newspapers, manufacturing plants, large iron and coke industries- and is one of the largest peach and strawberry centers in the State. Roane County has one of the best public health units in the State.

In the Spring of 1797 Prince Louis Philippe, later King of France, and his brothers Comte de Montpensier and Comte de Beaujolair, on their journey from Knoxville, where they had been entertained by Gov. John Sevier, to Nashville, stopped at South West Point (Kingston) and visited the site of a proposed Fort and the remains of prehistoric brestworks. Tradition says that some of the Indian Chiefs, among them Tulantuski who lived where Rockwood now stands, joined the party of distinguished visitors and the company drank at the Big Spring. The Princes were entertained at the home of Judge David Campbell. Thomas Norris Clark gave and deeded to Kingston this Big Spring early in 1880. It furnishes many gallons of good water each day.

The County was named for Archibald Roane, who was born in Pennsylvania 1759, coming to Tennessee in 1778. He was admitted to the Tennessee Bar at Jonesboro and Greeneville 1788 and the same year was appointed Attorney General of the district of Hamilton. He was a member of the Constitutional convention 1796, and was elected, one of the Superior Judges when the State was organized. He was elected the

THE HISTORY OF ROANE COUNTY

second Governor of Tennessee without opposition in 1801. During his administration the state was divided into three congressional districts, Washington, Hamilton and Mero. Knoxville was the Capitol of the State. He was reappointed a Superior Judge in 1815 which office he held until his death in 1819. He never lived in Roane County but was Governor when the County was erected.

BATTLE AT CRAB ORCHARD

The Soldiers stationed at the Garrison at South West Point were a great protection to the early settlers against the invasion of the Indians. On August 13, 1792 Lieut. McClellan, with thirty seven of Captain Evan's Company was attacked on the Cumberland road near Crab Orchard by about one hundred Indians. After twice repelling the warriors he was compelled to retreat with a loss of four men killed, Paul Cunningham, Daniel Hitchcock, William Flemming and Stephen Renfro. Abraham Byrd who was wounded and four others who were missing arrived at South West Point afterwards. William Lea, one of the number missing had been captured by the Indians, but escaped and reached the garrison on the 18th.

EARLY NEWSPAPERS

The first Newspaper published in Roane County was the Kingston Gazette and Register by N. A. Patterson in 1855.

Charles F. Brause established the "Daily News" in 1877 but after a few months' publication sold it to the Rev. G. W. Coleman who changed it to "The "Independent" and moved it to Maryville. In 1880 John J. Littleton began to publish a democratic newspaper "The Cyclone" which afterwards was bought by Hood Haggard, the name changed to "The Patriot" and politics to republican. Col. D. M. Coffman started "The Roane County Republican" in 1880.

EARLY LAWYERS

Early attorneys of the County were James, John and Andrew McCampbell, J. W. M. Brazeale, James Hope, J. Y. Smith, James Trimble, Thomas N. Clark, Samuel L. Childress, George L. Burk, James Sevier, E. E. Young, S. C. Clark.

EARLY COUNTY OFFICERS

Tht first clerks of the County were Henry Brazeale, who served thirty four years, H. H. Wiley, Austin L. Green, James T. Shelley, James Sturgess.

THE HISTORY OF ROANE COUNTY

The first Sheriffs were John Brown, who served twenty-three years, Robert Gilliland, Joseph Byrd, Lewis Burris, Ed. McDuffy.

Early Trustees were Isham Cox, W. C. McKamey, William Gilbreath, Thomas McConnell, William Work, George Yost, Robert Marney, J. W. McNutt.

Early Registers were John Stose, John McEwen, Henry Burris, H. H. Wiley, Robert Duncan, John A. Patton, John H. Taylor, Robert Allison, Walter H. King, G. A. Guenther, S. D. Standfield, Thomas Childress.

George Gordon and Robert Cravens built an iron furnace on Whites Creek which was called Eagle Furnace in 1828. They manufactured charcoal, pig iron, cooking utensils and other cast iron products which were shipped by boat to Chattanooga and Knoxville.

In 1867 the Roane Iron Co., was organized by Gen. J. T. Wilder, Capt. H. S. Chamberlain and Major W. A. Rockwood for whom the town was named. The company built two churches near the furnace, one for the whites, and the other for blacks. Coal was first discovered in 1840 by William Green an employe of Gen. John Brown. Green and William Brown soon entered the land and began mining the coal for local use. From the time the furnaces were started they did not stop day or night for fifty years.

PROPERTY TAXES RETURNED TO COURT 1802

(It was the duty of the Captain to collect the Taxes).

Richard Armstrong, Martin Armstrong, Robert Armstrong, Robert Bell, William Copeland, James DeArmond, Arthur Gilbreath, Heirs of George Doherty, George Ingram, William L. Lewis William Murphy, William Tyrtll, Robert Miller, James M. Lewis, Alexander Outlaw, George Waller, Robert White, John Wear, Thomas King, Edward Waller, John Smith T., Lewis Tiner, 1803-06 Jacob Brazelton. Thomas Gallaher, Thomas J. Van Dyke, William Black, James Blair, William Blair, Samuel McCall, Thomas Shelly, William Barnett, Jefferson Campbell, James Willet.

The merchants who paid taxes in 1805 and the first on record were:

James Jones and Richard Meredith	$ 25.00
James McNutt and Co.	25.00
James Willet	25.00
William McNutt	25.00

THE HISTORY OF ROANE COUNTY

John McEwen and Co.	$ 25.00
Hugh Beatty	25.00
William Black	25.00
Charles Milbanks	25.00
Cox and White	25.00
1806 Samuel Martin	25.00
1807 Thomas N. Clark	25.00

Sept. 18, 1808 Eli Talbut and Jacob Peck Esquires were admitted to the Bar.

Jesse McPherson, John Farnwalt and David Bailey were appointed Constables.

1807 the first licenses were issued to Ordinary (Inn) Keepers, who were Nelson, Smith and King, John Dowler, Josiah and John Nichols, John Eblen, John Stone, Jeremiah Buchanan, John Formwalt, Michael Arnold, John Love.

1808 Licenses were issued to B. F. Brazeale, Samuel Waddy, John Matlock, Moses Rawlings, Robert Caldwell. The Tax was $5.00 per year.

1806 Joseph Hardin paid tax on 200 acres.

In 1805 the following paid taxes:

Charles McClung	1575	acres
John Rhea	1750	acres
Richard Price	2500	acres
William Black	1000	acres
William Barnett	1000	acres
John Sterling	1000	acres
John Smith T.	42,000	acres
Anthony Street	15,000	acres

1803 Benjamin Roebuck, Samuel McCall, Jesse Dolozier.
1806 Joseph Hardin 200 acres on Clinch River.

ORDINARY KEEPERS (INN) IN 1812

Mathew Nelson, John Eblen, Gailbreath Barton, Abner Stout, John Loyd, David Haley, Richard Mtredith, Gideon Morgan, Samuel Eldridge, Thomas Childress, George Jack, Walter King.

LICENSE TO HOLD SHOWS IN 1812-1813

Dawson and Pardee, Peter Green.

EARLY MINISTERS

Thomas Brown, William Eagleton, Micaja Sellers, Charles Galloway, Henry Seward, Samuel Deatheridge, Samuel Harwell, Robert Hooper, James Mitchell, John Winton, William Magill, Darius Hoyt, Samuel Lvles, Elisha Turner, David Flemming, John Pope, William Pope.

THE HISTORY OF ROANE COUNTY

CAPT. JOHN WALKER'S CO. 1802

David Bartley, Nichodemus Barnes, John W. Burns, Isaac Brock, Reuben Brock, William Barnet, Philip Bashears, Thomas Capshaw, Robert Duncan, John Donnely, William Evans, James Garner, William Gardenhire, John Givens, Benjamine Greyson, Francis Johnston, John Kirk, Moses Looney, Andrew Lower, Francis Lee, Robert McCorkle, Roland McKinney, James Miller (Squarebottom), John McCain, Daniel Mason, Alexander Maughan, Nathaniel Mason, Samuel Miller, Nicholas Nail, John Neal, Elias Roberts, Thomas Robinson, Thomas Reece, John Sterling, Thomas Shye, Lewis Tiner, John Wear, Capt. James Walker.

CAPT. HUGH FRANCE'S CO. 1802

Zacheus Ayers, Jesse Blackwell, Hugh Beatty, Thomas Brown, Thomas Braley, Valentine Butler, Jesse Byrd, William Byrd, Jacob Clemmons, Micaja Carter, Alexander Cazey, Thomas N. Clark, William Coldwell, John Cotter, John Dudley, Azariah David, Jenkins David, David David, Owen David, Woodson Francis, Hugh Francis, Joseph Francis, Robert Houston, John Hackett, Sr., Joseph Henderson, Dickinson Hall, Joseph Hankens, Joseph Horton, Julias Hacker, William Henry, Jacob Jones, Thomas Jenkins, Peter King, Julias Klark, John Mckinney, James McClanehan, Thomas McMullen, Robert McCannon, John McKinney, Amos Marney, William Miller, Samuel McCall, William McDowell, John O'Neal, John Pembleton, William Peters, Rite Roberts, Stephen Rice, William Rorex, Zacheus Roberts, Isaac Shnall, John Sherky, Alexander Scott, John Stone, Davis Stockton, Allen Sneed, Anthony Street, Merreweather Smith, John Smith, Rubin Smith, James Thomas, Joseph Work, Joshua Washburn.

CAPT. RICHARD OLIVER'S CO. 1802

Joseph Anderson, Richard Allen, William Anderson, Patrick Burns, John Birdwell, Robert Burk, Nathaniel B. Buckingham, Alexander Brown, Robert Brown, Thomas Brown, William Brown, Henry Brazeal, Thomas Brady, David Bailey, Wilie Blount, William Campbell, Esq., Richard Cavett, John Crafton, Samuel Eblen, Jesse Eldridge, John Fulton, Francis Fulcher, Alexander Gamble, James Galloway David Henly, George Henshaw, Jesse Henshaw, Benjamine Henshaw, James Hankins, John Hankins, Daniel Hare, Paul Harelson, Esq., John Hugins, William Kitchen, Joseph Looney,

THE HISTORY OF ROANE COUNTY

George Light, Henry Landers, James McIntire, William Matlock, John Matlock, Henry Miller, James Miller, John Miller, James McNeel, Jason Matlock, Charles McClung, Nicholas Mansfield, Hugh McIntire, Robert Miller, Robert Miller, Jr., William Miller, James Morris, James Moore, George Moore, William Prewet, George Preston, John Rhea, James Rogers, William Ramsey, Cumberland Rector, Thomas Shoy, Jesse Stubs, Thomas Stafford, Reuben Simmons, John Thomas, Ephriam Walker, Thomas Walker, John Walker.

CAPT. GRAY SIMS' CO. 1802.

Robert Brashears, Isaac Brashears, Benjamine Blackburn, Jonathan Clenny, Thomas Carnes, James Caldwell, Peter Couch, Edward Davis, Benjamine Evans, Solomon Geren, James Glasgow, William Hueston, William Hogan, Henry Harmon, Thomas Jones, Robert Kirkpatrick, John Luster, William Luster, James Luster, 'George McPherson, Joseph McPherson, Solomon Mazer, Alexander Miller, David McGee, Abraham McClellan Esq., Edward Owen, Jeremiah Pate, John Parker, Clemmons Phillips, Jeffrey Potter, Joseph Robinson, James Robinson, Evan Shoemaker, William Shoemaker, Robert Shaddon, Adam Sherrel, Thomas Usury, Phillip Usury, James Whitson, John White.

CAPT. GEORGE INGRAM'S CO. 1802

Joshua Ashmore, Hugh Barton, William Curden, Aza Cobb, Jacob Cobb, John Davis, John Finley, David Gallaher, Thomas Gallaher, Solomon Greer, James Gibson, Alexander Howard, Elijah Hix, Allen Henson, Josiah Jent, Hugh Johnston, William Looney, James Mitchell, John Means, James Means, Samuel Oxshear, John Otter, Nathan Robinson, Joshua Renfro, William Standifer, Nathan Sullens, William White, Sr., Samuel White, Wesley Walker, William White, Jr., William Toomy.

CAPT. THOMAS COULTER'S CO. 1802

Robert Allison, James Blair, Darius Browder, John Brazelton, Peter Barger, Jacob Brazelton, William Black, Solomon Brewer, John Brown, Robert Brown, John Berford, John Browder, Jacob Cook, John Carmichael, William Cannon, James Copeland, Milton Center, Isham Cox, Judge David Campbell, Alexander Coulter, Jr., Daniel Derosset, Britton Davis, Brazzel Davis, William Davis, William Davidson, Nathan Eldridge, Simeon Eldridge, Thomas Eldridge, Josiah Elliott, Benjamine Flat, John Flat, Reece Gullick, Jacob

THE HISTORY OF ROANE COUNTY

Gardenhire, James Gilliland, Miars Gaspen, Henry Hartley, Spencer Haynes, James Hope, John Jones, Jared Hotchkiss, Eskridge Kenner, William Lampkins, William Long, Britain Mathis, Archalas Mathis, James McElwee, Daniel McPhail, Thomas Moore, Edward McFaddin, Samuel McSpaddin, Mathew Nelson, Benjamin Prater, James Preston, Richard Price, Daniel Rather, James B. Rogers, Andrew Richey, Nicholas Starnes, David Stuart, John Sutton, Willis Stockton, William Sherald, William Valance, John Warren, John Winton.

TAX LIST OF ROANE CO. MAY 10, 1808

Free Holders in Captain Wallis' Company.

John Birdwell
Rueben Brock
Robert Berk
Joshua Birdwell
Richard Cavit
James Cunningham
John Eblen
John Easley
Daniel Grub
Henry Riddle
William Punt
Weight Roberts
Thomas Rebourn
William Waller

Joseph Hankins
Benjamin Hardin
Thomas Hood
John Hood
William Holland
Henry Lauders
Jason Matlock
John Matlock
James Morrow
John Pickle
Jesse Stubbs
James Todd
James Thomas

CAPTAIN LEWELLEN'S COMPANY

Bazzle Bashears
Thomas N. Clark
John Formatt Jr.
Arthur Handley
Julius Hacker
James Moore
William D. Nelson

Meriweather Smith
John Wadly
David Patton
James Gorden
Adam Formatt
James Cain

CAPTAIN MCCORKLE'S COMPANY 1808

Michael Arnold
Joshua Christenbury
Robert Duncan
John Davis
Francis Erwin
William Evens

Thomas Galliher
James Galliher
John Givens
William Gardenhire
Alexander Howard
John Hickey

THE HISTORY OF ROANE COUNTY

Joseph Gilbreath
James Johnston
Andrew Lawer
Alexander Mahan
Rawling McKinny
John McGill
John Nail
Nicholas Nail
Jesse Rather
Thomas Reed
William White, Sr.
Robert Williams

Allen Hinson
G. W. Geen Henson
Samuel Miller
Robert McNeeley
Joseph Moore
John McKinny
Samuel Ashire
Gambal Richards
George Richards
John White
Samuel White
William White, Jr.

CAPTAIN BAKER'S COMPANY 1808

Jacob Anthony
Michael Baker.
David Baily
Benjamine F. Brageale
Isaac Baily
John Davis
John Flat
Thomas McMullen
James McMullen
James Morris
Isaac Morris
Cumberland Rector

William Erwin
John Fulton
Robert Gambal
James Hankins
John Hays
Thomas Littleton
William Matlock, Jr.
David M. Roberts
Amos Marney
Robert Man
Thomas Walker

CAPTAIN RATHER'S COMPANY

William Blair
Darius Browder
James Blair
Brien Breeden
John Brazelton
John Browder
Sterling Kemp
Simeon Eldridge
Nathan Eldridge
Robert Ellison
Daniel Carmichael
Joel Holt
David Stewart
Jacob Gardenhire
Mathew Gower
James Hope

Jesse Eldridge
John Freeman
Jared Hotchkiss
William Lampkins
James McGill
James McElwee
David Nowlan
Landon Rector
Nicholas Steens
George Cook
George Moore
Richard Meredith
Peterson Kimball
Milton Center
James Colter
Bartlett Cannon

THE HISTORY OF ROANE COUNTY

James Copeland
Britian Davis
William Davis
Bazzle Davis
John Winton

Adam Miller
James Preston
Benjamine Peters
Richard Swiger

CAPTAIN HOUSTON'S COMPANY 1808

Robert Brashears
Isaac Brashears
James Couch
Asa Cobb
James Dearmond
Edward Davis
Aden Evens
John Fooshee
Josiah Jent
John Lemons

William McCamy
Clemons Phillips
Mathew Pryor
Joseph Robertson
James Robinson
Joseph Sullins
Moses Winters
Alexander Wiley
Michael Horler

CAPTAIN ROGER'S COMPANY

Gilbreath Barton
Peter Couch
Joel Hembree
William Houston
Robert Randolph
Isaac Reece
James R. Rogers
Edward Smith
John Randolph

Jesse Casy
David McClelland
Henry McPherson
Abraham McClellan
Edward Owings
Elisah Randolph
Rector MacMillan
John McClelland

CAPTAIN MOORE'S COMPANY

John Berfit (Buford)
Sylvanus Hines
William Mitchell
Benoni Raymon
Jesse Rody
Mathew Wood

Thomas Harrison
Abner Magus
William Nail
George Rogers
George Sterns
Henry Wilkey

Names of Free Holders in different Companys that gave in taxes to Clerk in 1808.

Alexander Stewart
Robert White
John Love
John Hailey
Hugh Beaty

Joseph Stout
Robert White
Samuel Ward
Samuel·C. Hall

THE HISTORY OF ROANE COUNTY

SOME OF THE TAX PAYERS OF 1808

John Allen
Thomas Amey
 (a free man of colour.)
Catherine Arbuckle
William, Thomas and John Brown, Guardians
Elizabeth Preston (widow of George Preston)
Stephen Ammerman
William Campbell
Jacob Cook
Baracias Cope
Silas Coatney
John Eaton
Elijah Eaton
James Eaton
David Davenport
Stephen Duncan
Roger Gideon
Daniel Greib
Hugh Kelso
Elizabeth Preston
Talliaferro Richards
Thomas Shelley
Arnold Shields
James Labb
Robert Shields
Bartlett Robins
James Steele
Samuel Riley
Jacob Thrasher
Jenkins Whiteside
Jacob Watson
William Griffith
William Lewis
Samuel McCallie
Alexander Moore
John Nichols
Ephriam Pritchett
Samuel Ochsears

A LIST OF ALL WHO ARE ENTITLED TO VOTE IN CAPTAIN WILLIAM WHITE'S COMPANY 1809

John Walker
John Wray
James Noal
Nathanial Medlock
Jonathan Davis
James Davis
Asa Cobb, Esqr.
Josiah Sullins
Meshea Stevens
Mathew Pryor, Sr.
William Pryor
Mathew Pryor, Jr.
William Ervin
Ervin Evans
John Thompson
William White, Sr.
John Wiley
Ambrose Copeland
James Garner
Daniel Wilson
Joseph Sullins
Edward Morrison
David Thomas
Alexander Howard
Alexander Howard, Jr.
Alexander Willey, Sr.
Alexander Willey, Jr.
James Trimble, Esqr.
Asa Howard
Acquila Nail
Absolum Potter
Benjamin Brannon
Benjamine Draper
Francis Erwin
Francis Lee
George Crow
George White
Hugh Lackey
John Davis
John Gardiner

THE HISTORY OF ROANE COUNTY

John Nail
John Megill
Joseph Nail
Jesse White
John Young
John Hegley
John Rather
John H. Durret
James Scott
Joseph Bird
James Melentick
Jesse Cobb
John Morgan
William Gardenhire
William Dolton
William Cobb
Joseph Emery
James Ivey
James Massengail
John Crise
Jesse Corbin
James Jones
Jonathan White
Joshua Christenberry
Jeremiah Feils
Little B. Bryant
Michael Boyd
John Cravat
Jacob Miles
Calvin Johnson
William Scott

Mathew Nail
Marton Durret
Moses Looney
Michael Hostler
Maston Strong
Robert Dunken (Duncan)
Samuel Miller
Senders Cisco
Samuel Silvey
Thomas Corbin
William Ramsey
William Alexander
William Lilman
Thomas Gallaher
William Silvey
Willes Durret
Nicholas Nail
Menson Lingford
Robert Clough
William White, Jr.
William Jones
John Harris
Thomas Reed
Josiah Montgomery
Moses White
John Melton
Jesse Rather
Thomas Wiley
Thomas Gilbreath
William Draper
William Derrit

Jas. Gallaher, Justice of Peace

FIRST JURY

State of Tennessee)
Roane County)   June Session 1805
  To the Sheriff of Roane County Greeting, you are here by commanded to summons the following persons to wit:

William Peters
William Blair
John Nail
James Coulter
James Dearmond
John Flat

Jeames Galloway
Jeames Rogers
Robert McNealy
Joseph Looney
John Meriot

THE HISTORY OF ROANE COUNTY

William Houston
William Waller
William Sherold
Milton Center
George Cook
Mathew Goweros
John Hankins
George Moore
Richard Meredith
Mathem Sims
John Browder

John Matlock
James McMullen
Thomas Pritchet
Jesse Stubbs
Adam Carson
Jeames Gordon
David Patton
Solomon Geren
Richard Armstrong
Benjamin Grayson

JUNE SESSION 1805 JURY SUMMONS

Samuel Miller
Joshua Ashmore

Joshia Gent
John Parker

To appear at the Court House in Kingston the third Monday in September there to answer and attend as grand Jurors till discharged by the Court.

Henry Brezeal, Clk. of Roane Co.

1855 THE MEMBERS OF THE MILITIA OF THE 16TH CIVIL DISTRICT

Alexander Luck
James H. Johnson
S. A. Greasland
Jessey Reves
C. C. Ollis
Lewis Phillips
John Scarbury
William W. Adkinson
John H. Dickey
James Maguffee
John Bullard
H. L. Bullard
William C. Ritter
J. M. Bullard
John Barnet
Richard Barnet
B. M. Clark
Robert B. Clark
Samuel Bullard
Melton Suddeath
Joseph N. Love
Robert K. Byrd

James R. Crow
William G. Flinn
Jacob Davis
Simeon Hasler
John F. Williams
Samuel Mutney
Joel Solomon
Jessey Solomon
William Barnet
William A. Tedder
C. C. Crow
Robert Wilson
Wilkerson P. Adkinson
John M. Isbell
A. T. Sumter
James Tharkill
James P. Tedder
Morgan Harskins
Franklin Piddy
James Hammond
Jessey Hammond
John Hammond

THE HISTORY OF ROANE COUNTY

Robert Scarburay
William Durrett
S. B. Suddeath
Joseph B. Strickland
John Phillips
William Priddy
Josiah Haines
Newton Derrick
Martin Priddy
Lewis K. Night
Thomas Selvey
Nimrod Underwood
Samuel Dugger

JUSTICES OF THE PEACE IN 1819

Thomas Mullins, Abraham McClellan, Isaac Morris Samuel Eskridge, Thomas Blake, Alexander Nesmith, William Eblen, John Leftwich, William B. Lenoir.

Kingston was incorporated in 1820 with a Mayor and Aldermen.

SOME EARLY CITIZENS WHO PURCHASED LIBRARY VOLUMES IN EARLY DAYS

When the second Edition of Nicholson's British Encyclopedia or Dictionary of Arts and Science was published in 1818 the following Roane County Citizens were among those from various States who were purchasers.

Meriweather Smith
Walter King
Joshua Cox
William B. Lenoir
William Puris
William McClellan
James Sevier
George Morris
Benjamine White
John Puris
A. Carden
Samuel Brown
William Brown
Andrew Green

PART TWO

SOLDIERS OF THE REVOLUTION

Roane County can boast as many if not more Revolutionary soldiers than any county in the whole United States. While these brave men were not residents of Roane County during the Revolutionary War—for the simple reason that there was then no Roane County—they came to her soil in the years that immediately succeeded the War and remained to fight her battles with the Red Man and eventually to sleep beneath her beloved hills and valleys.

The records of some of these soldiers, although known to have served, can not now be established, many died before pensions were issued and many did not apply for or receive pensions. Some are mentioned in Ramsey's Annals where the fact that they were officers or performed some conspicuous service brought their names before the historian, but many died as they had served unsung.

This chapter includes the names of all whose Service in the Revolution is known, with reference for service.

LIST OF REVOLUTIONARY SOLDIERS LIVING IN ROANE COUNTY WHO WERE PENSIONED UNDER ACT OF MARCH 18, 1818

Pensioner	Rank	State
Crocomus Acree	Private	Maryland
John Bowman	Private	Virginia
Robert Crew	Private	Virginia
	died Feb. 2, 1843	
Valentine Cunningham	Private	Virginia
	died Oct. 17, 1832	
Samuel Evans	Private	Virginia
George Fuller	Private	North Carolina
William Mead,	Private	Virginia
	died Jan. 25, 1831	
John Parr	Private	New Jersey

THE HISTORY OF ROANE COUNTY

Uriah Rector	Private	Virginia
John Walker	Colonel	Virginia
	died July 7, 1829	
Samuel Walker	Captain	Virginia
	died July 7, 1830	
William Willis	Private	Virginia

LIST OF REVOLUTIONARY SOLDIERS LIVING IN ROANE COUNTY WHO WERE PENSIONED UNDER ACT OF JUNE 7, 1832

Pensioner	Rank	State in which Pensioner Served
John Algood		
Robert Allison	Private	North Carolina
James Aiken	Private	North Carolina
Richard Allen	Private	Virginia
James Allen	Private	North Carolina
Carter Barnard	Private	North Carolina
David Blackwell	Private	Virginia
Mattis Brashears	Private	Maryland
William Boyd	Private	North Carolina
Isaiah Brown	Private	North Carolina
	d. Apr. 29, 1833	
Laird Burns	Private	South Carolina
Robert Burke	Private	North Carolina
Enoch Bush	Private	Virginia
William Carroll	Private	North Carolina
Benjamin Chapman	Private	Maryland
John Cox	Private	Virginia
John Crenshaw	Private	Virginia
William Edgman	Private	North Carolina
Simeon Eldridge	Private	North Carolina
Ardin Evans	Private	Virginia
Solomon Geren	Private	North Carolina
Stephen Hancock	Private	Virginia
William Harvey	Private	Virginia
Jared Hotchkiss	Private	Connecticut
Meshack Henderson	Private	North Carolina
William Hyden	Private	Virginia
Charles Lain (Lane)	Private Corp. and Sergt.	Virginia
Joseph Lane	Private	Virginia
David Liles	Private	North Carolina

THE HISTORY OF ROANE COUNTY

Hesekiah Love	Private	South Carolina
	d. June 11, 1833	
Amos Marney	Private	Virginia
John McNutt	Private	South Carolina
Adam Miller	Private	South Carolina
John Parry	Private	North Carolina
Ebenezer Snow	Private	Pennsylvania
Benjamin Suddoth	Private	South Carolina
Benjamin Thacker	Private	Virginia
Peter Wees	Private	Virginia
John Woody	Private	North Carolina
Isham Young	Private	Georgia

LIST OF REVOLUTIONARY PENSIONERS LIVING IN ROANE COUNTY DRAWING PENSIONS UNDER ACT OF JUNE 1, 1840

Pensioners	Age	Pensioners	Age
James Acree	86	George Fuller	83
James Aiken	80	Solomon Geren	80
James Allen	81	John Hood	78
Carter Barnard	78	William Hyden	76
David Blackwell	82	Thomas Ives	86
John Bowman	86	Robert Liles	81
William Boyd.	86	Thomas Landrum	86
Laird Burns	85	John McNutt	78
Benjamin Clark	77	Adam Miller	83
Benjamin Chapman	78	William Moore	82
John Cox	82	Nathaniel Osbourn	89
David C. Denny	85	Tandy Senter	81
Samuel Evans	84	John Wood	81
	Edward Wyatt	81	

LIST OF ROANE COUNTY REVOLUTIONARY SOLDIERS NOT ON PENSION LISTS

Name	Reference For Service
Peter Avery	
John Bailey	Virginia State Library 9th Annual Report
John Blair	South Carolina
Nathaniel Buckingham	
Hugh Beattey	
David Campbell	Second Virginia State Regiment
Joseph Overton	
James Campbell	
Robert Overton	

THE HISTORY OF ROANE COUNTY

James Campbell	
Thomas Coulter	North Carolina Records Vol. 22. Page 722
Milton Center	Virginia
James Clark	2nd Virginia State Reg. War Dept. 351
Thomas Crumbliss	
William Davidson	North Carolina Regiment
Hugh Dunlap	D. A. R. Lineage Book
William Evans	Virginia State Records
Hugh Francis	
Joseph Francis	
Jacob Gardenhire	Virginia State Records
Joseph Green	Wayne County North Carolina
David Haley	
Alexander Gamble	
John Hackett	5th Virginia Regiment War Dept. 112
Robert Houston	Virginia Regiment
John Hinds	Virginia State Records
Sanford Ingram	North Carolina Regiment
Samuel Kendrick	Virginia State Records
Major Robert King	Virginia Letter from George Christian to Samuel Draper
Thomas Loyd	Pennsylvania
William Lewis	Virginia
James McElwee	Mecklinburg Co., North Carolina
Capt. Abraham McClellan	
Thomas McMullen	
Henry Miller	Virginia Regiment
David McClellan.	
Samuel McClellan	North Carolina
Gideon Morgan	Enlisted at New Mulford Conn.
Nicholas Nail	
Alexander Outlaw	North Carolina State Records
Richard Price	2nd Virginia Reg. War Dept. 33
Mathew Pryor	
William Repeto	10th Virginia Reg. War Dept. 284
John Rhea	7th Virginia Reg. War Dept. 148
William Randolph	Virginia Reg.
John Sharp	
John Staples	Virginia State Library Report
Jacob Smith	Capt. Jacob Sarer's Co. Virginia
Nathan Sullins	
Nathaniel Taylor	
William White	Virginia
Jesse Blackwell	

THE HISTORY OF ROANE COUNTY

REVOLUTIONARY SOLDIERS BURIED IN ROANE COUNTY—LIST NOT COMPLETE

Crocamus Acree, Buried in Bowers Grave Yard.
John Bowman, Buried in Stockton Valley Grave Yard.
Hugh Beatty, Buried in Cave Creek Grave Yard.
Thomas Crumbliss, Buried in Crumbliss Grave Yard.
Solomon Geren, Buried in Geren Grave Yard.
John Hood Buried in Wo'f Creek Grave Yard.
David Haley, Buried on Haley Farm.
Amos Marney, Buried near Riley's Creek.
Capt. Abraham McClellan, Buried in Post Oak Grave Yard
John McCoy, Buried in Post Oak Grave Yard.
James McElwee, Buried in Haley Grave Yard.
Hezekiah Love, Buried 8 miles above Kingston near Clinch River
Nicholas Nail, Buried in White's Creek Grave Yard.
Uriah Rector, Buried in Post Oak Grave Yard.
Cumberland Rector, Buried in Kendrick Grave Yard.
Tandy Senter, Buried in Harriman.
Jacob Smith, Buried in Post Oak Grave Yard.
Capt. Samuel Walker, Buried in Post Oak Grave Yard.
Samuel Kendrick, Buried in Kendrick Grave Yard.
Milton Senter, Buried in Center Grave Yard.
David McClelland, Buried in Post Oak Grave Yard.
Samuel McClelland, Buried in Post Oak Grave Yard.
Gideon Morgan, Buried in Kingston Grave Yard.

UNITED STATES SOLDIERS STATIONED AT SOUTH WEST POINT

Lieut Carrick 4th Reg U. S. Cavalry, age 19 died and buried at Post Oak Springs.

Capt. Samuel Walker   Daniel Hitchcock
Dr. Thomas J. Van Dyke   William Flennigan
Capt. Abraham McClellan   Stephen Renfro
Col. John McClellan   Abraham Byrd
              Paul Cunningham

THE HISTORY OF ROANE COUNTY

SOLDIERS OF 1812 AND CREEK WAR

Capt. Uriah Allison	David Haley
Capt. Allen Bacon	John Cloud Haley
William L. Brown	Joel Hembree
Darius Browder	Sylvanus Hinds
William Browder	James Lackey
William Breeden	John Loyd
John Blair	William Lenoir
Col. Joseph Byrd	Daniel Mason
Joseph Bryant	Thomas Jefferson Mason
Thomas Crumbliss	Thomas Margraves
John Clark	Robert Miller
Richard Dunlap	Gideon Morgan, Jr.
Samuel Owings	John McClellan
William McCall	Killed at New Orleans.
Capt. James Rogers	Anthony Smith
Jacob Shelley	Daniel Wester

Tandy Senter

REGIMENT, FIELD AND STAFF OFFICERS OF THE WAR OF 1812 ON RECORD IN ADJ. GENERAL'S OFFICE WASHINGTON D. C., AND TENNESSEE STATE ARCHIVES

2nd Regiment Mounted Gunmen East Tennessee Volunteer Militia Jan.,-May, 1814.

Colonel John Brown

Captains:
John Chiles, Chas. Lewen, James McCamy, Jesse G. Mains, John Trimble, William White.

REGIMENT EAST TENNESSEE VOLUNTEER MILITIA, SEPT. 1813 JAN. 1814

Colonel John Brown

Captains:
Allen S. Bacon, Hugh Barton, William D. Neilson, Lunesford Oliver, James Preston, James Standefer, William White, William Christan.

THE HISTORY OF ROANE COUNTY

WAR OF 1812

It was an eventful day, when the young Lieut. Uriah Allison, marched through the town of Kingston, with his fifers and drummer boy. He had been appointed 2nd Lieut. of the 8th U. S. Inf. March 15, 1812, had reported at Knoxville, by an order signed by Capt. John A. Rogers and had been instructed by Edmund P. Gaines, Lt. Col., U. S. Infty., to make all necessary provisions for recruits.

The men and boys gathered about the fifers and drummer in front of the Court House, while the women and children watched in the background with excitment. Bright new U. S. dollars lay upon the head of the drum, every man who stepped up and took a dollar became a volunteer in the War of 1812. The first to take a dollar from the drum was:
Stephen Smith age 24, 5 ft. 11 in. born in Dupland Co. N. C.
Nathan Fike age 19, 5 ft. 1 in. born in Chatham Co. N. C.
Joel McNutt age 22, 5 ft. 9 in. born in Maulbury Co. S. C.
Abner Senter age 25, 5 ft. 4 in. born in Surry Co. N. C.
Thomas Hibberts age 23, 6 ft. 2 in. born in Patrick Co. Va.
Solomon Moore, Sgt. age 21, 6 ft. 2 in. b. in Frederick Co. Va.
William Curry age 25, 5 ft. 7½ in born in —————Penn.
Henry D. Cooper age 30, 5 ft 8½ in. born in Hanover Co. Va.
Aquilla Churchwell age 19, 5 ft. 8 in. born in Loudon Co. Md.
Thomas White age 32, 5 ft. 8½ in. b. Cumberland Co. N. C.
Thomas Margraves age 22, 5 ft. 5½ in. b. in Rockbridge Va.
John Webber age 18, 5 ft. 6 in. born in Goochland Co. Va.
Hurd Price age 40, 5 ft. 9½ in. born in Fairfield Co. Conn.
Joseph Jenson age 23, 5 ft 8½ in. born in Chester Co. Eng.
John Ray age 42, 5 ft. 10½ in born in Halifax Co. N. C.
Hugh Lackey age 32, 5 ft 9 in born in Orange Co. N. C.
Elisha Pruet age 20, 5 ft. 11 in. born in ——— Co. N. C.
Elijah Pruet age 15, 5 ft. 5 in. born in——— Co. N. C.
John Dunkin age 27, 5 ft. 8 in. born in — ——— Va.
Alfred Reynolds age 29, 5 ft. 8. in. b. in Montgomery Co. Va.
John Clanter age 21, 5 ft 4½ in. born in Randolph Co. Va.
Mathew Graham age 24, 5 ft. 5 in. b. in Hawkins Co. Tenn.
John Holt age 18, 5 ft. 6 in. born in ————— N. C.
Andrew McDonough
James McDonough
John Hall age 19, 5 ft. 8½ in born in Randolph Co. N. C.
Abraham Wadkins, 22, 5 ft 7½ in. b. in Rockbridge Co. N. C.
Whitmill Brogdon age 19, 5 ft. 10 in. b. in Pendleton Co. S. C.
Jeremiah Jones age 21, 5 ft. 5 in. born in Lee Co. S. C.

THE HISTORY OF ROANE COUNTY

Daniel Wester age 26, 5 ft. 8 1-3 in. Edgecomb Co. N. C.
William Graham age 19, 5 ft. 5 in born in Pendleton Co. Va.
Henry Liggett
William Queen age 19, 5 ft. 10 in. born in Burk Co. N. C.
John Henderson age 19, 5 ft. 9 in. born in Burk Co. N. C.
Henry Miller age 17, 5 ft. 9 in. born in Augusta Co. Va.
Joseph Bledsoe age 35, 6 ft. 1 in. born in Orange Co. N. C.
Aaron Bledsoe age 15, 5 ft 11 in born in Orange Co. N. C.
Jeremiah Buchanan age 45, 5 ft. 5 in. born in Benkerse, Va.
and his sons:
Horeulas Buchanan age 16, 5 ft 11 in. born in Mont. Co. Va.
Moses Buchanan age 14, 5 fe. 2 in. born in Mont. Co. Va.
Jeremiah Buchanan age 12, 4 ft. 9 in born in Mont. Co. Va.

They were each paid $16. per month. They enlisted on July 24, 1812.

The fifers were paid $15. per month and were: Williamson Ladd and Archibald McCaleb.

The drummer boy was paid $10. per month and his name was Almerine Halley.

Lieut. Allison for doing his work faithfully, was commissioned Captain of the 2nd Reg. of Riflemen. Signed by James Madison President, James Monroe, Sec., of State, later commissioned a Col. and for distinguished services given several thousand acres of land on the Tennessee River.

MEXICAN WAR SOLDIERS

Capt. Robert King Byrd   Joseph Brown Martin
Col. Jonathan Barnard   Albert S. Lenoir
Samuel Houston   Joseph Parks
James Freeman   Daniel Wester
Col. Joel Hembree   John Wester
Dr. Lewis Jordon   Lewis Marshall Wester
            Major Thomas C. Lyon

WAR BETWEEN THE STATES

The men of Roane County were always ready to volunteer to defend any cause that they felt was just, so when war was declared in 1861 many of Roane County's sons volunteered either for service in the Federal or Confederate Army. Many families were split, brothers and cousins fighting against each other. When the election was held on May 6, 1861 for the people of the state to decide upon the question of secession, and the question of representation in the Confederate Congress and the adoption of the provisional Constitution of the Confed-

THE HISTORY OF ROANE COUNTY

erate Government the result in Roane County was as follows: Separation 454, Representation 436, No Separation 1568, No Representation 1580.

The first Union Regiment of Tennessee was organized by Robert King Byrd, of Roane County, at Camp Dick Robinson, August 1861. He was made a Colonel with James T. Shelley, of Roane Co., as Major.

In March 1862 Major Shelley organized the 5th U. S. Reg., Tenn., Inf., and was its Colonel. This Regiment was composed of soldiers from several Tennessee Counties and was in the battles of Stone River, Missionary Ridge, Nashville and other places.

The 1st. U. S. Regt., with Col. R. K. Byrd in command was under fire at Wild Cat, at Mill Spring, in the capture of Cumberland Gap, where it remained until the evacuation of the Post by General Morgan, who retreated to Ohio. Went on the expedition to Kanawah Valley, was at the Battle of Stone River. Entered East Tennessee under Gen. Burnside's Command and was at the seige of Knoxville. During the winter of 1864 was stationed at Kingston, and in the spring of 1865 entered the Atlanta Campaign, until just previous to the surrender of the City the greater portion of the regiment was discharged on account of the expiration of their term of service. While at Cumberland Gap a detachment of this and the 2nd. Reg. consisting of 69 men captured an important out post of the Confederates without a single loss. For this exploit a complimentary notice was read on dress parade by order of General Morgan.

The 43rd Tenn. Regiment (Confederate) was organized in November 1861 with J. W. Gillespie as Colonel. After service in East Tennessee, the Regiment was reorganized May 1862 and sent to Humphrey Marshall's Brigade in Virginia, but soon after joined Bragg's Kentucky Brigade. In December was transferred to Vicksburg to hard service. In May 1863 moved to Fort Gibson to oppose Grant's advance and fought at Champion Hill, then retreated to Vicksburg and surrendered early in July. The Regiment was exchanged and ordered to reenforce Longstreet at Knoxville. Seven months was spent in East Tennessee on out post duty. The 43rd. fought around Washington, Winchester, Cedar Creek, Fisherville, White Post and other places in Virginia, returning to East Tennessee in the fall of 1864, fighting at Morristown and Russellville. Learning of General Lee's surrender it moved south to join Johnson, but at Charlotte, N. C., met President Davis and served

THE HISTORY OF ROANE COUNTY

as his escort until his capture. Was paroled May 1865.

The 36th Tenn. Reg. (Confederate) was organized July 30, 1862 with R. G. Fain as Colonel and was composed of men from Roane and other Tenn. Counties. The Regiment operated in East Tennessee under Lieutenant Colonel W. H. Wilkerson, and was in the battles at Chickamauga Fort Sanders, Bean's Station, Dewy Bluff, Wathall's Junction and Petersburg in Virginia. Part were captured Apr. 5, 1865 and the remainder surrendered at Appomattox.

The 26th Tenn. Reg. (Confederate) was composed of men from Roane and other adjacent counties. It was organized Sept. 6, 1861 at Knoxville with John M. Lillard as Colonel. It was captured at Ft. Donaldson and taken to Northern prisons, exchanged and was at Vicksburg Sept. 1862 Col. Lillard was mortally wounded at Chickamauga and was succeeded by R. M. Saffell. It fought at the Battle of Missionary Ridge, spent winter of 1863-64 in North Georgia. Was in the battles of Atlanta, Jonesboro, Lovejoy, Nashville and Franklin. Col. Shaffell was killed at Bentonville, N. C., and was succeeded by Col. A. F. Boggess who also fell in a fight after Gen. Lee's surrender and before the troops at that point heard of it. The Regiment surrendered in April 1865.

WORLD WAR RECORD

Five months before the United States entered the World War, some of the women of Harriman organized a Red Cross Chapter and began sending supplies to the allies. At the first call for Volunteers the young men of Roane County, responded and organized the first Volunteer Company in the United States to offer its services to the War Department. The women of Rockwood organized a Red Cross Chapter at the same time. The records show that throughout the months that our Country was in the War that Roane County did not lag and equalled any in every phase of patriotic work.

The first Volunteer Company from Roane County was organized in June 1917. Left Rockwood for Camp Sevier, South Carolina, on September 10, 1917. Trained at Camp Sevier for eight months. Sailed from New York for France in May 1918. In France 11 months. Took part in five engagements. Three members of this Company, Curtis E. Smith, Fred C. Gouth and Joe Evans were killed in action. This Company was in the 119th Infantry, 30th Division.

THE HISTORY OF ROANE COUNTY

FIRST VOLUNTEER COMPANY FROM ROCKWOOD TENNESSEE. WORLD WAR

OFFICERS

Captain Timothy A. Wright

1st Lt. Robert H. Thompson

2nd Lt. Clarence G. Myers

Charles B. McCullough
Garrett H. Billings
Arthur L. Williams
Roscoe C. Hinds
Lester F. Powell
John F. McCullough
Rush W. Tedder
Harry H. Ficke
Elbert C. Etter
Bert Hicks
Oscar M. Patterson
Carl H. Kelton
Fletcher F. Scott
William R. Kindrick
Henry C. Tankersley
Taylor Hinds
Houston E. Powell
James Maricle
James A. Kizziah
Ford W. Arp
Rufus M. Rodgers
Samuel J. Pelfrey
Daniel C. Wolf
James P. Coleman
Isaac C. Clark
John E. Poland
Charles E. Foster
Guy S. Meadows
Ira Majors
Elmer Gallion
Jess Daniel
Tobias Daniel
Fred A. Taylor
Charles E. Fickey

Floyd Elliott
James P. Smith
Dorsey W. Hinds
Charles D. Nance
Clifford J. Morgan
Elmer Jones
Joe Farr
Samuel E. Kyle
Raymond Sherrill
James A. Bryant
Clifford H. Easter
Dallas A. Pope
Peter T. McGill
Paul McDaniel
Andrew Patterson
Evans Neal
Arch Howard
John J. Ingram
Thomas R. Kirkland
Dewey Ausburn
Ed Baldwin
Luther Evans
George F. Lyons
William H. Joseph
James Clowers
Creed Parham
Edgar Morgan
Ruben C. Doughey
Curtis E. Smith
Raymond F. Joseph
Arthur Brown
Edison Shamhart
Fred C. Gouth
Christopher C. Taylor

THE HISTORY OF ROANE COUNTY

Oscar Hampton
Sherman Doughty
George Phifer
William Cody
Robert R. Miles
Roy C. Henry
Doris C. Kelly
John E. Smith
Christopher C. Holloway
Wince Owens
William Bowling
Hobart DeLaney
Ed McCullough
Neal Collins
James Hinds
Claude Cook
George F. Clowers
Floyd Elliott
Patrick Vance
Andrew Lawson
Thomas R. Jett
Clyde Billings
Ralph Short
James Edgeman
John D. Ward
Edward Skeens
John Farmer
Ernest Pelfrey
Ervin B. Turner
Ernest R. Brady
Ernest Underwood
Joe Evans

SOLDIERS WHO MADE THE SUPREME SACRIFICE

Jesse Brannan
Jack Rayborn
James Wright
Charlie Gallion
John Henry Burchfield
Edward H. Hickey
George F. Clowers
Clifford Stegall
Joseph F. Evans
Oscar Hampton
Tillman Butler
Clarence F. Butler
Arthur Douglas
Curtis Smith

SOLDIERS WHO RECEIVED DISTINGUISHED SERVICE CROSS

Benjamine W. Diggs
Walter B. Stripling
Clarence S. Wright
Oliver Springs
Oliver Springs
Kingston

PART THREE

POST OAK SPRINGS

Though now a settlement of only four or five houses and one church it was at one time a very important village. It was on the public highway that was constructed in 1800 between South West Point (Kingston) and "Beans Lick" (near Nashville,) crossing Walden's Ridge over the present tunnel of the Tennessee Central Railroad. It was called Walton's road for Capt. William Walton who constructed it by the authority of an act passed by the Legislature in 1799. Another road leaving the Walton road at Post Oak Springs went in the direction of Ross' Landing. Captain McElwee, in writing of Post Oak and its people, has given some very interesting things of the locality. George Gordon got a charter from the State to construct a road from Post Oak Springs to White's Creek, crossing the mountain by way of Sparta and on to Nashville. The two roads were rivals for public travelers. Agents were engaged all along the road from Knoxville to Kingston to advertise each of these two routes. Each agent would furnish the traveler with a ticket; this ticket would be taken up by the first toll gate keeper and the agent paid a percent on the ticket. But the test of rivalry was at Post Oak Springs. Immense sign boards were erected for each road. The board on the Gordon road read:

"Gordon's Turnpike, Nearest and best road across Cumberland Wilderness. Fire and provender at each stop. Ordinaries and taverns every ten miles."

Joshua Moore was agent and drummer for the stage road. One night he tied a brush to a long pole and blackened out the sign board of the Gordon road. Gordon did not have it re-lettered but put up another board below with this:

"The above blackboard to be kept for erection over the grave of Joshua Moore upon which the devil will write his doom, Amen."

This board attracted much attention and turned a large amount of travel to Gordon's road.

THE HISTORY OF ROANE COUNTY

Gordon died and Moore moved away but the old sign post still stood during the 60's as a silent reminder of "things that."

Some of the early citizens of Post Oak Springs were: Thomas Hindman, Joseph Rentfroe, Thomas Brown, Eldbridge G. Sevier, John S. McMeans, Major John Smith, Mathew Allison, Edward Owings, Samuel Kendrick, Capt. Thomas McMullen, Capt. Samuel Walker.

The Post Oak Springs Christian Church was organized in 1812 by Major John Smith and the earliest members were the Smith, Owings (Owens) and Acuff families.

The Post Springs Academy stood across the road from the Christian Church near the home of Mathew Allison (now Staple's home). One end of the building was used for the boys and the other for the girls. Some of the teachers were Dr. Campbell Cawood, Martin Matlock, Dr. B. F. Davis, Rev. Nelson Roberts, R. P. Bayley, Col. John R. Neal, W. W. Millican, Miss Nannie Depew, of Amsterdam, N. Y., Maston Green, of North Carolina.

The War Between the States terminated school teaching in the Academy. It and the woodland to the south of it was occupied by Soldiers during war times. The building was used by the Federal Army as a Courier post, where the bearers of war dispaches changed. A fight occured here between the Federal and Confederate in a successful attempt of the Confederates to capture dispatches. Four couriers were killed and others captured. Within a year after this fight the Academy was burned and Post Oak Springs ceased to be the educational center of a large territory.

On the South of the same tract of land on which the Academy was located, stood the Methodist Church, and West of it the graveyard where lie the remains of several Revolutionary soldiers. The building and graveyard were badly abused during the War Between the States and afterwards was used as a school building. Among those who were members of the church were the families of:

Thos. A. Brown	Charles Haley
John Tedder	William Haley
John Pyott	W. L. Brown
Isaac Eblen	Maj. L. L. Thomasson
William McElwee	Esq. Kimbrough
Mathew Allison	Jacob A. Work
Jno. N. Moore	Dr. B. F. Davis
W. F. (Frank) Brown	Wm. C. Eblen

THE HISTORY OF ROANE COUNTY

Col. Hembree's daughter   Jno. W. Brown (Jack Brown)

Occasional attendants were the families of:

White	Alex Montgomery
Lintoln	Robt. Cravens
Sewell Phillips	Sherman C. Doughty
John A. Winton	Oscar Hampton
Elbert C. Montgomery	Shorts, and many others.

William McElwee, Franklin Brown, Maj. L. L. Thomasson, John Pyott, John Teddler, W. C. Eblen and others were official members, being Trustees and Stewards.

The sacramental unleavened bread was for a long time prepared by Mrs. Lucinda McElwee and the pure grape wine furnished or kept in custody of Steward William McElwee for many years.

METHODIST PREACHERS

The preachers serving in Post Oak Springs Church are recalled as:

Rufus Stephens	(a distinguished preacher)
David Flemming	Sewell Phillips
James L. Cash	William Tower
J. W. Dickey	Rev. Lowery
P. N. Price	———Belt
T. K. Munsey	Carroll Long
William Bowers	K. C. Atkins
Brandon and Patty	Jno. Y. Smith

Rev Bowers had a sleek bald head and during his preaching a sermon young John Davis, son of Dr. Davis, inquired in a loud voice, "Did the sheep eat the hair off that man's head" The inquiry produced some sensation.

Jerry Lamb and Andrew McCulley led the Singing Schools that were in operation in 1850.

THE HISTORY OF ROANE COUNTY

ASBURY CAMP GROUNDS

Located at Privett Springs, three miles south of Post Oak Springs and two and one-half miles east of the present Rockwood, this old time, ante-bellum popular religious camp meeting ground of the Methodists was named for a pioneer Bishop of the Church, Bishop Asbury.

This camp consisted of an assembly place under roof with seats without backs, and the floor covered with straw, that was renewed daily. There was a pulpit stand and a preachers' room on one side, and boxes in which were installed tallow dip candles for night services. Meetings and preachings and exhorations continued throughout the day and into the night. Great sermons were delivered.

The great preachers of the denomination from throughout the Holston Conference and beyond its limits, as all local preachers were in attendance and very active and enthusiastic, as were all the leading singers of the whole section and for great distances beyond.

The assembly shed was surrounded by the Camps of all the leading families of the churches of the whole district. Many brought their colored slave cooks and waiters and an immense supply of good things to eat of every character, which the region supplied in profusion. These negro slave servants attended the services, occupying the assigned section of the assembly shed. Many of them were members in good standing of the Methodist Church, as was usual during slavery times.

Some of the leading families camping here were the Browns, Pyotts, Tedders McElwees, Elbens, Wintons, Montgomerys, Whites, Haleys, Lincolns, Kimbroughs, Tommasons, Martins, Centers and many others.

Asbury Camp Ground and its great meetings came to an end when the black cloud of war burst upon the country. The great meeting became a memory only, and the buildings and appurtenances went to decay.

THE HISTORY OF ROANE COUNTY

HISTORY OF UNION LODGE NO. 38 F AND A. M.

Kingston, Tenn.
By James F. Littleton

The proceedings of the Grand Lodge, of Tennessee, or rather the Appendix thereto has the following entry on page 404 in the compilation of Past Grand Master, Wilkins Tannehill in 1824.

"Oct. A. L. 5821 at a grand annual communication, the M. W. Wilkins Tannehill, Esq. was re-elected, and charters issued to the following Lodges, Viz. Kingston Union, at Kingston; Nashville, at Nashville; Mount Moriah, at Dover and Washington Luminary, at Washington, in the State of Tennessee; to Franklin Lodge at Russellville, and Tuscumbia, at Courtland, in the State of Alabama. As I have before me a copy of the charter of the Lodge issued by the grand Lodge I am taking the liberty of copying it herein."

CHARTER

Sit. Lux. Et. Lux Fruit.

The M. W. Wilkins Tannehill, Esq. Grand Master. To all and every our right worshipful and loving brethern.

We, the M. W. W. Tanehill, Esq. Grand Master of the most Ancient and Honorable Society of Free and Accepted Masons in the State of Tennessee send greetings.

Know ye, that we, at the petition of our Right Worshipful and Well Beloved Brethern, John Brown, Gideon Morgan, Sr., Samuel Brown and several other Brethern, residing at or near Kingston in the State of Tennessee, do hereby constitute the said Brethern into a regular Lodge of Free and Accepted Masons, to be opened at Kingston, by the name of Union Lodge No. 38. And do further, at the said Petition, and of the Great Trust, and Confidence reposed in the above named three Bretheren, hereby appoint John Brown, Master, Gideon Morgan, Senior Warden and Samuel Brown, Junior Warden, for the opening of said Lodge, and for such further time only, as may be thought proper by the Brethern thereof. It being our will, that this our appointment, shall in no wise affect any further election of officers of that Lodge, but that the same shall be according to the regulations of that Lodge, and consistant with the general laws of the Society, contained in the Book of Constitutions.

And we do hereby charge you, the said Worshipful John Brown, to take special care, that all and every, the said Breth-

THE HISTORY OF ROANE COUNTY

ern, are and have been, regularly made Masons, and that they do perform, observe and keep all the Rules and Orders contained in the Book of Constitutions, and also such as may, from time to time be transmitted to you, by us. And further, that you do from time to time, cause to be entered in a Book, to be kept for that purpose, an account of your proceedings in the Lodge, together with such regulations, as shall be made for the good government thereof. A copy of which you are in no wise to omit laying before the Grand Lodge, once in every year, together with a list of the members of the Lodge: That you annually pay into the Grand Treasury, the sum of $10.00 toward the Grand Charity, as well as all further sum or sums, that may be required by our By Laws and Constitution. And moreover we hereby will and require of you the said Worshipful John Brown, as soon as conveniently may be, to send an account in writing of what shall be done by virtue of these presents.

Given at Nashvillt, Under our hand and Seal of Masonry, this 6th day of October, A. L. 5821. A. D. 1821.

                W. Tannehill   Grand Master
                John Rhea   Deputy Grand Master
                J. W. Wilson, Sr.   Grand Warden
                Stephen Cantrell, Jr. Grand Warden

Attested.
M. Norvel   Grand Sec'y

GRAND LODGE SEAL

The John Brown, who was the first Master of the Lodge was Sheriff of Roane County for 23 years and Gideon Morgan, the Senior Warden was one of the first merchants in the town of Kingston. In a short history of the Lodge it would be impossible to mention the names of all the notable men who have been members of the Lodge and held positions of honor in it and have gone into the world and made their mark in other fields.

The time of stated meetings of the Lodge when it was organized was on Friday preceeding the full Moon. In 1839 it was changed to the first Monday, and is so fixed at this time. The early meetings were held in the old brick Court house, until Oct. 1854, when they occupied what was known as the Long room in the present Court house, though the building was not accepted by the County until 1856. This room was the one formerly used as the Circuit Court Clerks office on the second

THE HISTORY OF ROANE COUNTY

floor, on the North side of the present Court room, the partition not being removed to form the present Court room until 1896.

In 1871 Bro. R. K. Byrd, and wife Mary L. Byrd gave the Lodge 3-4 of an acre, part of lots 1-2-15 and 16 as shown by the map of Kingston on the hill near where the M. E. Church now stands. A building was erected at a cost of $1,700.00 which the Lodge occupied until 1910 when it was destroyed by fire. Following the fire, the Lodge met for several months in the K. of P. hall, then removed to the third floor of the Court house, until 1908, when our present quarters were secured.

The Lodge had a membership of 30 in the year 1823 and up to 1839 had raised 43 members, yet in that year, its membership numbered 26. The largest membership in its first period of 18 years, was 39 in 1833, and the lowest was 18 members in 1835. From 1838 to 1847 its meetings were irregular, but from Sept. 7th, 1847 it continued to meet regularly until the War Between the States. Then from March 1861 until June 1866 no meetings were regularly held, and during this time part of its books and records were lost.

The earliest record of Minutes we now have is dated July 2nd., 1853, on that date following officers were officiating in the Lodge:

    W. M. Henry Liggett
    S. W. Henry Liggett, Jr.
    J. W. E. A. Yost
    Treas. James T. Asbury
    Sec'y John C. Gillespie
    S. D. Geo. W. Yost
    J. D. Thos. C. Center
    Tyler R. L. Cardwell

Then came for the periods set out the following who have been Master of the Lodge:

    1867 J. W. McNutt
    1871 James Sevier
    1880 E. E. Young
    1890 Geo. W. Henderson
    1900 J. G. Crumbliss
    1910 J. S. Parker
    1921 W. T. Ferguson

THE HISTORY OF ROANE COUNTY

1920 was the most active year, and there were conferred 80 degrees and had 7 admissions, with a gain in membership of 30. Since 1853 the roster shows 453 members, of whom 75 died while members of this Lodge. This has been the parent Lodge, of Stocton Valley Lodge, Rockwood Lodge, East Fork Lodge, Omega Lodge, South Gate Lodge, and Emerald Lodge, a part of the members of this Lodge becoming Charter members of each of them.

Union Lodge assisted in the erection of the Widows and Orphans home at Nashville, and contributed its part toward the building of the Washington Monument.

One of its members was honored in the Grand Lodge in the person of Henry Liggett, who served them as Jr. Grand Warden, as Sr. Grand Warden, and as deputy Grand Master.

In the years gone by a large number of strong men of the county have been the outstanding citizens of the county and at the same time devoted members of his Lodge and I cannot refrain from mentioning a few of the ones that have been in the writer's day: James Sevier, H. Crumbliss, Geo. L. Burke, who is still living, Col. J. M. Melton, Capt. W. H. Dietz, Will Shelley, W. L. Welcker, E. E. Young, and R. W. Gambill.

This Lodge has lived over a Century and its members have diffused Light. They have furnished the material that has established 6 other Lodges. They have extended their hands in public and private charity, upheld the everlasting truth of the Fatherhood of God, and the Brotherhood of Man, and have done other good acts which will never be known.

The writer is indebted to J. S. Parker, of Kingston, for a large part of the data upon which this short history of the Lodge is based. Bro. Parker has been a faithful member of Union Lodge for a long number of years from one station to another in Masonry he has advanced step by step until he has reached the highest degree in the institution and last year was called to the Ciy of Washingon where he had confered upon him the 33rd degree. He is the only Mason in this county, or in all this section of East Tennessee who has thus been honored.

THE HISTORY OF ROANE COUNTY
POST OAK SPRINGS CHRISTIAN CHURCH

The Church at Post Oak Springs is thought to be the oldest Christian Church in Tennessee, and the interesting facts of its early history deserve to be perpetuated in the records of Roane County, for the benefit of the present generation, and the future descendants of the pioneers of early days.

Among the early settlers who came into the lands and bought of the Cherokee Indians on the West side of the Tennessee River after the treaty of the Tellico in 1805, there was a group from Hawkins County, and among these Isaac Rice appears to have been the leader. Isaac Rice, William Matlock and Joseph Mee, with their families settled on "The waters of King's Creek." Isaac Rice built a log cabin on a small hill above the spring that now supplies water to Rockwood. William Matlock, a brother-in-law of Rice, and Joseph Mee, built cabins near by, and these three built a log cabin church house and organized a church membership about 1812.

It appears that Rice had learned new ideas and teachings of the gospel back in his home in Hawkins County or other sources, his instructors most likely being representatives of the movement that had organized from the preaching of Barton W. Stone. The enthusiasm and energy of Mr. Rice in preaching his views brought a good number of converts, but it also aroused the opposition of others.

In a few years the Church house was burned and the preacher Isaac Rice moved to McMinn County, to a place now called Riceville, and this left the membership to drift for some time. Major John Smith bought land near Post Oak Springs, and though he was not a preacher he became the leader of the work and would call the members together under some large oak trees, and have singing and prayer. The church was called "Schismatics," by other religious bodies in the country, thus indicating the attitude toward the people with the new ideas. The first Church building at Post Oak stood near the present structure.

It is not known just when the Church at Post Oak became acquainted with the teachings of the Campbells who were later than Stone, but as early as 1838 it is stated in the Millenial Harbinger that W. T. Owings had sent the money for the preaching of the gospel. The little flock was visited by Evangelists and traveling ministers at irregular and long distance occasions.

THE HISTORY OF ROANE COUNTY

In 1845 David M. Buck and Samuel H. Millard who were engaged as Evangelists by the East Tennessee and South West Virginia Co-operation traveled on horseback as far west as Post Oak Springs, preaching in Knox and Anderson counties, also others who preached for them in early days were Messers. Troutt, Eichbaum, Vermillion, Randolph, J. D. Billingsly Sr., Isaac Mulkey, J. H. Denton and others.

During the War Between the States the services of this church like many others were suspended and its members fought on both sides of the unpleasant fratricidal war. After the war was over it was with some difficulty that the members could be reorganized into a Christian fellowship. But under the ministry of John H. Acuff who had sons on both sides in the war, a communion service was held to which all persons, of whatever denomination, creed or belief, if they felt themselves worthy were invited to take the emblems of remembrance of the Savior who had suffered for all alike. Hatred and strife and the wounds of the War were healed and the Church began again to live and preach Christian Unity.

An event in the history of that early day that has its lessons for later time is that of the church undertaking to reproduce the communism of the Apostolic Church. This was undertaken by W. J. Owings who had earnest convictions that the experience of the early Church described in Acts 2:44, should be literally reproduced in the life of the Church of today, and that all should live as one family or community, sharing all alike in the common good of the community. After two or three years trial the experiment was abandoned as a mistaken conception of Christian fellowship and co-operation.

The Post Oak Church is called the Mother Church, and the growth from that small beginning has been remarkable. A little acorn planted by Isaac Rice has grown into a great oak with many branches.

BETHEL PRESBYTERIAN CHURCH

Seventeen years after Roane County was organized the first Church was started. History does not tell how or where worship was conducted, but it is probable that the Presbyterian families held services at their homes, until Rittenhouse Academy was built.

On June 6, 1818, six men and twenty women organized Bethel Church. The original records are still in existence.

The Rev. Isaac Anderson was present and ordained John Purris, Ruling Elder. John Walker, Samuel Walker, Abraham

THE HISTORY OF ROANE COUNTY

McClellan were ordained as Elders. The following were charter members:

John Purris, John Walker, Samuel Walker, Abraham McClellan, Roger Barton, George Manifold, Mary Manifold, Mrs. Margaret Walker, Jane Walker, Susan Walker, Sarah Purris, Jane Looney, Jane McCamey, Worthey Bailey, Mrs. Margaret Barton, Ruth Pride, Margaret McCamey, Eliza McClellan, Eliza McCuen, Betsy Walker, Jane Brown, Mary Small, Ann Tucker, Jane Tucker, Fannie Tucker, Mrs. Stephenson, David Patton, John McEwan, Thos. N. Clark, Walter King, Wm. C. McCamey, Trustees.

At the time of the organization of the Church the record gives the names of the following baptised persons not in full communion:

Edly P. Walker, James C. Walker, Samuel R. Walker, Margaret L. Walker, Elizabeth M. Walker, James B. Walker, Catherine O. Walker, Barbary M. Walker, John Blackburn Walker, Nancy R. Aberthnot Walker, John McClellan, Ruth A. McClellan, Catherine B. McClellan, Sarah H. Manifold, Mary B. Manifold, Zachariah J. Walker, John M. Walker, Theopheles Walker, Elizabeth Walker, Mary Walker, Michael Looney, William R. McClellan, Mary Ann McClellan.

On the day of organization Mrs. Ann Tucker brought for baptism her children, Rebecca, Esther, Samuel, James Sloan, Otis, Mary Ellender.

Mr. and Mrs. Olliver Wallace brought their daughter, Ruth.

George and Mary Manifold brought their son, William Fleming Calverey.

Mrs. Eliza McClellan brought her daughter Martha Eliza on November 5.

May 22, 1819 was a big day in the Church when Benjamine Moore, Nancy Gamble, Nancy Galloway, Mrs. Ann Byrd, Betsy Margraves, Patsy Small, Rebecca Tucker, Easter Tucker, Betsy Patton, Betsy Hanapan, Mrs. Margaret Eagleton, Margaret Gilliland, Mrs. Polly Gamble, Addison Carrick, Mrs. Rebecca Carrick, Mrs. Margaret Eagleton and Margaret Walker were received as members.

On November 7, were added the names of Nancy Bruce, Catherine Walker, Barbara Walker, Maria King and Morgan's Frankie, a woman of colour.

THE HISTORY OF ROANE COUNTY

THE RECORDS SHOW MEMBERS RECEIVED
June 4, 1820, Mrs. Susan Moore, Mrs. Patsy Arnold, Mrs. Patsy Pride, Mrs. McMeans, Mrs. Catherine Leftwich, Rebecca Woody, Eliza McCall.

October 22, Major John Leftwich, Alexander Galbraith, Sr., Betsy Galbreath.

June 16, 1821, Oliver Wallace, Mrs. Thankful Wallace, Samuel Pride, Mrs. Eliza McCampbell, Mrs. Sallie Hamilton.

June 9, 1822, Mrs. Nancy McCampbell, Miss Polie Wallace, Mrs. Buchanan.

October 27, Nathaniel Hewett, Mrs. Nathaniel Hewett, Betsy Jones.

1832, Ann Eve Moore, Thomas N. Clark, Susan Clark, Lucy Ann Kowsey, Sally Wallace, Polly McElwee, Eliza Bailey, Mrs. Polly Waters, Elijah McKee Eagleton, Margaret Kenner, Mrs. Ann Leftwich, Mrs. Sophia Eskridge, Mrs. Margaret Jones, Samuel Moore. Abagail Johnson, Mrs. Sarah Echard, Mrs. Betsy Morgan, Mrs. Byrd, Mrs. Moore, Catherine Wroe, Mrs. Sarah Wroe, Mrs. Nancy King, Nancy, a woman of colour, Mrs. Susan Dearmond, Ann Eve Bogart.

1824, Dr. Lewis Jordon, Thomas McConnell, Mrs. Catherine McConnell, Betsy Brazeale.

1825, Amanda Souke, Sarah Akard, Martin King.

1826, John Moore, Mary Looney, Betsy McDonnel, (a slave of Mrs. Eliza McEwen) George, (a slave of George Morgan), Amanda Smith, Alice Stephenson, from the Church at Leesbrough, Peggy McAdams, Alexander Galbraith, Eliza Galbraith, John Wallace, Mrs. Berry.

1827, Amanda Ashley, Jacob K. Spooner, Mrs. Spooner, Lewis Renfro, Mary Millican, Teresa Rebecca Patton, Mary Brazeal.

Amey, belonging to Mr. Gideon Morgan.
Sophia, belonging to Capt. Lyon.
Sidney, belonging to Mr. Gideon Morgan.
Cora Ann, belonging to Mr. Gideon Morgan.
Betsy a free woman.
Philip, belonging to Mrs. McElwce.
Ham, belonging to Mr. Walker.
John G. Liking and wife.

1828, William W. Berry, R. Caroline Berry, David Patton, Mrs. David Patton, Mrs. Nancy Brown, Mrs. Matilda Jordon, Maria, belonging to Gideon Morgan.

1820, John P. Patton, Nancy M. Patton, H. S. Purris, Jane M. Patton, John C. McElwee, Margaret McEwen, **Samuel**

THE HISTORY OF ROANE COUNTY

H. Smith, George Hawkins, (a man of colour).
1833, Sarah A. Pride, Harriett Jones, Jacob Moore, Esther A. Purris,
1835, Mrs. Lurana Rich, Pheobe Rich
1837, John Stephenson, James McCampbell, Jane Mc Campbell, William M. Steele, Mrs. Steele.
1839, Mrs. Mary B. Wiley, Eliza J. Wiley.
1840, Jesse Lincoln, Nancy Lincoln.
1841 Mrs. Jane Gallaher, Dr. William Rogers, Amanda Galbraith, Malinda Rogers, Thomas Moore, William E. McCampbell, James G. Patton, Ann E. McCampbell, Emily C. Gallaher.
1842, Mrs. Mary McClerestian,, Rebecca Lung, Lydia B. Smith.
1843, John N. Moore.
1844, Abiah K. Gallaher, Mary Wiley, Susan J. McCampbell, Barbary E. Myres.
1845 Amanda Love.
1856, Angeline M. Eastabrooke.
1858, William L. McEwen, David E. Patton, Robert K. Byrd, James F. Rouff, W. S. Patton, Mary H. Patton, Martha E. Geass, Thomas N. Clark, Mary A. E. Clark, Matilda H. McEwen, William J. Hornsby, Sarah P. Smith Angeline McConnell, Mrs. E. F. Patterson, Mrs. Frederica Meucke.
1859, William H. Boyd, M. J. McEwen.
1861, Mrs. H. B. Smith, Margaret F. Martin, Margaret J. Gillespie, Mary E. Patton, Joseph A. Muecke, Hugh Martin.
1866, Adelaide M. Meucke, Amanda Rhail, Jennie Colt, Charlie Brause, Gusavus Guenther.
1867, Mrs. Nancy Williams, Constantine Brouse, Eliza Brouse, Elizabeth White, Mrs. Mary Dietz.
1868, Joseph Martin, Mary Martin, J. D. Colt, Amelia Colt, Amanda Geren, Sarah M. McNutt, Mary Brouse.
1869, Mrs. Eblen, Mrs. Julia Zein, Mary Guenther.
1870, Thomas Sevier, Charles C. Hembree, Lillie Eblen, Mrs. Matilda C. Anderson, Mrs. Mary H. J. Roberts, Julia Reece Martin, Mary C. Sevier, Annie E. Sevier, Elizabeth C. Dietz, Matilda Eblen, Sally Roberts Martin, Mrs. Elizabeth Rains, Charlotte Gunther, Elizabeth C. Brouse, Emma Florence Reid, Annie Elizabeth McNutt, Christina M. Seinknecht, Patience Burnett, William H. Deitz, Ruthvin Morrow, Mathew

THE HISTORY OF ROANE COUNTY

P. McEwen, Charles Sevier, Samuel C. Martin, Richard W. Neergartte, Edward Mueche, Mary Bowling, Nannie Winston, Patton, David William Patton, Robert Rend, Paschal Colt, Alonzo Colt, Charles Nelson Martin, William H. McNutt, James R. Martin, Mary Ann Scales, Mrs. Emily C. Martin, Mrs. Mary Overton Patton, Mrs. Addia Patton, Miss Alice McEwen, James Sevier, Charles McEwen, R. L. Cardwell, William Jasper Hentley, Mrs. Louisa Hentley, Mrs. Elvira McCulley.

1872, Mrs. Myrtilla Dunning, Mrs. Mary Petty, Miss Sallie Martin were received into the Church.

EARLY CHRISTENINGS IN BETHEL CHURCH

The children of Mrs. Tucker, Oliver Wallace, George Manifold and Eliza McClellan have been mentioned.

1819, Mrs. Mary Small's son, George Washington, and daughter, Mary. Mrs. Ann Tucker's son, Adonifale. At the same time Margaret, daughter of Rev. William Eagleton, who had been christened at New Providence Church, John M. Gamble, Betsy Green Gamble, William Purris Gamble, Adolphus A. Gamble and Jane McDowell Gamble, who were christened in Knox County, were admitted into the Church.

1820, Mrs. Eliza McEwen's children, William Stephenson, Eliza Mary, Edminston, John Columbus, Robert Newton, Mathew, Margaret Ellis. Rev. William Eagleton's son, Samuel Ewing, Addison Carrick's, Rebecca McDowell and Sidney Gamble. Mrs. Betsy Purris Patton's children, Teresa Rebecca, John Purris, Nancy McClung, Jane McDowell. Oliver Wallace's son, Washington Wade. Mrs. Susan Moore's sons, William Adolphus and Samuel Pride. Mrs. Margaret Gilliland's daughter, Mary Bashears. Mrs. Nancy Bruce's daughter, Margaret Jane. Rev. William Eagleston's daughter, Elvira Hamilton.

1823, Mrs. Nancy McCampbell's children, Thomas Clark, John Andrew and Mary Louisa.

Mrs. Susan Moore's son, Samuel Perry. Mrs. Polly Water's son, Christopher Columbus. Benjamine Moore's children, Anthony Wayne and Mary Ruth. Mrs. Ann Leftwich's son, William John. Mrs. Betsy Harrison's children, Achilles Leonidas, Erasmus Darwin, Eliza Jane, John Koontz and William McEwen. Rev William Eagleton's son, Isaac Anderson. Mrs. Sarah Schard's daughter, Clarisa. Mrs. Sussan Dearmond's household, Esther, Peggy, Polly Elizabeth, John, Grizzy, Matilda Drusilla, Calhoun and Mahala.

THE HISTORY OF ROANE COUNTY

1824, Mrs. Buchanan's children, Mary Ann, Eliza Claris, John Whiteside, William Anderson, Eliza Jane and Sterling. Addison Carrick's son Sam Davis. Thomas McConnell's daughter, Betsy. Mrs. Sarah Schard's son, John.

1825, Mrs. Betsy Morgan Brazeales' daughter, Eliza Jane. Mrs. Buchanan's son, Lafayette. Mrs. Betsy Purris Patton's sons, William Steele and James Gamble. Mrs. William McCamey's son, William Cooper.

1826, Thomas McConnell's daughter, Peggy McAdams. Addison Carrick's son, Hugh Lawson White. John Wallis' son, William. John Moore's Thomas Jefferson and Eliza Ann. Mrs. James McCampbell's children, William Payne, Susan Ann, Mary Eliza and John. Mrs. McEwen's slave. Betty McDonnel's children: James Jackson, Charlotte, Betsy, William McDonnell, Frederick.

1827, Mrs. Betsy Brazeales' son, Columbus. Jacob Spencer's daughter, Elizabeth Wallis.

1828, William W. Berry's children, Elizabeth Walker, Thrusia Ruth Meredith, Sarah Meredith. Thomas David Patton's son, John Newton.

1829, Dr. L. W. Jordon's daughter, Saraphina Almyra. John G. Licking's son,—————. John Moore's daughter, Eliza. Mrs. Brazeales' son, Franklin. David Patton's son, Samuel Fisk.

1839, Mr. and Mrs. William Steele's son William Richard.

1840, son of Rev. Thomas Brown, named William Leonidas. Mrs. Nancy McEwen's daughter, Joana Columbia.

1841, James Hamilton, son of Jesse Lincoln.

1842, Mary Jane and Absolum, children of Mrs. Lung, also Joseph Luallen, son of Mrs. Lung. Joseph McEwen and George Lewis, children of Mrs. Margaret Gillespie. Mary Roxanna, daughter of Rev. Thomas Brown. Virginia, daughter of Dr. Rogers.

1858, Gustavas A. son of Mrs. Muecke. Susan E., William J., John L., Robert E., Mary A., Mathew P., and Charles, children of William L. McEwen.

1859, James C., Susan P., Thomas N., William B., John H., Samuel S., children of Thomas N. Clark. Anna Cora, daughter of N. A. Patterson. William Henry, Mary Alice, Eliza M., Ida Matilda, children of William L. and Martha Geese.

THE HISTORY OF ROANE COUNTY

OFFICERS OF BETHEL CHURCH

May 22, 1819, Addison Carrick was elected Ruling Elder and was ordained by Rev. Rob. Hardin. April 11, 1824, Thomas N. Clark was elected Ruling Elder, being ordained by Rev. William Eagleton. Oct. 2, 1824 Lewis W. Jordon was elected Ruling Elder, and was ordained by Rev. Isaac Anderson. December 27, 1827, David Patton, Thomas McConnell and James Moore, were ordained Elders by Rev. Thomas Brown.

The records show that Andrew Morrison was Moderator of Presbytery in 1820.

John Purris was the first Clerk of the Session, serving from the organization of Bethel Church until his death Sept. 1829, and was succeeded by Dr. Lewis Jordon, who was followed by John Moore as Clerk in 1820. Dr. Jordon's name is signed as Clerk in 1835 and on thru 1839, when John P. Patton was elected to the office and his name appears as clerk until Feb. 15, 1861, when the minutes close until April 1870 when the name of A. Phillips appears.

On October 16, 1870 James B. Martin and Constantine Brouse were ordained Elders by Rev. Thomas Brown and Rev. Thomas Roberts.

Nov. 12, 1870 Rev. E. W. Wyatt was ordained as pastor and continued his services with the Church until April 1872.

April 5, 1871 Mrs. Elizabeth Houston was given a letter of dismissal to the Church at Rockwood.

During the year the Church was most disturbed over the intemperance of one of its members. He had been brought before the session early in the year for drinking, he admitted his guilt but asked forgiveness and was forgiven. The second offence takes up most of the minutes of the year as his trial is written out in full. He was penitent but was excluded from the Church. The following sentence was published by the pastor from the pulpit. "With the earnest prayer that God in the abundance of his Grace and for the sake of our blessed Mediator and Advocate, the Lord Jesus Christ will lead our offending brother to repentance for all his sins, so for this, also his sin of continuance in refusing to hear the Church." W. S. Patton, Clerk.

March 27, 1872 is the next date of the meeting of the Session. Those present being Elders J. B. Martin, C. Brouse, W. S. Patton, with Rev. E. W. P. Wyatt, Moderator. J. P. Patton was absent on April 5. Alex Bartlett was Moderator

THE HISTORY OF ROANE COUNTY

and on April 13, William H. Deitz resigned as Treasurer and Rev. Wyatt resigned. It was decided at this meeting to hold two communion services a year. On April 17 at a congregational meeting Gustavus A. Gunter was elected a Trustee in place of Mr. Deitz and it was decided to fill the place of Rev. Wyatt as soon as possible. The minutes close with those of May 5, 1872 as follows "Communion Season. Rev. Wyatt submitted the following testimonials to the worth and services of our former minister, the late Thomas Brown. "As early as 1827 he entered upon his ministerial labors and only by the interruption of the late War and finally thru feeble health in 1867, did he cease to preach to us the unsearchable riches of Christ."

Rev. William Eagleton was probably the first regular pastor of the Church coming in 1819 and was President of Rittenhouse Academy. On account of failing health he resigned in 1826 or 27. He was succeeded by Thomas Brown who came a young man and stayed for forty years. He married Jane Patton. Rev. Wyatt was his successor in 1867 and remained until 1872. Thru the century of the Church's existence several of the male members were dismissed or reproved but the records show only one female who did not walk the straight and narrow path. In 1830 she was dismissed from the Church for being quarrelsome with her neighbors, and would not promise the Session that she would quit the bad habit. The first money shown on the Treasurer's book is "amount of collection after deductiig expenses $11. 39¾." Very little money was paid the early pastors most of it going for communion wine and material for church building. How interesting it would be to know more of the story of Bethel Church.

Addison Carrick m. Rebecca Gamble in Knox Co., Nov. 5, 1812.

THE HISTORY OF ROANE COUNTY

KINGSTON BURYING GROUND

This historic ground was given by John Riley to the trustees of Rittenhouse Academy for the right to send his children to the School. It adjoins the spot where the first Academy stood on a hill overlooking the town. The remains of many of the early settlers lie on this hillside which is covered by beautiful old trees, mosses and honey suckle. The only member of the Mereweather Smith family whose grave is marked is that of his son James Payne.

Rev. George Yost age 78, d. Oct. 28, 1865 and his wife Margaret, d. Nov. 11, 1858. On the same lot is the grave of Allen Hodges.

Near the lot of the Yost family markers show the graves of James C. b. April 1822, d. Oct. 26, 1880.

Manson S. b. April 12, 1826, d. March 1828.

Allen H. b. Sept. 5, 1837, d. Nov. 11, 1858.

Others are Col. Uriah Allison, b. Feb. 1, 1782, d. May 18, 1820. Robert M. b. 1829, d. 1892. His wife Lucy G. and their children Lida J. b. 1854, d. 1888. Lucy A. b. 1876, d. 1876, d 1876. Willis W. b. 1864, d. 1865.

James McNutt, his wife, Sarah Agnes b. Dec. 17, 1823. d. May 7, 1852. Their children Anna E. b. Dec. 22, 1854, d. Feb. 27, 1907. Robert B. b. Aug. 16, 1866, d. 1866. James, Jr., b. 1849, d. 1885. Anna dau of Dr. W. H. and M. L. McNutt b. Aug. 1888.

Col. Joseph Byrd b. Jan 8, 1795, d. Aug 5, 1858, his wife Ann Pride b. July 20, 1797, d. Aug. 24, 1885. Jesse, b. Mar. 20, 1820. Maria H. King, b. 1822, d. Nov. 24, 1852. Robert King, b. Nov. 1823, d. May 2, 1885. Mary Lea wife of Robert, b. Nov. 7, 1833, d. April 25, 1902. Thomas Brown, b. March 13, 1825. James Standifer, b. Dec. 28, 1828. Samuel Jackson, d. 1865, Mary Ellen b. March 21, 1831, Sarah Ruth b. August 3, 1830. Joseph Jr. b. Sept. 11, 1843, d. Nov. 29, 1870

Rev. William P. Lowery, b. 1812, d. 1892, a Methodist minister. Susan wife of Rev. W. P. age 57. d. Sept 6, 1874 Nancy Brown, mother of Rev. W. P. age 80. Martha J. b.1844 d. 1919. William, Jr., b. Feb. 10, 1840 at Loudon, d. Feb. 27, 1881. R. S. b. 1841, d. 1837

Mary, wife of A. J. Childress b. 1852, d. 1879. Henry Liggett, Sr., b. Jan. 11, 1795, d. Aug. 29, 1867. B. F. Walker

THE HISTORY OF ROANE COUNTY

b. April 5, 1821, d. Aug. 28, 1884. Matilda G., wife of Dr. L. W. Jordon, b. Jan. 26, 1805, d. April 1869. Mary, daughter of Dr. L. W. and Matilda G. Jordon, d. July 1830. Dr. J. W. Lea, b. Sept. 25, 1807, d. 1867. Mary Lea, b. Aug. 1811, d. Nov. 1865. Henry, b. 1845, d. 1846. Virginia, b. 1846, d. 1846. Levinia, b. 1843, d. 1846.

Rev. Daniel Flemming, b. May 4, 1799, d. Aug 28 1868. Mary Burem, his wife b. Feb. 29, 1808, d. April 4, 1884. Charles Rhoton, b. July 23, 1832, d. 1856. Andrew Foster, b. June 29, 1841, d. Oct. 1871.

Thomas N. Clark, Sr., b. May 5, 1763, d. Oct. 13, 1827. Susan Payne, b. Jan. 21, 1768, d. 1812. Thomas Morris Clark, Jr., b. Feb. 28, 1803, d. March 6, 1855. William B. b. ———— d.————. Elizabeth, b. June 20, 1799, d. Dec. 2, 1880. M. A. E., wife of Thomas N. Clark, Jr., b. May 1823, d. Dec. 23, 1899. Children of Thomas and M. A. E., Louie, Willie, Charlie. James C. Clark d. March 8, 1888, age 44. Susan Clark Phillips d. 1826.

Enclosed by an iron fence stands the monument erected over the graves of Gen. Thomas Brown, b. in Green County, N. C., Sept. 15, 1779 and his wife Jane McElwee, b. March 22, 1782, d. May 6, 1860, and that of his twin brother Gen. John Brown who died in 1845.

On the Tomb of Gideon Morgan who died November 15, 1830 is the following:

"Here reposes in the Silence and Tranquility of the Tomb the body of Gideon Morgan, Sr. age 60."

Near lie the remains of his son Rufus who died August 16, 1826, and Elizabeth the wife of Rufus who died Nov. 19, 1859.

THE HISTORY OF ROANE COUNTY

RITTENHOUSE ACADEMY AT KINGSTON

The records of the academy show the first trustees to be Thomas J. Van Dyke, Samuel Eskridge, Jacob Jones, Zachariah Ayers and Jesse Byrd. These were appointed by an act of the legislature in 1806. The names of John Purris, M. Smith, Thomas N. Clark, Thomas Brown, John Brown, Mathew Nelson and Samuel Martin were added to the board in 1809.

Like a good many valuable records the story of the academy for several years was lost, but the minutes of the board meeting of Feb. 1819 show that the trustees present were John Brown, Thomas Brown, Thomas N. Clark, Robert Gilliland, Henry Liggitt, Noah Ashley and Samuel Ewing.

Rules governing the academy, many setting forth duties required of the students, were adopted, that would seem amusing if used today. Each pupil was required to contribute one dollar annually for fire-wood. Those in the English class paid $3.75 for a session of three months, those in the higher classes were charged $5.00.

All students were required to attend public worship on the "Lord's Day." Any student tardy or absent without an excuse from the parent was required to "perform a portion of the menial offices of the academy." Public examinations were held at the end of each session for the "animation of the students in literary pursuits." Students were "not allowed to fight, use profane language, speak obscenely, get drunk, gamble, frequent taverns or associate with base, abandoned characters." Nor were they allowed to smoke paper or tobacco within the walls of the academy or wear their hats while school was in session.

At a meeting of the board Oct. 29, 1822, those present were Thomas N. Clark, Solomon Geren, Gen. John Brown, Thomas Brown, Samuel Martin, Merriweather Smith, Jesse Byrd, Henry Liggett, Noah Ashley, Robert Gilliland and Hugh Dunlap.

William Egleton was made president and the price of tuition was put at $6 per session. One of the duties of the president was to advertise the school for six weeks in the Knoxville papers.

At the November meeting of 1823 William S. McEwen was added to the board and in 1824 James McPherson and Lewis Jordon were elected. The health of the Rev. William Egleton had failed and Allen G. Gallaher was elected president of the academy in his stead.

THE HISTORY OF ROANE COUNTY

During the year the trustees met several times, but little business was recorded in the minutes except that the secretary, Robert Gilliland, was instructed to call on the East Tennessee bank for funds due the academy from that state school fund. William B. Clark was added to the board, which again ordered the president to advertise in the Knoxville paper.

In December, 1825, Mr. John Hook was elected president.

The records show that the trustees met often in the next two years with the names of those present, but little of interest transpired except that William Clark and William McEwen were appointed to visit the school once a month and see if the by-laws were carried out. Jacob Spooner was elected president in 1827 and the following report was sent to the house of representatives:

Nov. 15, 1827. "Trustees met and the following report was sent to the house of representatives:

"In obedience to a resolution of Sept. 27, we, a committee appointed by the trustees of Rittenhouse Academy to make a report of this institution to your honorable body, make leave to report the following:

"This academy is now in operation, and we are flattered with the prospects that it will add much to the interest and welfare of the rising generation.

"The branches taught are orthography, reading, writing, arithmetic, English, grammar, geography, with the use of maps and globes, astronomy, mensuration, trigonometry, geometry, moral intellectual and natural philosophy, belles-letters, the Latin and Greek languages.

"As to funds, which are at present available, the trustees are unable to make a report, as an act of the general assembly of 1821 appropriating the rent of certain lands to the institute, which has since been repealed, the sum received by the trustees has been $289.50. Said sum having been appropriated for repairs.

"The trustees beg leave to represent to your honorable body that our buildings are much out of repair, the institution is now in debt, no means available by which we can be relieved. We beg leave to suggest to your honorable body the expediency of fostering and cherishing such institutions as are most likely to secure permanent harmony and welfare of the yeomanry of our country. Trusting that the confidence which we entertain in the guardians of our liberty, we beg leave to call your legislative attention to the furtherance and promotion of edu-

THE HISTORY OF ROANE COUNTY

cation, impressed with the assurance that a subject fraught with so much good to the rising glory of our republic, will meet with the warmest co-operation of an enlightened legislative body.
"Thomas Brown, W. S. McEwen, William B. Clark, Jacob K. Spooner, committee."

Mathew Sullivan was an assistant teacher at this time, but was succeeded in 1828 by L. J. Likins. Jacob Spooner and his assistant had classes in the following books:

Murray's Grammar,, S. Pike's Arithmetic, Adam's Geography, Blair's "Lectures," Paley's "Moral Philosophy," "Conversation on Natural Philosophy," "Conversation on Chemistry," Euclid (three books), Gibson's "Surveying," Hedges "Logic," Locke's "On the Understanding," "Rudduman's Grammar, Crowder's Greek Testament, John and the Acts (historear sacre), Ovid's "Lucian" (half through; "Xenophon" (Ceasar's Commentaries) : Homer's "Virgil and Sallust" Cicero's Oration (Latin prosedy) : Horace's "Oration."

The same year Jacob Spooner resigned, L. J. Likens was made president with Albert Allcorn as assistant. Ill health caused Mr. Likens to resign the next year and William J. Keith succeeded him.

In 1831 William Wilson brought a recommendation from the Rev. Isaac Anderson and was employed as president.

Thomas N. Clark, Sr., had deeded 1½ acres of land to the trustees of Bethel Presbyterian church in 1823 for the sum of $1. In 1832 the contract was let to Thomas Crutchfield to erect a new academy in Kingston, Joshiah Smith, who was teaching a private school in the academy in 1832, was elected president and a female school was allowed the use of the old building. The president was ordered to advertise in the Knoxville Register the commencement of the next term.

The record of 1835 shows William Brown, John Byrd and William B. Clark as having been made trustees, George Rich as president with Miss Pheobe Rich assistant. The academy continued under their management until 1837 when Mr. Rich removed from Kingston and his daughter was allowed the use of the building for a primary school until another teacher could be found.

In 1838 Dr. Richard Richards and Phillip Beddo were appointed trustees by the legislature and Benjamin F. Smith elected president. He was succeeded in 1845 by Benjamin V. Irvine and the minutes say that it was agreed by the trustees that

THE HISTORY OF ROANE COUNTY

females would be admitted to the academy, although the list of students of 1828 included girls.

Mr. Irvine served four years as president. Henry W. Von Alderhoff, a Prussian nobleman, who had taught at Forest Academy at Athens when Senator J. T. Morgan was a student, was given the office with a salary of $300. per session.

In 1852 Athens made an effort to secure Mr. Von Alderhoff, and as an inducement to remain in Kingston, his salary was raised to $400, with John Fleming as assistant at $100 per session. The school had grown until there was not room in the academy and the board rented a house from George Yost until an addition could be built.

When Mr. Von Alderhoff resigned in 1856, his place was filled by William G. Loyd, of Chattanooga. George McDuffee, John Y. Smith, Samuel DeArmond, W. S. Center and James McNutt were trustees appointed by the court during the late 40's and during the 50's. In 1861 the court added the names of A. O. Fisher, James Martin, Newton Patterson, William Gurscot and Freemoten Young and the board advertised for a suitable teacher.

In January, 1862, the Rev. Samuel Roberts was employed as principal, and then the record of the school ends, to be closed until the war is over.

The academy was re-opened in 1871 with John R. Neal, who had returned a Colonel from the Confederate Army as Principal.

PUPILS ENROLLED AT RITTENHOUSE ACADEMY
APRIL 16, 1828

ENGLISH CLASS
Betsy M. Carrick
Nancy Patton
Mary Brown
Jane Patton
Jane Harrison
Archilles Harrison
Andrew McCampbell

READING CLASS
Jane Patton
Nancy Patton
Amanda Jones

Betsy M. Carrick
Jane Harrison
Mary Brown
Mary Gilliland
Amanda Gilbreath
John Jordon
William McCampbell

Jacob Moore
Andrew McCampbell
Wyley Tuttle
William Liggitt
William Brown

THE HISTORY OF ROANE COUNTY

GEOGRAPHY CLASS
Betsy M. Carrick
Nancy Patton
William B. Ayers
Mathew McEwen
Mary Brown

VIRGIL CLASS
J. T. McCampbell
J. T. Smith
John P. Patton

NATURAL PHILOSOPHY
Miss Nancy Patton

HORATIO CLASS
W. P. Gambell
Frances A. Brown

ARITHMETIC CLASS
Andrew McCampbell
Jacob Moore
Aaron Rollins
Mathew McEwen
Archilles M. Harrison

STUDENTS SEPTEMBER 25, 1828

HISTORY OF ROME CLASS
Nancy Patton
Mary Brown
Elizabeth Carrick

CORDERIE
A. S. Harrison
M. P. McEwen
A. H. Gambell
J. A. McCampbell

ENGLISH GRAMMAR
Betsy M. Carrick
Mary Brown
Nancy Patton
Archilles S. Harrison
John W. Brown
Jacob Moore

VIRGIL CEASAR AND HOMER
P. Patton

ERASMUS CLASS
A. S. Harrison
A. H. Gambell
M. P. McEwen

ARITHMETIC CLASS
Archilles Harrison
Jas. Moore
J. W. Brown
J. P. Patton

GEOGRAPHY CLASS
Nancy Patton
Mary Brown
Elizabeth Carrick

THE TREASURER'S BOOK SHOWS THE FOLLOWING WHO PAID TUITION
1832

Rachel Loyd	$ 3.00	Andrew Jack	5.00
Hugh L. McPherson	1.00	John Moore	2.00
P. T. Beddo	2.00	Wm. Galbraith	2.00
E. D. Murray	2.00	H. H. Wiley	3.00
Sam'l. H. Smith	5.00	H. S. Purris	2.00
Wm. Musgrove	1.00	David Patton	7.00

THE HISTORY OF ROANE COUNTY

1846

Jessie Allison	$ 4.29
Robert Allison	4.86
Lucinda Brown	4.86
George Gillespie	3.00
Katherine Green	4.86
Sarah Kirkpatrick	4.86
Sarah Brown	6.48
Wm. A. Kirkpatrick	8.00
S. L. Suddath	8.00
Henry Smith	8.00
Caroline P. Smith	8.00

W. M. McEwen
D. Welcker
Matilda Richardson
Mary Nicholson
John Cox
Andrew C. Wiley
Robert N. McDuffee
Sarah P. Smith
Angeline McDuffee
John M. Staples
Thos. T. Brown
Thos. Center
Henry Liggett, Jr.
H. C. Sevier
M. P. Smith
Wm. L. Smith
Wm. Welcher (Welker)
Thos. B. Brown
Thos. B. Sevier
Dr. James W. Lea
R. D. Duncan
Robert Kimbro
S. M. Matlock
Dr. Welcker (Welker)
D. Asbury
Jas. Hamilton
Elizabeth Cosby

Rachel Wester
Samuel Smalley
John Fundley
T. B. Matlock
William A. Smith

1847

Jas. Stephenson
Sam Childress
Martin Matlock
Dewitt Welcher
W. S. Senter
J. C. Plumlee
A. L. Green
H. Liggett
Wm. Staples
John White
Allen Yost
Thos. B. Brown
Henry Sevier
J. W. Pyott
T. White
C. D. Talliafero
D. Patton,
Jesse Delozier
John Y. Smith
Julian Scott
D. G. Taylor
David Fleming
Sam'i Pyott
Thos. Childress
Thos. A. Brown
Martha Childress

1848

W. S. McEwen
R. D. Fleming
Samuel Eblen
Charles Gallaher
Fleming Work

THE HISTORY OF ROANE COUNTY

James Lea
Thos. Childress
James McNutt
George Brown

Sam'l Pyott
R. N. McDuffee
James Asbury
Elizabeth Patton

The Treasurer's records show that more money was spent on window panes than almost any one thing. One old rule was that the students were not to study aloud. An old story that has been handed down from the early days of the Academy is amusing. Mrs. B. was passing the school one day just as the school closed, and the larger boys rushed out, some reciting "Alpha-Beta-Chi-Delta-Gamma at the top of their voices, and scared the old lady so much that she rushed into the house next door crying "Sister S. save me, they are running after me yelling "catch her, beat her, kill her, dam her."

COL. JOHN R. NEAL TAUGHT IN 1871, SHOWING THE FOLLOWING PUPILS ENROLLED

CLASS NO. 1.

Nannie Roberts
Asa Williams
John O. Patton
Henry Hedgecloth
Martha Renfro
Flora McCully
Nannie Center
John B. Green
Charlie Allison
John Nichols
Columbus Renfroe

CLASS NO. 2.

Ella DeArmond
August Lindbury
Charles Deitz
Ida May Reno
Mary Steinwehr
E. C. Strurges
Sallie Nelson
John M. Sturges
Catherine Senknicht
Christine Lindbury
James D. Colt

Paul J. Nearguard
Maggie Wester
O. C. Clark
Scott Martin
Austin Green

CLASS NO. 3.

John Rothe
Mollie Tipton
Martha Hood
James Allison
Charles Steinwher
Matilda Hood
Mary Hood

CLASS NO. 4.

Willie Eblin
Anna McNutt
Allen Barnwell
Richard Nearguard
Walter Henderson
Alonzo Colt
Pascal Colt
May Wester
Henry Biss

THE HISTORY OF ROANE COUNTY

R. T. Barnard
James Young
Wlliam McNutt
Alice Barnwell
Theo Neerguard
R. J. Eblin
Freddie Colt
David Patton
Thomas Gipton
Sam C. Clark
Mathilda Fritts

CLASS NO. 5.
Sallie Brown
George W. Nixon
Lillie Deitz
Robert F. Brown

CLASS NO. 6.
Charles Sevier
Charlotte Guenther
John W. Hood
Matilda Bowers

Charles Martin
J. W. Crowder,
Columbus Reagan

RHETORIC CLASS
Sallie Brown
Matilda Bowers
Anna McNutt
Charlotte Guenther
J. W. Crowder
John Hood
Richard Neerguard
Lena Colt
Columbus Reagan
Robert Brown

ALGEBRA CLASS
John Hood
J. W. Crowder
Robert Brown

ASTRONOMY CLASS
Charlotte Guenther

THIRD QUARTER COMMENCING NOVEMBER 1 1871

6TH CLASS

Sallie Brown
Lillie Deitz
George W. Nixon
Robert F. Brown

5TH CLASS

Charles Sevier
Charles Martin
Charlotte Guenther
J. W. Crowder
John W. Hood
Columbus Reagan
Mathilda Bower

CLASS NO. 4.
Willie Eblin
James Young
Anna McNutt
William McNutt
Allen Barnwell
Alice Barnwell
Richard Neerguard
Theo Neerguard
Walter Henderson
R. J. Eblin
Alonzo Colt
Freddie Colt
Pascal Colt
David Patton
May Wester

THE HISTORY OF ROANE COUNTY

Thomas Gipton
Henry Biss
Sam C. Clark
R. T. Bernard
Mathilda Fritts
Maggie Wester
CLASS NO. 3.
John Rothe
Charles Steinwehr
Mollie Tipton
Mathilda Hood
Martha Hood
Mary K. Hood
James Allison
CLASS NO. 2.
Ella DeArmond
Catherine Senknicht
August Linbury
Christine Linbury
Charlie Deitz
James D. Colt
Ida May Reno
Paul J. Neerguard
Mary Steinwehr
Maggie Wester
E. C. Sturges
O. C. Clark
Sallie Nelson
Scott Martin
John M. Sturgis
Austin Green

CLASS NO. 1.

Nannie Roberts
Nannie Center
Asa Williams
John B. Green
John O. Patton
Charlie Allison
Henry Hedgecoth
John Nichols
Martha Renfroe
Columbus Renfroe
Flora McCulley

RHETORIC

Sallie Brown
Mathilda Bowers
Anna McNutt
Charlotte Guenther
I. W. Crowder
John Hood
Richard Neerguard
Lena Colt
Columbus Reagan
Robert Brown

COMPOSITION

Alice Barnwell
Lillie Deitz
May Wester
Pascal Colt
W. Eblin
David Patton

ASTRONOMY

Charlotte Guenther

HISTORY

Charlotte Guenther
Sallie Brown
Lillie Deitz
Anna McNutt
W. McNutt
Pascal Colt
Freddie Colt
Sam Clark
W. Eblin
I. W. Crowder
John Hood
Columbus Reagan
Thomas Gipton

6TH READER

Martha Hood
Mathilda Hood
Kate Hood
Mathilda. Fritts

Maggie Wester
May Wester
Mollie Gipton
Flora McCully
James Allison
Henry Biss
August Linbury
R. T. Barnard
J. M. Sturges

ALGEBRA

John Hood
J. W. Crowder
Robert Brown
Charlie Sevier

GEOGRAPHY

Mary Wester
Maggie Wester
Henry Biss

FOURTH QUARTER COMMENCING FEB. 12, 1872

CLASS 6.
Robert F. Brown
Sallie B. Brown
Lillie Deitz
Charles Martin

CLASS 5.
Charlie Sevier
W. Margraves
Belle French
Columbus Renfroe

3RD CLASS

John McNutt
Willie Wright
Charlie Steinwehr
August Linbury

4TH CLASS

Walter Henderson
W. M. McNutt
Anna McNutt
Theo Neerguard
Richard Neerguard
Mary Wright
Annah Rhoel
James DeArmond
Mathilda Fritts
Mathilda Hood

John Rothi
Felix Center
Frank Fritts
Maggie Coleman

2ND CLASS

Belle Rhoel
E. C. Sturges
Maggie Wester
Robert Seinknicht
Richard J. Neerguard
Charlie Deitz
Mary Steinwehr
H. M. Hedgcoth
Lizzie Harris

1ST CLASS

Nannie Roberts
Anna Wester
Willie Ferguson
Charlie Eblen
Tennessee Burnette
Samuel Rothe

COMPOSITION

Mary Wright
Lilly Deitz
Mathilda Fritts

THE HISTORY OF ROANE COUNTY

Mathilda Hood
W. McNutt
James DeArmond
August Linbury

LATIN
Robert Brown
Charlie Martin
Lillie Deitz

ASTRONOMY
Sallie Brown
Nannie McNutt
Belle French

ENGLISH GRAMMAR 1
Richard Neerguard
Charlie Martin

ENGLISH GRAMMAR 2
Willie Wright
John McNutt
James DeArmond
Annie Rothe
John Roth

ENGLISH GRAMMAR 3
Theo Neerguard
Walter Henderson
W. M. McNutt
Mary Wright
Lillie Deitz
Mathilda Fritts
Mathilda Hood

GEOMETRY
Charlie Sevier

RHETORIC
Columbus Reagan
Richard Neerguard
Robert Brown
Belle French
Anna McNutt

HISTORY
Lillie Deitz
James DeArmond
Mary Wright
Sallie Brown
Anna McNutt
W. McNutt
Richard Neerguard
Theo Neerguard
Walter Henderson
W. Margraves
Charlie Sevier
Richard Neerguard
Columbus Reagan
Mathilda Hood
Mathilda Fritts
Maggie Coleman

GEOGRAPHY
Willie Wright
John McNutt
Anna Roehl
Flora McCulley

ARITHMETIC
Lizzie Harris

6TH READER
Anna Roehl
Flora McCully
Willie Wright
John McNutt
August Linbury

ALGEBRA
W. Margraves
Belle French
Robert Brown

BOOKEEPING
Charlie Martin

Bud J. Neerguard
Nannie Patton
Teresa Patton
John Patton
Columbus Reagan
Frank Rhoel
Anna Rhoel
Belle Rhoel
Asa Williams
May Wester
Maggie Wester

Anna Wester
Arthur Smith
Josephine Green
Sallie Brown
Kate Kimbrough
Mary Wright
Willie Wright
Mathilda Fritts
Carrie Brown
Lizzie Nicholson

FIFTH QUARTER COMMENCING APRIL 29.

Tennie Burnette
Sam Clark
Eugene Clark
Charlie Clark
Maggie Coleman
James DeArmond
Ella DeArmond
Lillie Deitz
Carl Deitz
Belle French

Willie Ferguson
Mary Gibbs
Henry Hedgcoth
Willie Liggett
W. Margraves
W. M. McNutt
John McNutt
Charlie Martin
Felix Center
Frank Fritts

PART FOUR

EARLY MARRIAGE LICENSES

From 1801, when the County was organized until 1838 no record was kept and the Marriage Licenses were scattered. They have lain for many years in the dust and trash of the third floor of the Court House and some are so faded that it has been almost impossible to read. In some of the names and dates, therefore some mistakes may have been made.

("M. G." abreviation for Minister of the Gospel.)
("J. P." for Justice of the Peace.)

These lines are written on the back of the marriage license of Joseph Nail and Alonia Nimsco married March 14, 1817.

"With pleasure I record the tale,
This day was married Joseph Nail,
To Miss Alonia Mimsco White.
Both were agreed, 'twas there for right,
By me, Alex Nesmith, a Justice of Peace
For the County of Roane, I did act in this case,
And tho' I believe no one there wished me harm
Not a nerve in my body but took the alarm.
Oh! sensibility, offspring of Jove,
Thou source of wildest wrath and softest love,
By these we are taught to tell another's woe,
And just as keenly taste his pleasures too."

March 14, 1817   Alexander Nesmith, J. P.

EARLY MARRIAGE LICENSES OF ROANE COUNTY

NAMES	BONDSMEN
	1801
Dec. 22. John Powell Ann Carter	Micajah Carter Henry Brazeal, Clerk
	1802
Oct. 25, John Mear Mary Burnes	John Mear Hugh Mear
Mar. 27, William Davis Betsy Roberts	James Hankins
March 1, William Walker Feby Horton	Thomas Walker William Walker
June 22, Samuel Williams Nancy Haskins	Samuel Williams James Haskins
March 15, James Dearmond Suckey Shaddon	
July 10, John McCord Betsy Sharkey	
	1803
Jan. 4, William Matlock Sally Walker	William Matlock Ephriam Walker
April 4, Augustus Strong Louisa Shepherd	Augustus Strong Townley Deakins Thomas Olliver
July 12, John Gambell Betsy Evins	John Gambell James Gallaher

THE HISTORY OF ROANE COUNTY

NAMES	BONDSMEN
	1804
Feb. 11, Townley Deakins Agness Rainfrow	married by Jesse Byrd, J. P.
Mar. 19, Daniel Durne Sarah Stone	Daniel Durne Edward Waller
Mar. 9, John Walker Ginney Galloway	John Walker James Galloway
Feb. 9, Hugh White Mary Johnson	Hugh White William Barnett
July 24, Thomas Bozeman Ammy Miller	Thomas Bozeman Alex Miller
Nov. 29, William Pruitt Sally Cavett	William Pruitt Richard Cavet
Sept. William Johnston Matty Rogers	
	1805
Dec. 28, John Prater Peggy Wood	John Prater John Wood
Nov. 8, James James Nancy Givens	James James Eama Walker
Nov. 16, James Luster Anv Jones	James Luster John Luster David Lee

THE HISTORY OF ROANE COUNTY

NAMES	BONDSMEN
	1805

Aug. 26,
George Graves — Jacob Work
Sarah Willet — James Willet
(married by James M. Watt)

July 20,
John Johnson — John Johnson
Lydia Copeland — William Hellums

Aug. 8,
James Brazeale — James Brazeale
Peggy Miller — Thomas Pritchett

Aug. 20,
Simpson Eldridge — Simpson Eldridge
Fannie Simmons — Jesse Eldridge

Nov. 30,
Richard Oliver — Richard Oliver
Elizabeth Allen — John Wood

Jan.
John Crsery — John Crsery
Susanah Hahins — Daniel Hare

Sept. 25,
James Miller — James Miller
Mary Fendley — Frances Miller

June 20,
Thomas Upton — Thomas Upton
Emmey Wilson — John Brown
— Mark Renfroe

Oct. 28,
William Brown
Stacey Grason

Sept. 16,
Thomas Laye — Thomas Laye
Sarah Smith — Daniel Hare

1806

Feb. 2,
Daniel Brown — Daniel Brown
Jane Ellender — Robert Nobles
married by John McEwen J.P.

THE HISTORY OF ROANE COUNTY

NAMES	BONDSMEN
	1806

Nov. 6,
Morris Moore Morris Moore
Dianah Adams Thomas Moore
 James Nail

Nov. 22,
Thomas Stafford Thomas Stafford
Rosey Baskin Frances Fulcher

Aug. 19,
Samuel Dudley Samuel Dudley
Martha Sherard Jesse Sherard

Aug. 10,
William Richards William Richards
Polly Phillips Joel Holt

June 10,
James Roberts James Roberts
Delilah Woods Joseph Hankins

1807

Nov. 27,
David Dean David Dean
Gracey Joiner Winniam Joiner

Jan.
Daniel Self Daniel Self
Ann Robinson John Jones

March 7,
Henry Self Henry Self
Betsy Allin Levi Self
 Mathew Nelson

May 11,
David Lee David Lea
Judith Dwire (Dyer) Thomas Young

THE HISTORY OF ROANE COUNTY

NAMES　　　　　　　　BONDSMEN

1807

Dec. 7,
John Derick
Caty Bird

John Derick
George Derick
Henry Derick

May 22,
William Ballard
Polly Eblen

William Ballard
Hugh Frances

May 23,
Phillip Burch
Polly Paine

Phillip Burch
Abraham Shafer

Aug. 6,
Jeremiah Hynson
Fannie Lyles

Jeremiah Hynson
Isaac Shualt
Robert Lyles

June 6,
Wiley Tuten
Rachel Cody

Wiley Tuten
John Riley
Absolum Dixon

Feb. 15,
William Goodrich
William L. Lovely

July 14,
John Husk
Nancy Thompson

John Husk
James Thompson

Feb. 24,
Peter Berry
Rebecca Buchanan

married by
Jesse Byrd, J. P.

1808

Aug. 23,
Henry Haynes
Lucinda Neal

Henry Haynes
Abner Majors

March 26,
George Vaugn
Caty Roberts

THE HISTORY OF ROANE COUNTY

NAMES	BONDSMEN

1808

April 9,
William Holland
Patty Short

Nov. 10,
James Trimble   William Lyons
Letitia Clark   Richard H. Love

April 2,
Samuel Keys   Samuel Keys
Polly Riley   Gilbert Pool
    (Married by Abner K. Shaifer, J. P. at South West Point. Witnesses: C. M. Thouston Samuel Riley Samuel Keys, Sr.)

Jan. 7,
Lewis Widener   Lewis Widener
Anna Click   Peter Wingener

Sept. 28,
Samuel Bradley   Samuel Bradley
Peggy Taylor   Littlepage Sims

Sept. 6,
Bartlett Robins   Bartlett Robins
Catey McNutt   Samuel Waddy

March 25,
Yaza Bashears   Yaza Bashears
Polly Rice   John B. Rice

July 12,
Elijah Evans   Elijah Evans
Nancy Fouche   Henry Brazeale

Nov. 11,
Daniel Little   Daniel Little
Polly Tunnmins   Samuel Tunnmins

Nov. 11,
Robert Bashears   Robert Bashears
Sallie Hankins   James Hankins
    Betsy Puris

THE HISTORY OF ROANE COUNTY

NAMES	BONDSMEN
	1808
Jan. 2, George Delozier Perina Rouder	
Oct. 8, James Lappington Polly Dickson	
	1809
Jan. 25, John Riley Suckie Walker	John Riley Gilbert Pool
March 13, John Neal Ellender Harrison	John Neal William Thomas
April 19, George Stephens Polly Moore	
Nov. 16, Alexander Russell Betsy Rice	
Nov. 18, William Adair Nancy Rather	William Adair Samuel Riley
Dec. 25, Thomas Moore Polly Kindrick	married by William McCamey, J P.
Nov. 11, Alpha Kingsley Eliza Ayers	Alpha Kingsley E. Pritchett
March 13, John Gillespie Nancy Gallaher	John Gillespie Mathew Donaldson
Oct. 11, Thomas Craig Peggy Stonecipher	Thomas Craig Andrew Pruitt

THE HISTORY OF ROANE COUNTY

NAMES	BONDSMEN
	1809
Nov. 3, James Green Susan Rowden	James Green Ekale Rowden
Sept. 27, Thomas Harvey Rachael Carter	Thomas Harvey Edward Eblen
Nov. 13, Stephen Wright Jeminia Buchanan	Stephen Wright Samuel Stout
Jan. 24, David Patton Betsy Purris	David Patton John Purris
March 6, Christopher Robinson Sally Rector	Lewis Robinson Abraham Shaefer
Oct. 29, Julius Hacker Sarah Hagerty	Julius Hacker Samuel McCall
Dec. 26, Absolom Eakin Jane Sutton	Absolom Eakin Thomas Blackstone
Oct. 20, Jonathan Clenny Jinny Husett	Jonathan Clenny John Dirgin
March 14, John Kennedy Eady Dunlap	Married by A. K. Shaefer, J. P. Col. John McClellan William McClellan Hugh Dunlap and others
Nov. 17, William Parker Cilby Barnett	
Oct. 3, Elias Allen Sally Holly	

THE HISTORY OF ROANE COUNTY

NAMES	BONDSMEN
	1810
Dec. 10, Calvin Johnson Nancy McKamey	Calvin Johnson William McCamey
Jan. 19, Wiley Walker Patsy Robertson	Willie Walker Charles Codey
Feb. 5, John Moton Jenny Kelly	
Jan. 12, William Oliver Peggy Lacefield	William Oliver John Allen
Aug. 21, Isaac Keys Elizabeth Riley	Isaac Keys Gilbert Pool
Feb. 16, Jesse Pellum Peggy Culp	Jesse Pellum Mathew Wood
Oct. 1, John Hart Ruth Stout	John Hart James Dearmond
Nov. 7, James Preston Jinney Allison	James Preston Uriah Allison
Feb. 23, James Warren Nancy Evans	James Warren Arden Evans
Dec. 22, Reuben Phillips Kitty Bowers	Reuben Phillips James Robinson
Aug. 27, Hugh Crumbliss Betsy Bashears	Hugh Crumbliss Isaac Rashears

THE HISTORY OF ROANE COUNTY

NAMES	BONDSMEN
	1810

Sept. 3,
Alexander Galbreath
Polly Gallaher

Alexander Galbreath
James Gallaher

Aug. 16,
Samuel Nipp
Elizabeth Riley

Samuel Nipp
Charles Cody
John Odin

March 13,
Robert Hewett
Rebecca Phillips

Robert Hewett
James Robinson

July 4,
Moore Matlock
Lucy Knight

Moore Matlock
William Anderson

May 20,
Elisha Williams
Sally Matlock

Elisha Williams
James Matlock

April 7,
John Haggart
Sarah Smith

John Haggart
James Haggart
John Smith

Feb. 17,
James Bailey
Polly Rector

James Bailey
John Rector

Nov. 2,
Charlie Burk
Nancy Bowman

Charlie Burk
John Bowman

Jan. 24,
Isaac Bullar
Sally Geren

1811

May 26,
James Rogers
Nancy Cody

James Rogers
Wiley Tuten

NAMES	BONDSMEN
	1811
Dec. 7, John Dauret Elizabeth Coatney	John Dauret John Doss
Sept. 11, Alexander Powell Patsy Browder	Alexander Powell Britton Mathews
July 16, Clemmens Phllips Drusilla Prewett	Clemmens Phillips John W. Bowers
July 16, Daniel Hastler Nancy Noel	Daniel Hastler David Thomas
Oct. 4, Charles Hickey Lucinda England	Charles Hickey Jeremiah Fielder
Aug. 1, Thomas Richardson Elizabeth Ellison	Thomas Richardson Ambler Casey
Sept. 6, Reuben McKinnie Jenny Lyle	Reuben McKinnie Robert Lyle
June 29, William Pimerlore Mary Corey	
Aug. 28, John Thacker Nellie Brazelton	John Thacker James Hunt
Dec. 11, Ethereld Taylor Catherine H. Arbuckle	Ethereld Taylor John Brown
Oct. 11, Abner Waters Betsy Reyburn	
March 8, John Black Peggy Eldridge	

THE HISTORY OF ROANE COUNTY

NAMES | BONDSMEN
1811

Sept. 11,
Joseph Thompson
Polly Hopkins

1812

Jan. 7,
William Kelley
Ruth Prigmore

William Kelley
James May

Jan. 4,
William Bogart
Jenny Preston

William Bogart
James Preston

March 25,
Ephriam Bridges
Betsy White

Ephriam Bridges
Benjamin Shields

Sept. 5,
James Wilkinson
Lucy Rice

James Wilkinson
James Rice

Sept. 7,
Silas Luttrell
Stacey Burnett

Silas Luttrell
Moses Burnett

Oct. 16,
Samuel Hope
Agnes Duncan

Samuel Hope
Jeptha Dugger

Feb. 26,
Moses Cavett
Polly Pickle

1813

Sept. 23,
Larkin Sawyer
Elizabeth Childs

Larkin Sawyer
William D. Neilson

Jan. 10,
William Bowman
Levisy Edmonds

William Bowman
Mathew Edmonds

THE HISTORY OF ROANE COUNTY

NAMES -- BONDSMEN
1813

Sept. 11,
Joshua Dover
Passy Rice

Joshua Dover
Abraham Stout

Sept. 9,
Alexander Casey
Nanny Ross

Alexander Casey
William Brown

Dec. 24,
Adam Gardenhire
Absey Tippet

Sept. 10,
James Cooper
Mary Weir

James H. Cooper
Andrew Weir

Feb. 1,
George Pickle
Sussanah Haggard

1814

July 9,
Isaac Roberson
Nancy Talbot

Isaac Roberson
Frances Erwin

Feb. 16,
Charles Mitchell
Framina Perriman

Charles Mitchell
Louis Combs

June 22,
William Breeding
Patience Phillips

William Breeding
James Hope

June 7,
William Bowers
Betsy Phillips

William Bowers
John Bowers

Dec. 1,
Nathaniel Aplegate
Elizabeth Smith

Nathaniel Aplegate
Richard Fairies

Dec. 1,
John Thomas
Barbara Casey

John Thomas
Anthony Casey

THE HISTORY OF ROANE COUNTY

NAMES	BONDSMEN
	1815
Oct. 17, James Flatt Rebecca Rice	James Flat John Rice
Jan. 6, John Hill Virry Lane	John Hill Joseph Graham
	1815
Jan. 19, Fielding Balden Nancy Stean	Fielding Balden Thomas York
Aug. Joel Oliver Celia Vaughn	
Sept. 14, William Eblen Lucretia Smith	
July 24, Gabriel Richards Peggy Ayers	married by Richard Richards, M. G.
Dec. 1, Edward Warren Polly Eldridge	
Sept. 30, James Matlock, Jr. Betsy Hicks	
May 2, Elijah Farmer Jane Preston	
	816
Dec. 16, Solomon Potter Esther Melton	married by Alexander Nesmith, J. P.
Dec. 23, Abraham Adkinson Sally Adkinson	married by William McKamey, J. P.

THE HISTORY OF ROANE COUNTY

NAMES	BONDSMEN
	1816

May 3,
Mishac Rowden
Sarah McNabb

Jan. 28,
Lewis Robinson
Betsy Starks

Nov. 22,
James Hamilton   Jas. Hamilton
Nancy Childers   Samuel Stout
   married by
John Purris, J. P.

Oct. 12,
Wyatt Gallaher   married Feb. 6, 1817 by
Sally Dalton   Asa Cobb, J. P.

Dec. 17,
Nicholas West   Nicholas West
Polly Jackson   John West

Aug. 3,
Thomas Oden
Nancy Miller

1817

Mar. 10,
Eli Oliver
Essie Ellis

Dec. 24,   married at home of John Puris
Nathan Game   J. P. Witnesses:
Sarah Delaney   George Davis
    Betsy Margraves

Feb. 27,
Moses Looney   Moses Looney
Patty York   Joseph Lacey

THE HISTORY OF ROANE COUNTY

NAMES BONDSMEN

1817

April 20,
Andrew Nail
Sally Harvey

Andrew Nail
Allen Hill

Oct. 11,
Isaac England
Rebecca Rector

Isaac England
Thomas England

May 8,
John Rather
Nancy Nail

John Rather
Williom Gardenhire

Mar. 25,
Samuel Woody
Hannah Woody

Nov. 24,
Alexander Casey
Eany Whith

Alexander Casey
Samuel Tucker

Nov. 26,
James Moore
Nancy Lanston

James Moore
Benjamine Hagewood
Philip Stephens

Jan. 16,
Peter Upshaw
Jeney Fields

married by
Robert Williams, J. P.

Feb. 17,
Alexander Kelly
Sally Prigmore

Alex Kelly
George Gregsby

Feb. 27,
Bevinds Brown
Jennie Mathews

Bevinds Brown
Nicholas Mansfield

Aug. 28,
Seaborn Center
Nancy Carson

Seaborn Center
George Arnold

April 5,
Arthur Cody
Cynthea Garrett

Arthur Cody
Thomas Clark

THE HISTORY OF ROANE COUNTY

NAMES	BONDSMEN
	1817
April 4, Jesse Casey Patsy Coe	married by Joseph McPherson
Dec. 5, Phillip Stephens Mary Oliver	Phillip Stephens George Stephens
Sept. 10, John Breeden Nancy Frost	John Breeden William McKamey
Dec. 30, Jonathan Dildine Nancy Garrett	Jonathan Dildine Gillesreath Barton
Feb. 16, Peter Johnson Keziah Berry	Peter Johnson John Leftwich
March 14, Joseph Nail Albina Mensco White	married by Alexander Nesmith, J. P.
Dec. 17, William Bailey Betsy Lawson	William Bailey Bartley Lawson
Jan. 29, Edward Crow Jinsy Burns	married by M. C. McKamey, J. P.
May 11, Thomas Cox Nancy Vaughn	Thomas Cox Isaiah Brown
Dec. 5, Joseph Knox Margaret Erwin	
Dec. 5, Phillip Stephens Mary Ann Oliver	
	1818
Jan. 7, Luke Lytle Mary Castil	

THE HISTORY OF ROANE COUNTY

NAMES　　　　　　　　BONDSMEN

1818

June 12,
Edward Musgrove
Nancy Stout

Jan. 27,
Luther White　　　　　　Luther White
Isabella McCamey　　　　William White

March 8,
William Erwin
Drucilla Hannah

March 23,
John Shields　　　　　　John Shields
Nellie Delozier　　　　　James Kennan

March 18,
Alexander Brown
Polly Sharp

May 6,
John Leadsinger
Joanna Bucklen

Aug. 19,
William Bailey　　　　　William Bailey
Frankie Reyborn　　　　Daniel Bailey

Aug. 19,
Jesse Power
Betsy Bakon

Sept. 4,
George Renolds　　　　 James Renolds
Rachel Smith　　　　　　James Moore

Dec. 23,
Jacob Fritts　　　　　　 Jacob Fritts
Sally Sexton　　　　　　John Fritts

Dec. 29,
Osy Dixon　　　　　　　Osy Dixon
Jinny Boden　　　　　　 Benjamine Porter

THE HISTORY OF ROANE COUNTY

NAMES	BONDSMEN
	1818
Dec. 29, Thomas Branham of Knox Co. Nellie Branham	Thomas Branham Nicholas Mansfield
June 27, Edward Merritt Sallie Carden	Edward Merritt Samuel Grisley
May 6, Abner Staples Elery Toomey	Abner Staples Ambrose Toomey
Oct. 16, Oxley Johnson Catey Rogers	Oxley Johnson Richard Dickens
Oct. 26, Elijah Williamson Rebecca Mann	
Nov. 23, David Shaw Chryleena Vickey	David Shaw James Lackey
Dec. 7, John M. Staples Polly Bryant	married Dec. 10, by Abraham McClellan, J. P.
March 28, Rudolph Moorman Rebecca White	Rudolph Moorman Martin Durrett
March 17, Joseph McClelland Jenny Moore	
Sept. 11, James Cox Barbara Gardner	James Cox James Gardner
Feb. 3, Henry Hart Polly Snow	Henry Hart James G. Williams
March 4, David McDaniel Mary Buchanan	married by William Eblen, J. P.

NAMES	BONDSMEN
	1819
Dec. 1, Willes Crow Nancy Tedder	
Oct. 19, Green M. Bruce Nancy McCube	Green M. Bruce Robert S. Gilliland
Feb. 16, John Vincent Anna Mapee	John Vincent John Thomas
Feb. 22, John M. Wilson Anna D. Rogers	married Feb. 25, by William Eblen, J. P.
May 6, Joseph Byrd Ann Pride	Joseph Byrd Thomas Brown
Dec. 16, William Crow Patsy Bowers	William Crow James Bowers
Feb. 20, Nicholas Mansfield Jinny Morris	married by William Eblen, J. P.
Nov. 19, Caleb McDaniel Susannah Carter	Caleb McDaniel David McDaniel
March 17, John Coulson Sallie Ketching	John Coulson William Long
Aug. 18, John Rice Tabitha Dodson	John Rice William Matlock
Jan. 11, James Larrimore, of Knox Co. Kitty Thomas	James Larrimore James Nipper
Aug. 17, William Arnold Martha D. King	William Arnold Rufus F. King

THE HISTORY OF ROANE COUNTY

NAMES	BONDSMEN
	1819
Feb. 2, Abner Parks Viney Lane	
March 27, Thomas Coppage Betsy Allison	Thomas Copage John McEwen
March 15, William Green Mary Smith	William Green Anthony Dickey
March 1, Alexander McCullock Lucy Robinson	Alexander McCullock Levi Wheat
Dec. 21, Samuel Swan Nancy McElwee	married by William Eagleton, M. G.
Nov. 29, Richard Card Polly Eldridge	Richard Card Benjamine Eldridge
Nov. 8, Samuel Harris Peggy McVey	married by Abraham McClellan,, J. P.
Sept. 1, Louis Derosset Isabel Lane	
March 12, William Headrick Matilda Short	William Headrick William Cornealison
Feb. 10, Joseph Bryant Patsy Hart	Joseph Bryant John Loyd
Jan. 23, William McConnell Jane Scott	William McConnell John Potter
April 10 Benjamine Haygood Polly Robinson	Benjamine Haygood Edward Warren

THE HISTORY OF ROANE COUNTY

NAMES　　　　　　　　BONDSMEN
　　　　　　　　1819

Aug. 6,
Claborn Kinnan　　　　　married by
Betsy Bowers　　　　　　John W. Durrett P. R. C.

Oct. 10,
James Humphries　　　　James Humphries
Polly West　　　　　　　George Branham

March 25,
John McNatt　　　　　　John McNatt
Lucroso Rayburn　　　　 Thomas Rayburn

Dec. 16,
John Bowers　　　　　　John Bowers
Polly Crow　　　　　　　James Bowers

Nov. 13,
Jesse Waten　　　　　　Jesse Waten
Mary Moore　　　　　　 William Leftwich

May 1,
Samuel Marney　　　　　married by
Elizabeth Spence　　　　 Richard Richards, M G.

Aug. 4,
William Mason　　　　　William Mason
Sophia Work　　　　　　William C. McKamey

March 20
Hezekiah Quick　　　　　Isham Cox, Sr.

May 4,
Arthur Bane　　　　　　Arthur Bane
Elener McPherson　　　　William Jent

Sept. 13.
William Sloane　　　　　William Sloane
Eliza Rector　　　　　　 John Jackson

Feb. 4,
John Tedder　　　　　　married by
Mary Robinson　　　　　Abraham McClellan, J. P.

THE HISTORY OF ROANE COUNTY

NAMES	BONDSMEN
	1820
Feb. 26,	
Samuel Ramsey	Samuel Ramsey
Nancy Gardner	Michal Sellers
Jan. 27,	
James Hankins	James Hankins
Rebecca Fulton	Robert Stout
July 31,	
Jesse West	Jesse West
Susannah Carrol	John Harrison
June 22,	
Solomon Forrester	Solomon Forrester
Sarah Marney	John Loyd
Sept. 7,	
William Bogart	William Bogart
Polly Preston	Abraham Bogart
Oct. 27,	
Phillip Harmon	
Sarah Clark	
Oct. 13,	
Isaac Anderson	Isaac Anderson
Julian Fout	William Berry
Sept. 9,	
John Selbe	John Selbe
Rhoda Cunningham	Edward Warren
Nov. 1,	
John Moore	married by
Charity McDaniel	Jesse Byrd, J. P.
March 18,	
Jesse Preston	Jesse Preston
Nancy Bogart	Abraham Bogart
Jan. 29,	
Uriah Allison	Uriah Allison
Mary Cox	Thomas Brown
Jan. 15,	
Andrew Nail	married by
———— Stubbs	Alexander Nesmith, J. P.

THE HISTORY OF ROANE COUNTY

NAMES	BONDSMEN
	1820
Nov. 24, Michael Ethridge Charity Horn	
Dec. 23, Abraham Miller Patsy West	
Sept. 5, John Mapes Betsy Pelfry	John Mapes Nathan Turner
Dec. 23, Nelson Ladd Jenny Rogers	married by James Johnston, J. P.
Sept. 26, Isaac Brown Margaret Sharp	Isaac Brown James Buchanan
March 27, John Clark Jinny McPherson	John Clark Rudolph Moorman
Feb. 22, Alfred Owings Polly Long	Alfred Owings Martin Center married by Solomon Geren, J. P.
Jan. 8, Samuel Burnett Sally Davis	Samuel Burnett Thomas Spence
Aug. 22, Thomas Edminston Nancy Box	Thomas Edminston John Edminston
Jan. 10, James Moore Jenny Woody	married by James McMullen, J. P.
Dec. 23, Robert Madrin Patsy Nance	Robert Madrin Joseph Ashley

THE HISTORY OF ROANE COUNTY

NAMES	BONDSMEN
	820
Nov. 24, Benjamine Howard Mahaly M. Conk	Benjamine Howard Samuel Side
July 24, William Beavers Betsy Crevet	William Beavers James Beavers
Jan. 5, Benton Draper Lucinda Williams	
Nov. 20 William Cavy Jenny Ireland	
May 16, Henry Kendrick Nancy Smith	
March 29, William Green Ruth Westmorland	married March 30, by James Johnston, J. P.
	1821
John Riddle Juda Easely	John Riddle Jonathan Harvey
Feb. 4, Armstead Blackwell Betsy Galloway	Armstead Blackwell Jesse Galloway
May 21, Audley P. Walker Polly Noel	——— Walker William McKamey
Aug. 5, James Mond Polly Williams	married by Thomas Stockton, J. P.
Jan. 10, Samuel Vance Polly McComb	
Feb. 8, Nathan Paget Kiziah Allen	married at the home of William Gilbreath at Kingston by William E. McKenney

THE HISTORY OF ROANE COUNTY

NAMES	BONDSMEN
	1821

April 5,
Adam Houston
Zilpe Good
    married by
    William McKamey, J. P.

Oct. 29,
Samuel Robinson
Matilda Powell

Dec. 17,
Stephen Killingsmith
Nancy Hart
    married by
    Richard Richards, J. P.

March 21,
Solomon Collins
Catey Arsterton
    Solomon Collins
    Moses Stout

Dec. 11,
William Jolly
Nancy Etheridge

Jan. 29,
John Brazeal
Annie Essary
    John Brazeal
    John Essary

April 13,
William Wilson
Jenny Kimbull
    William Wilson
    William Crow

Feb. 7,
James Adkinson
Patsy McCabe

Feb.
James Tedder
Elizabeth Todd

April 13,
William Wilson
Jennie Kimbrell

April 5,
Rowland Childs
Nancy Galloway
    married by
    James McMullen, J. P.

THE HISTORY OF ROANE COUNTY

NAMES	BONDSMEN
	1821

Jan. 24,
Joseph Henry
Scyrethea Herbert

Joseph Henry
Michael Arnold

May 12,
Robert Gamble
Betsy Lamb

Robert Gamble
Gideon Morgan

Jan. 3,
William Pritchett
Viney Keaner

William Pritchett
Phillip Pritchett

April 14,
John Hendreck
Mariah Work

John Hendreck
Samuel Woody

Aug. 28,
William Hall
Sarah Buchanan

married by
Micah Sellers, M. G.

Oct. 17,
James Freeman
Axey Ponder

married by
James Johnston, J. P.

Jan. 24,
Samuel Erwin
Sally Ingram

Samuel Erwin
Joseph Hankins

April 4,
Robert Allison
Nancy Byrd

married by
William C. McKamey, J. P.

May 5,
Thomas McNabb
Betsy Poor

Thomas McNabb
Ethelridge Taylor

March 2,
Henry Brazeale
Betsy Morgan

married by
James McMullen

1822

Sept. 9,
William Edwards
Polly Parks

married by
James Johnston, J. P.

June 15,
Nehemiah Grasham
Polly Clark

Nehemiah Grasham
Phillip Stephens

THE HISTORY OF ROANE COUNTY

NAMES	BONDSMEN
	1822
April 14, Leonard Asher Polly Clift	Leonard Asher Charles Asher
Nov. 28, Henry Jolly Polly McCullum	William Jolly ———— Taylor
Nov. 10, Henry Newman Sally Brazeale	
Oct. 22, Isaac Sellers Nancy Todd	married by Micah Sellers, M, G.
	1823
Feb. 5, Waddy Thompson Patsy Birdwell	Waddy Thompson Thomas Cox
Nov. 3, Thomas Farman Rachel Murrey	Thomas Farman Edward Roberts
July 31, William Wilkison Sally Tyler	William Wilkison John Brown
Oct. 21, Samuel Harwell Sophia Ayers	Samuel Harwell J. W. M. Brazeale
April 29, Jonathan Underwood Polly Staton	married by Thomas Stockton
Oct. 9, William Roath Lydia Elkins	William Roath Jacob Warren
Jan. 23, Hyram Berry Nancy Eblen	married by Richard Richards, M. G.
Sept. 9, John Bowers Nancy Morgan	married by Tomas Stockton J. P.

THE HISTORY OF ROANE COUNTY

NAMES	BONDSMEN
	1823
Nov. 25, Abner Deatherage Rebecca Davis	Abner Deatherage John M. Hale
Aug. 19, Benjamine Crow Betsy Sutton	Benjamine Crow John Crow
Oct. 28, Larkin Forrester Sarah Tuten	
Aug. 3, Thomas Gallaher Amelia Williams	Thomas Gallaher William Carroll
Nov. 12, Isaac Hembree Mary Blake	Isaac Hembree Joseph. M. Clark
Sept. 2, William Sutton Reyna Clemmons	married by James Johnston, J. P.
Nov. 6, Jesse Carter Betsy Sutton	married Nov. 20, by James Green, J. P.
June 5, Thomas Lane Judy Robinson	
Aug. 30, John Wrinkle Polly Hunter	
	1824
Jan. 2. John Nesmith Phebe Roberts	
Sept. 6, Abraham Odum Sally Henderson	Abraham Odum Alex Forrester William C. McKamey

THE HISTORY OF ROANE COUNTY

NAMES	BONDSMEN
	1824

March 4,
William Clift   married by
Mary Penland   Henry Liggett, J. P.

March 5,
William Nickand   married by
Elizabeth Brazeale   James McMullen, J. P.

Nov. 12,
George Decker   George Decker
Jane Branham   Phillip Huff

Aug. 19,
William W. A. Bensete (?)
Lody Johnson

July 17,
James Crew   married by
Anna Lawson   James Johnston, J. P.

Jan. 27,
George Blackwell
Olsey Mantin

Jan. 28,
John Woody
Elizabeth Farmer

Oct. 2,
Andrew Stansberry   Andrew Stansberry
Jane Carroll   Edmond Davis

Dec. 30,
Phillip Prititch   Phillip Prititch
Charity Etheridge   Peter Manning

Oct. 6,
Byrd Delaney
Alyse Muns

March 30,
Robert McHenry   Robert McHenry
Patsy Hightower   Samuel Andrews

Nov. 8,
Willis Evans   Willis Evans
Rebecca Shadwick   William Kane

THE HISTORY OF ROANE COUNTY

NAMES	BONDSMEN
	1824
July 21,	
Benton Lanston	Benton Lanston
Betsy Haskins	James Harrison
Nov. 6,	
James Lackey	
Jane Matlock	
Feb. 5,	
J. W. M. Brazeale	J. W. M. Brazeale
Betsy Margraves	Addison Carrick
Nov. 27,	
Jacob F. Kindrick	Jacob F. Kindrick
Margaret McPherson	Allen Haley
Aug. 15,	
Richard Morehead	
Polly Berry	
March 10,	
Isaac Matlock	married by
Jane Selvidge	Little B. Roberts. J. P.
Jan. 15,	
Richard Reves	married by
Eliza Miller	Thomas Stockton
Jan. 26,	
Samuel Lane	married by
Milly Robinson	Samuel Dauthel
July 16,	
Joseph Lyles	married by
Nancy Cofer	Charles Galloway, M. G.
Jan. 24	
John Wheat	John Wheat
Nancy Rather	Levi Wheat
Feb. 11,	
John Mee	married by
Sarah McElwee	William Eagleton, M. G.
June 1,	
Benjamine Dunkin	Benjamine Dunkin
Jane Hannah	William G. Blake

THE HISTORY OF ROANE COUNTY

NAMES	BONDSMEN
	1824
April 11, Robert H. Brazeale Anna McKamy	Robert H. Brazeale J. W. M. Brazeale
Nov. 4, William Sawords Mary Manning	William Sawords Peter Manning
Jan 27, Jesse Lowe Prudence England	
Sept. 6, Abraham Odum Sally Henderson.	married by Joseph Bryant, J. P.
	1825
Oct. 5, James R. Hines Rachel Abeel	James Hines John Hamilton
Nov. 30, Peter Perry Barbary Ann Bonds	Peter Perry Edward Pritchett
Dec. 15, William Sexton Susan Pennick	
Sept. 26, Abraham Rowden Ann Brandon	Abraham Rowden Adam Brandon
July 23, Jacob Phillips Jane Miller	married Aug. 2, by James Burselly
Feb. 24, John Wallace Eliza McCowl	married by William Eagleton, M. G.
Oct. 27, William D. Phillips Susan P. Clark	married by William Eagleton M. G.

THE HISTORY OF ROANE COUNTY

NAMES	BONDSMEN
	1825
Jan. 3,	
William McNutt	William McNutt
Sarah Weiss	Wiley Luten
July 15,	
John Haster	married by
Elizabeth Dore	Charles Galloway, M. G.
Sept. 27,	
Jacob Winter	
Jane Frazier	
Nov. 29,	
William Young	married by
Polly Alif	Bashears Roberts, J. P.
Feb.	
James Russell	married by
Elendor Russell	Charles Galloway, M. G.
April 8,	
Thomas Bell	
Polly McNight	
June 25,	
Allen Bolten	Allen Bolten
Margaret Gardenhire	William Harvey
Oct. 5,,	
Reuben Evans	Reuben Evans
Rebecca Lauston	Daniel Mizell
Sept. 6,	
William Anderson	married by
Eliza M. E. McEwen	William Fagleton, M. G.
June 8,	
Robert McNutt	
Nancy Eldridge	
Jan. 11,	
Thomas McNutt	Thomas McNutt
Agnes Solomon	Thomas Nelson
Dec. 14,	
Jacob Rinkle	married by
Levisy Webb	Thomas Stockton

THE HISTORY OF ROANE COUNTY

NAMES	BONDSMEN
	1825

Aug. 28,
Moses Caps
Dicey Cane

Moses Caps
William Cane

Dec. 25,
Peter Fritts
Parmelia Williams

Oct. 29,
David Haley
Betsy Fleiner

Witnesses: Robert Haley, James Good, Richard Fleiner, Sally Fleiner

Dec. 30,
Michael Anderson
Patsy Pritchett

married by
James McMullen, J. P.

Feb. 18,
John Davis
Frances Duncan

married by
William Magill

1826

Feb. 4,
William Yates
Eleanor Cagnee

Dec. 2,
John Julan
Jane Taylor

John C. Julian
Wentley Sturges

Sept. 6,
William Jones
Lydia Moon

William Jones
Jonas Moon

Dec. 14,
William Booth
Eliza Litbull

married by
Henry Soward, M. G.

Jan. 3,
Titas Lacey
Malinda T. Hamilton

married by
James McMullen

July 27,
John Oliver
Barbary McCrery

John Oliver
John Hope
Lewis Bowman
William Weese

THE HISTORY OF ROANE COUNTY

NAMES	BONDSMEN
	1826

Nov. 20,
John Stubbs
Mariam Nail

John Stubbs
John Nail

Dec. 6,
Samuel Evans
Arty Lawson

Sept. 26,
Peter Tyler
Sally Adams

Peter Tyler
John Loyd

March 11,
Milo Luckjon
Polly Huff

Jan. 26,
Samuel Davis
Jane Smith

married by
Thomas Stockton, J. P.

Nov. 1,
Elisha Turner
Jane Ward

Dec. 29,
Charles Adkins
Margaret T. McMinn

Charles Adkins
James P. Haynes

Seb. 11,
Edmond Ford
Phebe Butler

Edmond Ford
Thomas Blake

Aug. 22,
Isaac Gallion
Nancy Johnson

Isaac Gallion
Benjamine Hensley

Sept. 28,
William Day
Patty Shahan

William Day
George Sims

May 5,
Absolum Hicks
Cretora Molting

married by
Jonathan Barnard

March 14,
Joel Hood
Nancy Haskins

married by
George Gamble

THE HISTORY OF ROANE COUNTY

NAMES	BONDSMEN
	1826

Feb. 9,
James Wiseman
Polly Spind

    married by
    Henry Liggett, J. P.

Sept. 1,
B. L. Mullins
Beamy Sharp

Jan. 24,
Joseph Parker
Betsy Thalkill

    married by
    Charles Galloway, J. P.

Oct. 2,
John Grunant
Sally Boman

Spt. 12,
John Gennings
Jane Eatain

June 1,
Henry Davidson
Patsy Marney

March 14,
Joel Hood
Nancy Haskins

March 25,
Alexander Hyden
Margaret Wrinkle

1827

Sept. 20,
Josiah Perry
Tempy Lewallin

    married by
    Ben J. Lonacre

March 2,
William Brown
Polly Weese

    married by
    Thomas Stockton

Nov. 13,
Eldridge G. Sevier
Mary C. Brown

    Fldridge Sevier
    W. C. Dunlap

Dec. 27,
Zadak Loveless
Martha Falton

    William Loveless
    Zadak Loveless

THE HISTORY OF ROANE COUNTY

NAMES	BONDSMEN
	1827
June 5, Arthur McFarland Elizabeth Sherrill	married by Joseph Bryant
Dec. 31, Joseph J. Monnger Nancy S. Yanf	Joseph Monnger Samuel Harvey Isaac Burris John Cove
Feb. 21, Stephen Fortsen Peggy West	Stephen Fortsen Hezekiah Hotchkiss
July 7, William Scott Elizabeth White	William Scott Luther White
Sept. 7, Henry Cluck Ludy Wells	Henry Cluck William Cluck
Dec. 7, John Browder Minerva Matlock	married by Samuel Detherel, Methodist Church.
June 11, Thomas Donohoo Marian Harris	
Jan. 8, Benjamine Kimbrell Katherine Luttrell	Benjamine Kimbrell Peterson Kim
Aug. 24, Joseph Shadwick Susan Selvey	Joseph Shadwick Willis Evans
August 8, Cory A. James Catherine E. Car	married by S. B. Howerwell, M. G.
Oct. 12, Lear Wheat Katie Isham	

NAMES	BONDSMEN
1827	
June. 23, Alexander Gilbreath Peggy Snodgrass	Alexander Gilbreath John B. Mason
Jan. 23, James Grammer Susan McCulley	
David Ambrose Kesiah Robb	married by Jonathan Barnard, J. P.
Nov. 13, John Harvey Abigial Cole	married by Bashears Roberts
Dec. Welding Keeling Elizabeth Hiden	Welding Keeling Abraham Rinkell
March 13, Elijah Row Sinthy Juet	married by James Pursley
July 27, Alexander Gilbert Susan Burk	Alexander Gilbert James Dalton
Feb. 19, Jacob Utley Nancy Williams	married on the 23rd by Thomas Spence, J. P.
March 25, Nathan Watson Lucy Steels	
1828	
May 14, Albert Hurt Sally Garrett	married by Rev. R. Hooper

THE HISTORY OF ROANE COUNTY

NAMES   BONDSMEN

1828

Jan. 1,
Elijah Rector
Nancy Mann

Dec. 30,
James Qualls   James Qualls
Eliza Snow   James Taylor

Oct. 18,
Barton Phillpot   married by
Catherine Funderburk   William Brown, J. P.

July 26,
Benjamine Cates   married by
Catherine Poindexter   James Briggs

Oct. 11,
Alexander Black   married by
Sarah Ann Smith   William B. Clark, J. P.

May 28,
William McCally   William McCally
Polly Rather   Waddy Thompson

Feb. 28,
John Rathers   married by
Peggy Reyburn   William Eblen, J. P.

June 28,
Henry Brazeale   Henry Brazeale
Syntha Ann McKinney   Robert Brazeale

Dec. 11,
James Stephenson
Nancy Crow

Dec. 26,
Morris Mitchell   married by
Annie Ewing   James Mitchell, M. G.

Feb. 1,
Owing Gentry
Martha J. Brazeale

THE HISTORY OF ROANE COUNTY

NAMES	BONDSMEN
	1828
July 9, William Loveless Polly Minton	William Loveless Silas McGee
Sept. 10, Joshua Casey Anna Haile	Joshua Casey Solomon Stow
August 4, Ornson Harris Nancy Rector	married by William Brown, J. P.
March 26, Thomas Woodburn Polly Griffy	married April 1st by George Donnell, M. G.
Oct. 25, Samuel Edington Sarah Hinds	married Nov. 9th by William Brown, J. P.
Dec. 20, Moses Lewis Lucinda Shell	
Nov. 5, William Goddard Nancy Evans	William Goddard Nathan Goddard
March 10 Hezikiah Smith Anna Ralston	married by Thomas Stockton, J. P.
Sept. 28, George Martin Elizabeth McIntire	married by Joseph Bryant
August 19, John Jolly Polly Detheridge	marred by Jonathan Barnarl, J. P.
March 18, Nicholas Ward Margaret Queener	married by James Mitchell, M. G.

THE HISTORY OF ROANE COUNTY

NAMES	BONDSMEN
	1828
August 17, Albert Henderson Elizabeth Hawks	married by Buckner Walker, J. P.
July 31, Drury Robinson Polly Hamilton	married by Rev. Joseph Mounger
Jesse Carter Betsy Sutton	J. Carter Louis Sutton A. M. Brazeale, Clerk
	1829
Jan. 15, Moses Crevat Nancy West	
June 30, William H. Gardner Ann Galloway	William Gardner Thomas Gardner
Jan. 26, Richard Clark Ann Smith	Richard Clark James Cofer
Jan. 21, David Roberts Patsy Bailey	David Roberts Isaac Bailey
Jan. 24, Milton Burk Phebe Hatley	Milton Burk Lewis Renfro
Feb. 5. John Taylor Sally Lamb	married by Henry Soward, J. P.
Feb. 5, John Covington Nancy Guffy	John Covington Jesse King James Hankins

THE HISTORY OF ROANE COUNTY

NAMES   BONDSMEN

1829

Dec 18,
John Renfro   John Renfro
Polly Snow   M. K. Selvidge

Sept. 24
William Huff   William Huff
Keziah Tunnell   James Freeman

March 11,
William Hughs
Jane Beverly

August 11,
Henry Lyles   married by
Jenny Laney   John Tedder, M. G.

March 24,
James Fell   James Fell
Rebecca Tate   Elijah Longbottom

Oct. 27,
Noah Miller   Noah Miller
Rachel Carter   James Gambrill

Jan. 22,
Archibald C. Rogers   married by
Sarah P. Clark   William Eagleton, M. G.

Jan. 22,
Joel Wright   married by
Amanda Westbrook   Robert Marney, J. P.

Feb. 24,
Jesse McKinney   married by
Matilda Harvey   John S. Henley

March 4,
Abraham Caphers
Frances Willis

Nov. 5,
George Mitchell   married by
Sarah Ewing   M. R. Jarrett

THE HISTORY OF ROANE COUNTY

NAMES	BONDSMEN
	1829
Dec. 7, Joseph Overton Polly Blevens	
Oct. 20, William Owings Abigail Randolph	
Feb. 20, John Houston Margaret Riddle	John Houston Robert Stout
Dec. 19, Evans Breeding Abigail Hinds	married by B. Longacre
Oct. 29, Joseph Lorance Mary Ann Hyten	Joseph Lorance Anderson Hyten
August 19, John W. Winton Eliza Browder	married by Samuel Deatheridge, M. G.
April 7, Isaac Welhite Sussanah Harris	
	1830
Sept. 23, John D. Harbert Elizabeth Dalton	John Harbert Rial Silvey
Sept. 9, John McKane Elizabeth Dawson	John McKane Wiley Tuten
Dec. 15, Phillip Fritts Frances Jane Williams	Phillip Fritts Peter Fritts
March 31, James Wilmot Maria Burnett	
August 2. William H. Burns Susan Roberts	married by William Magill

THE HISTORY OF ROANE COUNTY

NAMES   BONDSMEN
                          1830

March 24,
Joseph Brashears
Mary Dickey

July 19,
Pleasant Cosey
Lucy Webb

Nov. 20,
Alfred Thompson   Alfred Thompson
Julia Woody   Brice Woody

March 5,
J. A. James   married by
Casandree Kennedy   William Brown, J. P.

Oct. 23,
Samuel Grubb   married by
Sarah Roach   Robert Williams, M. G.

July 30,
Thomas Jones   Thomas Jones
Harriett Haggard   Dudley Snow

Dec. 16,
John A. Hook   married by
Polly Gambell   Thomas Brown, M. G.

Dec. 25,
Jefferson Stoner
Vanilia Patty

Dec. 6,
Joseph Parks   Joseph Parks
Margaret Fain   Robert Blackstone

March 8,
John Smith   married on the 25th by
Julia Davis   William Eblen, J. P.

Sept. 10,
William Hutson   William Hutson
Matilda B. Wright   Hansel Wright

THE HISTORY OF ROANE COUNTY

NAMES	BONDSMEN
	1830
Oct. 8,	
John G. Clark	John G. Clark
Winney Jones	Stephen Honey
Nov. 30,	
Jacob Funk	Jacob Funk
Emily Hastler	David Patton
Jan. 28,	
William S. Weese	William S. Weese
Nancy Weese	William Weese
August 9,	
John Collier	John Collier
Polly Hankins	David Roberts
August 2,	
Ebenezer Johnston	E. Johnston
Hannah Huff	Robert Johnston
Dec. 23,	
James Oliver	
Anna Seltz	
Dec. 8,	
Josiah Danforth	married by
Letitia Prater	Darius Hoyt, M. G.
	1831
Jan. 25,	
London Rector	married by
Betsy Taliferro	B. Longacre, J.P.
Jan. 31,	
Louis M. Sumpter	Louis Sumpter
Lidia Geren	John Smithy
Oct. 8,	
Lutherate Grigsby	L. Gregsby
Patsy Bailey	George Good
Oct. 24,	
Leander Watson	
Mary Ann Suttle	

THE HISTORY OF ROANE COUNTY

NAMES	BONDSMEN

1831

March 20,
James Martin
Evaline Gossett

    married by
B. Longacre, J. P.

July 2,
James Yandall
Polly Williams

James Yandall
Solomon Row

June 22,
Edward Bowman
Sally Cooper

Edward Bowman
Jesse M. Low

Feb. 20,
David Burnett
Patsy Burnett

    married by
George Luttrell

Oct. 25,
Moses Carter
Cynthia McCarroll

    married by
Thomas Spence

Nov. 1,
Robert Thornton
Sarah Hagler

Jan. 6,
Isaac Griffith
Catherine Howard

Isaac Griffith
Josiah Sullens

Feb. 15,
Lemaster U. Hornsby
Polly Donaldson

    married by
B. Longacre, J. P.

May 29,
William Brown
Lititia Knidred

married by Samuel Lyles
Minister of the Baptist Church.

Oct. 10,
James Melton
Eliza Foster

James Melton
Alexander Nail

Oct. 5,
David Dearmond
Sarah Hinds

David Dearmond
Zacheus Ayers

THE HISTORY OF ROANE COUNTY

NAMES	BONDSMEN
	1831
Sept. 14, Isaac Smith Flora McMillan	married by William Brown, J. P.
Oct. 11. John Easton Polly Clark	married by W. B. Clark, J. P.
March 12, Charles Ellis Vicey Turner	Charles Ellis Achilla L. Harrison
Jan. 15, John Cox Ana Crow	married by Robert Marney, J. P.
April 14. William Branham Rebecca Lyles	William Branham William Brock
Oct. 30, Jacob Mesamore Lettice Tunnell	married by John Carter, J. P.
Sept. 12, James Hackney ———— Longean	James Hackney D. Parkings
June 18, Abrabam Fuller Nancy Scott	
July 11, Richard Earp Sarah Tolbert	
	1832
Aug. 28, Andrew McNabb Frances Christian	married by Joseph Robinson, J. P.
March 30, William Gilbert Elizabeth Hurt	married by Robert Marney, J. P.

THE HISTORY OF ROANE COUNTY

NAMES	BONDSMEN
	1833
Dec. 26, William Lacey Kiziah Grinsley	married by Jonathan L. Barnard, J. P.
July 25, Allen Letsinger Elizabeth Cole	License issued in Knox Co., by Charles J. McClung. Married by Robert Williams.
	1834
Dec. 21, Andress McCullock Elvira Underwood	married by Isaac Eblen, J. P.
Oct. 30, John Morgan Mary Ann Highton	
Nov. 5, Mathew D. Russell Charlotte Dunwold	Mathew Russell Bryson Hood
Nov. 22, Benjamine Gilbert Malinda James	B. Gilbert George W. Smith
Dec. 23, John Mahaffee Malinda Brandon	J. Mahaffee Joshua Moore
Oct. 15, Zachariah Shackleford Mary Ann Cox	married by Richard Richards, M. G.
Nov. 26, William A. Thompson Elizabeth Gibbons	W. A. Thompson Ralph Smith
	1835
Jan. 9, Hiram Carroll Sarah Perry	

THE HISTORY OF ROANE COUNTY

NAMES	BONDSMEN
	1835
August 8. Samuel H. Davis Elizabeth C. Evans	married May 2, 1836 by William Reed, J. P.
August 5, Massey Bishop Mary W. Gideon	
June 9. Overton Goodwin Elizabeth Hotchkiss	
Nov. 18. Samuel Dearmond Grizzy B. Dearmond	
Aug. 6. William Lea Sarah Clark	William Lea John Clark
Jan. 21, Abraham Weece Polly Braham	married by Josiah Patty
July 27, Joshua Gordon Polly Grammer	
March 3, Thomas Kitchen Margaret Bogart	married by Elisha Turner
August 17, Campbell Simpson Eliza Boman	C. Simpson Elias Lane
Oct. 2, Jeremiah Rich Emily Bond	
Nov. 11, William Silvey Nancy Solomon	W. Silvey Jacob Tower
Feb. 28, William James Jane Renfro	W. James Edward McDuffer

THE HISTORY OF ROANE COUNTY

NAMES	BONDSMEN
	1835
Nov. 10. James K. Robertson Frances R. Lockett	J. Robertson John H. Wright
Jan, 17, William M. Grubb Prudence Scarbrough	W. M. Grubb John Edwards
Nov. 5, John C. Terry Matilda Christian	J. C. Terry Hezekiah Love
Nov. 5, Thomas J. Johnston Harriet G. Johnston	T. J. Johnston Henry Liggett
June 8, Levi Voiles Omy Shaw	married by Solomon Geren, J. P.
Aug. 13, John Vann Tibitha Williams	John Vann Dennis Vann
May 6, Linsey Branham Betsy Cooley	married by Joseph Robinson, J. P.
June 27, George W. Stout Jane Greer	G. W. Stout William Davis
Oct. 20, Ephriam Huffine Hanover Ingram	E. Huffine Thomas Melvin
Nov. 26, Levi Jackson Jane West	married by William Reed, J. P.
Sept. 15. John West Jane Eldridge	John West John Eldridge

THE HISTORY OF ROANE COUNTY

NAMES	BONDSMEN
	1835

Oct. 29,
Wesley Middleton
Polly Easter
    married by
    William Reed, J. P.

August 13,
John Finley
Gabriella M. Hotchkiss
    John Finley
    Samuel Hotchkiss

August 17,
William Pearson.
Mary McBath
    married by
    ———— McBath

Feb. 23,
Lewis M. Roberts
Mary Eleanor Stewart
    L. M. Roberts
    John Shields

March 9,
John Alford
Sarah Maddy

Feb. 17,
Elias Lane
Mahala Bowers
    Elias Lane
    Littledery Johnston

Sept. 10,
Robert Wilson
Eliza Scarbrough
    R. Wilson
    William Hapler

Jan. 6,
William Underwood
Elizabeth Young
    W. Underwood
    Andrew McCullock

Dec. 9,
George McNabb
Catherine Perkepile
    married by
    John Blair, J P.

Jan. 3,
Jacob Lowery
Keziah Gossett
    married by
    William B. Clark, J. P.

THE HISTORY OF ROANE COUNTY

NAMES	BONDSMEN
	1835

July 5,
Wade Narramore
Polly Tenn————

   married by
Elisha Turner, M G.

Oct. 22,
John G. Magill
Polly Lovelace

J. G. Magill
A. S. Lenoir

Feb. 11,
Albert Howard
Levinia Bowling

A. Howard
John W. Rhea

Nov. 19,
John A. Mathaney
Lucinda Deatherage

J. A. Mathaney
Abner Deatherage

April 4,
William Weese
Amanda J. Wester

W. Weese
Absolom Tuttle

Oct. 5,
Jacob Delmon
Margaret Keelaugh

   married by
William B. Clark, J. P.

May 2,
Samuel Weese
Rebecca Brackett

S. Weese
William Weese

1836

March 17,
Mark C. Capps
Dellia Towers

M. C. Capps
Gideon Capps

Nov. 15,
George Towers
Elvira Carter

George Towers
John A. Sharp

Oct. 29,
Roger Wilkey
Mariah West

Nimrod Newman

March 23,
Anderson Jones
Frances Lewallen

A. Jones
Jesse Owings

THE HISTORY OF ROANE COUNTY

NAMES	BONDSMEN
	1836

Sept. 2,
George Cook   George Cook
Sattira Haggard   John Cook

April
Michel Cook   married by
Ann Mullins   William G. Ellis

April 7,
Major M. Dobbins   Major M. Dobbins
Evaline F. Miller   Epriam Miller

Sept. 25,
William Shackelford   W. Shackelford
Elizabeth Reeder   Edmund Pryor

Feb. 25,
Enoch H. Willett
Savilla H. Russell

Jan. 24,
William Y. Dryskill   W. Dryskill
Martha Johnston   Samuel T. Childress

Dec. 9,
Thomos Purcey   married by
Mary Ann Breeden   Micale H. Sellers, M. G.

Sept. 23,
Joseph Lane   J. Lane
Rebecca Baldwin   Jesse Baldwin

Sept. 10,
James Lynn
Nancy Dickson

Oct. 11,
George Arnold
Nancy Cook

Jan. 19,
Samuel Thompson   Samuel Thompson
Margaret McKamey   William N. McKamey

THE HISTORY OF ROANE COUNTY

NAMES   BONDSMEN

1836

Oct. 1,
John Burkett
Parmelia Burkett

July 11,
Nelson Munds   N. Munds
Anny Clark   Austin L. Green

Jan. 14,
Chastain Freeman   married by
Beckey McMullens   Elisha Turner, M. G.

March 6,
Jesse Hays   married by
Eveline Keith   Richard Richards

August 11,
Thomas Napier
Ethalenda Underwood

March 23,
David Turpin
Dillia Wyatt

1837

Nov. 7,
Thomas Coffer   married by
Jane Martin   Henry Liggett

Jan. 2.
George Bowers   married by
Mary Armstrong   William C. Julian, J. P.

Nov. 2?
John Williams   J. Williams
Mahaley Jane Stennett   Martin Williams

Aug. 31,
John Umphris   J. Umphris
Patience Richards   Richard Watt

Sept. 2,
Caswell Allen Niper   C. Niper
Anny King   William Griffen

THE HISTORY OF ROANE COUNTY

NAMES   BONDSMEN

1837

Nov. 16,
James Scarborough
Ann Davis

    married by
    J. M. Butler, J. P.

Oct. 20,
Richard Simpson
Martha E. Johnson

1838

April 15,
Abraham Howard
Kezziah Thrailkill

1839

March 26,
Thomas Gallaher
Elizabeth Williams

April 24,
Joseph Graham
Polly Thrailkill

March 23,
John Garabrant
Elizabeth Thrailkill

Aug. 18,
John Renfro
Hannah Evans

Sept. 18,
William Hunt
Elizabeth Hope

Jan. 24,
Joseph Lacey
Susan Tuten

1840

Dec. 17,
James Gallaher
Elizabeth Burris

THE HISTORY OF ROANE COUNTY

NAMES	BONDSMEN

1841

Oct. 10,
Joseph Wilson
Elizabeth Rose

Dec. 2,
Eli Hembree
Nancy M. Ballew

1842

Jan. 25,
Samuel Todd
Caroline Newberry

Sept. 10,
Wiley Tuton
Susan Marney

1843

Jan. 22,
William Haggard
Nancy Deatheridge

July 15,
John Cave
Elizabeth Preston

August 18.
George T. Fry
Elizabeth Bogart

Sept. 30.
Joseph Strange
Sarah McGuffey

The exact spelling of names as they appear in the marriage bonds has been followed, E. M. W.

On the back of the marriage records of Jesse Hays and Eveline Keith are the following lines.

March 6, 1836.
"Comments by Richard Richards, M. G."
Said Jesse to Eveline, "let's us marry,"
Said Eveline to Jesse. "You might be sorry,
You are only seventeen,"
"Yes", said Jesse the not to fasten,
Children to marry are very keen.
"We will send for the Parson."
The work was done, the not was tied
Between the boy and his bride.

PART FIVE

EARLY FAMILIES OF ROANE COUNTY

ALLISON

1. Thomas m. Susan Howard. Issue, Robert, Samuel,
2. Robert, from Chester Co., N. C. Settled in Greene Co., Tennessee. M. Jane Moore Lambkin, dau. of Alexander and Roxie Cowan Moore. Issue (a) Mary Moore, b. Feb. 1, 1774, (b) Uriah (b. Feb. 1, 1782, (c) Margaret, (d.) Susan, (e) Annie, (f) Robert, b. 1805 (g) Jane.
3. (a) Mary Moore, m. Gen. John Brown (See Brown)
3. (b) Uriah served under Gen. William Henry Harrison in subduing the uprising of the Indians under Tecumseh. Also served under Capt. James Rogers, Capt. James O. Anderson, Col. Elmund P. Gaines and Brig. Gen. James Winchester in War of 1812; m. 1822 Nancy Clark Cox, b. 1800. Issue: (a) Mary, (b) Mariah, (c) Catherine Jane (d) Uriah.
3. (c) Margaret, dau. of Robert m. Moses Preston.
3. (d) Susan m. John Council
3. (e) Annie, m. James Craig
3. (f) Robert M. m. April 4, 1821 Nancy Byrd. Issue (a) Jesse Byrd, (b) Robert, (c) William, (d) Ruff, (e) Mary, (f) Sarah, (g) Lou, (h) Maria (i) Edna, (j) Uriah.
4. (a) Mary, dau. of Col. Uriah m. Dec. 3, 1840 John Doss. Issue.
5. (a) Margaret m. Standifer Peak. Issue, Walter.
5. (b) Eliza, dau. of John and Mary Doss m. William Craighead. Issue (a) Jack, (b) William Alexander, (c) Gillespie, (d) James R., (e) Charles C., (f) Libbie Kate.
5. (c) Mary Kate m. Tyler Crawford 5. (d) Georgia.
4. (b) Maria Louise, dau. of Col. Uriah m. George Nicholson. Issue.

THE HISTORY OF ROANE COUNTY

 5. (a) Mary m. Breckenridge, of Ky.
 5. (b) Annie m. first Jacob Fritts, Issue Elizabeth, Second Thomas Gibson.
 5. (c) Hugh, 5. (d) Henry, 5. (e) Elizabeth, 5 (f) John.
 4. (c) Catherine Jane, dau. of Col. Uriah m. Dr. John W. Wester. (See Wester.)
 4. (d) Uriah m. Jan. 29, 1820 Mary Cox.
 4. (a) Jesse, son of Robert and Nancy m. 1827 Eliza Ann Hill Issue. (a) Joseph Hill, (b) Elizabeth.
 5. (a) Joseph Hill m. Maria Mathews, Issue (a) Elizabeth Lee. (b) Benjamine.
 5. (b) Elizabeth m.
 6. (a) Elizabeth Lee m. Hugh Brown.
 6. (b) Benjamine m. Pansy Saunders.
 2. (b) Samuel Son of Thomas and Susan m. Margaret Dickson. Settled in Kentucky. Issue 3 (a) Nancy R. m. Samuel Jackson.
 3. (b) Charles McLean, 3. (c) William Dickson, 3. (d) Young Ewing.
 3. (e) John Adair, 3. (f) Samuel Henley.

THE HISTORY OF ROANE COUNTY
BARNARD

1. John came from England. m. 1st Anna Carr. Issue a (a) Reuben,, (b) Hyre, (c) Anna, (d) Mary, (e) Rachel. 2nd m. ———— Bachman. Issue (f) Zedic, (g) John C., (h) Jonathan, (i) Polly, (j) Lydia.

2. (h) Jonathan b. Jan. 1, 1790 came to Roane Co., 1820, d. April 1875 m. Sarah Jolly b. Oct. 24, 1794, d. Sept. 3, 1875. Issue 3 (a) John Anderson, (b) William, (c) James, (d) Reuben, (e) Samuel, (f) George, (g) Jonathan M., (h) Nancy, (i) Margaret, (j) Sarah, (k) Elizabeth, (l) Lucinda.

3. (a) John Anderson b. May 31, 1800, d. Jan. 3, 1904, m. Nov. 20, 1838, Eliza Campbell. Issue.

4. (a) Jonathan Robert Campbell, (b) Seraphine, (c) James, (d) Alexander, (e) Newton, (f) Albert, (g) John Anderson, (h) Samuel, (i) Eliza, (j) Almarinda. Anderson, (h) Samuel, (i) Elija, (j) Almarinda.

3 (f) George, son of Jonathan m. Cardine Crowder. Issue (a) Crowder, (b) Alice, (c) Sallie, (d) Thomas, (e) Walter, (f) Eblen, (g) May.

3. (g) Jonathan M., son of Jonathan I, m. Rebecca Weiss. Issue 4 (a) Richard, (b) Sallie, (c) Arch, (d) Mack, (e) Cora, (f) Laura (g) Bertha, (h) Charles.

3. (h) Nancy, dau. of Jonathan I, b. 1814 m. Oct. 8, 1841, William Breeden, b. in Virginia 1803.

3. (i) Margaret, dau. of Jonathan I, m. ————Ponder.
3. (j) Sarah, dau. of Jonathan I m.   Johnson.
3. (k) Elizabeth, dau. of Jonathan I m.   Kincaid.
3. (l) Lucinda, dau. of Jonathan I, m.   Rushing.
3. (d) Reuben, son of Jonathan I, m. Dec. 11, 1832, Rachel Sparks.

3. (b) William J. son of Jonathan I m. Dec. 20, 1843, Mary Ann Puree.

4. (b) Seraphine, dau. of John Anderson m. March 25, 1853, Arthur Ewing (see Ewing).

THE HISTORY OF ROANE COUNTY

4. (j) Amarinda, dau. of John Anderson m.   Harmon.
4. (e) Cora, dau. of Jonathan and Rebecca m. Billingsly.
4. (g) Bertha, dau. of Jonathan and Rebecca m. Crabtree.
4. Samuel, son of Nancy B. and William Breeden, b. July 25, 1852, m. 1884, Hester Marrell, dau. of Eldridge and Susan Allison Marrell. Issue. William E.

5. (h) Samuel T., son of Jonathan R. C. b. April 16, 1855 m. Margaret Lydia Williams b. May 27, 1864. Issue 5 (a) Robert Arthur (m. Flora Hurst, 5 (b) Fred, 5 (c) Henry Gibson m.) Whitlow Betterton. Issue 6 (a) Henry Gibson, Jr., 5 (d) Marjorie m. George Thomas Margraves. Issue (a) William Thomas, (b) James Barnard, (c) Harry Eugene, (d) Robert Erwin, 5 (e) Jack Carson m. Claire

5 (f) Lula May.

5. (g) Morgan Clack m. Ruth Cummings. Issue 6 (a) Caroline Lee, 6 (b) Morgan Clack, 5 (h) Hazel Genevieve, 5 (i) Helen Marie

THE HISTORY OF ROANE COUNTY

BLAIR

1. John b. in South Carolina, a soldier at King's Mt., m. Feb. 9, 1771, Jane Gamble, Guilford Co., N. C. Issue 2 (a) Thomas, 2 (b) Hugh, b. 1774, (c) William, b. 1775, (d) James b. 1777, (e) John b. April 20, 1783, (f) Samuel b. Sept. 5, 1784, (g) Jane b. Oct. 6, 1781, (h) Mary Dawson b. July 2, 1789, 2nd wife Hannah Caruthers Issue (i) Polly, (j) Rachel, (k) Martha Patsy, (l) Elizabeth.

1. John settled in Roane Co. in 1790
Issue of Hugh b. 1774.
3. (a) John b. March 31, 1808, (b) Polly b. Jan. 5, 1810, (c) Jenny, b. Nov. 3, 1811, (d) James b. Sept. 9, 1813, (e) Frankie b. Sept. 27, 1815, (f) Vinson b. Jan. 23, 1819, (g) Betsy, b. May 25, 1821, (h) Hugh b. Jan 11, 1825, (i) Patsy Ann b. June 11, 1831.

2. (e) John b. April 20, 1783, son of John and Jane m. March 29, 1827 Elizabeth Johnson, Issue (a) James Thomas b. Aug. 29, 1828, (b) William Wiley b. July 2, 1830, (c) Hugh Allen b. Feb. 14, 1832, (d) Mary Jane b. Feb. 21, 1834, (e) Nancy Isabelle b. Jan. 3, 1836, (f) John Johnson b. Dec. 8, 1837, (g) Elizabeth Ann b. Oct. 1839, (h) George M., b. Nov. 18, 1841, (i) Martha b. Dec. 17, 1843, (j) Elizabeth Caroline b. Nov. 14, 1845.

2. (c) James b. 1777 d. Nov. 6, 1826, m. Jane Carmichael b. Jan. 11, 1775, d. Mar. 26, 1841. Issue (a) John b. July 19, 1800 m. Elizabeth Scales b. June 25, 1808 d. Feb. 23, 1868. Issue (a) Isabelle b. July 6, 1801 m. ─────── Prater, (b) William (Wiley) b. Feb. 13, 1803 d. Jan. 1, 1865, (c) Betsy b. Feb. 16, 1805, (d) Allen b. Nov. 9, 1807, (e) Mahala b. Jan. 8, 1810, (f) Hugh b. April 16, 1811, (g) Wiley b. Feb. 19, 1813, d. Aug. 2, 1854, (h) Jenny, b. July 29, 1815.

2. (c) William, son of John and Jane Gamble m. Sarah Simmonds. Issue (a) John b. 1808, d. 1875, m. Mary Edwards of Virginia. Issue:

3. (a) William R., (b) Sarah, (c) Vincent, (d) Hugh, (e) Elizabeth.

3. (b) Sarah m. John Hall.
3. (e) Elizabeth m. Andrew Allen.

4. (a) Dr. James Thomas, son of John and Elizabeth m. 1st. Oct. 18, 1853 Margaret Lucinda Barkley. Issue:

5. (a) Lilliam Olivia b. July 23, 1856 (b) Arthur b. Aug. 10, 1858, (c) Jessie b. June 9, 1862, (d) Finnie b. Aug. 16, 1864, (e) Walter b. Jan. 15, 1867. 2nd. m. June 11, 1872 Lucy George Osborne. Issue (f) Fannie b. March 21, 1873, (g) Lucy b. Jan. 3, 1875, (h) Jimmie Hugh, b. Oct. 31, 1878, (i) Callie Alice b. July 22, 1881, (j) Samuel Douglas b. Dec. 4, 1883, (k) Martha Eliza (l) John Allen b. Sept. 29, 1888.

4. (b) William W., son of John and Elizabeth m. Winn.

4. (c) Dr. Hugh Allen m. Margaret —————.
4. (d) Mary Jane m. James L. Johnston.
4. (e) John Johnson m. Mary Osburn.
4. (f) Martha m. May 10, 1866, George W. St. John, M. D.
4. (h) Callie m. William D. Johnston.

Issue of John J. and Mary Osburn Blair:
5. (a) Lula m. Dr. A. B. Ramsey.
5. (b) John J. m. Addie Rogers.

5. (b) William Wiley, son of James and Jennette b. 1803 m. March 3, 1843, ————— Martha F. Johnston. Issue.

4. (a) Rachel, (b) Laura, (c) James M. b. 1844, (b) Wiley W. b. 1851, (e) Hugh E. F.

4. (b) Laura m. William R. Blair.

THE HISTORY OF ROANE COUNTY
BLAKE

Thomas came from Virginia in 1810.
1. Thomas m. ———— King, a sister of Major Robert King and settled on King's Entry, now part of the Clack farm. Issue: Mary, William G., Nathan, John.
2. Mary m. March 12, 1823 Isaac Hembree.
2. Nathan m. Betsy Summers. Issue.
3. (a) John H. (b) William A., (c) Charles C., (d) George Washington, (e) James F., (f) Elija, (g) Robert K., (h) Benjamine F., (i) Joseph, (j) David, (k) Mary J.
3. (a) John H., m. Mary Staples. Issue, (a) Samuel Monroe, (b) William Anderson, (c) Susan Elizabeth, (d) Velia M., (e) Joseph Frederick, (f) Anna Laura, (g) Georgia Fay, (h) Charles, (i) Ruth.

 3. (b) William Anderson
 3. (c) Charles C. m. Rachel Snow.
 3. (d) George Washington m. Louise Snow.
 3. (g) Robert K. m. Paralee DeLaney.
 3 (h) Benjamine F. m. Della Upshaw
 3. (i) Joseph m. Rachel Snow.
 3. (j) David m. Kitty Staples.
 3. (k) Mary J. m. William F. Seaver. Issue (a) William, (b) Fannie.

(a) Samuel Monroe, son of Mary and John H. Blake m. Sarah E. McGuffey. Issue (a) Charles Edward, (b) James Morgan, (c) J. Alvin.

(a) Charles Edward Blake m. Margaret Middleton Wells.

(b) William Anderson, son of Mary and John H. Blake m. Barbara McGuffey. Issue: Willie May m. Dr. Welch.

(c) Susan Elizabeth m. James H. Bowman. Issue, (a) James, (b) Linnie Fay, (c) Wendel.

(d) Velia m. Joseph Powell. Issue (a) Josie May, (b) Asa A.

(e) Joseph Frederick m. Anna Lewis. Issue, (a) Joseph Frederick, (b) Mary Thelma.

(f) Anna Laura m. Allen Montgomery. Issue, Ellen Fay.

(g) Georgia Fay m. Rue H. Haggard. Issue, (a) Allen Halen, (b) Frederick.

(h) Charles m. Dorothy Golston. Issue (a) John, (b) Frank.

(i) Ruth m. Edgar Siler. Issue, (a) Edgar Allen, (b) Edwina.

THE HISTORY OF ROANE COUNTY

BOWERS

1. Green b. Orange Co., N. C., was Sheriff of the County for seven years. Moved to Roane Co., in 1814.
2. Benjamine b. in North Carolina m. Mary Cloud and moved to Roane Co., in 1827. Issue:
3. (a) David G. b. 1826 in Orange Co., N. C., m. 1848 Eliza Bowman. Issue (a) Samuel, (b) Mary E., (c) Sarah, (d) John W., (e) Rufus S., (f) James J., (g) Thomas L.
3. (b) Mary m. Patrick W. Evans (see Evans).
3. (c) Sarah m. Aug. 3, 1842 Charles S. Howard.
3. (d) George m. Oct. 30, 1844, Jane Milsap.

Sam B. Bowers m. 1892 Cora Owings.
Issue:
    a. Raymond S.
    b. Elmer O.
    c. Sam B., Jr.
    d. J. D.
    e. Jesse M.
    f. Alice Ruth.

John W. Bowers m. Mary M. Acuff.
Issue:
    a. Nellie.
    b. Tom R.
    c. Alice.
    d. Will S.
    e. Myrtle.
    f. David G.
    g. John Ed.

Charles E. Delozier m. Nelle Bowers.
Issue:
    a. Edward W.
    b. Helen.
    c. Claude B.
    d. Paul.

Thomas L., son of David G. m. Polly Nelson, Issue. (a) Thomas, (b) Rose.

(a) Thomas m. Mary Ingram.
(b) Rose m. Fielding Brown.

THE HISTORY OF ROANE COUNTY
BOWMAN

1. John b. in Virginia a Revolutionary Soldier.
2. Samuel b. in Virginia m. Elizabeth Morgan, of Virginia. Issue, William, Nancy, Eliza, John.
3. William m. Jan. 10, 1813 Levisy Edwards.
3. Nancy m. Nov. 2, 1810 Charlie Burk.
3. Eliza m. David Bowers.

Children of John W. and Myra:
4. (a) Saunders m. Anna Poole.
4. (b) Anna m. 1st. Oscar Evans, 2nd. James Delaney.
4. (c) James Harper m. Susan Elizabeth Blake

(See Blake).

4. (d) Lennie m. Robert H. Alford.
4. (e) John W. m. Frankie Eblen.
4. (f) David Franklin.

Children of Saunders and Anna:
5. (a) Frank m. Elsie Thompson.
5. (b) Thomas Leeper m. Elizabeth Street.
5. (c) Lennie m. ———— Farnum.
5. (d) Ruth m. Robert H. Tilley.
Helen.
5. (e) Grace, 5 (f) Saunders, 5 (g) Mildred, 5 (h)

Chillren of Anna and Oscar Evans.
5. (a) Rupert, (b) William, (c) Alice, (d) Thomas, (e) Patrick.
5. (c) Alice Evans m. Oscar Rose.

Children of Lennie and Robert H. Alford.
5. (a) Myra m. ———— Eblen (b) Paul, (c) Robert, (d) Elsie.

Children of John W. and Frankie.
5. (a) Owenby, (b) Dixie Lynn, (c) Mary Frabk, (d) Bettie, (e) James.

THE HISTORY OF ROANE COUNTY

BRAZEALE

1. (a) Henry came from South Carolina and settled in Knox Co., was appointed assistant Dist. Attorney July 3, 1797. Moved to Kingston 1797. Issue (a) Willis, (b) Henry, (c) John W. M., (d) Sarah, (e) Carrick, (f) Robert.
2. (a) Willis m.
2. (b) Henry m. March 2, 1821 Betsy Morgan.
2. (c) John W. M. m. Feb. 5, 1824 Betsy Margraves.
2. (d) Sarah m. Nov. 10, 1822 Henry Newman.
2. (f) Robert m. 1824 Anna McKamey.
2 (b) James, brother of Henry, m. 1805 Peggy Miller.

Issue:
2. (a) Henry Miller who m. Syntha McKinney June 28, 1828.
  (b) Martha who m. Owing Gentry 1828.
3. (a) Elijah W., son of Willis, m. Nancy McMullen.
3. (b) Jane, dau. of Willis, m. Isaac McCoy.
(c) Elizabeth, dau. of Willis m. Isaac Eblen.
(d) Adaline, dau. of Willis m. ———— Duncan.
(e) Amanda, dau. of Willis m. Moses Ingram.
(f) Willis, Jr., m. Nancy Bogart.
(g) James, m. Susan Munger.
(h) Sarah Woods m. Stephen Ingram.

Issue of Elijah W. and Nancy:
4. (a) Amanda, (b) Thomas B., b. 1835 m. Jane Young, b. 1841. Issue 5. (a) Samuel Alexander, (b) Oscar, (c) Elizabeth, (d) Hortense, (e) Martha.
4. (a) Samuel Alexander m. Lou Ralston.
4. (b) Elizabeth m. Samuel Wilkerson.
4. (c) Hortense m. Charles Henderson.
4. (d) Martha m. William Wilkerson.

Elizabeth Brazeale m. William Nickard.
Alezander Brazeale m. Jan. 8, 1842 Elizabeth Stow.
Robert H. m. Nov. 14, 1841 Elizabeth Wells.
Henry Brazeale m. Louisa Luttrell Oct. 5, 1850.
J. H. Brazeale m. Susan Delozier June 3, 1880.
William Brazeale m. Julia Narramore Sept. 30, 1881.
David R. Brazeale was in the County in 1823.
Hugh L. Brazeale practiced law in Roane Co., in 1834.

THE HISTORY OF ROANE COUNTY

BROWDER

1. Edmund, of Guilford Co., N. C. Issue.
2. John and Darius brothers came from Cheatham Co., North Carolina about 1796.
    2. John m. Miss Richardson. Issue: 2 (a) Darius, m. Miss Matlock.
        2. (b) James m. Susan Johnston. Issue (a) John, (b) William, (c) Darius.
        2. (c) Jeptha.
        2. (d) Ginsie m. ———— Eldridge.
        2. (e) Julia m. Thomas Prater (See Prater).
        2. (f) Nancy (Polly) m. Bowman.
        2. (g) Fannie m. Eddington.
        2. (h) Eliza m. John Wesley Winton (See Winton).
        2. (i) Mary m. Josiah Jackson b. Dec. 25, 1800, d. Jan. 17, 1877.
        2. (j) ———— m. ———— Wilson.

1. Darius, son of John m. Jane Crump and came from North Carolina in 1796. Issue.
    2. (a) William, (b) Darius, (c) John, (d) Betsy, (e) Jane.

    2. (a) John m. 1828 Minerva Matlock. Issue (a) Theresa, (b) William J., (c) Darius, (d) Samuel, (e) Mary, m. W. R. Harvey, (See Harvey) (f) John F., (g) Martha J. m. James Reynolds), (h) Julia, m. George D. Rogers, (i) Minerva E. m. Rev. L. K. Haines, (j) Ellen m. W. L. Gallaher, (k) Joseph Crump.

    3. (f) John F. b. Oct. 15, 1840 m. Mar. 12, 1862, Sarah Gallaher. Issue 4. (a) Joseph Rowan, (b) George L., (c) Lula May m. J. R. Giddings, (d) Maud m. W. R. Dougthit, (e) William H.

    4. (a) Joseph Rowan b. Aug. 28, 1863 m. Dec. 18, 1889 Nellie Dyer Issue 5 (a) Sarah J., (b) Willie Rice, (c) Frank Vaughn, (d) Joseph G., (e) Robert H., (f) Nellie B., (g) John, (h) Mattie Elizabeth.

    2. (a) William, son or Darius b. in Chatham Co., N. C., Feb. 10 1792 m. 1814 Elizabeth, daughter of James Lackey in

THE HISTORY OF ROANE COUNTY

Roane Co. Issue 3 (a) John Jefferson b. Nov. 9, 1818, (b) William D. b. Jan. 1822 (c) James Madison, b. Oct. 16, 1824, (d) Darius, (e) David A., (f) Nancy Jane b. May 17, 1839, (g) Maryline.

3. (a) John Jefferson m. Dec. 22, 1844 Elizabeth Lotspeich b. May 7, 1825. Issue.

4. (a) Elizabeth, (b) Mary, (c) Amanda, (d) William, (e) Sarah, (f) John W., (g) Charles D., (h) Nancy, (i) Alice, (j) Samuel.

3. (b) William D. m. Jan. 1823 m. Sarah Deatherage Oct. 24, 1844.

3. (c) James Madison m. Nov. 29, 1849 Letitia Patterson. Issue. 4 (a) Mary m. J. L. Suddath, (b) David Newton m. Emma Byrd, (c) Elizabeth m. J. N. Heiskell, (d) Ellen m. Austin A. Green, (e) James Patterson m. Maud Critchell, (f) John Jefferson m. Bettie Taylor, (g) Horace Lackey m. Hulda Cleveland, (h) Lucy m. W. K. Horton, (i) Robert, 2nd wife of James M. was Elizabeth Armstrong Issue: (j) Samuel, (k) Clyde.

3. (e) David A. b. Mar. 2, 1835 m. Rachel Dickey Oct. 12 1858. Issue.

3. (f) Nancy Jane m. John H. Pickel.

3. (g) Maryline m. James Stone. Issue (a) Malinda (b) Elizabeth.

4. (a) Malinda m. William McMurray.

4. (b) Elizabeth m. Estel Lowe. Issue: (a) James, (b) David, (c) William, (d) Samuel, (e) Lee, (f) Josephine.

4. (c) Amanda, dau. of John J. m. April 16, 1872 Andrew J. Dickey.

THE HISTORY OF ROANE COUNTY

BROWN

1. James b. in Rockbridge Co., Va., Scotch-Irish.
2. Thomas b. 1800, was the pastor of Bethel Presbyterian Church from 1827 to 1872. m. 1834 to Jane N., dau. of David and Elizabeth Patton. Issue. (a) Ignatius Cyprian, (b) Mary, (c) Rowena, (d) William L., (e) Nancy, (f) David J., (g) Mary E., (h) Eusannah, (i) H. Virginia, (j) Laura.

) 3. (c) Ignatius C. m. Ruth Hamlet. Issue: Jennie, William L., Harry L., Hadly.
3. (c) Rowena m. Thomas J. Moore. Issue: Susan, Thomas J.

3. (d) William L., m. Sydney Hood. Issue: Clara Maud, Cecil, Thomas John P., Huldah, Jane S., Lois Amanda.

3. (i) Virginia m. ——— Hall.
Cecil m. Buena V. West.
Thomas, son of William m. Nettie Walker.
John P., m. Hazel Jones.
Susan, dau. of Rowena and Thomas J. Moore, m. J. B. Siezer.

Thomas J. Moore, Jr., m. 1st. Helen Swalm, 2nd. Ella Hastings McGinness.

BROWN

1. Edward b. in Wales came to Northampton Co., Va., m. Miss ——— Brown. Issue: (a) Samuel, (b) William, (c) John, (d) Henry (e) Benjamine, (f) Beverly, (g) Robert.

2. (b) William m. Sarah Long of Culpepper Co., Va. and moved to North Carolina, Issue: (a) Henry, (b) William, (c) Benjamine, (d) Samuel, (e) John.

3. (e) John enlisted as Ensign 1775 in North Carolina. Commissioned Captain in 1st. N. C., Apr. 26, 1777. Served in N. C. Dragoons 1778. m. Mary Little Tarver, of Snow Hill, Greene Co., N. C. and settled at Contentnea Creek. He was killed by a Tory about 1792. Issue (a) Robert Tarver, (b) John and Thomas, (twins) (c) William, (d) Rebecca, (e) Mary Ellen.

THE HISTORY OF ROANE COUNTY

4. (a) Robert Tarver b. Nov. 19, 1775, d. Jan. 14, 1846. m. June 1, 1807 Catherine Valle at Station Genevieve (St. Louis, Mo.) Catherine d. Sept. 4, 1842.
4. (b) John Brown m. 1st. Mary Moore Allison, 2nd. Nancy Clark Cox Allison, widow of Col. Uriah Allison.
4. (b) Thomas Brown m. Jane Adams MeElwee.
4. (e) William Brown m. Sarah Kimbrough.
4. (d) Rebecca Brown m. Robert Taylor.
4. (e) Mary Ellen Brown m. May 14, 1803 1st. Zacheus Ayers. 2nd. Dr. Richard Richards.

In 1798 Mary Tarver Brown, after the death of Capt. John Brown moved to Roane Co. Her son, John, was made a Brig. Gen. by Andrew Jackson in the War of 1812. He raised a Regiment of Soldiers known as the "Second Regiment Mounted Gunmen, of East Tennessee Volunteers" and went to the assistance of Gen. Jackson at the "Battle of Horseshoe Bend." Mary T., died 1800 and is buried at Muddy Creek Cemetery.

Issue of Gen. John and Mary M. Allison Brown.
5. (a) Robert Allison, (b) Sarah Tarver, (c) Thomas Albert, (d) Mary Jane, (e) John W., (f) William L., (g) Susan Howard.

Issue of Gen. John and Nancy Cox Allison Brown.
5. (a) Benjamine, (b) Rachel Jackson, (c) Eliza Jane, (d) George Bartlett.

4. (b) Thomas, the twin brother of Gen. John Brown. was a soldier in the War of 1812 and was commissioned a Major. b. Sept. 15, 1779; m. Jane Adams McElwee 1800. Issue: (a) William Franklin, (b) John Smith T., (c) Mary Caroline.

5. (a) Robert Allison, son of Gen. John and Mary Brown, b. Feb. 8, 1808, d. Sept. 7, 1886, m. Oct 27, 1836, Mary Jane Gillenwaters b. Dec. 30, 1819. Issue: (a) William G., (b) John, (c) Robert A., (d) Elizabeth Gillen Waters, (e) Samuel Eskridge, (f) Walter Roddye.

5. (b) Sarah Tarver Brown m. Nathaniel R. Jarrett. Issue: (a) Mary Comelia, (b) Jerome, (c) Robert, (e) Susan. (f) Eliza, (g) John.

5. (c) Thomas Albert m. Edna Trowers. Issue: (a)

THE HISTORY OF ROANE COUNTY

Matilda, (b) Victoria, (c) Mary Ellen, (d) Thomas (e Wilbur, (f) George, (g) Edna.

    5. (d) Mary Jane, dau. of Gen. John m. Dr. John Wesley Wester, (See Wester).

    5. (e) John Winston m. Sarah Matlock.

    5 (f) William L. m. Caroline Gamble. Issue: William.

    5. (g) Susan Howard m. Dr. Benjamine F. Davis. Issue: (a) John, (b) Jennie Medora.

    5. (a) Benjamine, son of Gen. John and Nancy Brown, m. Sarah M. Ellis. Issue: (a) John Ellis, b. May 4, 1857, (b) Carrie Meadors, b. Apr. 1858, (c) George, b. Apr. 1859, (d) Thomas W., b. Dec. 5, 1860, (e) Caleb, b. June 13, 1864, (f) Ernest, (g) Wilbert Otho, b. 1868, (h) Charles Robert, b. 1871, (e) Gypsie, b. May 30, 1874, m. J. W. Prater.

    5. (b) Rachel Jackson m. John Coleman. Issue: (a) Margaret, (b) Ella, (c) Addie, (d) James, (e) Mamie.

    5. (c) Eliza Jane m. William Martin d. June 2, 1927, (See Martin).

    5. (d) George Bartlett b. June 2, 1839, d. Feb 21, 1924.

    4. (e) Issue of Mary Ellen and Zacheus Ayers, 5 (a) Alexander, (b) William, (c) Alpha, (d) Sophia, (e) Zacheus.

    5. (d) Sophia m. Rev Samuel Harwell.

    5. (a) William Franklin, son of Major Thomas and Jane Brown, m. Amanda Renfro. Issue: (a) Thomas J., (b) Catherine Jane, (c) John Smith, (d) Rebecca, (e) Polk, (f) Amanda, (g) Sarah, (h) Robert, (i) Mary Caroline.

    6. (a) Thomas J. m. Martha Almeda Owings. Issue: 7 (a) William Jackson b. 1868, 7 (b) George Franklin, b. 1870, m. Maud Sewell.

    Issue: 8 (a) Emma Frances, 7 (c) Thomas Jefferson b. 1873, 7 (d) James Polk b. 1875).

    6. (b) Catherine Jane m. Robert m. Kimbrough. (See Kimbrough).

    6. (c) John Smith m. ―――――

    6 (d) Rebecca m. William McElwee (See McElwee).

    6. (e) Polk m. Mary Roddye. Issue: (a) Florence, (b) Elizabeth.

THE HISTORY OF ROANE COUNTY

6. (f) Amanda m. Dr. William Wilson. Issue: (a) William. (b) Caroline, (c) Robert, (d) Mamie.

6. (g) Sarah m. Henry Patton. Issue: (a) Frank m. Florence —————, (b) Neal m. Etheleen Upshaw.

6. Mary Caroline m. John R. Neal. Issue: (a) Amanda B., (b) John R., (c) Mary P., (d) Nora K., (e) George F.

7. (a) Amanda m. William Wheelock. Issue: (a) William Neal, (b) John S.

7. (e) George F. m. Mattie S. Milton.

5. (b) John Smith T., son of Major Thomas m. Elizabeth Tarver.

5. (c) Mary Caroline m. Elbridge Gerry Sevier (See Sevier).

6. (a) Victoria, dau. of Thomas Albert and Edna Brown m. George Gillespie, (See Gillespie).

6. (b) Mary Ellen m. Jesse Cravens, (See Cravens).

6. (a) William, son of William L. and Caroline Gamble Brown m. Janie Ford. Issue: (a) William, (b) Ella, (c) George, (d) Vassie, (e) Zollicoffer.

7. (a) Florence, dau of Polk and Mary Roddye m. Charles Mills. Issue: (a) Ruth, (b) Elizabeth.

7. (b) Elizabeth m. James Crumbliss, (See Crumbliss).

6. (a) Matilda, dau. of Thomas Albert and Edna Brown m. Thomas Roberts. Issue: (a) Thomas, (b) Nancy Ann.

4. (d) Children of Rebecca Brown and Robert Taylod (a) Etheldred, (b) John, (c) William, (d) Kinchen, (e) Polly, (f) Sarah, (g) Clasky, (h) Jincy, (i) Rebecca.

5. (2) Etheldred m. Dec. 11, 1811, Catherine Arbuckle.

Children of Robert Tarver and Catherine Valle Brown.

5. (a) John Fenwick b. 1810 m. Miss Grass. Issue: (a) Cora A., (b) Robert Tarver, (c) Charles.

THE HISTORY OF ROANE COUNTY

 6. (a) Cora A. Brown m. James Defani. Issue (a) Esther, (b) Cassie, (d) Bernard.
 6. (b) Robert Tarver m. 1st. Laura Montgomery, 2nd. Theresa Berdendistle.
 5. (b) Walter b. 1812 m. Mary J. Rochford. Issue: (a) Catherine, (b) Harriett, (c) Susan, (d) Cora, (e) Mary.
 6. (b) Harriett m. Louis Schaff. Issue: (a) Edward, m. Ida Cox, (b) Walter m. Matilda Jordon, (c) Mary m. Sylvester Rozier, (d) Cecelia m. Frank Rozier, (e) Carl, (f) Caroline m. Henry Rhem.
 6. (c) Susan m. Joseph Faina. Issue: Joseph.
 6. (d) Cora m. Jasper Menord. Issue: (a) Stella, (b) Rochford, (c) Nora, (d) Agnes, (e) Lucille, (f) Henrietta, (g) Rose, (h) Catherine, (i) Edward.
 6. (c) Mary m. John Reel. Issue: Jennie and others.
 5. (c) Robert T. m. Jan. 22, 1838, Mary E. Holden. Issue: (a) Ellen m. Jonah Sappington, (b) Julia, m. 1st. Cissil, Issue (a) Carrie, (b) Robert; 2nd. m. ——— Stocker. Issue: (c) Charles Stocker.
 5. (d) Francoise Valle, b. July 19, 1822 m. Sarah Harwell. Issue:
 6. (a) Barton, (b) Robert T. m. Bell Howard. Issue: (a) Howard, (b) Bell, (c) Valle, (d) Genevieve.
 6. (c) Thomas m. Celeste Murphy, 6 (d) Ada m. Joseph Weber. Issue: (a) Nellie, (b) Ada, (c) Sarah, (d) John.
 5. (e) William A. b. Aug. 21, 1818, m. Ann S. Noel Mar. 4, 1839. Issue: (a) Mary, (b) Emely m. James Burgees. Issue: Mattie, Catherine, Charity, Elizabeth, Joe, James, Henry, Zeno, Valle.

(c) Catherine, (d) Laura, (e) Ann.
 5. (f) Louis Franklin b. Dec. 1832 d. Apr. 1840.
 5. (g) Charles C. b. Nov. 24, 1830 m. Mary de Lossus, Jan. 12, 1858.
 5. (h) Zeno b. Oct. 9, 1826 d. Mar. 7, 1874.
 5. (i) Thomas Joseph b. Nov. 22, 1824 d. 1904.
 5. (j) Evariest Ambrose b. Dec. 7, 1828.

THE HISTORY OF ROANE COUNTY

5. (k) Mary E. b. July 22, 1814 m. Francoise Gregoire Dec. 28, 1831, d. Oct. 17, 1848. Issue: (a) August and others.

5. (l) July Mary b. Aug. 3, 1820 d. July 10, 1861 m. Francis H. Wilkerson, Jan. 23, 1838.

5. (m) Catherine Emely b. Aug. 1,.1835 m. 1st. Richard Waters Apr. 13, 1854. Issue: (a) Julia, b. Apr. 22, 1855, 2nd. J. Barton Cox, Jan. 11, 1859. Issue: (b) Louisa Catherine m. Henry B. Lawrence, (c) Phillip Shaw, (d) George W., (e) Ida M. m. Edwarl Schaff, (f) William B. m. Lula Maud Staunton, (g) Anne E. m. Peter Huck.

6. (a) William Gillen Waters, son of Robert A. b. Apr. 11, 1838, d. Mar. 19, 1914, m. Elizabeth Glenn. Issue: 7 (a) Robert Hugh m. Ida Morris. Issue: Susan Elizabeth, 7 (b) William m. Ida Horn. Issue 8 (a) Frank, 7 (c) Albert m. Bess Cowden. Issue 8 (a) George Albert.

6. (b) John b. Mar. 29, 1840, d. Mar. 4, 1864.

6. (c) Thomas b. Mar. 20, 1842, d. Apr. 21, 1862.

6. (d) Robert Allison b. Dec. 3, 1844, m. Mary Agnes Stephens, Oct. 14, 1866, b. Mar. 16, 1850. Issue: (a) Nellie, (b) Mary, b. Sept. 3, 1869, m. John H. Preston Nov. 14,, 1901. Issue: 8 (a) Hester Elizabeth, (b) Thomas Benjamine b. May 20, 1874. (c) Walter Roddye b. Dec. 12, 1877, m. Lou Halton Apr. 26, 1900, (d) William Brady b. Sept. 12, 1880, d. Dec. 25, 1905 m. Mabel Hurst Apr. 12, 1903, (e) Elizabeth Gertrude b. Mar. 22, 1885 m. A. Lafayette Todd, May 12, 1909. (f) Hetha Hill b. Feb. 15, 1888, m. Arthur S. Prettyman Aug. 2, 1908. Issue 9 (a) Thomas Brown.

6. (c) Elizabeth Gillenwaters Brown, b. Oct 25, 1847, Cass County, Mo., m. Oct. 29, 1868 to H. Clay Daniel (1842-1925) b. Trigg Co., Ky. Issue: 1. Pearl Hall Daniel, m. Austin H. Merrill. Issue: 1. Austin H. Merrill, Jr. m. Levine Shinn, Issue :Patrica Ann Merrill, 2. Elizabeth Brown Merrill, m. Crawford Duncan Everett. Issue, Merrill Everett.

11. Charles Hardin Daniel m. Jessie Harriett. Issue: 1. Ruth Daniel m. Delmas Gives, Jr., 2. Naomi Daniel m. (1) Andrew Womack. Issue: Dorothy Womack, m. (2nd). Daniel m. (1) Andrew Womack. Issue: Dorothy Womack, m. (2nd).

THE HISTORY OF ROANE COUNTY

III. Robert Brown Daniel m. Lilian Boswell. Issue: 1. Robert Edwin Daniel, 2. Grace Daniel.

IV. Mary Brown Daniel, second wife of John Trotwood Moore. Issue: 1. Austin Merrill Moore, 2. Helen Lane Moore, (twins) 3. Mary Daniel Moore.

V. H. Clay Daniel, Jr., m. Effie Ervin. Issue: 1. Frances Daniel, 2. H. C. Daniel III.

VI. Elizabeth Daniel m. Wm. Barnes.

VII. William Gillenwaters Daniel, 1882, 1911.

VIII. Louise Merrill Daniel, m. Charles Owen Crawford. Issue: 1. Anna Dale, 2. Elizabeth Waite, 3. Mary Louise, 4. Charles Owen, Jr.

6. (f) Samuel Eskridge b. Feb. 1, 1850 m. Dec. 3, 1870 Zada Robinson, b. Sept. 30, 1853. Issue: 7 (a) Lena b. Oct. 14, 1871 m. Nov. 1901, Henry Shanks. Issue: 8 (a) Margaret Shanks, (b) John Winton b. Aug. 30, 1875 m. Feb. 22, 1917 Mrs. Mabel Hager, 7 (c) Ida m. Apr. 17, 1901 Frank Armstrong. Issue: 8 (a) Samuel B., (b) James B., (c) Frances Lucille, 7 (d) Harriet Ethel b. Oct. 4, 1879 m. Edward Woodson Ragsdale June 27, 1898. Issue: (a) Edward Brown, 7 (e) Lucille b Dec. 23, 1887 m. Charles Dean Eidson Nov. 26, 1908.

6. (g) Walter Roddye b. July 18, 1853 m. Margaret Lisle. Issue: 7 (a) Glessner m. Coates S. Cockrill. Issue: 8 (a) Woodson, 8 (b) Joe Brown, 8 (c) Billy, 7 (b) Leslie, m. Corinne Connely, 7 (c) Margaret Roddye.

6. (a) Mary Cornelia Jarrett m. Dr. Wm. Vonnah Taylor 2nd. Issue: 7 (a) Wm. Vonnah Taylor 3rd. m. Sarah Davis. Issue: 8 ( )a) Wm. Vonnah Taylor, 4th., m. Roberta Burton; 8 (b) Allen Davis Taylor m. Kate Prudence Smith; 8 (c) Arthur Jarrett Taylor m. Lucille Brown. Issue Arthur Jarrett Taylor, Jr., Emily Taylor; 8 (d) Lois Taylor m. Norman Crawford. Issue: Norman Crawford, Jr., Wm. Vonnah Crawford. Frances Eva Taylor m. Robert Prestedge. Issue: Frances Davis Prestedge, Robert Prestedge, Leonard Henderson Taylor m. Bessie Kincaid. Issue: Elise Taylor, Martha Henderson Taylor, William Vonnah Taylor, 5th.

THE HISTORY OF ROANE COUNTY

7. Arthur Robert Taylor m. Timmons Lewis Treadwell. Issue: Starnes Treadwell Taylor m. Mary Podester. Issue: Mary Frances Taylor.

7. Mary Emmet Taylor m. William Marshall Rees. Issue: Marshall Stroud Rees, Arthur Wilbur Rees, d. Young.

7. Nena Lee Taylor m. Thomas Bass Jones, Issue: Irma Lee Jones, m. T. N. Buckingham. Issue: Irma Jones Buckingham.

6. (b) Jerome Jarrett m. 1st. Adeline Cassey, 2nd.—— Casey. Issue Jerome.

6. (c) Robert Jarrett m. ———————— Issue Mary.

6. (d) Sarah Jarrett m. ————— Kellogg.

6. (e) Susan Jarrett m. ————— Robinson. Issue: 7 (a) Jessie, (b) Paul.

6. (g) John B. Jarrett m. Lula Jones. Issue: 7 (a) John Brown, (b) Louise.

6. (a) John Davis, son of Dr. B. F. and Susan Brown Davis, m. Zilphia Amanda Huggins.

6. (b) Jennie Medora Davis b. Aug. 10, 1857 m. Andrew Gordon Deacon. Issue: (a) Robt. Richardson, b. May 23, 1877 m. May 23, 1905, May Hall b. Nov. 23, 1897, (b) Helen Davis b. Jan. 9, 1881 m. June 20, 1910 George B. Spivey, b. Oct. 31, 1875, (c) William Cory b. Jan. 1879 m. June 25, 1902, Mattie Zimmerman, (b) Mary Belle b. 1883, (e) Elizabeth S. b. 1886, (f) Andrew Gordon b. Feb. 16, 1891 m. Nellie Louise Coward b. Nov. 3, 1899.

Robert Allison III b. Nov. 18, 1891 m. Nina L. Hunt June 9, 1921. Issue Mary Louise.

Agnes Nelson b. Dec. 17, 1895.

Helen Holton, dau. of Walter Roddye Brown m. Glenn Maddox, Nov. 26, 1920. Issue, Louise.

Children of William Brady and Mabel Brown.

(a). Nell Christie, (b) Harry Hurst.

Children of Elizabeth and Lafayette Todd.

(a) Agnes Loretta, (b) Howard Allison, (c) John Silas. (d) William Brady, (e) A. Lafayette.

THE HISTORY OF ROANE COUNTY

(a) Thomas, son of John Smith T. Brown m ―――. Issue: Daisy m. Dr. Purifoy. (d) Bessie, dau. of John Smith T. m. Jones Tyson, (h) Mary Ellen, dau. of John Smith T. m. Judge B. F. Saffold. Issue: (a) Marion, (b) Burney m. Margaret Parsons, (c) Roy m. Camille Robins. Issue: Ray J. m. Mary Tait, (d) Ida m. ――――― Heidt. Issue: Marion m. C. W. Mimms.

Children of John Brown and Zilpha H. Davis.
(a) Arthur L., m. Lane Hughes, (b) Susan Jennie m. E. R. Ginn, (c) Charles Betts, (d) Nellie May m. Lewis Price Gattis, (e) Curtis L., (f) Gilbert L., (g) Leona M., (h) Cecil.

Margaret dau. of John H. and Rachel Brown Coleman m. ――――――― Morrow.

Ella, dau. of John H. and Rachel Brown Coleman m. ――――――― Hoyle.

Addie, dau. of John H. and Rachel Brown Coleman m. ――――――― Greer.

Mamie, dau. of John H. and Rachel Brown Coleman m. J. C. Grant.

THE HISTORY OF ROANE COUNTY

BYRD

1. Jesse b. in Virginia came in a flat boat down the Tennessee River and settled on the site of Kingston about 1795 and established the first ferry at that point. Issue, (a) Joseph, (b) Eliza.

2. (a) Joseph b. Jan. 8, 1795 m. May 6,, 1819 in Roane Co., Ann Pride b. July 20, 1797. Issue:

3. (a) Jesse b. Mar. 20, 1820, m. Mar. 11, 1843 Mary McDuffie.

(b) Mariah King b. June 1, 1822.

(c) Robert King b. Nov. 4, 1823 m. July 23, 1861 Mary Lea.

(d) Thomas Brown b. Mar. 13, 1825 m. Savannah Margraves.

(e) James Standifer b. Dec. 28, 1828 m. Oct. 18, Narcissa Tennessee McMillan, b. Aug. 27, 1844.

(f) Samuel Jackson b. 1830.

(g) Mary Ellen b. Mar. 21, 1831 m. Sept. 11, 1855 Henry Monger.

(h) William Hardin b. Dec. 31, 1832.

(i) John Hamilton b. Jan. 29, 1835 m. Mary Ann Ballard.

(j) George Gillespie b. Dec. 15, 1836.

(k) Sarah Ruth b. Aug. 3, 1839.

(1) Eliza b. Jan. 23, 1841, m. James Bohannon.

(m) Joseph, Jr., b. Sept. 11, 1843.

3. (k) Sarah Ruth m. 1860 Dr. Paul Gregory. Issue: Eugene Hamilton. They were separated and she changed her son's name to Byrd. 2nd. she m. John H. Billingsley.

4. (a) Dr. Eugene Hamilton Byrd m. May 19, 1892 Canis Blanch Hasinger. Issue: Sarah Ruth.

Children of Thomas and Savannah.

4. (a) Emma, (b) Vada, (c) Lou, (d) Sarah, (e) Robert, (f) John L.

THE HISTORY OF ROANE COUNTY

  5. (a) Emma m. Newton Browder. Issue, (a) Byrd, (b) Thomas.
    5. (b) Vada m. Dewitt Dickey. Issue, three children.
    5. (d) Sarah m. Thomas Hardin. Issue, four children.
    5. (e) Robert m. Elizabeth Smith.
    5. (f) John L. m. Dora Cook. Issue, four children.
  Children of Sarah Ruth and John H. Billingsley.
    5. (a) Joseph Byrd, (d) Margaret Wray, (c) Mary Ann.
    5. (b) Mary Ann m. Oct. 10, 1896, Theron Browne. Issue:
      6. (a) Brownie m. Alberta Holmes.
      6. (b) Evelyn Ruth m. Albert m. Johnson.
      6. (c) Marguerite Blanch m. Fred L. Campfield.
      6. (d) Anne Pride m. John Paul Jones.
      6. (e) Mary Louise m. Albert W. Allison.
      6. (f) Jane Leatherwood.
    5. (a) Joseph Byrd m. Madie Gibson.
    5. (b) Margaret May m. William Browder.
  4. (a) Nancy dau. of Jesse and Mary m. Robert M. Allison (See Allison).
  Children of James Standifer and Narcissa.
  4. (a) Joseph Rush, (b) Sam Lee, (c) Flora Nelissa, (d) James Standifer, (e) Mary Lea, (f) Nena Terressa, (g) Ben Augustus.
  Children of John Hamilton and Mary Ann.
  4. (a) Charles m. Jennie B. Wilson. Issue:
    5. (a) Mary, (b) Francis.
  4. (b) Oscar m. Mary Cope. Issue:
    5. (a) Shannon, (b) Robert, (c) Mary Louise, (d) Frank.
  4. (c) Ethel May Lida m. Tie Blair. Issue:
    5. (a) William, (b) Anne, (c) Grace, (d) Laura, (e) Ruth, (f) John, (g) Francis.
  4. (d) Emma m. Samuel Wilson. Issue:
    5. (a) Helen, (b) Robert, (c) John, (d) Mary.

THE HISTORY OF ROANE COUNTY

4. (e) Samuel m. Annie Hood. Issue, three children.
4. (f) Robert m. Frankie Jones. Issue, one child.
4. (g) Rose m. Benjamine Huffine. Issue, seven children.
4. (h) Newton.
4. (i) Ernest m. Maud Pickel.

NOTE: Abraham Byrd was wounded when in company with Lieut. McClelland on Aug. 13, 1792, they were attacked by Indians near Crab Orchard on Cumberland Mountain.

THE HISTORY OF ROANE COUNTY

CENTER

1. Milton Center, a brother of Tandy Senter, came to Roane Co. before 1802, d. 1848. Came from Virginia and settled on Emory River. m. 1790 in Carter Co., Nancy Keener. Issue. 2. (a) Milton, (b) Willis, (c) Thomas, (d) Elizabeth, (e) Frank, (f) Caroline, (g) Levina.

2. (b) Willis b. ———— m. Jane, dau. of James Gallaher. Issue:

3. (a) Thomas Clark, (b) Nancy, (c) Frank Keener, (d) Willis Stephens, (e) George Washington, (f) Sarah Elizabeth. (g) Mary Gallaher, (g) James Gallaher, (h) Virginia, (i) Felix.

3. (a) Thomas Clark m. Johanna McEwen, Issue:
4. (a) Thomas C., (b) Elizabeth, (c) Willis, (d) Nancy Jane, (e) William Stephens, (f) Charles McEwen, (g) James Gallaher, (h) Anna, (i) Margaret, (j) George G., (k) Ira, (l) Felix, (m) Hugh Martin.

3. (b) Nancy, dau. of Willis and Jane m. Eldridge Yost. Issue:

4. (a) Adelaide, (b) Katherine, (c) George Center, (d) James Yost, (e) Sarah Elizabeth, (f) Alma.

3. (c) Frank Keener, son of Willis and Jane m. Sarah Crow.

3. (e) George Washington, son of Willis and Jane m. Mary Overton Bacon.

3. (f) Sarah Elizabeth, dau. of Willis and Jane m. Hugh Martin (See Martin).

Children of Frank Keener and Sarah Center.
4. (a) Eliza m. Eugene Clark (See Clark).
4. (b) Martha m. Blair.
4. (c) Willis.
4. (d) Georgia.
4. (e) Perrin.
4. (f) Katherine.
2. (e) Frank m. Eliza Gallaher.
2. (f) Caroline m. Robert S. Gilliland.

THE HISTORY OF ROANE COUNTY

2. (g) Levina m. Thomas Knight.
2. (d) Elizabeth.

Children of George Washington and Mary Center.

4. (a) Mary Gallaher, (b) George W., (c) James.

4. (d) Nancy Jane, dau. of Thomas and Joanna Center m. Samuel P. Spark.

4. (e) William S., son of Thomas and Johanna Center m. Florence Jenkine. Issue: Gladys McEwen.

Martha Center m. Jan. 22, 1840 William Barnett.

Byrd Center and Stephen Center are on the Tax list of 1813.

Evelyn Center m. John Sudath. Issue (a) Stephen B. m. Sarah Elizabeth Mayberry, (b) Frank S. m. ——— Hasler, (c) Milton Graves, (d) Evelyn m. ——— Standfield, (e) Margaret m. William Henley, (f) Nancy.

Willis, son of Milton, is said by a member of the family to have changed the name Senter to Center.

Milton and Nancy are buried in the Center graveyard on the Mahoney farm near Harriman.

THE HISTORY OF ROANE COUNTY
CLARK

Thomas Norris came from Scotland an orphan when a small boy to Petersburg, Va., m. Susan Payne, a first cousin to Dolly Payne Madison. Moved to Kingston soon after and was one of the first merchants. Issue: (a) Mary, (b) Letitia, (c) William, (d) Nancy, (e) Susan, (f) Elizabeth, (g) James Payne, (h) Thomas, (i) Louisa, (j) Sally Payne, (k) Matilda.

2. (a) Mary m. Thomas Lyon, of Knoxville. Issue: (a) Thomas L. (b) Susan Clark, (c) Mary, (d) Louisa, (e) Washington, (f) William.

3. (a) Thomas Lyon was engaged to Miss McClung, who died a few days before the time set for the wedding.

3. (b) Susan Clark Lyon, m. Campbell Wallace.

3. (c) Mary Lyon m. J. J. Craig.

3. (d) Louisa Lyon m. A. A. Barnes, of Memphis.

2. (b) Letitia Clark m. James Trimble. Issue. (a) John, (b) Thomas, (c) Susan, (d) Mary Ann, (e) Eliza, (f) Andrew, (c) Louisa.

2. (c) William m. Nov. 11, 1813 Nancy White in Knox Co.

2. (d) Nancy Clark m. Thomas McCampbell. Issue: (a) Thomas, (b) Andrew, (c) Louisa.

2. (e) Susan Clark m. William Phillips.

2. (f) Elizabeth Clark m. James McCampbell.

2. (h) Thomas Norris m. 1st. a niece of Dolly Madison who died childless, and he m. Mary Clowney. Issue: (a) James, (b) Susan, (c) Louisa, (d) Thomas III, (e) John, (f) Samuel, (g) Eugene.

2. (i) Louisa Clark m. John Brown Rogers. Issue: (a) Thomas, (b) William, (c) Annie Clark, (d) Josephine Virginia, (e) John Thomas, (f) James Edgar, (g) Mary Louisa, (h) William Thomas.

2. (j) Sally Payne Clark m. Archibald Rogers. Issue: (a) Eustace, (b) Archibald, (c) Frank, (d) Thomas, (e) Dewitt, (f) Lelie, (g) James.

3. (b) Susan, dau. of Thomas and Mary Clowney m. Major Murphey. Issue: (a) Florence who m. Fisher, (b) Alice

THE HISTORY OF ROANE COUNTY

m. Tomlinson, (c) Annie Belle m. Kirkpatrick, (d) Nell m. Robert O. Gallaher.

2. (k) Matilda Clark m. William McEwen.

3. (a) John, son of Letitia C. and James Trimble m. Marguerita McEwen.

3. (b) Thomas Trimble m. Penelope Williams.

3. (c) Susan Trimble m. Col. William Ramsey.

3. (d) Mary Trimble m. Neil S. Brown, Governor of Tennessee, Minister to Russia under President Fillmore.

3. (e) Eliza Trimble m. Adrian Van C. Lindsley.

3. (f) Louisa Trimble m. John Reed. Issue: (a) Frank Trimble Reed.

3. (c) Louisa McCampbell m. Enock Ensley.

Children of Mary Ann Trimble and Neil Brown. (a) James Trimble, b. Feb. 25, 1842, (b) George Tully b. Dec. 1843, (c) Neil b. Feb. 1, 1846, (d) Duncan b. Aug. 4, 1848, (e) Susan Louisa b. Nov.), 1850, (f) Henry b. May 7, 1854, (g) Myra Letitia b. June 27, 1856, (h) John C. b. Dec. 28, 1858.

4. (a) James Trimble Brown m. Jennie Nichols. Issue: (a) William Lytle, (b) Elizabeth Trimble, (c) Trimble.

4. (b) George Tully Brown m. Lou Ezell.

4. (c) Neil Brown m. Susan Walton. Issue: (a) Neil, (b) Walton.

4. (g) Mary Letitia Brown m. Capt. Vinet Donaldson.

5. (b) Elizabeth Trimble Brown, b. Mar. 22, 1876 m. first Feb. 17, 1897 Archibald J. Majoribank, Gov. Gen. of Canada. Issue: a son and a daughter. 2nd. 1905 Sir Douglas McGarel Hogg, Attorney General, of England. Issue, two sons.

3.f (f) Samuel, son of Thomas II, m. Miss Doak. Issue: (a) Annie May, (b) Helen.

3. (g) Eugene, son of Thomas II, and Mary Clowney,

THE HISTORY OF ROANE COUNTY

m. Eliza Center. Issue: (a) Charles, (b) Willis, (c) Estelle, (d) Thomas N.

2 (g) James Payse, son of Thomas N. b. Oct. 5, 1759 d. Feb. 6, 1863, m. June 20, 1820, Susan Hunt McCorry b. 1802 d. 1844. Issue:

    3. (a) Thomas b. May 24, 1821.
    3. (b) Benjamine Parker b. Mar..2, 1823.
    (c) James Trimble b. Dec. 31, 1824.
    (d) George Shall b. Feb. 7, 1827 d. 1906.
    (e) William Henry b. Feb. 23, 1829.
    (f) Adelaide Frances b. Nov. 5, 1830, d. 1860.
    (g) Edward b. Oct. 14, 1832.
    (h) Frank b. Sept. 1834.
    (i) Alice McCorry b. May 1, 1836 d. Aug. 12, 1915.
    (j) Mary Florence b. Apr. 1839.
    (k) Sallie Parker and Patsy Paine b. May 29, 1841.
    (l) Henry Wood McCorry b. Aug. 14, 1843.
    (m) Carlos Smith b. Nov. 5, 1845.

James Payne Clark was Clerk of the Supreme Court at Nashville for many years.

    3. (a) Thomas Norris, son of James Payne and Susan McCorry Clark m. Issue:

    4. (a) Albert, (b) James Payne, (c) Thomas Norris, (d) Edward (e) Marina, (f) Fannie, (g) Addie, (h) Susan McCorry.

    4. (a) Albert m. Sally Stephens. Issue: 5 (a) Frances, (b) Louise (c) Mary, (d) Barbara, (e) Albert.

    4. (e) Marina m. Clark Pybas. Issue: 5 (a) Francis, (b) Adelaide, (c) Clark.

    4. (f) Fannie Clark m. Ellis Pearson.

    4. (g) Addie Clark m. Dr. Moore. Issue: 5 (a) Adelaide,

    4. (h) Susan McCorry Clark m. ——— Marks. Issue: 5 (a) Thomas Clark.

    3. (b) Benjamine Parker, son of James Payne Clark m. Henrietta Morgan. Issue: 4 (a) Fannie, (b) Adelaide.

THE HISTORY OF ROANE COUNTY

4. (a) Fannie m. Thomas Kendrick. Issue 5 (a) Henrietta, (b) Adelaid.

4. (b) Adelaid Clark m. William Eastman.

3. (1) George Shall, son of James Payse Clark m. Elizabeth Terrill, b. 1840, d. 1877. Issue: 4 (a) Harry Terrill, (b) Susan McCorry, (c) George Shall, (d) James Payne, (e) Florence, (f) Sheffield, (g) Elizabeth Payne.

4. (a) Harry Terrill m. Samantha Hudson. Issue: 5 (a) George Shall, (b) Henry Terrill, (c) Charles Spurgeon, (d) Robert, (e) James Payne, (f) Grady.

4. (b) Susan McCorry m. Robert Meade Patterson. Issue: 5 (a) James L., (b) Clark, (c) Robert Mead, (d) William Gleaves.

4. (d) James Payne, son of George Shall m. Beatrice— Issue: 5 (a) Beatrice, (b) Mary Elizabeth.

4. (f) Sheffield m. Idella Sawrie. Issue: 5 (a) Margaret McAlister, (b) Thomas Sheffield.

3. (e) William Henry, son of James Payne and Susan Clark m. Margaret ———, Issue: 4 (a) William Henry, (b) Thomas Norris, (c) Jennie, (d) Margaret m. Dr. M. E. Link.

3. (f) Adelaide Frances m. William A. Gleaves Aug. 14, 1851. Issue: 4 (a) Susan Clark, (b) James C., (c) Mary T., (d) William A.

3. (i) Alice McCorry m. Samuel Van Leer. Issue 4 (a) John, (b) Samuel, (c) Carlos Clark.

THE HISTORY OF ROANE COUNTY

COX

Isham m. Catherine Cox, dau. of Bartlett Cox who lived near Washington on the Potomac River. Issue: ten children, (a) John, (b) Joshua, (c) Mary, (d) Nancy, (e) Thomas, (f) James. Isham was Trustee of Roane Co., 1802 to 1820.

2. (c) Mary m. Jan. 29, 1820 Uriah Allison.
2. (e) Thomas m. May 11, 1817, Nancy Vaughn.
2. (f) James m. Sept. 11, 1818, Barbara Gardner.
2. (l) Nancy m. 1st. Col. Uriah Allison, 2nd. Gen. John Brown.

3. (a) Abner Jackson Cox, son of Thomas Cox and Nancy Vaughn was born Jan. 12, 1826, at Kingston, Roane Co., Tenn., m. Elizabeth Wilson, dau. of Samuel Wilson and Margaret Clark, was born at Kingston Aug. 13, 1832.

Issue:

4. (a) Lafayette Bryson, Feb. 11th, 1855.
(c). Carrie Myra, Jan. 22, 1860.
(b) Leander Monroe, Aug. 25, 1857.
(d) Thomas Samuel, May 22, 1862.
(e) Emma, Dec. 6, 1864.
(f) Charles W., Oct. 30, 1867.
(g) Alice Letitia, Nov. 2, 1869.
(h) Newton Hamilton, Aug. 8, 1873.
(i) Alma Lee, Aug. 24, 1880.

4. (c) Carrie Myra Cox m. Edward H. Henry. Issue: (a) Frances, (b) Marie, (c) Reita.

(g) Alice Letitia Cox m. M. H. Shoemaker. Issue: Richarl, Clinton, Robert and Elizabeth.

(h) Newton Hamilton Cox m. Elizabeth Bartlett.
(i) Alma Lee Cox m. Wm. P. D. Moross. Issue: Elizabeth Dwight, Frances Dwight.

5. (a) Frances Henry m. Leon Jarrett.
(b) Maria Henry m. Roy' Justin McCormick.
(c) Reita Henry m. Walter L. Bryant.
5. (a) Elizabeth Moross m. Cooper O'Grady.

THE HISTORY OF ROANE COUNTY
CRAVENS

1. Robert settled in Orange Co., Va., 1873. m. Mary Harrison.
2. (a) Robert m. Hester Harrison.
2. (b) John, son of Robert and Mary m. Margaret Hiatt Dyer.
4. James, son of John, m. Dec. 20, 1791, Ann dau. of Thomas Love, of Fauquier Co., Va. He was b. Apr. 12, 1737,. d. July 12, 1821. Issue:

5. (a) Mary m. Jacob Shelley.
5. (b) Margaret m. Samuel Swan.
5. (c) Patsye m. Pleasant Lea.
5. (d) Robert b. May 5, 1805 m. Catherine Cravens.
5. (e) Dorothea m. Thomas Ball.
5. (f) Eliza m. Jack Haley.
5. (g) Hannah m. ———— Roberts.
5. (h) Sallie.

(d) Robert b. May. 5, 1805 in Rockingham Co., Va. moved when a young man to Roane Co., where he, with his uncle, George Gordon, built the first iron furnace in the State and probably in the South, known as Eagle Furnace.

Robert m. 1st. Oct. 6, 1830 Catherine, dau. of Jesse and Jennie Mahaffa Roddye.

Catherine, b. Aug. 3, 1806 d. Sept. 28, 1845. Issue:
6. (a) Nancy J. b. Aug. 10, 1832. m. J. P. McMillen.
6. (b) Ann E. b. Nov. 7, 1843, d. Aug. 25, 1885, m. 1854 George Wasington Lyle.
6. (c) James Reagan b. 1837 m. 1st. Harriet Newell Rogers. 2nd. Mary D. Lyle.
6. (d) Lydia b. 1839 m. W. W. Anderson.
6. (e) Jesse Roddye b. 1843 m. 1st. Mary Ella Brown, 2nd. Ida Miller.

Robert m. 2nd Caroline Cunningham 1847.

Children of Nancy and Jonathan P. McMillen.
7. (a) James b. 1856.
7. (b) David Caldwell b. 1859.
7. (c) Ann Craven b. 1870 m. Atwell Thompson.

THE HISTORY OF ROANE COUNTY

Children of Ann and George W. Lyle.
7. (a) Thomas, (b) George W., (a) Katherine.
1. (c) Katherine m. 1890 George R. West, M. D. Issue.
8. (a) Lyle B., (b) George R.
Children of James Reagan and Harriet Rogers.
7. (a) Robert Spencer who m. Evelyn Gordon. Issue:
8. (a) Hattie.
7. (b) Mary m. 1886 William J. Sawyer. Issue:
8. (a) Robert Cravens who m. Rosalie Cunningham.
7. (c) Jane Harriet d. 1864.
Issue of James Reagan and Mary Lyle.
7. (d) Henry Lyle, (e) Ruth L., (f) Jesse P., (g) James R., (h) George L., (i) Joseph, (j) Marvin, (k) Charles, (1) Lucy.

Dr. James Reagan d. Oct. 23, 1911. Mary L. d. Feb. 28, 1918.

8. (a) Henry. Lyle m. Evelyn Mathew.
8. (g) James R. m. Elizabeth Thomasson.
8. (j) Marvin. m. Rosa B. Pulliam.
Issue of Jesse Roddye and Mary Ella Brown.
7. (a) James, (b) McMillin, (c) Tarver, (d) Roy, (e) Katherine.
Issue of Jesse Roddye and Ida Miller.
7. (f) Mary E., (g) Robert, (h) Nancy.
Children of Lydia Love Cravens and William W. Anderson.

(a) Charles E. who m. Mary Bachman. Issue:
8. (a) John Bachman Anderson m. Dorothy Morgan.
(b) William Dulaney Anderson m. Rosalie Slaughter.
(c) Margaret Anderson m. Charles Coffee.
Chillren of Nancy Jane and Jonathan P. McMillin
8. (a) James P. b. 1856, (b) David b. 1859, (c) Anna C., b. 1870.

8. (a) James P. m. 1882 Elizabeth Armstrong. Issue: (a) Robert, (b) Laura who m. T. H. Wagoner, (c) James P.

8. (b) David C. m. Feb. 17, 1886 Minnie B. Newman. Issue:
9. (a) Douglas N. m. Ariel Stephenson.
9. (b) Edwin W. m. Margaret Davies.

THE HISTORY OF ROANE COUNTY

CRUMBLISS

1. Thomas came from Ireland was a Revolutionary Soldier. Issue: James.

2. James, a soldier of the War of 1812 a native of Ireland, emigrated to America in his youth, d. 1839 m. Ann Goddard. Issue: Hugh.

3. Hugh m. Aug. 27, 1810 Betsy, dau. of Isaac Bashears. Was Clerk and Master of Roane Co., for several years.

4. (b) Henry b. 1834, m. Apr. 3, 1867, Nellie Penelope Griffin, of Somerset, Ky. Children:

5. (a) James Griffin m. Elizabeth, dau. of Polk and Ann (Roddy) Brown. Children: (a) James B., (b) Florence M., (c) Virginia, (d) Hugh Polk.

(b) Hugh, died May 10, 1918.

(c) Henry, m. Mabel Muse. Children: (a) George Muse, (b) Henry.

(d) Roy m. Margaret McFarland, Children: (a) Roy, (b) Mary, (c) Margaret.

(e) Raleigh m. Vera Trimby. Issue: Vera Trimby.

(f) Penelope m. George Gordon Stiles. Issue: (a) Penelope Elise, (b) Ethel Gordon.

(g) Rosa m. Alexander Lawrence Roberson. Issue: (a) Alexander Lawrence, (b) Nell, (c) Ruth, (d) Mariana, (e) Hugh.

(h) Lucile, m. John Sherman Shaw, Issue: (a) John Sherman.

4. (a) George Washington b. Mar. 10, 1831 in Roane Co., m. Cordelia, dau. of Richard and Polly (Turnley) Luttrell.

4. (c) Alice m. ——— Hasler.

4. (d) Caroline m. ——— Walker.

THE HISTORY OF ROANE COUNTY
DEARMOND

1. The first of family by this name of French origin came to Knox Co., and from there moved to Mississippi in 1790, then on to Louisiana.
2. Thomas b. 1795 in Mississippi went to Louisiana with his parents and there m. Julia A. White. Issue: Samuel Jackson b. 1816 in Louisiana moved to Roane Co., in 1837, m. Nov. 1835 G. B. DeArmond. (Goodspeed).
James b. July 3, 1771, d. Mar. 1, 1831, m. Susan Shadden, b. Sept. 1, 1786, d. Feb. 18, 1869. Issue:
- (a) Esther m. ——— Bashears.
- (b) Elizabeth m. Thomas DeArmond.
- (c) Drucilla m. Paul Frost.
- (d) Matilda, m. John G. D'Armond.
- (e) Susan m. John G. D'Armond.
- (f) Grizzie m. S. J. D'Armond.
- (g) Jane m. Owen Flucker.
- (h) Mahala m. William B. Nichols July 28, 1866.
- (i) Mary and Margaret.
- (j) Elizabeth.
- (k) Jackson.
- (l) Calhoun.
- (m) James.
- (n) Wylie.
- (o) John b. Oct. 31, 1808, d. May 21, 1896, m. Oct. 28, 1860 Caledonia Bowers.

Issue: (a) Annie Laurie, (b) Susan Hannah, (c) John, (d) Lewis, (e) James, (f) Fred, (g) Richard, (h) Lula, (i) Margaret.

(a) Annie Laurie m. B. A. Tedder. Issue: (a) Ella Blain, (b) Will, (c) Bessie, (d) John.

(b) Susan Hannah m. Charles B. Robinson. Issue: (a) Blanch, (b) Billie, (c) John, (d) Eva.

(c) John m. Laura Watson. Issue: (a) John, (b) Grace, (c) Spurdgram.

(d Lewis m. Elizabeth Bailey.

(f) Fred m. Verne Oliver. Issue (a) Lester, (b) Fred (c) Margaret, (d) Anna Ruth.

THE HISTORY OF ROANE COUNTY

(e) Richard m. Eugenia Graves. Issue: (a) Merrill, (b) Jack.

(h) Lula m. John D. Chandler. Issue: (a) Archie, (b) Wade.

Blanch, dau. of Charles B. and Susan H. Robinson, m. Egbert B. Stowers. Issue: (a) Helen B.

Billie m. James Waterhouse. Issue: James Franklin.

John m. Vida Law.

THE HISTORY OF ROANE COUNTY

DUNLAP

1. Hugh b. 1763 n Londenderry, Ireland, m. Susannah Harding Gilliam in Knoxville. Moved to Roane Co., at the time of its organization 1801, where he lived in what is now Rockwood until 1826, He died 1846 and is buried at Paris, Tenn. Issue: (a) John H., (b) Richard G., (c) William C., and Hugh W., twins, (d) James Trimble, (e) Eady, (f) Nancy, (g) Devereaux, (h) Martha, (i) Ripley.

2. (a) John H. a soldier in the Seminole War, m. Mary Etta Beauchamp. Issue: 3 (a) Susan, (b) William, (c) Bethenia, (b) John, (e) Hugh, (f) Richard.

3. (a) Susan m. June 17, 1851, John Davis Porter, Ex. Gov of Tenn. Issue: (a) Susannah, (b) Charles, (c) Dudley, (d) Thomas Kennedy.

3. (d) James Trimble b. 1810, m. 1839, Mrs. Jane Blount Thorpe. Their daughter, Susan Gilliam, m. Jonathan Smith Dawson. Issue: (a) Darling m. A. T. E. Morton, (b) Hallie m. C. D. M. Greer.

3. (e) Eady.

3. (f) Nancy m. Jan. 19, 1813 Henry Clair.

3. (b) William m. Sandal Stewart. Issue: (a) John, (b) Marie.

3. (c) Bethenia m. Dr. W. Harcourt. Issue: 4 (a) Johnetta, (b) Martha.

3. (e) Hugh m. Sarah Atkins. Issue: (a) Clinton, (b) Hugh, (c) John (d) Porter, (e) Evelyn, (f) William.

3. (f) Richard m. Charlie Stewart. Issue: 4 (a) Richard, (m) Benjamine.

4. (d) Porter Dunlap m. Mignonie Maiden. Issue: (a) Mignomie, (b) Porter.

4. (e) Evelyn m. Thomas Austin Miller. Issue: (a) Susanna, (b) Evelyn, (c) Dunlap.

THE HISTORY OF ROANE COUNTY

EBLEN

1. William emigrated from England and settled in Va.

2. John m. in Loudon Co., Va., about 1870 and settled in Roane Co. Issue:

3 (a) Isaac b. Oct. 26, 1781, d. Mar. 25, 1860 m. Mar. 6, 1806, Elizabeth Wilson, b. Oct. 25, 1785, Loudon Co., Virginia.

3. (b) Keziah b. May 12, 1783, m. 1st. Hiram Berry, 2nd. Peter Johnson in 1818, d. Aug. 1, 1873.

3. (c) William b. Sept. 15, 1784 m. Sept. 14, 1815, Lucretia Smith 2nd. ——— McMullen.

3. (d) Isreal b. Mar. 7,1786 d. Apr. 20 1863, m. Barbara Ernest b. Oct. 24, 1789, d. May 26, 1882.

3. (e) Mary b. May 20, 1787.

3. (f) Edward b. April 15, 1789.

3. (g) Sarah b. June 14, 1791.

3. (h) Anna b. Jan. 9, 1793, m. Jonas Arnold.

3. (i) Samuel b. July 30, 1794, d. Oct. 28, 1878 m. Martha Young Feb. 4, 1818.

3. (j) John b. Feb. 16, 1796.

3. (k) Elizabeth b. Feb. 17, 1798.

Children of Isaac and Elizabeth.

4. (a) Nancy m. Jan. 23, 1823, Hiram Berry d. Mar. 1875.

4. (b) Lucinda b. Mar. 6, 1811, m. William McElwee Mar. 24, 1829, d. Dec. 3, 1904. (See McElwee).

4. (c) Mary Jane . June 17, 1813 m. Mathew Allison Nov. 1838.

4. (d) William Carr, b. April 1818, m. 1st. Margaret Gamble 1848. 2nd. Cherokee Morgan McElrath.

4. (e) John b. Feb. 1816, d. Aug. 1840, m. Eliza Berry Jan. 29, 1839.

Children of Nancy and Hiram Berry.

5. (a) Isaac, (b) John, (c) Annie, (d) Hiram, (e) Elizabeth, (f) Lucy.

Children of Mary Jane and Mathew Allison.

5. (a) Elizabeth, (b) Thomas, (c) James, (d) William, (e) Frank.

Children of William Carr and Margaret.

James Gamble m. Sophia Work.
Polly, dau. of John, Jr., m. 1807, William Ballard.
Sarah Eblen m. Dec. 20, 1838 Edward Mounger.
Anna Eblen m. Nov. 7, 1839, William Tallent.
Eliza Eblen m. June 11, 1842 John Miller.
John Eblen m. Feb. 9, 1843, Martha Eblen.

4. (a) Samuel, son of Samuel, m. Sarah McGowan, was the father of sixteen children, all lived until grown except one. (5 (a) Glen, (b) Samuel, (c) Hiram, (d) John L., (e) M. S., (f) Isham, (g) Joseph, (h) Walker, (i) Isaac Newton, (j) Mack, (k) Sallie, (l) Jane, (m) Mattie, (n) Belle, (o) Nettie, (p) Y. B.

5. (d) John Lewis m. Julia Malinda, dau. of Robert Newton Johnson. Issue: 6 (a) Effie, (b) Susan, (c) Lelia, (d) Elmer Lewis, (e) Mae.

5. (i) Isaac Newton b. June 16, 1837, d. Dec. 14, 1903. m. Mary Florence Post, July 8, 1880 who was b. Oct. 12, 1857. Issue 6 (a) Sarah McGowan, b. Sept. 24, 1888, (b) James, b. Feb. 12, 1890, (c) Newton Colvin, b. Mar. 13, 1895.

6. (b) James, m. Florence Strickfuss.

6. (c) Newton C., m. Frances Ellison.

6. (a) Effie, dau. of John Lewis m. Loyd Arwood.

6. (b) Susan m. Garland Prim.

6. (d) Elmer Lewis, m. Wilma E. Scott.

5. (k) Sallie, dau. of Samuel and Sarah m. Frank Tutterow.

5. (l) Jane, dau. of Samuel and Sarah m. S. W. Briggs.

5. (m) Mattie, dau. of Samuel and Sarah m. J. D.

5. (n) Belle, dau. of Samuel and Sarah m. ——Huffine. Littleton.

5. (o) Nettie, dau. of Samuel and Sarah m. Balser Tutterow.

5. (p) Y. B. Eblen m. Sallie ———— Issue: (a) George, (b) Wilma, (c) Blanch.

Elijah Eblen m. 1889 Zorilda Owings. Issue:
(a) Wilkey Al, (b) Pearl Grady, (c) Olney Arthur, (d) Terra Franklin, (e) Thomas Byron, (f) Pauline Elizabeth, (g) James Buren.

THE HISTORY OF ROANE COUNTY

ELLIS

1. Francis b. in South Carolina m. Sarah Breedlove about 1814. Issue: (a) Caleb, (b) Monroe, (c) William, (d) Benjamine.

2. (a) Caleb m. ———— Wakefield.

2. (c) William M. b. in Roane Co., May 4, 1818 m. March 26, 1839 Lucy Bowlin. Issue: ten sons, 3 daughters.
Rebecca m. William Kimbrough.
Sarah m. Benjamine Brown (See Brown).
Thomas.
John.
William.

Frank Ellis m. Parthenia Kendrick. Issue: (a) C. J., b. 1853, (b) Uriah Samuel m. 1879, Jane Geneva Buttram b. 1861.

Uriah Samuel Ellis m. Jane Geneva Buttram. Issue:

(a) William Elbert b. 1880 m. 1910 Beulah Dial b. 1887.

(b) Aimee Parthenia b. 1881 m. 1903 Thomas William Knight b. 1874.

(c) Maud Elizabeth b. 1883 m. 1908 Thomas Washington Caudle b. 1881.

(d) Mary Bessie b. 1884 m. 1919 Howard P. Arrowood b. 1884.

(e) Minnie Samantha b. 1886 m. 1911 Kelly M. Chambers b. 1889.

(f) Vera Ethel b. 1837 m. 1908 Robert Purser b. 1884.

(g) Kate Isabel b. 1889 m. 1920 J. Harrison Shields b. 1896.

(h) Chrissie Winnie b. 1891, m. 1911 Roscoe Jaco b. 1885.

(i) Samuel Franklin b. 1893 m. 1920 Anna Shields b. 1898.

(j) Foster Kendrick b. 1896 m. 1917 Lella Green b. 1894.

THE HISTORY OF ROANE COUNTY
ENGLAND

1. Dabney England was stolen when a child and brought to Virginia. As his name was not known he was given the name of his country. He married Nancy Kindreck. Issue: (a) Lucinda, (b) Pauline, (c) Prudence, (d) St. Claire, (e) John, (f) Thomas, (g) Isaac, (h) William, who was killed at the battle of New Orleans.

    2. (a) Lucinda m. Oct. 4, 1811 Charles Hickey.

    2. (b) Pauline m. 1st Samuel Ladd, 2nd Tolbert Mccall b. in North Carolina, whose mother was ——— Candance. Issue: (a) Sarah, (b) William Wade, (c) Henry Puris, (d) Candance Ann, (e) Susan, (f) Samuel.

    4. (b) Candance Ann m). William Groffith Flinn. Issue: 5. (a) Roxanna, (b) Carrie, (c) Corena.

    2. (b) Prudence m. Sept. 6, 1824 Jesse Lowe.

    2. (f) Isaac m. Oct. 11, 1817 Rebecca Rector.

THE HISTORY OF ROANE COUNTY

EVANS

1. Samuel of Welsh and Irish descent emigrated with his parents when very young to this country locating in Cocke County, Tennessee. He marries Elsie Ogle. Issue: (a) Keziah, (b) Polly, (c) Abby, (d) Patrick Henry. Samuel d. about 1800 ad Elsie m. Frank Padgett. The family moved and settled in Stamp Creek Valley coming down the river in a flat boat.

 2. (a) Keziah m. Hugh L. Hartley, of Roane Co.
 2. (b) Polly.
 2. (c) Abby m. Thomas Dalton.
 2. (d) Patrick Henry b. Feb 11, in Cocke Co., m. Rebecca Parks Nov. 10, 1830. Patrick H. volunteered as a soldier in 1836 and went with U. S. troops under command of Gen. Wingfield Scott and was stationed at Ross' Landing during the removal of the Indians. He d. Feb. 22, 1875. Rebecca d. July 12, 1873. Issue:

 3. (a) Alcy b. June 13, 1832, m. Robert Alford.
 3. (b) Thomas H., b. Aug. 15, 1834.
 3. (c) Mary E., b. Oct. 9, 1836 m. William Bowman, Aug. 3, 1854.
 3. (d) Samuel P., b. June 6, 1838 m. Emma Godby.
 3. (e) Nehemiah O. b. June 22, 1840 d. April 28, 1862 in U. S. Army.
 3. (f) Patrick W., b. Jan. 24, 1844 m. Mary E. Bowers Oct. 1866 who d. Aug. 28, 1916. Issue: 4 (a) Thomas Oscar, (b) William S., (c) Alice, (d) David H., (e) John C.

 (d) David H., m. Mary McNutt Pope.
 4. (e) John C. m. Dixie Eblen.

THE HISTORY OF ROANE COUNTY

EWING

1. James born in Ireland settled in Virginia.

2. (a) Jacob b. Mar. 15, 1802 came to Roane County in 1809 m. Anna Mathaney b. Mar. 15, 1800, dau. of Elijah Mathaney, a native of Virginia.

3. (a) Elijah M., b. Nov. 25, 1830 m. Oct. 13, Nancy Murphy, dau. of Benjamine and Nancy Murphy.

3. (b) Arthur C. b. Feb. 24, 1837, m. Mar. 25, 1858 Saraphine, dau. of Col. John A. and Elizabeth Campbell Barnard.

Children of Elijah and Mary Ewing.

4. (a) John M., (b) Martha J., (c) Nellie, (d) Sarah M., (e) William A.

Children of Arthur C. and Seraphine.

4. (a) James A., (b) Jacob, (c) Elijah B., (d) Lulini Leati.

4. (b) Martha J., m. Elisha, son of Abijah and Levina Sharp Boggess. Issue: (a) Sudie, (b) Catha, (e) Dixie.

THE HISTORY OF ROANE COUNTY
FLEMING

1. James and Martha Fleming emigrated from Tyrone Co., Ireland 1787. James d. 1830 in Washington Co., Va. Martha d. 1854 in Sullivan Co., Tenn. Issue:

2. David b. 1799 in Chester Co., Penn, Moved to Roane Co., 1850 d. 1868. Was one of the founders of Holston Methodist Conference having entered the Ministry in his youth, was a circut rider and presiding Elder in Western Virginia and East Tennessee, m. 1829 Mary Buren dau. of John and Cynthia Miller of Hawkins Co., Tenn. b. 1808 d. 1884. Issue:

3. (a) John Miller, (b) James Clarke, (c) Charles Rhoton, (d) Wilbur Fisk, (e) Andrew Foster, (f) Martha Elizabeth.

3. (a) John Miller b. 1832 d. 1900. Was Editor of several leading newspapers of the State, being first Editor of the Knoxville Sentinal, a member of Legislature 1861. State Superintendant of Public Schools 1872-74,putting into operation the present school system and is described in Notable Men of Tennessee as a man of superior intellect and of a superior legal mind. m. 1860 Anna Howard, dau. of Judge Samuel and Susan Mason Boyd. Issue: 4 (a) David, (b) Samuel, (c) Mary Miller.

5. (c))Mary Miller m. John Lamar Meek. Issue: John Fleming.

3. (f) Martha Elizabeth b. 1845 d. 1919 m. 1871 in Kingston, Rev. Grimsfield Taylor of Blount Co., Tenn. Issue:

4. (a) Mary Elizabeth m. Harry Preistly Driver: Issue:
5. (a) Martha Elizabeth.
4. (b) Franklin m. Katherine Hayter. Issue:
5. (a) Jean, (b) Joseph.
4. (c) Nancy Susanna m. Hilton Screven Hampton.
4. (d) James Fleming m. Alice Smith. Issue
5. (a) Elizabeth, (b) Virginia, (c) James Fleming, (d) Nancy.

THE HISTORY OF ROANE COUNTY

FORRESTER

1. Marcus, of South Carolina soldier in Black Hawk War. Issue: (a) Mildred, (b) Martha, (c) Nancy, (d) Thomas, (e) Alexander, (f) Solomon, (f) James, (g) Larkin.

2. (d) Thomas m. Margaret (Peggy) Marney. Issue: (a) Solomon.

2. (e) Alexander m. Sallie Harvie. Issue: (a) William, (b) George, (c) Marshall H. and James, (d) Nancy, (e) Eliza.

2. (f) Solomon b. 1803, in S. C., d. 1863, m. 1852 in Roane Co., Sarah Marney, b. 1807, d. 1852. Issue: (a) Rufus, b. 1824, (b) James, (c) Caroline, (d) Joseph Bryant, (e) Polly Ann, (f) Martha, (g) Belinda, (h) William, (i) Alexander, (j) Robert, (k) Benjamine Franklin b. 1844.

3. (b) James m. Louella ———. Issue: (a) Eva, (b) Ethel, (c) Frank, (d) William.

3. (d) Joseph Bryant b. 1834 m. 1855 Maria Shannon. 2nd Hannah Hale, 3rd. Eliza Forrester.

3. (g) Belinda m. David McWilliams. Issue: (a) Thomas

3. (k) Benjamine F., m. Frances Green. Issue (a) Josephine, (b) Edna, (c) Benjamine, (d) Emma, (e) Louella.

2. (f) James m. Patsy Bryant. Issue: (a) Polly, (b) Bettie, (c) Nancy, (d) Jane, (e) Deborhah, (f) Maria.

2. (g) Larkin m. Tuton. Issue, (a) Wiley, (b) Thomas, (c) Menerva, (d) Rachel.

4. (a) Josephine, dau. of Benjamine m. J. D. Dunnaway. Issue. (a) Maurine, (b) Waldo, (c) Frances, (d) Ruth.

4. (b) Edna, dau of Benjamine F. m. ——— Orr.

4. (c) Benjamine, son of Benjamine E. m. Dahlia Ezell.

4. (d) Emma, dau of Benjamine E. m. ——— Hampton.

4. (e) Louella, dau of Benjamine m. ——— Hancock.

3. (c) Marshall H. m. ——— Wilkey. Among his children were William, James, Isham G. and daughter, Mrs. C. W. Mathaney.

M. Hazeltine, dau of Joseph Bryant and Marie S. b. 1858 m. June 1876 John Calvin Keeney, b. 1847. Issue, Marie K. m. A. M. Patterson, John, Guy, Mrs. Guy C. Phillips.

THE HISTORY OF ROANE COUNTY
FRITTS

1. Jacob emigrated from North Carolina and settled 8 miles above Kingston on what was known in early history as the Buttermilk Road. His brothers and sisters were Peter, Phillip, Henry, Katie, Christiana.

Peter m. Dec. 15, 1825 Parmelia Williams.
Phillip m. Dec. 15, 1830 Frances Jane Williams.
1. Jacob m. Dec. 23, 1818 Sally Sexton. Issue: (a) Isham, (b) John, (c) David, (d) Joseph, (e) Jacob, (f) Mary Ann, (g) Kate, (h) Henry.

1. Henry m. Annie Johnson. Issue: (a) ——————— (b) George W., (c) William, (d) ———, (e) ———, (f)

2. (e) John, son of Jacob m. Lorena Elizabeth Stallcup, Oct. 9, 1866.

2. (b) George Washington m. Martha Helen Bunn. Issue: (a) Robert, (b) William, (c) John, (d) Henry, (e) James, (f) Martin, (g) Phillip, (h) Mary.

2. (c) William, son of Henry m. Martha Hunnicut. Issue: (a) Albert, (b) Dock, (c) Mitchell.

3. (f) Martin, of George W., m. Matilda Pickel. Issue: 2 sons, 2 daughters.

3. Issue of John and Elizabeth Williams, 7 sons and 2 daughters.

3 William M., m. 1875 Sallie Norton. Issue, (a) Jesse R., (b) John W., (c) William N., 5 daughters.

Henry son of George W. and Martha m. Mar. 5, 1840 Ann Turnbull.

2. (a) Isom G. son of Jacob and Sally m. Lucy Whittle. Issue: (a) Wylie, H., (b) Jacob, (c) John, (b) Thomas, (e) Henry, (f) Benjamin Franklin, (g) Matilda.

2. (c) David, son of Jacob and Sally, m. May 4, 1844 Catherine Beard.

2. (f) Mary Ann, dau of Jacob m. John Hood.

2. (g) Katie, lau. of Jacob m. James Burnett.

2. (h) Henry, son of Jacob m. Polly Williams.
John Fritts m. Mar. 8, 1843 Mary Ann Luttrell.
George Fritts m. May 28, 1839 Sarah Spoon.
Mary Fritts m. Mar. 14, 1844 Richard Williams.

3. (a) Wylie H., son of Isom m. ――― Murray.
3. (b Jacob m. Anna Nicholson.
3. (d) Thomas Wilson b. Oct. 1, 1849, son of Isom m. Annie Kyle. Issue: (a) Annie Mary m. Leon D. Bailey. Issue Thomas Fritts, (b) William J., (c) Thomas Wilson, (d) Lena m. E. R. Blair. Issue: Virginia Blair.
3. (f) Benjamin Franklin b.――― son of Isom m. Inez King. Issue: (a) Fred A. Weil m. Elizabeth Mynders, (b) King, m. Helen Arnold, (c) William m. Vance Talbot.
3. (g) Matilda, dau. of Isom m. Thomas E. Roberts.

Jerry and Ransom Fritts were half brothers of those who came from North Carolina about 1810. Isaac and John were their cousins, who came at the same time. Isaac m. Apr. 11, 1836 Frankie Fortner. John Fritts m. Rhoda C. McDuffie Oct. 4, 1859. Benjamin Fritts m. Martha Moses Mar. 8, 1871. Mary Fritts m. Columbus Motes July 30, 1887. John Fritts m. Jane Coker June 3, 1863.

THE HISTORY OF ROANE COUNTY

FULLER

1. George came from North Carolina.

2. Joshua 1790 in North Carolina m. 1820 Mary, b. May 10, 1892, dau. of James Clark and widow of Rev. James Moore, who d. 1816 Mary d. 1881. Joshua d. 1858.

3. James b. May 20, 1822 m. 1845 Lucinda, dau. of William and Nancy Jolly b. 1825.

GAMBLE

1. Samuel b. 1785, d. 1855, m. Aug. 19, 1823 Matilda Riggs, b.Nov. 29, 1803, d. Oct. 15, 1855. Issue: ten children.

2. James b. Apr. 1793, d. Jan. 1875 m. 1st 1818 Ann Dickey, b. 1800, d. Jan 1849. 2nd ———— Beeler.

Robert L.., son of Samuel b. Dec. 10, 1836, m. June 29, 1859 Parmelia Tillery.

3. (a) William M., son of James b. Oct. 11, 1832 m. Jan. 12, 1868 Margaret Denton, b. Feb 18, 1848.

3. (b) Caroline, dau. of James m. William L. Brown. (See Brown)

3. (c) Margaret m. William Carr Eblen. (See Eblen.)

3. (d) James.

3. (e) Victoria, dau of James and his second wife m. Capt. Williams.

THE HISTORY OF ROANE COUNTY
GILLESPIE

1. George b. 1867 m. Anne Neilson b. 1872. Issue: 2 (a) William N., (b) Thomas Jefferson, (c) Robert N., (d) Jane Harriet, (e) Charles, (f) George Lewis, (g) John Cessna, (h) Archibald D., (i) James Wendel, (j) Joseph Strong, (k) Elbert Dave.

2. (a) William N., m. Sidney Ann Lutey. Issue:

3. (a) George m. Aug. 12, 1863, Victoria Brown. Issue: (a) Etta, (b) Alice, (c) Thomas, (d) George, (e) Gay.

2. (b) Thomas Jefferson b. 1805 m. Lucinda McCaleb. Issue: 3 (a) George Thomas m. Laura Peters, Issue: 4 (a) George Thomas, (b) Jean Neilson.

2. (c) Robert N., b. Feb. 14, 1807 m. 1826 Hannah Luety. Issue: 3. (a) Robert N. b. May 28, 1846 m. 1st. Dec. 31, 1867, Emma Frazier, 2nd. May 1878 Lilie Wilshire. (b) Thomas Jefferson, (c) William (d) Adelia.

2. (d) Jane Harriet m. James Holman Blain.

2. (e) Charles m. Evelyn Taylor.

2. (f) George Lewis b. 1832 m. May 15, 1838 Margaret Alice, dau. of John and Elizabeth McEwen. Issue: 3 (a) John, (b) George Lewis, (c) Anna Neilson, (d) Elizabeth.

2. (g) John Cassna m. Margaret Alice, dau. of John Columbus and Nancy P. McEwen. Issue 3 (a) Margaret Alice, (b) Nellie, (c) Nancy Elizabeth, (d) James W., (e) Anna Neilson, (f) Thomas J., (g) Lewis, (h) Mary Blain.

2. (i) James Wendel m. Nancy Brazelton.

2. (k) Elbert Dave m. Sarah C. Cleage.

2. (j) Joseph Strong m. Feb. 10, 1848 Penelope Whiteside. Issue: a. Anna Penelope, b. James Whiteside, c. Joseph Anderson, d. Jean Neilson, e. Florence.

3. (a) Anna Penelope m. John Hooke.;Issue: a. Mary Porter m. R. A. Stigler, b. John Anderson (m. Margaret ——— c. Carl (m. Julia.———).

3. (b) James Whiteside b. Mar. 25, 1853 m. May 1, Virginia Swan. Issue: a. Hugh Swan, b. Joseph Strong, e. Penelope Whiteside d. Annie Dent, e. Luther L., f. James Anderson.

THE HISTORY OF ROANE COUNTY

3. (c) Joseph Anderson m. Margaret Mitchell. Issue: a. Kyle, b. Joseph (m. Mary House.)

3. (d) Jean Neilson m. G. Allison Holland.

4. (a) Hugh Swan, son of James and Virginia m. Maud Berry.

4. (b) Joseph Strong, son of James and Virginia, m. Rose Gallaher.

4. (c) Penelope Whiteside, dau. of James and Virginia m. Thomas Basil Smith. Issue: a. Hugh Craig, b. Virginia Louise, c. Thomas Basil.

4. (d) Anna Dent, dau. of James and Virginia, m. Louis Edward Brading.

4. (e) James Anderson, son of James and Virginia, m. Nell Randle.

3. (a) John M., son of George L. and Margaret Alice Gillespie, m. Amelia King. Issue: John King b. Sept. 1871.

3. (b) George L., m. Miss McMasters.

3. (c) Anna Neilson m. Arthur Watkins.

3. (d) Elizabeth m. James A. Caldwell. Issue: 4 a. Percy, b. Rhobie ,c. Elsie.

3. (a) Margaret Alice, dau. of John C. and Margaret, m. William A. Martin. Issue: 4 a. William A., b. John C., c. Anna Neilson, d. Ernest.

3. (b) Nellie m. L. Japheth Sharp. Issue: a. Margaret, b. Ellen, c. John Cessna, d. Alice Neilson, e. Elizabeth.

3. (c) Nancy Elizabeth m. Eugene Thomasson.

3. (d) Anna Neilson m. William W. Roof. Issue 4 a. Mary.

3. (e) Lewis G. m. Sue Reese.

3. (f) Mary Blain m. Joseph H. Davenport. Issue: 4 a. Joseph H., b. Margaret McEwen.

4. (a) Joseph m. Laura Voigt, b. Margaret McEwen m. William Carswell.

4. (a) William, son of William A. and Margaret Alice Martin, m. Mary McGruder. Issue: a. William McGruder.

4. (b) John G. son of William and Margaret Alice m. Gladys Brown. Issue: Alice.

4. (a) John King, son of John M. and Amelia m. Oct. 24, 1895 Hortense Booth. Issue: 5 a. John King II. b. Booth, c. Hortense.

4. (b) Rhobie, dau. of Elizabeth Gillespie and James A. Calldwell m. Frederick Smallman.

4. (c) Elsie Caldwell m. Roland Olmstead.

4. (a) Margaret, dau. of J. P. and Nellie Gillespie Sharp, m. Robert H. Williams. Issue: 5 a. Eleanor m. Hardwick Caldwell, b. Margaret Cornelia m. Scott Livingston Prob co, c, Robert Patten.

4. (b) Ellen m. John S. Poindexter. Issue 5 a. Jane, m. Pauling Shri r Steward, b. John, c. Mary Lee.

4. (c) John Cessna m. Rachel Cook. Issue, John Cessna.

4. (1) Alice Neilson m. Samuel Bartow Strang. Issue: 5 a. Samuel Bartow, b. John Cessna, c. Frances Thornton.

4. (e) Elizabeth m. Carl Eberling, M. D. Issue: Carl.

3. (d) Adelia dau. of Robert N. Gillespie m. William Perry Darwin. Issue: 4. a. William Peyton, b. James Robert m. Margaret Jaspheth Sharp, dau. of E. Frank Sharp. c. Hannah m. Jesse Brown Swafford, d. Ella m. Dr. Walter F. Thomison, e. Nell m. Jacob M. Gass, f. Jennie m. Dr. William L. Abel, g. Thomas Albert m. Elizabeth————, h. Frederick Perry m. Alexander Arrants, i. Bertha m. William W. Henry.

4. (a) William Peyton m. Caroline Waterhouse, Issue: 5 a. Cyrus, b. Adelia m. Frederick Stout, c. Eleanor d. Darius, e. Alice m. Edwin Brady, f. Audrey m. ——— Denton.

Children of James Robert and Margaret S. Darwin.
5. a. Frank Sharp m. Katherine Sulte.
b. Gordon Gillespie m. Caroline Wilson.
c. James Kenneth m. Ruth Wilkey.
d. Margaret Elizabeth m. Noel S. Walters.
Children of Hannah Darwin and Jesse B. Swafford.
5. a. Samuel Perry m. Pauline Morgan.
b. Jesse Lucille m. Oliver Hamilton Altridge.

Children of Ellen Darwin and Dr. Walter F. Thomison:
5. a. Maud, b. Clara m. Peyton Brown c. Walter Agnew.

Children of Jennie Darwin and Dr. William Abel.
5. a. Thelma.

Children of Frederick P. and Alexandria Darwin:
5. a. Arrant, b. Sidney.

Children of Bertha Darwin and William W. Henry:
5. a. Gladys.

THE HISTORY OF ROANE COUNTY

GREEN

1. Thomas b. in Virginia where he m. Keziah Avery. Issue:

 2. a. Avery b. in Virginia. Issue: 3 a. Obey, b. John.
 2. b Thomas.
 2. c. Bluford m. Betsy Underwool. Issue: a. Thomas b. Mary, m. Fred Isham, c. Jane m. Alexander Wolf.
 2. d. Theodric.
 2. e. Austin Letheridge, b. in White Co., Virginia 1811, m. 1st. Delia Crow in Roane Co. Issue: 3 a. Katherine m. Alexander Harwell.
 b. Henry Pierce m. Mary Barnett, c. William, C. d. Leonodas m. Calisty ————, e. Rebecca m. ————, Beard. 2nd. wife, Emily Liggitt. Issue f. Jennie, m. John T. Mahoney, g. Willis Center m. Sarah Brown, h. Austin Avery m. Ella Browder, i. John B., j. Charles W.

Children of Katherine and Alexander Harwell.

 4. a. Austin b. Sarah, c. William, d. Susan, e. Alice f. Charles, g. Pierce, h. Herbert, i. Jennie.

Children of Henry Pierce and Mary Green.

 4. a. George, c. Mattie m. George Bender.

Children of Leonidas and Calisty.

 a. Surry m. Elizabeth Glover, b. Minnie m. Dr. W. C. Huddleston, c. Maud m. Professor Laney.

Children of Jenny and John Mahoney.

 4. a. Edger, b. Wilbur, c. Charlie, d, James, e. Guy f. Ray g. Emma, h. Cora m. ———— Strong, i. Nell m. Roland Duffy.

Children of Willis and Sarah:

 4. a. Ernest, b. Harold, c. Blanch.

Austin L. Green with a goosequill pen wrote the code of Tennessee in 1858. He was for six years in the Legislature and held different offices in Roane Co., for forty years.

THE HISTORY OF ROANE COUNTY

HALEY

1. David Rev. Sol. came from Ireland m. Letitia Cloud. Issue: a. John Cloud, b. James.

2. John Cloud b. Feb. 7, 1777 d. Sept. 3, 1840, m. 1812 Elizabeth Matlock, b. Nov. 3, 1781, d. Dec. 12, 1848. Issue: a. John, b. Sarah, c. Martha, d. Allen, e. Charles, f. Elijah. g. James, h. Leathy, i. William B., j. Ward.

3. a. John m. Polly Smith, of McMinn Co.
3. b. Sarah m. ———— Stevens, of McMinn Co.
3. c. Martha m. ———— Foster, of Marshall Co., Ala.
3. d. Allen m. Betsy Rice, of McMinn Co.
3. e. Charles m. Margaret Smith.
3. f. Elijah m. ———— Rice, of Mcminn Co. 2nd. Sept. 25, 1839 Letitia Winton.
3. g. James m. Mary Clark.
3. h. Leathy m. Miller Rice, of McMinn Co.
3. i. William B. m. Sydney R. Smith, of McMinn Co.
3. j. Ward m. Mary Roddy.

3. a. Children of Charles and Margaret. a. Elizabeth, b. Henry.

4. a. Elizabeth m. James Woods Wilson. Issue a. James, Charles, b. Margaret Lyon, c. Henry Haley, d. Robert, e. Isabelle, f. John, g. Claud, h. Mabel, i. George Edward, j. Elizabeth.

4. b. Henry m. 1st. Emma Riggs. Issue Charles Smith. 2nd. Victoria Frazier. Issue: a. Henry, b. Rosco, c. Margaret, d. Clara, e. Robert, f. James. g. Kenneth, h. Sarah.

5. a. James Charles, son of Elizabeth and James Woods Wilson m. Florence Warner. Issue: a. Charles, b. Mary, c. Willard Warner, d. Florence Woods.

5. c. Henry m. Emily Ashe.

5. d. Robert m. Mary Elizabeth Kimbrough.

5. e. Isabella m. 1st. Herbert Black. Issue: Margaret Elizabeth, 2nd. Felix Zollicoffer Martin.

5. g. Mabel Claire m. James Anderson Huff. (See Huff).

5. h. George Edward m. Madge Tarwater. Issue: George Edward.

THE HISTORY OF ROANE COUNTY

Children of Robert and Mary Elizabeth Wilson.
6. a. Katherine, b. James Charles, c. Margaret, d. Mabel Claire, e. Warren.

Children of William B. and Sydney Haley:
4. a. John Cloud, m. Mary Jane Montgomery.
4. b. Margaret m. Frank Suddath.
4. c. Sally T. m. Jerome King, son of Charles King.
4. d. Charles B. m. Stacia Ingram.
4. e. Jackson m. Nancy Montgomery.

Children of John Cloud and Mary Jane.
5. a. Eugene, b. Alexander, c. Nellie, d. Joseph, e. Frances, f. George, g. John.

Children of Margaret and Frank Suddath.
a. William, b. Charles.

Children of Sally and Jerome King.
5. a. Beulah, b. Sidney, c. William, d. Charles, e. Addie, f. Margaret, g. Neal, h. Iola, i. Eula Lee, j. Elizabeth.

Children of Charles B. and Stacia Haley.
5. a. Pearl, b. Elizabeth.

5. b. Alexander, son of John Cloud and Margaret, m. Nancy Doyle.

5. e. Sidney Frances, m. Thomas C. Goodner. Issue: Mary Rebecca, m. John F. Devaney.

5. f. George m. Margaret Carter. Issue. a. George, b. Raymond Carter, c. Margaret, d. John Cloud, e. Milton, f. Robert, g. Frank, h. Marion.

5. g. John Henry m. Anna Dancliffe. Issue: a. Milton J.

6. b. Raymond Carter Haley m. Edith King.

6. c. Margaret Haley m. Clarence Slaughter.

6. a. Milton J. Haley m. Lola Briggers.

5. a. Pearl, dau. of Charles anl Stacia m. Taylor Boyd.

5. b. Elizabeth, dau. of Charles and Stacia m. Walter Clack.

Major David Haley owned a large grist mill during the War of 1812. He and his son, John Cloud Haley sent wheat

THE HISTORY OF ROANE COUNTY

and other grains free of charge on flat boats to the soldiers in 1812, they built the stopping wall at the Suck Creek in the effort to help General Jackson's Army. When Andrew Jackson was President, Elbert G. Sevier drafted a petition which was signed by every land owner in the County asking President Jackson to recommend to Congress that Major Haley and his son be paid for the work they did. Mr. Sevier wrote the President that these men made it possible for him to fire the first powder in the Creek War.

THE HISTORY OF ROANE COUNTY
HART

Henry b. in London, England, 1761 came to Charleston, S. C., 1786. m. ———— Sawyer.

a. Martha b. 1802 m. Joseph Bryant, b. John Sawyer m. Letitia Marney, c. George m. Serena Neal, d. Deborah m. 1st. Howell, 2nd Howell, 3rd. Couch. e. Sarah m. Sauterland, g. Amanda m. ———— Howell, h. Ely m.———— McWilliams, f. William m. ———— Williams, i. Henry m. Feb. 3, 1818 Polly Snow.

Henry Sr. came to Roane Co. 1804. Settled on Long Island in the Tennessee River.

John Sawyer and Letitia were the parents of 14 children, among them, Samuel, George, Henry.

Samuel's son, John Jay, is the father of Samuel Henry Hart.

Henry Jr. was a soldier of 1812.

THE HISTORY OF ROANE COUNTY

HARVEY

1. Thomas came from North Carolina, m. ———Smith. Settled at Shady Grove, Tenn. Issue: a. a son who moved to Middle Tennessee, b. Dicie m. Thomas Hunt. Thomas Harvey was a preacher and built a log meeting house where Shady Grove Church, Knox Co., now stands. After the death of his first wife he m. Sarah Smith, her sister. Issue: a. Oney, b. James, d. James, e. Rufus, f. Susannah, g. Wilson, h. William.

2. c. Oney m.——— Issue: a. Henry, b. Jackson, c. Eliza Jane, d. daughter who m. Frank Roe, e. Oney, Jr.

2. d. James m. Elizabeth Birdwell. Issue: a. John R., b. Tressie, c. Joshua B., d. Smith, e. James W., f. Mrs. Newton Johnson, g. Mrs. Peter Johnson, h. Mrs. William Pickel, i. Mrs. John Robinson, j. Mrs. Elizabeth Amos.

2. e. Rufus m. ——— Issue: a. George killed in the War at Nashville, b. John F., c. Samuel, d. Hope, e. Frank f. Walker A., g. Albert, h. Mrs. William Crowder, i. Mrs. Henry McKinney, j. Mrs. J. M. Crowder, k. Sarah.

2. f. Elkanah m. ———. Issue: a. William b. Charles, c. Minnie.

2. g. Wilson m.——— Issue: a. John, b. George, c. J. Monroe, d. Elkanah, e. Mrs. Polk Freeman, f. Mrs. James Collock, g. Mrs. Charles Eldridge, h. Mrs. John Ingram.

2. h. William, son of Thomas moved to Hillsboro, Tex.

3. a. Henry, son of Oney m. ——— Issue: a. Robert J., b. Mrs. Lena Taylor, c. Samuel.

3. e. Oney J., m. ———. Issue: a. Frank, b. Nancy, c. Josephine, d. James R., e. Mrs. Mollie Shaw, f. Mrs. Dollie Baldwin, g. Ernest, h. Freeland.

3. b. George, son of Elkanah I., m. ———. Issue: a. Jackson, b. Oliver, c. Charles, d. Joseph, e. Sanford, f. Mrs. Laura Littleton, g. Mrs. Maud Hall, h. Mrs. Callie Dutton.

3. c. James Monroe, son of Wilson, m. ———: Issue: a. Wallace, b. Wilson, c. Mrs. S. H. Anderson, d. Mrs. C. A. Phillips, e. Mrs. J. L. Reaves.

3. c. Joshua B., m. ―――. Issue: a. John W., b. Fred O., c. James N., d. Charles, e. Joshua, f. Mrs. S. M. Brooks, g. Isaac, h. Mrs. Lissie Tutterow.

3. d. Smith, m. ―――. Issue: a. Edgar N., b. Lewis W., c. Mrs. L. L. Thomas, d. Mrs. John Norman.

3. b. John F., son of Rufus m. .... Issue: a. Rufus, Jr., b. William, c. Samuel, d. Cynthia, e. John, f. Charles, g. Mrs. William Gilliland, h. Wesley, i. Frank, j. Susan.

3. c. Dr. Samuel, son of Rufus, m. ―――. Issue: a. Charles B., b. Burton, c. Mrs. R. P. Eaton, d. Eloise, e. Mrs. Charles Hornsby.

3. f. Walker A. son, of Rufus, m. ―――. Issue: a. Thomas, b. Lee, c. Rufus, d. Clyde, e. Mrs. Bessie Jenkins.

3. b. Charles, son of Elkanah m. ―――. Issue: a. William, b. Stella Lane, c. Hugh, d. Ulys, e. Hobart, f. Dortis.

3. a. John son of William m. ―――. Issue: a. Joseph, b. Elmer, c. Esper, d. John Jr., e. Mrs. Alice McNabb, f. Mrs. Maggie Hatfield, Mrs. Kate Vann.

3. d. Elkanah, son of Wilson m. ―――. Issue: a. Charles, b. Fred, c. Ralph, 1. Martin, e. Mrs. Minnie Matlock, f. Mrs. Effie Malone, g. Mrs. Ida Mills.

1. Thomas was a Baptist Preacher.
Elkanah, his fourth son was a Baptist Preacher.
Wilson, his fifth son was a Baptist Preacher.
Elkanah, Wilson's son was a Baptist Preacher.

THE HISTORY OF ROANE COUNTY

HILL

Barney Hill was the first of the family to come to Roane County. He is descended from Colonial and Revolutionary stock, being a son of Jacob and Elizabeth (Lane) Hill of North Carolina and Tennessee.

Barney Hill b. 1804, d. 1849 married 1840 Nancy Green Millican, dau. of William and Mary Millican b. 1809, d. 1875.
Their children were:
a. William Columbus, m. Nancy Rector.
b. Isaac Alexander, m. Margaret Amanda Kendrick.
c. John Nelson, m. Mary Dorcas Dixon.
d. Elizabeth, m. Albert Marion Owings.
e. James Moses, m. Katherine Matilda Absten.

William Columbus Hill, son of Barney and Nancy (Millican) Hill b. Apr. 25, 1824, m. Nancy S. Rector, b. July 23, 1846 living.
Their children were:
a. Nancy D., b. July 16, 1867, m. George Shillings.
Nora E., b. Mar. 13, 1869, m. Joseph Tedder
c. James B., b. Jan. 21, 1871, m. 1st. Nina Kindred, 2nd. Amanda Stokes,

d. Samuel R., b. March 8, 1872, d. Sept. 7, 1914, m. Belle Raines.
e. Wm. Columbus, b. Feb. 9, 1874, m. Tempe Hickman.
f. Mary Margaret, b. June 11, 1875, m. R. T. Sisco.
g. Absalom F., b. Nov. 11, 1876, m. Elizabeth Tedder.
h. Wiley H., b. July 22, 1879, m. Mamie Branam.
i. Isaac A., b. Feb. 8, 1880, m. Ethel Qualls.
j. Robert L., b. Feb. 8, 1880, m. Margaret Anderson.
k. Liddy M.
l. Myrtle M., b. Mar. 28, 1886, m. Alonzo Tedder.
m. John A.
n. Walter E., b. Nov. 19, 1889,
o. Frank, b. June 25, 1891, m. Elsie Lane.

Isaac Alexander Hill, son of Barney and Nancy (Millican) Hill, b. June 28, 1844, d. Jan. 22, 1916, m. Margaret Amanda Kendrick, b. Sept. 23, 1851.

Their children are:
a. May, b. Dec. 6, 1871, m. June 2, 1892, Dr. W. W. Hill, b. Oct. 24, 1861.

THE HISTORY OF ROANE COUNTY

b. Pearl, b. Feb. 22, 1874, m. June 22, 1905, Robert Bryan Cassell, b. July 29, 1868. Issue: a. Margaret Bryan.

c. Charles L., b. July 20, 1876, m. May 6, 1900, Ruth Tyler Davis, b. Nov. 14, 1879.

d. Nannie Ellen b. Sept. 24, 1879, m. April 5, 1903, Allen Russell Davis b. June 5, 1878. Issue: a. Dorothy Randolph.

e. Robert Kendrick, b. Feb. 27. 1882, m. May 14, 1909, Abbie Fay Jewett. Issue: a. Vara Kendrick, b. William Leslie.

f. Cap Kendrick, b. Oct. 7, 1884.

g. John Paul, m. Laura Silvey.

Children of May and Dr. W. W. Hill:
a. Ivy, b. Pauline, m. William Rayborn Massey. Issue: a. Margaret Kendrick.

c. William Walter.

d. Nancy Pearl.

John Nelson Hill, son of Barney and Nancy (Millican) Hill, b. 1848, m. March 26, 1871, Mary Dorcas Dixon, b. Mar. 2, 1856, d. Oct. 20, 1922.

They had the following children.
a. William Edward m. Sudie Ellis. Issue: a. Ellis Dixon, b. Ruth Irene.

b. Gilbert Isaac, m. Bessie Serrill.

c. Daisy Dorinda.

d. Virgil Albert m. Addie Huffman. Issue: a. Mary b. Helen.

e. Mary Elizabeth m. Apr. 22, 1915, Howard M. Lancaster. Issue: a. Howard, b. Elizabeth.

f. Grace Dixon m. May 25, 1908, Ernest W. Hall. Issue: a. Elizabeth, b. Catherine, c. Billie.

g. James Rupert, m. Dec. 25, 1977, Leona Summers. Issue: a. Wesley, b. Russell.

James Moses Hill, son of Barney and Nancy (Millican) Hill b. Feb, 26, 1849, d. Nov. 30, 1889. m. Sept. 1, 1881 Katherine Matilda Absten, b. Sept. 1, 1849, living.

Their children were:
a. Barney B.

b. Roy R., m. Elizabeth C. Walker. Issue: a. Mary Walker, b. Roy C.

c. Anne C. m. James Boyd. Issue: a. Catherine E. b. Margaret A., c. Mary Helen, d. Anne Eugene.

THE HISTORY OF ROANE COUNTY

HINDS

In 1792 John Hinds a Revolutionary Soldier came with his sons, Sylvanus, Joseph, Simeon, and John, Jr. and two daughters to Roane Co. He made an entry for one thousand acres of land which became known as Hinds Valley.

Sylvanus Hinds was a soldier in the Creek and Indian War and that of 1812.

Issue of Sylvanus Hinds
a. John, m. Sarah A. Hickey.
b. James C., m. Rachel Abels.

John Hinds, m. Sarah A. Hickey Issue:
a. Mary E. m. Willey Doughty.
b. James Carter, m. 1868, Rutha Caroline Hinds, b. 1838 d. 1917.
c. Lou m. 1st. ———— Wilson. 2nd ————Redferrin.
Wiley Doughty and Mary E. Issue:
a. Thomas J., b. 1855, d. 1856.
b. Sarah Ann b. 1856, d. 1901, m. John Evans.
c. Margaret E. b. 1858, d. 1895 m. Hugh Boyd.
d. John William b. 1860, m. 1883, Celia East, b. 1870 d. 1922.
e. Lousinda C.
f. Mary Eauline.
g. Sidney Caroline, b 1867 d. 1885 m. Sidney Bledsoe.
h. James Isaac, m. 1st. Amanda Wallace. 2nd. Julia Hyde.
i. Minnie C. b. 1872. m. William Cobb.
j. Charles Franklin, b. 1874.
k. Mattie Pearl b. 1876, d. 1882.

John W. and Celia East. Issue:
a. Lewis m. 1904, Dora Tausher.
b. Sam, m. 1906, Corrie McPherson.
c. Pearl.
d. Carl.
e. James.

f. Ella Mae, m. 1911, C. L. Wilson.
g. Sewell.
g. Reuben, m. 1920 Jennie Mae Lawson.
i. Sherman.
k. Kate, m. 1916 Roy Wells.
l. Velma.
m. Nell.
n. Willard.

Lewis, m. Dora Tausher. Issue:
a. Carl.
b. Louise.
c. Raymond.
d. Edna.
e. John.
f. Ruth.

Sam, m. Corrie McPherson. Issue:
a. Floyd.
b. Clarence.
c. Kathleen.
d. Dorothy.

C. L. Wilson m. Ella Mae Doughty. Issue:
a. Violet.
b. Woodrow.
c. Mildred.
d. James.
e. Mary Edna.
f. Frances.

Reuben m. Jennie Mae Lawson. Issue:
a. Paul.
b. Kathleen.
c. Bailey.

Roy Wells, m. Kate, dau. of John and Celia (East) Doughty. Issue:

THE HISTORY OF ROANE COUNTY

a. Pearl.
b. Lucile.
c. Margaret.

William Cobb m. Minnie, dau. of Wiley and Mary E. (Hinds) Doughty. Issue:

a. Mary Lizzie, m. William Edward Crabtree.
b. George R., m. May Doughty.
c. Maud, m. Ben Goss.
d. Raymond.
e. Roy Fred, m. Thelma Bowling.
f. Ann Lou.
g. Perry, m. Raymond Blackwell.
h. Aileen m. Bert Brown.
i. Billie.
j. Luretha.

William Edward Crabtree, m. Mary Lizzie, dau. of William and Minnie (Doughty) Cobb. Issue:

a. Cathryn Reece.
b. Woodrow.
c. Edward.

Ben Goss, m. Maud, dau. of William and Minnie (Doughty Cobb. Issue:

a. Bennie.

George Robert, son of William and Minnie (Doughty) Cobb m. May Doughty. Issue:

a. J. W.
b. Cathryn.
c. Robert.

Roy Fred, son of William and Minnie (Douhgty) Cobb m. Thelma Bowling. Issue:

a. Roy.

Bert Brown, m. Aileen, dau. of William and Minnie (Doughty) Cobb. Issue:

a. Billie.
b. Joe.

THE HISTORY OF ROANE COUNTY

James Carter, son of Sylvanus and ———— Hinds m. Rutha Caroline Hinds. Issue:

   a. William Crawford.

   b. Rilla Catherine b. 1871 m. Elisha Turner Ingram b. 1860. (See Ingram).

   d. Samuel Burgess, b. 1877 m. 1900 Sarah Dorinda King, b. 1879.

   e. Martha Elizabeth b. 1880, m. 1920 John Richards.

   f. Katie Kimbrough.

   g. Ella May, b. 1885, m. 1907 Theodore Ewing Hamby.

   h. James Lewis, b. 1888, d. 1918, m. 1907, Anna Rose.

Samuel B. Hinds m. Sarah Dorinda King. Issue:

   a. Bruce S., b. 1901.

   b. George C.

Theodore Ewing Hamby m. Ella May Hinds. Issue:

   a. Evelyn May.

   b. Theodore Ewing, Jr.

   c. Eleanor.

   d. John Leslie.

   e. Caroline Hinds.

   f. James Arthur.

James Lewis m. Anna Rose: Issue:

   a. James Lewis.

   b. Ewell.

Joseph, son of John Hinds, m. Susan Hankins. Issue:

   a. Levi Jackson m. 1843 Minerva Owings b. 1822 d. 1851.

   b. Sarah, m. Carter Hickey.

   c. Susan, m. John Fooshee.

   d. Annie, m. Christopher Abels.

   e. Joseph.

   f. George m. Elizabeth Abels.

   g. Henry P. W., m. Margaret Delaney Harner.

THE HISTORY OF ROANE COUNTY

Levi Jackson, son of Joseph and Susan (Hankins) Hinds m. Minerva Owings. Issue:

a. Albert N., m. 1866, Susan M. Harner.

b. Rutha Caroline Hinds m. 1st. 1864, Joseph Bacon b. 1845 d. 1909. 2nd 1868 James Carter Hinds b. 1838 d. 1917. See Hinds Family above.

c. Sarah Annie m. 1st 1867 Absalom Rector, b. 1850. d. 1911. 2nd 1882 David Billingsly b. 1851. d. 1921.

Albert, son of Levi Jackson and Minerva (Owings) Hinds, m. Susan M. Harner. Issue:

a. Annie C., b. 1867, m. 1882 Thomas C. Hickey
b. M. Malissa, b. 1869.
c. W. Jack, b. 1871, d. 1924, m. 1898, M. Jane Long.b. 1878.
d. Almeda M., b. 1873 d. 1901, m. 1899 Stephen Long.
e. Ida D.
(e) Ida D. b. 1878 m. 1895 Marquis D. L. Brawn.
(f) Otis A. b. 1882 d. 1925 m. 1915 Vinnie Ragsdon.
(g) Clay H. b. 1886 d. 1922 m. 1918 Jennie Goodson.

Children of W. Jack and Jane Hinds.
(a) Homer H.
(b) Clifford C.
(c) Martin C., m. Matsy Fulks.

Clifford C., son of W. Jack and Jane (Long) Hinds m. 1919 Iona Audrey Crisp. Issus:
(a) Clarence.
(b) Harry.
(c) Ruth.
(d) Billy.

Children of David and Sarah Billingsly:
(a) Mary Elizabeth.
(b) John Reuben.

Mary Elizabeth, dau. of David and Sarah Billingsly, m. 1904 David W. McReynolds b. 1884. Issue:
(a) Dorothy.
(b) Elinore.

(c) Evelyn
(d) David W. Jr.

John Reuben, son of David and Sarah A. (Hinds) Billingsley m. 1917, Nora Cowen b. 1888. Issue:

(a) John Reuben, Jr.
(b) Mary Lorraine.

Carter Hickey m. Sarah, dau. of Joseph and Susan Hinds, Issue.

(a) Henry.
(b) Elizabeth.
(c) Susan.
(d) Joseph, m. Annie Cassey.
(e) Thomas, m. Annie Hinds.
(f) Anna Elizabeth
(g) Mary m. ———— Witt.
(h) Jane, m. ———— Witt.

John Fooshee m. Susan, dau. of Joseph and Susan Honds issue:

(a) Jonas.
(b) Mary.
(c) Ab.

Annie, dau. of Joseph and Susan Hinds m. Christopher Abels. Issue:

(a) Susan m. John Millican.
(b) Louisa m. Wattson Robbs.
(c) George, m. Frankie Robbs.
(d) William, m. Emma Narramore.
(e) Robert.

George, son of Joseph and Susan Hinds m. Elizabeth Abels. Issue:

Holman Blaine, m. 1st. Susie Millard. 2nd Mattie Snodgrass Baker.

(b) Nancy, m. John Montgomery.

Holman B., son of George and Elizabeth (Abels) Hinds m. Susie Millard. Issue: Pearl m. James Abels.

(a) A. Pearl, m. James Abels.

Holman B. Hinds m. 2nd Mattie Snodgrass Baker. Issue:
(a) Holman Blaine Jr., m. Frances ?
(b) George Washington,m. Ruth Cooper.
(c) Henry Clay.
(d) Virginia.
(e) Eliza May.
(f) Kathleen, m. Walter Clyde Weatherford.

Henry P. W., son of Joseph and Susan Hinds m. Margaret Delaney Harner. Issue:
(a) Ruth Caroline, m. Absalom Pinkeny Thompson.

Issue: (a) Margaret Minerva, m. 1st. James Coleman Smith T. 2nd. William Martin Hicks.
(b) Robert William, m. Gertrude Williams.
(c) Laura m. 1st William H. Fisher. 2nd. Carl Mee.
(d) Lillie May, m. David Drips.
(e) Dyke Thompson.

Joseph Hines son of John I., m. June 9, 1812 Susannah Hawkins in Knox Co. (Records of Miss Kate White.)

THE HISTORY OF ROANE COUNTY
HUFF

1. John b. in Virginia m. Mary Yates. He came to Roane Co. 1822 as agent for King Salt Works, of Virginia. He died 1830. Mary died 1850. Issue, William Yates, Hannah, James H., John, Elizabeth, Prudence, Polly.

2. (a) William Yates b. in Virginia 1809 m. Keziah, dau. of William Tunnel, of Fredricksburg, Va., Issue, a. James White, b. Mary, c. Emely, d. Eliza, e. Elizabeth, f. William, E., g. Margaret, h. Sarah. William Yates served as County officer for 14 years, d. 1870.

3. (a) James White m. Elizabeth McIlwaine Anderson. Issue, a. Bessie, b. William E., e. James Anderson, d. Mamie.

3. b. Mary Angeline m. Hiram Bogart. Issue, a. Mary K., b. Robert, c. William Huff, d. Robert, e. Joseph, f. Lida.

3. (c) Emily Jane m. R. R. Anderson. Issue: a. Bessie, b Rhea, c. Adah, d. Emma.

3. (d) Eliza Rebecca m. James Mahoney.

3. (f) William Ebenezer m. Rachel Johnston. Issue, a. Mary, 6. William E., c. Sallie, d. Lenna.

3. (g) Margaret Katherine m. Samuel Anderson. Issue a. Emma, b. Joseph, M., c. Addie, d. Reece.

3. (h) Sarah Ellen Augusta m. Samuel Reese. Issue, May.

4. (a) Bessie, dau. of James and Elizabeth Huff m. Dr. J. R. Jump.

4. (b) William Ebenezer m. Lucy Gallaher.
4. (c) James Anderson m. Mabel Wilson.
4. (d) Mamie m. James F. Littleton.
4. (a) Mary K. dau. of Mary Huff and Hiram Bogart, m. Benjamine F. Smith.
4. c) Robert m. Mary Maxey.
4 (e) Lida m. Joseph E. Thompson.
4. d) Emma, dau. of Emely and Robert Anderson m. O. E. Mahoney.

4. (b) William E., Jr., son of William E. and Rachel J. m. Ada McCroskey.

4. (c) Sallie m. Will Kline.
4. (a) Emma, dau. of Margaret and Samuel Anderson m. Samuel O. Henley.

THE HISTORY OF ROANE COUNTY

4. (b) Joseph M. m. 1st. Lucy Cook, 2nd. Mary Belle Blair.
1. (b) Hannah Hughes m. August 21, 1830 Ebenezer Johnston.
Children of James Anderson and Mabel Huff.
5. (a) James Anderson, (b) Florence Elizabeth, (c) Woods Wilson, (d) Mable Claire, (e) Margaret Ann, (f) Isabelle Rhea.
Children of William E. and Lucy G. Huff.
5. (a) James Gallaher, b. Hugh McCrosky.
2. John, son of John and Mary m. 1st. Emeline Tunnel. Issue, a. James David, 2nd. Sarah Woodridge.

2. Elizabeth, dau. of John and Mary m. 1st. Robert Johnston. Issue a. James Hervey, b. Pelma, 2nd. Henry King.

2. James Hervey Huff, son of John, b. 1818 in Loudon Co., Va. came with his parents to Roane Co. Settled in Georgia. m. Margaret McGaughey, b. 1826 in Murray Co., Ga. Issue, a. John Ira, b. William C., c. Hannah, d. Mary, e. James Ransom.

3. (b) William E. m. Lida Emmons.
3. (d) Mary m. William Ransom.
3. (e) James R. m. Ann Willis.

William Tunnell, whose daughter Keziah, m. William Yates Huff, was the first settler south of the Tennessee River, now Loudon.

THE HISTORY OF ROANE COUNTY

HORNSBY

1. William moved from North Carolina to Roane Co. in 1808, m. April 14, 1831 Rachel Longacre.
2. (a) James b. in Wake Co., N. C. October 25, 1792 d. Oct. 22, 1863. m. Eleanor McCidy, b. in South Carolina 1880. Issue: James W. b. March 30, 1831 m. March 29, 1855. 1st. Martha L. Brady, b. May 20, 1832, d. December 7, 1871. Issue, a. Mary, b. Ellen, c. Margaret, d. Martha, e. Susan, f. Laura, m. 2nd. Martha Burkett Wasson.

THE HISTORY OF ROANE COUNTY

HOTCHKISS

1. Jared b. in New Haven, Conn. was a tailor for the Revolutionary soldiers. Moved to Roane Co. and kept a tavern on the Knoxville and Kingston Road. m. Betsy Knight b. at New Glasgow, Va.

2. C. M. b. 1802 in Roane Co. m. Sallie Ann Wyley b. 1811. Issue,

3. (a) Louisa, b. Isabella, c. Sallie. Louisa m.————Lauderdale. Isabella m. 1st. John Anderson, 2nd. John Hill. Sallie m. ————Johnson.

THE HISTORY OF ROANE COUNTY

INGRAM

1. Garland came from Wythe Co., Va., m. Miss Mays. Issue.
   2. (a) Sanford m. Mary Burnett.
   2. (b) David moved to Middle Tennessee.
   2. (c) Larkin moved to Alabama.
   2. (d) Sally m. January 24, 1821 Samuel Erwin.
   2 (e) Hanover m. October 20, 1835 Ephriam Huffine.

Children of Sanford and Mary.

3. (a) Stephen Harrison m. Sarah Woods Brazeale. b. Samuel; c. Elisha m. Maraline Brazeale. d. Moses b. 1845 m. Amanda W. Brazeale. e. Jack b. 1845 m. Mary Susan Smith. f. Hannah G. m. Thomas Jefferson Littleton (See Littleton). g. Mary m. Dock Littleton. Issue a. Samuel, b. John. h. Penelope. i. Lucinda m. Van Stowe. j. Jefferson m. Sallie Smith.

Children of Stephen and Sarah B.

4. (a) Elizabeth Ann b. 1849 m. Pleasant Littleton, (See Littleton) ; b. Samuel Houston b. 1851 m. Rosa Arabella Sparks. c. Mary b. 1849 m. 1870 John Collett b. 1844. d. Nancy Adeline b. 1857 m. 1876 Henry D. Biss. e. Amanda Clementine b. 1858 m. 1876 Thomas B. Morrison. f. Elisha Turner m. 1889 Rilla Catherine Hines. g. Stacia Maraline m. 1883 Charles W. Haley (See Haley). h. Lucinda Catherine b. 1867 d. 1918. i. Sanford Harrison m. 1st. Hattie Gibson, 2nd. Edna Melton. j Sarah m. John Vaden Tedder.

Children of Samuel H. and Rosa Sparks Ingram.

Lela Emma m. William Martin.
Ella May m. William B. Qualls.
Callie Lucile m. Charles Thomas Tedder.
Bonnie Jean m. Elbert Qualls. Issue: a. Jack.
Albert Ernest m. Elizabeth Jones.
David Carson.
Maud Blanch m. James King.

Children of May and John Collett.

5. (a) William, b. John m. Margaret Martin.

Children of Elisha and Rilla Hines Ingram.

Reece m. James Charles Acuff (See Owings.)

Lenice Wood m. Frederick Sayford Bacon.
Elisha Turner.
Rilla Catherine.
Children of Sanford H. and Hattie G. Ingram.
5. (a) Stephen, b. Raymond, c. Larry, d. Alice.

Children of John and Margaret Collett.
John William m. Mary Benson.
Robert m. Kate Bristow.
Ralph.
Mary Catherine.
Charles.
Raymond.
Howard.

Children of Moses L. and Amanda Brazeale Ingram.
Thomas Franklin b. 1860 m. 1st. Adeline Hall, 2nd. Margaret Allison.
    Jack m. Annie Vann.
    James m. Laura Caldwell.
    Sue m. Frank Duff.
    John m. Jane Harvey.
    Elisha W. m. Ida Vann.
    Margaret m. Frank Brown.
    Robert m. Myra Martin.
    Lucinda m. George Vann.
    Julia m. Alvin Weber.
    Henry m. Alma Gurley.

Children of Thomas F. and Adeline H. Ingram.
Charles m. Goldie Martin.
Lillie m. John Rose.
Moses E. m. Mina DeYoung.
Amanda W. m. William B. Ladd.
Annie Jackson m. Joseph Hartman.
Margaret Lee m. Hal M. Rose.
Thomas Reed m. Bernada Hill.
Frank m. Beatrice Tooten.
Herbert.

THE HISTORY OF ROANE COUNTY

Issue of Thomas F. and Margaret Allison, a. James Melton.

Issue of Jack and Annie Vann Ingram.
5. (a) Martin, b. Mae, c. Tom.

Issue of James and Laura C. Ingram.
Marcus m. Ruth Neal.
Fred m. Annie England.
Floyd m. Elizabeth Holland.
Julia m. Hugh Wyatt.
Teresa m. Logan Christopher.

Issue of Sue and Frank Duff.
William m. Mattie Douglass.
Margaret m. Fred Hackney.
Stella m. George Henshaw.
Addie.
Clara.
Raymond.
Robert.

Issue of Jack and Jane Harvey Ingram.
Jack m. Minnie Billingsly.

Issue of E. W. and Ida Bann Ingram.
Dora m. Barclay Blair.
Mae m. Thomas Bowers.
Robbie.
Henry.
Vann.

Issue of Margaret and Frank Brown
Georgia m. Fred Hall. Lunn, Elijah, and Frank.

Issue of Lucinda and George Vann.
John.

Issue of Julia and Alvin Weber.
Catherine and Alvin.

Issue of Charles and Goldie Martin Ingram.
Mary, Charles and Thomas F.

Issue of Jack and Susan Smith Ingram.
Mollie m. Robert Millican.
Oscar m. Lou Austin.
Louella m. John Johnston.
Wagly Dove m. Isaac Johnston.
Ida m. James L. Johnston.
Alma m. James L. Childress.
Pearl m. Algie B. Crawford.
Robert m. Edith Blizzard.

THE HISTORY OF ROANE COUNTY

Issue of Mollie and Robert Millican.
Annie m. Wiley Marney.
Roscoe m. Mary Meadows.
Reece m. Loyd Turner.
Issue of Oscar and Lou Austin.
Floyd m. Mary Pardue; Fred, Spencer, Mary Robert, and Rena.
Issue of Louella and John Johnston.
Jack, Grace m. Carl Preston.
Issue of Wagly Dove and Isaac Johnston.
Frank m. Eleanor Sawyer.
Isssue of Ida and James L. Johnston.
Ruth m. Robert A. Rowlette.
Dorothy.
Issue of Alma and James Childress.
James.
Issue of Pearl and Algey Crawford.
Lindsay.
Issue of Robert and Edith Ingram.
Elwin and Mabel.
Issue of Lucinda and Vann Stowe.
Savannah, Elizabeth and Catherine.
Elizabeth m. John Barxtol Goodwin. Issue:
Ada Frank m. John Roberts.
Kate m. Edwin Porter Allen.
Luther m. Bonnie Ewing.
Gilbert.
Joe E.
Catherine m. James E. Pickel. Issue:
Charlie m. Adeline Harris.
Tom m. Lee Miller.
Joe m. Elizabeth Carthcart.
Lillie m. Ralph Neerguard.
Jessie m. Albert Hartsooh.
Gilbert m. Eva Dereux.
Vann m. Rose Patton.
Issue of Jefferson and Sallie Smith Ingram.
  a. George, b. Martin, m. Harriet Harvey. Issue: a. Murray. Martin, c. John, d. Samuel m. Mary Heury. Issue, a. Murray.
  Laura m. George Graham. Issue a. Laura m. Yerb Roberts.
  George Ingram, Captain of a Company 1802 m. March 5, 1797 Nancy Granme in Knox Co. (Record of Miss Kate White.)

THE HISTORY OF ROANE COUNTY

JOHNSTON

1. Joseph b. in Ireland about 1755 settled in Rockbridge Co., Va. 1780 where he married Margaret Graham. Later moved to Blount Co., Tenn. Issue, a. James, b. Joseph, c. Josiah, d. Samuel, e. Robert, f. Frances, g. Ebenezer, h. William, i. Jane, j. Margaret, k. Hugh.

2. (b) James b. May 6, 1784 in York District, S. C., m. March 21, 1805 Rachel Martin, of same place. His brothers Francis and Hugh settled in Roane Co., about 1801. James came in 1808. Issue of James and Rachel, a. Margaret, b. Robert M., c. Joseph A., d. Martha, e. James M., f. Anne J., g. Rachel Louise, h. Mary M., i. William F., j. Ebenezer, k. Elizabeth.

2. (a) Margaret m. William Gammon.
2. (c) Joseph A. m. Jane Cowan.
2. (d) Martha m. James Johnson.
2. (f) Annie J. m. John Carmicheal.
2. (g) Rachel Louise m. Jeremiah Johnson.
2. (h) Mary M. m. Wiley Blair.

2. (j) Ebenezer m. Hannah Hues Huff, August 2, 1830. Issue, a. Melisa Clementine, b. Mary Jane, c. Robert Franklin, d. Joseph Marshall, e. John Yates, f. James Harrison, g. Jerome, h. Milton Graham, i. William McEwen, j. Hannah Elizabeth.

2. (k) Elizabeth m. John Blair.
2. Issue of Joseph and Jane, a. Nannie E., b. Rachel A., c. Hettie, d. Robert, e. Martha, f. Andrew H., g. Lennie Bell, h. Josie.

3. (b) Rachel A., m. William E. Huff. (See Huff).
3. (c) Hettie m. L. T. Blair. (See Blair).
3. (a) Melissa C., dau. of Ebenezer and Hannah m. December 22, 1852 Richard T. Wilson.
3. (b) Mary Jane m. S. D. Reynolds.
3. (c) Joseph Marshall m. Martha Hugenor.
3 (d) John Yates m. Susan Ayers.
3. James Harrison, b. January 22, 1842, m. October 1866 Mary Kline.
3. (i) William McEwen m. Flue Reese.
3. (j) Hannah Elizabeth m. Cook.
3. (f) Children of James Harrison and Mary Johnston.
4. (a) Sarah m. John Griffiss.
4. (b) Elizabeth m. Hugh M. Thomas.

THE HISTORY OF ROANE COUNTY

JORDON

1. Dr. Lewis W. Jordon b. in Marion, Va., m. Sarah Yancy, of the same place. Moved to Roane Co. 2nd. wife Sophia Matilda Ayers. Was surgeon of 14th Reg of Infantry in the Mexican War.

2. Sarah Saphina, daughter of Lewis and Sophia Jordon m. Thomas Jefferson Tifton at Selma, Ala. Issue a. John Yancy, b. Thomas Grayson, c. Mary Molett, d. Douglass Elma, e. William Pope, f. Lewis W., g. Ida Alice.

3. (a) John Yancy m. Mollie Womble.

3. (b) Thomas Gayson m. Sarah Garrett.

3 (c) Mary m. C. W. Stewart.

3. (g) Ida Alice m. 1st. Walter L. Martin. Issue, a. James Edward, b. Walter L., 2nd. husband, Roy Simpson.

4. (a) James Edward m. Virginia Hardwick. Issue James Edward, Jr.

4. (b) Walter L. m. Anna Jones.

THE HISTORY OF ROANE COUNTY

KENDRICK

Samuel Kendrick was born in Virginia. He was the son of Edom Kendrick and both were Revolutionary Soldiers. Samuel Kendrick married Margaret Fauby and they were among the earliest pioneers of Roane County.

Samuel Kendrick b. 1752; d. 1850; m. 1790 Margaret Fauby, b. 1772; d. 1856. Issue.

(a) Absalom, b. 1792. d. 1817.
(b) Mollie b. 1794, m. Enoch Rector.
(c) Henry,   b. 1796, m. Nancy Smith.
(d) Elizabeth, b. 1798.
(e) Nancy, b. 1800, m. Willis Short.
(f) Jacob Fauby, b. 1802, m. 1824, Margaret McPherson.
(g) William Edom, b. 1804,
(h) Diana, b. 1807, m. 1840 Richard Rector.
(i) Samuel b. 1809, m. Mary Rector.
(j) John, b. 1810, d. 1888, m. 1838, Martha Susan Owings. b. 1820, d. 7893.
(k) Margaret Fauby, b. 1815, d. 1898, m. 1839 William Jackson Owings b. 1815, d. 1895. (See Owings Family)

Henry, son of Samuel and Margaret Kendrick m. Nancy Smith. Issue:

(a)   John m. Jane Emery.
(b) Lucretia, b. 1821, d. 1872, m. 1840 William Evans b. 1821, d. 1897.
(c) Margaret
(d) Melcenia, m. William Emory.
(e) Elizabeth, m. Anderson Grassham.
(f) William.
(h) Henry d 1837. m. Callie Norman, d. 1917.
(g) Joseph, m. Sarah Brown.
(h) Mary, m. William Clift.

Lucretia, dau. of Henry and Nancy (Smith) Kendrick m. William Evans, Issue;

(a) Andrew Jackson m. Catherine Ragel.
(b) Mary E. m. James Glover.

(c) Nancy Ann m. 1st. Evan Davis. 2nd. George Buries.
(d) William.
(e) Hugh Campbell, m. Mary Ann Davis.
(f) Thomas Witherspoon m. Matilda Davis.
(g) Albert Newton.
(h) John Evan, m. Sarah Doughty.
(i) Joseph S. b. 1858, m. 1884 Sarah L. Rayder. b. 1867, d. 1925.
(j) Martha Susan m. Press Hickey.

Joseph S., son of William and Lucretia Evans m. Sarah L. Rayder. Issue:
(a) Bessie M. m. 1902 William Henry Polston.
(b) Jack Frederick.
(c) Harry Robert.
(d) William Fred.
(e) Henry Clay, m. 1911, Mary Phillips.
(f) Julia m. 1914, Frank Goddard
(g) Carl Samuel, b. 1896, m. 1918 Audrey Page.
(h) Arthur L., m. 1923, Pauline Davis.

Bessie M., dau. of Joseph and Sarah L. Evans m. William Henry Polston. Issue:
(a) Clarence Franklin.
(b) Fred Lewis.
(c) Joseph Daniel.
(d) Lucille Elizabeth.
(e) Bonnie May.

Henry Clay, son of Joseph and Sarah L. Evans m. May Phillips. Issue:
(a) Mary Elizabeth.

Julia, dau. of Joseph S. and Sarah L. Evans m. Frank Goddard. Issue:
(a) Frank Lewis.
(b) Joseph Paul.

Carl, son of Joseph S. and Sarah L. Evans m. Audrey Page. Issue:
(a) Carl Samuel.
(b) Ruth Catherine.
(c) Nancy Jean.

THE HISTORY OF ROANE COUNTY

Henry, son of Harry and Nancy (Smith) Kendrick m. Callie Norman. Issue:
(a) William, b. 1866, d. 1918. m. 1892 Ida Powell.
(b) Louisa.
(c) John, m. Emma Mehlhorn.

William, son of Henry and Callie (Norman Kendrick m. Ida Powell. Issue:
(a) Lena May.
(b) Doyle, m. 1923 Nellie Fritts.
(c) Leona Iris.
(d) Joseph Burton.
(e) Corrie Lou, m. 1925 Chas. Monroe.
(f) Clifford Lee.
(g) William Charles.

Joseph, son of Henry and Nancy Kendrick, m. Sarah Brown. Issue:
(a) Rebecca, m. John Benson.
(b) Walter.
(c) John Henry, m. Della Robbins.

Nancy Kendrick, daughter of Samuel and Margaret, Kendrick m. Willis Short. Issue:
(a) Franklin, m. McPherson.
(b) Elias, m. McCully.
(c) Samuel m. O'Bryn.
(d) John, m. Betty Coleman.
(e) Jasper.
(f) Edom, m. 1st. Rooker. 2nd. Stanchell.
(g) William.
(h) Jackson.
(i) Standifer.
(j) Julius.
(k) Melthenia m. Wesley McCully.
(l) Laura, m. F. A. Chapman.
(m) Diana, m. John Roberts.
(n) Margaret, m. Hiram Bailey.

Jacob Fauby Kendrick, son of Samuel and Margaret Kendrick b. 1802, m. Polly Mc Pherson. Issue:
(a) Louallen.
(b) Eliza.
(c) Elizabeth.
(d) Enoch.

THE HISTORY OF ROANE COUNTY

Diana Kendrick, dau. of Samuel and Margaret (Fauby) Kendrick, b. 1807, m. Richard Rector 1840. Issue:

(a) Absalom, m. 1867, Sarah Annie Hinds, b. 1850.
(b) Frankie, m. 1867 John Smith.
(c) Nancy Short, b. 1864 m. 1866 William C. Hill b. 1842, d. 1925. (See Hill Family.)

Samuel Kendrick, son of Samuel and Margaret Kendrick b. 1809, m. Mary Rector. Issue:

(a) Parthenia, m. Frank Ellis. (See Ellis).
(b) Jacob F., b. 1834,
(c) Lethe M., b. 1835, d. 1895. m. 1859, Samuel Acuff b. 1836. d. 1908.
(d) Enoch Jackson, b. 1838, d. 1906, m. 1862, Eliza Cornelia Owings b. 1841.
(e) Rufus F. b. 1840, m. 1st. Eleanor White Cunningham. 2nd. Louisa Bailey Owings.
(f) John W. b. 1841.
(g) Samuel. b. 1843.
(h) Thomas A., b. 1845, m. 1877 Molly Foust.
(i) James Richard, b. 1847, m. Samantha E. Whitlock b. 1859.
(j) Mary Elizabeth b. 1850, m. John Montgomery.
(k) Martha Susan, b. 1852, m. Allen Detheridge.

Lethe M., dau. of Samuel and Mary (Rector) Kendrick. Issue:

(a) William J., b. 1863, m. 1887, Mary L. Lewis b. 1872.
(b) Mary M., b. 1866, m. 1884 John W. Bowers b. 1855, d. 1925.
(c) Elizabeth, b. 1872, m. 1895, W. F. Millican b. 1862, d. 1821.

William J., son of Samuel J., and Lethe M. (Kendrick) Acuff, m. Mary L. Lewis. Issue:

(a) Robert Rilla.
(b) Minnie Murray Acuff, m. 1911, Wilmer H Shamhart.
(c) Harry.

217

(d) Joe Donley.
(e) Nelle.

Madge,, dau of W. F. and Elizabeth (Acuff) Millican m. Tom Ferguson. Issue.

(a) Rose.
(b) Billy Tom.
(c) Charles Fred.

W. F. Jr., son of W. F., and Elizabeth Millican, m. Susan Wyrick. Issue:

(a) Mabel Frances.

Enoch Jackson, son of Samuel and Mary (Rector) Kendrick m. Jan. 2, 1861, Eliza Cornelia Owings, Issue:

(a) Mary Lee b. 1862.
(b) Sarah Almeda, b. 1864,
(c) Martha Alice, b. 1866, m. 1897, Luke H. Montgomery, b. 1859.
(d) Columbia Eleanor, b. 1896.
(e) Lethe Maud b. 1871, d. 1901, m. 1895 Arch Frizzell, b. 1852.
(f) Nancy Araminta. b. 1874.

Mary Lee, dau. of Enoch and Eliza (Owings) Kendrick m. 1885, Beauregard G. Adcock, b. 1861. Issue:

(a) Etoile May, m. 1907, William Lee Weir.
(b) Milburn Kendrick.
(c) Bula Maud.
(c) Tula Claude.
(d) Lorelle Cornelia.

Bula Maud, dau of B. G. and Mary Lee Adcock, m. 1910, Harvey Thurman Whitson. Issue:

(a) Mary Frances.
(b) Jere B.
(c) Jean.

Tulla Claude, dau. of B. G. and Mary Lee Adcock, m. 1917, David Campbell Lee. Issue:

(a) Lucy Randolph.

THE HISTORY OF ROANE COUNTY

Lorelle C. dau. of B. G. and Mary Lee Adcock m. 1914, Robert Lee Maddux. Issue:
(a) David Haywood.
(b) Ledora Maddux.

Sarah Almeda, dau. of Enoch and Eliza Kendrick m. 1882 Neil S. Brown Payne b. 1857, d. 1911. Issue:
(a) Lester Lavins, m. 1916, Samille Amanda Dodson.
(b) Otis Kendrick, m. 1910 Margaret Dealy.
(c) Vera Maud, m. 1913, Walter E. Richardson.
(d) Robert Carney, m. 1915, Leola Williams.

Martha Alice, dau. of Enoch and Eliza C. Kendrick, m. Luke H. Montgomery. Issue.
(a) Rita Cornelia.
(b) Thelma Maud, b. 1901, m. Charles Waterfield.
(c) Robbie Randolph, m. Carl Rose.
(d) Luke Hamilton.

Rufus, son of Samuel and Mary (Rector) Kendrick m. Eleanor White Cunningham. Issue:
(a) Benjamin.
(b) William, m. Elizabeth West.
(c) Ida, m. Thurston Bowman.
(d) Frank m. Mollie Blankenbecker.
(e) Charles.
(f) George, m. Kate Benson.

Thomas, son of Samuel and Mary Kendrick m. Molly Foust. Issue.
(a) Samuel M.
(b) Ira. E.
(c) Mary Margaret.
(d) Clovie.

James Richard, son of Samuel and Mary Kendrick, m. Samantha Elizabeth Whitlock. Issue:
(a) Malissa Caroline b. 1879.
(b) Thomas Allen, b. 1881.
(c) Bertie Lee, b. 1884.
(d) Ida Alice, b. 1866, m. John Lentz.
(e) James Carlysle, b. 1889.
(f) William Edward b. 1891, d. 1918. Died in France World War.

THE HISTORY OF ROANE COUNTY

(g) Robert Otis.
(h) Iva.
(i) Clifford Jennings, b. 1898.
(j) Ruby Rae.

Samuel, son of Samuel and Mary Kendrick m. Susan Burford. Issue:
   (a) Stonewall Jackson m. Minnie Greenwood.
   (b) June m. Hugh H. McAllister.
   (c) Goldie m. M. Lucian Cartwright.
   (d) Sam Tilden m. Littie Collins.
   (e) Horace C. m. Hazel Tauchton.

Stonewall Jackson, son of Samuel and Susan (Burford) Kendrick m. Minnie Greenwood. Issue:
   (a) Henry B.

June, daughter of Samuel and Susan. Hugh H. McAllister Issue:
   (a) Hilliard H. m. Blanch Derr.
   (b) Sidney.
   (c) Wanda.
   (d) Ruby.

Hilliard, son of Hugh H. and June McAllister m. Blanch Derr. Issue:
   (a) June.

Sam Tilden, son of Samuel and Susan Kendrick m. Lottie Collins. Issue:
   (a) Sam Collins.
   (b) Mary Frances.

Horace C., son of Samuel and Susan m. Hazel Tauchton. Issue:
   (a) Horace Keith.

Thomas Allen, son of James Richard and Samantha Kendrick m. Elizabeth Detheridge. Issue:
   (a) Ruth.
   (b) Richard.
   (c) Lewis
   (d) Pauline.
   (e) Marshall.
   (f) Wallace.
   (g) Alice Jean.

Bertie Lee, dau. of James.Richard and Samantha Kendrick m. Thomas McBroom. Issue:
- (a) Eugene.
- (b) Christine.
- c( ) Iva Nelle.
- (d) Louis.
- (e) Richard.
- (f) Betty Lou.

James Carlysle, son of James and Samantha m. Hazel Reese. Issue:
- (a) Beth Oleta.
- (b) Alma Rose.

Robert Otis, son of James Richard and Samantha, m. Mabel Brown Issue:
- (a) Wanda Marie.
- (b) Glen.

Iva, dau. of James Richard and Samantha, m. Henry Lehman. Issue:
- (a) Edna Rose.
- (b) Erma.
- (c) Norma May.
- (d) Cornell.

Clifford Jennings, son of James Richard and Samantha, m. Maud Whitaker. Issue:
- (a) Carlysle.

John, son of Samuel and Margaret (Fauby) Kendrick, m. Martha Susan Owings Issue:
- (a) Sarah, b. 1839, d. 1840.
- (b) James Polk, b. 1844, d. 1875.
- (c) Robert Samuel, b. 1844, d. 1875.
- (d) William Edom.
- (e) Mary Ellen, b. 1849, d. 1891.
- (f) Margaret Amanda, b. 1851, m. 1870, Isaac A. Hill
- (g) Rebecca Ann b. 1853.
- (h) Nancy Jane, b. 1856.
- (i) Melissa Cornelia, b. 1858.

THE HISTORY OF ROANE COUNTY

James Polk, son of John and Martha (Owings) Kendrick m. 1877 Mary A. Dugger, b. 1842, d. 1905. Issue:

(a) Cynthia, m. 1910 James M. Wester. Issue: Mary Josephine.

Robert Samuel, son of John and Martha (Owings) Kendrick, m. 1870, Alice Wester, b. 1851. Issue:
(a) Willie T.
(b) Charles Winthrope, b. 1873, d. 1905.
(c) Robbie May.

Charles W., son of Robert S. and Alice Kendrick m. 1898, Edith Margaret Morris, b. 1877. Issue:

(a) Margaret Kendrick, m. 1921 Timothy Asbury Wright, Jr.

Robbie May, dau. of Robert S. and Alice Kendrick m. 1903, John Morgan Clack b. 1863. Issue:

(a) John Morgan Clack, Jr.

Mary Ellen, dau. of John and Martha Kendrick, m. 1868 Darius M. Acuff, b. 1844, d. 1897. Issue:
(a) John R. b. 1869.
(b) Lillie A.
(c) Margaret.
(d) Emaline.
(e) Willie.
(f) James Blaine, b. 1884, d. 1910.

Margaret A., dau. of Darius M., and Mary Acuff, m. 1902, Sewell Howard. Issue:

(a) Margaret Ellen, m. 1924, Thomas Scott Lowry III,
(b) George S.
(c) Cornelia Kendrick.
(d) Martha Christine.

James Blaine, son of Darius M. and Mary Kendrick Acuff m. Artie Blevins. Issue:
(a) Mary Ellen.
(b) Martha Ann.

THE HISTORY OF ROANE COUNTY

Rebecca Ann, dau. of John and Martha (Owings) Kendrick, m. 1871 James F. Tarwater, b. 1847, d. 1915. Issue:
- (a) Polk.
- (a) Martha.
- (b) Cora Ellen.
- (c) Maud Catherine.
- (d) John Kendrick.
- (e) Thomas William.
- (f) Dorothy.
- (g) Nellie Jane.
- (h) Madge Cornelia, m. 1920 George Edward Wilson (See Wilson.)
- (i) Reba Ann.

James Polk, son of James F. and Rebecca Tarwater m. 1904, Grace Kendrick Spears b. 1878. Issue:
- (a) James Lawrence.
- (b) Rebecca Josephine.
- (c) Penelope Maud.

Maud Catherine, dau. of James F. and Rebecca (Kendrick) Tarwater m. 1894 Timothy Asbury Wright b. ―――. Issue:
- (a) Timothy Asbury, Jr. m. 1921 Margaret Kendrick.
- (b) James Tarwater.
- (c) William Polk.
- (d) Dorothy Spearman.
- (e) Bardon Absalom.

John Kendrick, son of James F. and Rebecca (Kendrick) Tarwater, m. 1906 Ava Howard. Issue:
- (a) Mildred Rebecca.
- (b) John Kendrick.

Thomas William, son of James F. and Rebecca Tarwater m. 1920, Katherine Jane West. Issue:
- (a) Thomas William, Jr.

Nancy Jane, dau. of John and Martha (Owings) Kendrick, m. 1875 John H. Haggard, b. 1851 d. 1907. Issue:
- (a) Hobart, m. 1903 Alma Smith.
- (b) Frederick G., m. 1901 Kate Crowder.
- (a) Claude (Jerry) m. 1913 Mabel Tracy. Issue: a. Jerry, b. Frank.

THE HISTORY OF ROANE COUNTY

(d) Rue, m. 1913 Fay Blake. Issue a. Allen Hale, b. Frederick.

(e) Nancy Jane, m. James O'Neal Kimbrough. Issue: Nancy Jane.

Melissa Cornelia, dau. of John and Martha (Owings) Kendrick m. 1884, James A. Ervin, b. 1858. Issue:
(a) Alma.

Martha Susan dau. of Samuel and Margaret Kendrick m. Allen Deatherage b. Dec. 17, 1845. Issue:
(a) Laura Olive, b. Aug. 6, 1873, d. Jan. 27, 1922, m. Sept. 9, 1897 Robert Hicks b. July 8, 1868.
(b) Sexon A., b. Oct. 6, 1874, m. Dec. 27, 1905, Emma Denton, b. Oct. 8, 1882.
(c) Virginia, b. Feb 15, 1874.
(e) Ella, b. Oct. 23, 1879.
(e) Alice, b. Aug. 21, 1881.
Children of Laura Deatherage and Robert Hicks.
(a) Mamie Sue, b. May 2, 1898.
(b) Emma Jean, b. Sept. 30, 1900.
(c) Linda, b. Mar. 4, 1903.
(d) Reba Kendrick, b. June 5, 1906.
(e) James Russell, b. Nov. 16, 1912.

Children of Sexon A., and Emma Deatherage.
(a) Mary Sue, b. July 19, 1907, m. Aug. 12, 1925, William Perry b. Feb. 4, 1903.
(b) Paul b. Aug. 8, 1909.
(c) Browder Kendrick b. June 10, 1915.
(d) Robert Allen, b. Feb. 18, 1924.

Martha Kendrick Detherage, m. Second, Thomas H. Small, March 26, 1883. Issue:
(a) Samuel H. b. Feb. 2, 1884, m. July 22, 1918, Effie Lee Plemons, b. Dec. 14, 1884.
(b) Pearl Ada, b. May 18, 1886.
(c) Chloe Rector, b. Sep. 16, 1887.
(d) Mary Kendrick b. Dec. 1, 1890.

(e) Clarence, b. Oct. 24, 1893, m. Apr. 2, 1916, Viola Newman, b. Oct. 30, 1897.

Children of Samuel and Effie Lee Small.
(a) Wilma Sue.
(b) Alma Ray.
(c) Ella Jane.
(d) James Thomas.

Children of Clarence and Viola Small.
(a) Thomas Edward.
(b) Lora Louise.

THE HISTORY OF ROANE COUNTY

KIMBROUGH

1. Robert came from Virginia to Roane Co. in 1805.
2. Joseph b. in Virginia 1799 m. October 15, 1823 Mary Lord Hazen, b. in Knoxville 1808. Joseph was clerk of Quarter Session (now County Court) and moved to Roane Co. at the time of his marriage. Issue:
   (a) William b. Oct. 5, 1824.
   (b) Robert b. Sept. 19, 1827.
   (c) Joseph b. August 26, 1829.
   (d) Sarah A. b. October 26, 1831.
   (e) Gideon H. b .December 12, 1833, d. July 26, 1923.
   (f) Rufus M. b. February 9, 1836, d. July 23, 1922.
   (g) Calvin Morgan b. June 11, 1838 d. July 22, 1862.
   (h) Mary M. b. October 24, 1842.
   (i) Asa Hazen b. Feb. 12, 1845.
   (j) George Washington b. September 4, 1847.
   (k) Martha (Mattie) b. March 12, 1852.
   (a) William m. Rebecca Ellis.
   (d) Sarah Ann m. Lemuel Thomasson.
   (e) Gideon m. ————McMahan.
   (f) Rufus m. Catherine Jane Brown, November 23, 1840.
   (g) Calvin Morgan killed in Claiborne Co. July 1862 during War Between The States.
   (h) Mattie m. ————Roddye.

Issue of Sarah Ann and Lemuel Thomasson.
   (a) Mary Kimbrough, b. Eugene Barnard, c. Joseph, d. Leona, e. William K., f. Elma.
   (a) Mary K. Thomasson m. William S. Neighbors. Issue Sarah Armor.
   (b) Eugene Barnard m. Nancy Elizabeth Gillespie. Issue a. Margaret, b. Eugene Morgan, who m. Ruth Richmond, e. William K., m. ————Cady, f. Ema m. Hugh Banks Chapman.
   Sarah Armour Neighbors m. Eugene G. Woolwine.

Issue of Rufus and Catherine Brown Kimbrough.
   (a) Calvin Morgan b.————d. February 28, 1896, m. December 1889 Fannie Hamby.
   (b) Mattie b. September 16, 1867 m. December 26, 1889 George Ault, b. September 13, 1862.

(c) Bessie b. April 20, 1870 m. December 1891 E. F. Dodson.
(d) Rufus Franklin b. November 26, 1873.
(e) Mary b. May 22, 1875.
(f) Katherine b. 1878.
(g) Mary Elizabeth b. October 18, 1881 m. November 25, 1898 Robert Wilson. (See Haley.)

Issue of Mattie Kimbrough and George W. Ault.
(a) Katie Rebecca b. 1891.
(b) Edith b. 1894 d. 1916, m. September, 1911, William Watts.
(c) Rufus W. b. Jan. 27, 1896 m. Dec. 4, 1921 Edith Baldwin.
(d) George D. b. Oct. 19, 1899, m. Nov. 4, 1917 Delia Baldwin.

THE HISTORY OF ROANE COUNTY

KING

1. Walter m. Feb. 19, 1795 Nancy, dau. of John Sevier, b. 1779. Issue:

    2. (a) Thomas, b. Amanda, c. Martha, d. John Sevier, e. Austin b. September 21, 1801, d. April 22, 1870, was Governor of Missouri where he died. m. 1st. Nancy Roberts, 2nd. Mattie Woodson.

    2. (b) Amanda m. ———Brazeale.

    2. (c) John Sevier b. May 30, 1814, d. April 15, 1884 m. December 2, 1834 Martha Ernest, b. April 1, 1814 d. May 30, 1880.

    (Martha Earnest was a descendant of General Joseph E. Warren who was killed at the battle of Bunker Hill.)

    Issue 3. Walter H. b. 1843 m. 1st. Cynthia P. Fryar b. 1847, d. 1883. Issue a. Walter H., b. Charles W., c. Martha, d. Ann, e. Nancy Sevier, 2nd. m. Sarah Foster.

    2. (e) Austin Augustus. Issue:
    3. (a) Walter m. Annie Miles. Issue 4 a. Annie.
    3. (b) Thomas m. 1st. Emma Childs, 2nd. Clara Bingham.

    3. (c) Fannie b. November 30, 1830 m. Allen P. Richardson.

    3. (d) William m. 1st Guthrie. Issue 4 a. Edward, 4. b. Clarence, 2nd. Kate Clark Issue c. Allene.

    3. (e) Edward Livingston m. Eliza Jane Lisle.
    3. (f) Austin Augustus b. Dec. 5, 1841, d. May 30, 1886.

    Children of Fannie King and Allen P. Richardson.
    4. (a) Allen Preston m. 1st. Margaret Keefe. Issue 5 a. Robert, b. Preston, c. William, 2nd. Annette King. Issue 5 d. Walter, e. Allene.

    Children of Edward L. and Eliza Lisle King.
    4. (a) Annette m. Allen P. Richardson, Jr.
    4. (b) Benjamine.
    4. (c) Walter m. Dora Nummert. Issue: 5 a. Frances, b. Jane..

    3. (f) Austin Augustus Jr. m. Dorothea Elizabeth Lisle, twin sister of Eliza Jane Lisle. Issue:

4. (a) Margaretta b. Oct. 11. 1868, m. October 26, 1893 Joseph Warren Pitcher b. Dec. 18, 1867 d. May 5, 1917. Issue 5 a. Margaret Lisle, b. Robert Warren m. Ruth Genoa Moorman.

4. (b) Ella, c. Austin Augustus III b. 1872 d. 1899, m. Anna Hannagan. Issue a. Austin Augustus.

4. (d) Jennie Lisle.

3. (g) Elizabeth m. 1st. ———Moore 2nd. Lackey 3rd. Richbery. Issue Elsie, Fannie and Roland.

3. (h) Mary Belle dau. of Austin Augustus and Matilda Woodson, m. Milton Tootle. Issue 4 a. Harry, b. Lillian, c. Mary.

Walter and Nancy King lived in Kingston for about twenty-five years where their children were all born and were members of Bethel Presbyterian Church.

THE HISTORY OF ROANE COUNTY
KING

Major King came from Virginia. m. 1st.─────── Issue: (a) Charles (b) William moved to Roane Co., 1834 m. 2nd. ─────── Spaggins. Issue:
   (c) Joe W. King, m. Priscilla Hodge. Issue:
   (a) William Henry.
   (b) Joe W.
   (c) James B.
   (d) George Washington, b. 1852, m. Mary Elizabeth Hamby, b. 1850.
   (e) Sarah, b. 1854, m. 1875, Gilbert Randolph Hamby b. 1854, d. 1896.

William Henry King m. 1876, Martha Jane Hamby b. 1847, d. 1916. Issue:
   (a) Virgil Allen.
   (b) Julius Jerome.
   (c) Charles Franklin.
   (d) Harry Gilbert, m. 1910 Bertha McDonald.
   (e) Nellie Clarinda.

Charles Franklin King, m. Ella Hicks. Issue:
   (a) Evelyn.
   (b) Wilma Margaret.
   (c) Charles Franklin.
   (d) Ruth.

Harry Gilbert King m. Bertha McDonald. Issue:
   (a) Mary Juanita.
   (b) Myra Genevieve.
   (c) Martha Carita.
   (d) Harry Gilbert, Jr.
   (e) Virgil Leon.

James B. King, m. 1885, Lou Ann Owings. Issue:
   (a) Joseph Malcolm, m. Alice Easter.
   (b) Charles Franklin, m. Bessie Wren.
   (c) Carrie Zorilda, m. Robert Gideon Tedder.
   (d) James William, m. Maud Ingram.
   (e) Tom Owings, m. Tilla Tindell.
   (f) Lutie Ruth.
   (g) Rilla Almeda.

George Washington King m. 1873 Mary Elizabeth Hamby b. 1850. Issue:

THE HISTORY OF ROANE COUNTY

(a) Mattie Viola.
(b) Sarah Dorinda, m. 1900 Sam B. Hinds.
(c) Inez Gilbert.
(d) James Burns, m. 1920, Frances Young. Issue James Burns Jr.
(e) Joe Sam, m. 1913 Ida Parker. Issue: a. Allen George, b. Thomas Edward, c. Joe Sam.
(f) Ora Lynn, m. 1924, Robert Hicks.
(g) Ed George, m. 1920, Ora Belle Davis. Issue: a. Ed George, Jr.

Mattie Viola, dau. of George W. and Mary (Hamby) King m. 1895, Sam Goddard. Issue:
(a) Mary Elizabeth, m. 1915, Johnny Martin.
(b) Kathleen Bayless, m. 1919 Wilson Lane.
(c) Olive.
(d) Marvin Wiley.
(e) Eva Rose.
(f) Ora Frances.

2. Charles m. Julia Rather McElwee, Issue: 3. (a) James, b. Newton, c. Jerome, d. Thomas, e. Penelope, f. Feruby, g. Mary Jane, r. Ellen, i. Adelaide, j. Julia.

3. (a) James m. Mary McClesky, Issue: 4 (a) Charles, b. Rhoda, c. Campbell, d. Benjamine.

3. (b) Newton, m. ——————— Issue: (a) Edgar.

3. (c) Jerome, m. Sally Haley. Issue: 4. (a) Sidney, b. Adelaide, c. Iola, d. Viola, e. William, f. Charles.

3. (d) Thomas, m. 1878, Addie Wester. Issue: 4. (a) Maud, b. Alice, c. Boyd.

3. (e) Penelope, m. Noah J. Wagner, Issue: 4. (a) Charles, b. Hugh, c. Julia, d. Caroline, e. James, f. Adelaide, g. King.

3. (h) Ellen, m. Joseph Pyott.

3. (i) Adelaide m. Thomas Boyd, Issue: 4 (a) Frank.

4. (b) Rhoda, dau. of James and Mary King m. Milton Shields.

4. (a) Edgar, son of Newton m. Sidney, dau. of Jerome King.

4. (a) Maud, dau. of Thomas and Addie m. Frank Robinson.

4. (a) Charles Wagner, m. 1st. Mary Murphy. Issue: 5 (a) Paul, b. Edith, c. Kathleen. 2nd. m. Elizabeth Whitaker

5. (a) Paul, m. Ruth Sorrell.

4. (c) Julia Wagner, m. William W. Newberry, Issue 5 (a) Nelly White, b. Wagner.

4. (d) Caroline Wagner, m. Richard Donelly, Issue 5 (a) Pauline m. Roy Machamer. (b) Janice m. Robert Cox.

4. (e) James Wagner, m. May Hill, Issue. a. Louise.

4. (f) Adeline,m. Robert P. London, Issue a. Robert P. Jr., b. Marjory.

4. (g) King Wagner, m. Mattie Sorrell. Issue: a. Martha King, b. Richard.

LACKEY

1. James b. 1786 in Virgina moved to Roane Co. about 1800. m. Jane Matlock. Was for many years Deputy Sheriff and d. 1873. Issue:

2. (a) Samuel, b. Jackson, c. James, d. William e. John, b. 1825, d. 1879.

2. (e) John m. 1849 Margaret, dau. of John L. and Rosanna Gillespie Russell, b. 1827.

3. (a) John R. b. 1850 d. 1873, b. James m. b. 1852 d. 1874. (c) Laura b. 1854 m. 1873 Thomas W. Kellar.

3. (d) Jane b. 1859 m. 1880 Andrew C. Montgomery.

3. (e) Annie, 3 (f) Melinda b. 1866 m. 1886 Oscar B. Prater.

3. (g) Samuel, b. 1868, m. 1892 Flora Kizer. Issue, John K. b. 1893.

Children of Laura Lackey and Thomas W. Kellar.

4. (a) Ernest R. b. 1874, b. Mary M. b. 1877, c. Lena L. b. 1879, d. Maud, b. 1883, e. Howard R. b. 1886, f. Ethel, . 1889, g. Rosa L.

Children of Jane Lackey and Andrew C. Montgomery.
4. (a)) Beulah M. b. 1882, b. Margaret, P. d. John C.

Children of Jane Lackey and Andrew C. Montgomery.
4. (a) Beulah M. b. 1882, Margaret P. d. John C.

Children of Melinda Lackey and Oscar B. Prater.
4 (a) Walter L. b. 1868, b. William W. b. 1890, c. Margaret b. 1892.

LEA

1. Herndon.
2. James W. M. D. b. 1807 d. 1867. m. 1831 Malvina Wear dau. of Robert and g. dau. of Samuel Wear. Issue:
3. (a) Mary L. b. 1833 m. Robert K. Byrd.
3. (b) Robert L. b. 1836.
3. (c) Myrtilla A. b. 1838.
3. (d) Albert T. M. D. b. 1840, d. 1870 m. 1865 Virginia A. Darnell Issue: 4 (a) Albert E., b. Mary Malvina.
3. (e) Aurelia Jane, f. Henry, g .Virginia.
4. (a) Albert Eugene b. 1866, m. 1890 Deborah S. Wear, b. 1872. Issue 5, a. Virginia L. b. Isaac D.
4. (b) Mary Malvina m. John Purris Patton. (See Patton.)

THE HISTORY OF ROANE COUNTY
LENOIR

1. General William, Rev. Sol. b. in Brunswick Co., Va. May 20, 1751 m. 1771 Ann Ballard, b. July 11, 1851, d. Oct. 9, 1833 in Halifax, N. C. William d. at Fort Defiance, N. C. May 6, 1839.

2 (b) William Ballard, b. Sept. 1, 1775 m. 1802 Elizabeth, dau. of Waightstill Avery, of Burk Co. N. C., moved to Roane Co. 1810, d. Dec. 11, 1852. Issue.

(a) Albert Sobieski, b. Aug. 30, 1833 d. Nov. 23, 1861.
(b) Louisa Caroline b. 1805 d. Aug. 12, 1841.
(c) Isaac Thomas b. 1807 d. Dec. 7, 1875,
(d) Leah Adeline b. 1809 d. July 22, 1879.
(e) Myra Ann b. 1811 d. Mar. 8, 1879.
(f) William b. Jan. 20, 1813 d. June 16, 1787.
(g) Waightstill Avery b. Jan. 15, 1815 d. Mar. 6, 1884.
(h) Walter Franklin b. Nov. 21, 1816 d. Sept. 1, 1878.
(i) Eliza Martha b. Dec. 23, 1818 d. Mar. 4, 1894.
(j) Benjamin Ballard b. Mar. 5, 1821, d. Mar. 13, 1905
(k) Israel Pickens b. Sept. 21, 1823 d. Dec. 21, 1876.
(l) Julia Joyce b. 1826 d. Dec. 18, 1841.

(2) Albert Sobieski m. Mar. 2, 1837, Catherine Freeling Welcker. Issue:

3 (a) Elizabeth b. Jan. 28, 1838 m. July 1, 1857 David M. Key.

3. (b) Margaret m. James A. Lyons. Issue: (a) Adelaide (3) Kate, (d) Frederick, (e) Mary, (f) Laura, (g) Julia.

Children of Elizabeth Lenoir and David Key.

4 (a) Emma, (b) Albert, (c) John S. (d) Kate, (e) Sarah A., (f) David, (g) Margaret, (h) Henry Lenoir, (i) Elizabeth.

4 (b) Albert m. Grace Condit-Smith. Issue: Albert Lenoir, Jr., d. y., David M. m. Marjory Wright. Issue: Albert Lenoir.

4 (c) Kate m. Samuel R. Read.

THE HISTORY OF ROANE COUNTY

4 (d) Sarah Avery m. Z. C. Patten. Issue, (a) Cartter.

4. (g) Elizabeth m. Garnett Andrews. Issue, Betty m. Beren Waters, (b) Katherine m. Samuel C. Hutcheson, Garnet, (d) David.

4. (d) Frederick, son of Catherine Welcker and Albert Lenoir m. Mrs. Carot. Issue, (a) Kate.

4. e. Mary, dau. of Catherine Welcker and Albert Lenoir m. James S. McDonough, M. D. Issue, a. Mary, b. Albert, c. Katherine (m. Frank Vorhees). Issue, Frederick, James, d. Margaret.

4. (f). Laura Lenoir m. Henry Chambers. Issue, Joseph.

4. (g) Julia Lenoir m. James A. Conizer. Issue, a. Sarah, b. Albert, c. Paul, d. James, e. Katherine, f. Adeliade.

2 (b) Louisa Caroline m. Reynolds A. Ramsey. Issue:
3 (a) William Lenoir b. Apr. 1, 1829 d. Feb. 14, 1896.
3 (b) Waightstill Avery b.———, d. Aug. 3, 1866.
3 (c) Elizabeth b. Oct. 26, 1833 d. Dec. 3, 1864.
3 (d) Thomas Isaac b. Oct. 13, 1835.
3 (e) Julia Ann Campbell.
3. (a) William Lenior m. June 23, 1858. Louisa Mccampbell. Issue: 4 (a) Jennie m. James Faucette, (b) Lula.

3 (c) Elizabeth Ramsey m. Newton A. Patterson. Issue, 4 (a) Cora m. James Hardin, (b) Edward.

3. (b) Thomas Isaac m. Amelia Boyd, of Texas. Issue: (3) Annie, (b) Waightstill, (c) Thomas.

3 (e) Julia Ann Campbell m. Jan. 21, 1863, Gideon Caldwell. Issue:
4. (a) Allen b. Mar. 18, 1864.
(b) Catherine b. July 1, 1869, (c) Louisa b. Sept. 24, 1869.
(d) Mary Elizabeth b. Feb. 6, 1872.
(e) James Harvey b. Aug. 18, 1875.
(f) Addie Ellen b. Oct. 6, 1880.

2 (c) Isaac Thomas Lenoir m. Mary Caroline Hogg. Issue, 3 (a) William Ballard.

2 (d) Leah Adeline Lenoir m. Rev. John Y. Smith. Issue, 2 (a) Merriwether P. (b) Caroline P., (c) William

THE HISTORY OF ROANE COUNTY

Lenoir, (d) Waightstill Avery, (e) John, (f) Elizabeth, (g) Laura.

3 (a) Merriwether P. m. ——Martin.

3. (b) Caroline P., m. 1st. J. A. Corry. Issue: (a) Thomas. 2nd. John W. Winton. (See Winton).

3. (d) Waightstill Avery m. Mary Hill, of Petersburg. Virginia.

3. (g) Laura m. Rev. J. W. Robertson.

2. (e) Myra Ann Lenoir m. Gen. James A. Reagen. Issue, 3 (a) William Ballard Lenoir, (b) Julia, b. Sept. 4, 1844, (c) James Avery b. Jan. 7, 1846, (d) John Martin, (e) Frank H.

3. (b) Julia Reagen m. Col. James R. Love. Issue 4 (a)

4. (a) Myra Lenoir b. June 19, 1872 m. May 8, 1902 James W. Lowery. Issue 5 (a) Joseph Walker, (b) Julia Love, (c) James Robert.

4. (b) Margaret Bell.

4. (c) Julia Burgwin b. Mar. 30, 1876 m. Nov. 1894 Frank St. John. Issue: 5 (a) Frank Love, (b) Louise Avery, (c) Julia Love.

4. (d) James Reàgen b. Sept. 3, 1877.

4. (e) Elizabeth Avery b. Sept. 3, 1879, a teacher in Soochow, China.

4. (f) Robert John b. Sept. 19, 1881 m. July 3, 1915 Lillian Dee Warrell. Issue 5 (a) Robert John.

4. (g) Hallie Frank b. Feb. 6, 1884, Dean of Medical School at Soochow, China.

2. (g) Waightstill Avery Lenoir m. Aug. 20, 1857 Isabella Jane Hume. Issue, 3 (a) Eliza Hume.

3 (a) Eliza Hume b. June 1, 1852 m. June 13, 1873 Dr. George M. Burdett. Issue 4 (a) James, (b) Margaret, Isabella, (c) Eliza Lenoir.

2 (h) Walter Franklin Lenoir m. 1st. Elizabeth Campbell Goddard b. Jan. 10, 1855. Issue: 3 (a) Walter Thomas m. Lona Edwards, (b) William Goddard m. 1st. Alice Osborne, 2nd. Fannie Adkins, (c) John Albert, (d) Thornton Pickens.

THE HISTORY OF ROANE COUNTY

W. F. Lenoir m. July 17, 1857 Hattie Osborne. Issue, (a) Frank, (f) Rose, (g) Henry Lee, b. Dec. 6, 1863 m. May 23, 1888 Annie Gannon.

2 (i) Eliza Martha Lenoir m. Col. John Martin. Issue, 3 (a) Hugh, (b) Elizabeth, (c) John b. Oct. 28, 1845 m. Oct. 27, 1869 Fannie Dallom. (d) James Reagen b. Mar. 17, 1850 m. June 17, 1878 Ada S. Winston. (e) Sallie Russell b. Oct. 10, 1852 m. Apr. 14, 1880 Joseph D. Thomas. Issue John Martin b. Jan. 30, 1881.

Children of John and Fannie D. Martin.
4. (a) Herbert Dallom b. Nov. 11, 1871.
4. (b) Hugh b. May 11, 1874.
4. (c) Fannie Inman.

Children of James and Ada W. Martin.

Rachel Winston b. Dec. 20, 1879 and others.

2 (j) Benjamin Ballard m. Nov. 26, 1855 Henrietta Rutlelge, dau. of Dr. J. G. M. Ramsey. She d. May 25, 1864. Issue 3 (a) James Ramsey b. Aug. 26, 1859.
3 (b) William Ballard b. Aug 2, 1860.
3 (c) Charles Barton b. Dec. 9, 1861.
3 (d) Henry Ramsey b. Apr. 6, 1864.

Benjamin B. m. May 14, 1872 Margaret Virginia Siler. Issue. (e) John Siler, (f) Mary Elizabeth, (g) Benjamin B., (h) Louisa, (i) Myra Florence.

3 (b) William Ballard m. Florence Siler. Issue.
3 (d) Henry Ramsey m. Bessie Campbell. Issue.
3 (i) Myra Florence m. Avery Burdett.

THE HISTORY OF ROANE COUNTY

LIGGITT

Henry, son of Perrin, a Revolutionary Soldier in Virginia, moved to Knox County, where he died.

2. (a) Henry b. in Smith Co., Va., Jan. 11, 1795, d. Aug. 29, 1861, moved to Maryville, Tenn., 1812. Enlisted in U. S. Army Nov. 13, 1814, was a Sergeant in Capt. Alexander Brigg's Co., of Infantry, 5th Regt. East Tenn. Militia. Col. Booth in command. Served until May 10, 1815. When peace was declared he received an honorable discharge in Blount Co. In January 1816, moved to Kingston, m. Aug. 14, 1817, Elizabeth, dau. of Milton and Nancy Keener Center. Issue:

    3. (a) William Milton b. Dec. 26, 1818.
    3. (b) Nancy Keener b. Mar. 9, 1820, m. —— Duncan.
    3. (c) Emily R. b. May 26, 1821, m. Austin Green (See Green).
    3. (d) Caroline M. b. Apr. 25, 1823.
    3. (e) Sarah Elizabeth b. Dec. 4, 1825, d. Dec. 30, 1874.
    3. (f) Henry Jr., b. Aug. 3. 1828, d. Oct. 26, 1882.

    3. (e) Sarah Elizabeth m. June 6, 1849 Richard Livingston Cardwell, b. 1824, d. July 23, 1896. Issue:

    4. (a) Susan Ann b. Aug. 17, 1857 m. Nov. 29, 1876 Thomas Walter Carter b. Jan. 31, 1854. Issue:

    5. (a) Bonna Rozine b. Jan. 2, 1893 m. Jan. 2, 1919 Dr. Nelson Henry Rankin b. Oct. 29, 1892. Issue,
    6. (a) John Carter.
    5. (b) Paul Dillard b. Jan. 2, 1893.
    5. (c) Hal Dismuhes.

THE HISTORY OF ROANE COUNTY

LITTLETON

1. William emigrant from England to North Carolina. m. Sarah Cottingham.

2. (a) Thomas b. 1772 m. 1794 Mary Matlock in North Carolina. Moved to Hawkins Co. 1797.

3. (a) James m. Katherine Brown in Hawkins Co. Moved to Roane Co. Issue: (a) Jesse M., (b) George P., (c) Pleasant Green, (d) Thomas Jefferson, (e) William, (f) Dock, (g) Amelia, (h) Eliza Jane.

4. (a) Thomas Jefferson m. 1851 Hannah Ingram. Issue (a) William Frances, (b) Sanford Nelson, (c) Mary Katherine, (d) John Jackson), (e) James J., (f) Moses L., (g) Jesse M., (h) Charles C., (i) Martin L. After the death of his wife, Thomas J. m. 1879 Anna McNutt. Issue, (j) Albert, (k) Thomas, (l) Addie, (m). Robert, (n) Benjamine, (o) Pessie, (p) Morton, (q) Minnie, (r) Rachel.

5. (a) William F. m. Nancy Jane Eblen. Issue, (a) Hannah, (b) Charles, (c) Elizabeth, (d) Tom Wilk, (e) Sallie, (f) Addie Lou.

5. (b) Sanford m. 1st. Pearl L. Pickle. Issue (a) Emma, (b) Martin, (c) Cora, (d) Mary, (e) Hannah, (f) Burton. 2nd. wife Lois Mays. Issue (g) Reece, (h) Irene, (i) Joe.

5. (c) Mary m. J. C. Lewis. Issue Mary Katherine.

5. (d) John J. m. Mary Brabson. Issue, (a) Carlyle, (b) Augustine.

5. (e) James Joseph.

5. (f) Moses L. m. Eva Smith. Issue (a) Ester, (b) Maud, (c) Lincoln, (d) Minnie, (e) Jack.

5. (g) Jesse M. m. Katherine Estill. Issue: Jessica.

5. (h) Charles m. Pearl Corn. Issue, Hester.

5 (i) Martin W. m. Maud Wilson, (a) Martin, (b) Douglas.

Issue of Thomas and Annie McNutt Littleton.

5. (j) Albert F. m. Stella Estes. Issue, (a) Albert M., (b) Virginia.

5. (k) Thomas J. II m. Zoe Sublette. Issue (a) Thomas J. III, (b) Virginia, (c) Bettye Grey.

THE HISTORY OF ROANE COUNTY

5. (l) Addie m. J. D. Rose. Issue (a) Edward, (b) Ellen, (c) Clarice, (d) Robert, (e) Frank, (f) Francis, (g) William.
  5. (m) Robert A.
  5. (n) Benjamine H. m. Clarice Lee.
  5. (o) Bessie M.
  5. (p) Morton.
  5. (q) Minnie A., m. Richard Burke. Issue (a) James Donahue.
  (r) Rachel E. m. Cornelius Vanderbilt, Jr.

  3. (c) Pleasant Green Littleton, son of James Littleton, m. Elizabeth Ingram, daughter of Stephen Ingram. Issue:

  1. James Franklin m. Mamie Huff. Issue: (a) Elizabeth, (b) Mabel Huff.

  2. Jennie Littleton m. John Arthur. Issue: (a) Bessie, (b) Mamie, (c) Johnnie.

  3. Kate Littleton m. Lewis Arthur. Issue: (a) Flora.

  4. Addie Littleton m. Fate Schrimphser. Issue: (a) Addie, (b) Mary, (c) Jane.

  5. Amanda Littleton m. John McNabb. Issue: (a) Sam, (b) James, (c) Nathaniel.

  6. John J. Littleton m. Lula Smith. Issue: (a) Lee, (b) Frank, (d) Lula.

  7. Henry Littleton m. Louis Arthur.

  8. Mary Littleton m. John Blackburn.

  3. (e) William, son of James m. Oct. 24, 1840 Elizabeth Ingram.

  3. (f) Dock m. Mary Ingram.

  3. (g) Amelia m. July 27, 1841 Ephriam Miller.

  (h) Eliza Jane m. Dec. 22, 1849 John J. Hart.
Florence Littleton m. Nov. 15, 1884 W. P. Miller.
John Littleton m. April 17, 1884 Mary Lee.

THE HISTORY OF ROANE COUNTY

LOVE

1. Robert m. Violet Wilson 1718 at the forks of the Brandywine River, Chester Co., Penn. Issue:

2. (a) James, (b) Margaret, (c) Robert, (d) Viola, (e) John, (f) William, (g) Joel, (h) Mary, (i) Samuel, (j) Hezekiah.

3. (j) Hezekiah b. 1751, d. 1833. Was a Soldier in the Revolutionary War. m. 1st. Elizabeth Cartamount 1783. 2nd. 1789 m. Nancy Duren. Issue: (a) Joel, b. 1791, (b) John M., b. 1793, (c) Hezekiah, b. 1796, (d) Jesse b. 1798, (e) Elizabeth, b. (f) William b. 1804, (g) Wiley b. 1812.

4. (c) Hezekiah moved to Roane Co. (accompanied by his father who died in 1833). m. Martha Terry. Issue: (a) Elizabeth, (b) Robert, (c) Mary, (d) Josiah T., (e) Hezekiah, (f) William,) (g) John C., (h) Jesse Richard and Hannah Price, (e) Wiley B.

5. (h) Jesse Richard b. Oct. 13, 1837 m. Mar. 7, 1867 Margaret Louisa Hotchkiss. Issue: (a) Hannah Mary, (b) Martha Matilda, (c) Jessie Louise, (d) Josie Elizabeth, (e) Jennie, (f) Carrie May, (g) Herbert Hezekiah, (h) Katherine Ethel, (i) Robert Wiley, (j) William Lee, (k) Walter.

5. (i) Wiley B. m. 1878 Sarah Wester. Issue: (a) Mary Brown, (b) Sarah, (c) Lura W., (d) Thomas.

Elizabeth Love m. Daniel R. Dugger Dec. 12, 1839.

Melissa Love m. John Angel Dec. 26, 1867.

Robert Love in 1783 with James White and F. A. Ramsey explored a large part of East Tennessee including Knox and Roane Counties.

THE HISTORY OF ROANE COUNTY

LOYD

1. Thomas of Dutch decent, a Revolutionary Soldier in Col. Chapman's Co., m. Mrs. Peaycord. Issue:

2. John b. 1762. Rev. Sol. in Capt. Griffith's Co. 4th. Ba. Chester Co., Penn. 1780. m. 1787 Rachel Vanderverr b. 1768. They were m. at Guilford Court House, N. C. Their daughter, Elizabeth m. Daniel Wester. (See Wester).

William, brother of John, m. Mary Ann Stearns in Knox Co. June 29, 1798.

THE HISTORY OF ROANE COUNTY

MARNEY

1. Amos of Fredrick Co., Va.

2. Amos b. Sept. 1760 was a soldier in the Revolution, enlisting June 1770 in Va. Div. as a private. Was stationed about Richmond until 1781 when marched with the army to Yorktown and remained until the surrender. m. Apr. 22, 1784 Sarah, b. 1764 dau. of Gen. Samuel Vance of Shenandoah Co., Va. Moved to Tennessee 1788 and settled on Clinch River. Amos d. in Roane Co. Aug. 1839. The father of 14 children. Sarah d. 1858.

3. (a) Betsy, (b) David, (c) Robert b. July 8, 1795, m. Anna Stevenson, (d) Amos b. Jan. 15, 179— m. Patsy Young, (e) Elizabeth Spence b. Nov. 22, 1801 m. Isaac Bailey, (f) Letitia b. 1806 m. 1820 John Sawyer Hart, (g) Sarah b. Feb. 10, 1807 m. Solomon Forrester, (h) Samuel b. Feb. ——— m. Betsy Marr, (i) Rebecca, (j) Pheby, (k) Polly m. Joseph Rayburn, (l) Margaret m. Thomas Forrester, (m) Malinda m. John Wilson, (n) Patsy m. June 1, 1826 Henry Davidson.

3 (c) Robert's and Ann's children (a) Mary m. ——— Childress. Samuel Marney m. May 1, 1819 Elizabeth Spence.

Samantha Marney m. Charles M. Rose. Issue:

(a) Hal. m. Margaret Ingram.
(b) Helen m. Ralph McMurray.
(c) Hugh m. Flo Parker.
(d) Emma m. Ernest Foster.
(e) Donald, (f) Mary Ruth, (g) Rachel, (h) Roscoe m. Mamie Huffine, (i) Susan, m. George W. Galyon.

THE HISTORY OF ROANE COUNTY
MARTIN

1. Samuel m. Julia Reese. Issue (a) James, (b) Eliza, (c) William P., (d) Nancy, (e) Joseph, (f) Mary, (g) Samuel, (h) Hugh, (i) Margaret.
3. William Porter b. Oct. 18, 1823 m. Oct. 8, 1856 Eliza Jane Brown, b. Oct. 11, 1835. Issue: (a) Lida, (b) Zollicoffer, (c) William Porter.
3. (a) James Reese m. 1st. Nancy Ames Gallaher. 2nd. Mrs. Metcalf McLester.
3. (b) Eliza m. Dr. Charles Nelson.
3. (d) Nancy m. Coleman Williams.
3. (e) Joseph m. Mary Hicks.
3. (f) Mary m. ——— Williams.
3. (h) Hugh m. 1871 Sarah Elizabeth Center. Issue: (a) Mabel, (b) Olive, (c) Jack, (d) Hugh, (e) Jean, (f) Grace Elizabeth.
4. (a) Mabel m. Asa Coleman Williams, Jr. Issue: (a) Sarah Elizabeth, (b) Hugh Martin.
4. (d) Hugh m. Marie Paulus.
4. (i) Jean m. Harry L. Cory. Issue (a) Hugh Martin, (b) Julia Reese, (c) Jean.
4. (f) Grace Elizabeth m. George B. Gallaher. Issue: (a) William Thomas, (b) Sarah Elizabeth.

Issue of Nancy McIlwaine and Coleman Williams.
4. (a) Julia Martin, (b) Asa Coleman, (c) Timothy Clarence.
4. Issue of James Reese and Nancy G. Martin: (a) Adelia, (b) Margaret, (c) Sarah, (d) Samuel, (e) Julia Reese, (f) Charles Nelson.

Issue of James Reese and his 2nd. wife Mrs. Metcalf McLester: (g) Scott.

Issue of Eliza Martin and Charles Nelson.
4. (a) William, (b) Julia Reese.
4. (a) Adelia, dau. of James and Nancy Martin m. William S. Patton.
4. (b) Margaret m. William Helicus Deitz.
4. (c) Sarah m. Gusta A. Guenther. Issue, (a) Margaret.
4. (b) Julia Reese, (c) Fannie.
5. (a) Margaret, dau. of Sarah and Gusta m. Harry L. Durell.
5. Issue of Margaret and William H. Deitz: (a) William, (b) Margaret Martin.

THE HISTORY OF ROANE COUNTY

MATLOCK

1. Jason b. in Virginia July 18, 1769, d. in Roane Co. Nov. 29, 1848. Issue: (a) James, (b) Moore. His second wife was Mary Miller, b. Sept. 30, 1783, d. Aug. 2, 1859. Issue: (a) Absolom, (b) Jane, (c) Malinda, (d) Amanda, (e) Ann, (f) Eveline, (g) Louisa.
2. (a) Absolom b. Aug. 12, 1819 m. Margaret Russell, b. May 14, 1845. Issue.
3. (a) Ann, (b) William, (c) Jane Lackey, (d) Avery Lenoir, (e) Mary, (f) Abbie, (g) Robert, (h) John.

2 (b) Jane b. 1807 m. James Lackey Nov. 6, 1824.

2 (c) Malinda b. 1814 m. Isaac Low. Issue, (a) Dolph.

2 (d) Amanda b. 1822 m. S. D. W. Low.

2 (e) Ann m. 1st. Darius Browder, 2nd. Asa Ambuster.

2 (f) Eveline m. ——— Osborne.

2 (g) Louisa m. Hamilton Russell.

3 (a) Ann, daughter of Absolom and Margaret m. William Keller. Issue: (a) Frank, (b) William, (c) Robert, (d) Avery, (e) Ted, (f) Margaret, (g) Mary.

3 (b) William m. Barbara George. Issue: (a) Lena, (b) Mary, (c) Maude.

3 (c) Jane Lackey m. W. Edward Foster. Issue: (a) Snow A., (b) Annie Myra.

3 (d) Avery Lenoir m. 1st. Annie Herbert, 2nd. Alice Hyatt, 3rd. Susan Hymon. Issue, Ruth Russell.

3 (e) Mary m. Marcellus Gomly. Issue, (a) Nellie, who married Victor Seilay. (b) Grover, (c) John, (d) Marcella.

3 (f) Abbie, (g) Robert.

3 (h) m. Roe March. Issue: (a) Lottie, (b) Beulah.

4 (a) May, dau. of William and Barbara m. Providence Mounts.

4 (b) Maud m. A. H. Watson.

Richard, Rev. Sol., b. April 1761, in Granville Co., N. C. (d. Nov. 4, 1847) while residing in Burke Co., N. C. served from April 1, 1779 to July 1, 1779 in Capt. John Montgomery's Co., Col. Joseph McDowell's Reg., and other companies to 1781. Allowed a pension Oct. 4, 1832 in Hawkins Co., m. May 10, 1804 in Hawkins Co., Mary Waddel.

THE HISTORY OF ROANE COUNTY

McELWEE

1. John, the emigrant, settled in South Carolina.
2. James, Rev. Sol. was at the Battle of King's Mountain and was present in Charlotte, N. C. April 1775 when the Declaration of Independence was signed. He m. 1st May 10, 1781 Nancy Johnston, of Va., d. 1810. Issue: (a) Jane Adams, b. March 22, 1782, (b) Mary, b. April 8, 1784, (c) John, b. Oct. 31, 1785, (d) William, b. May 1787, (e) Elizabeth, b. Jan. 22, 1789, (f) Margaret, b. Jan. 10, 1791, (g) Polly Gilmore, b. Feb. 23, 1797, (h) William II, b. June 28, 1798, (i) James, b. Jan. 16, 1800, (j) Nancy, b. Nov. 24, 1801, (k) Sally Johnston, b. Aug. 19, 1803, (l) Polly, b. May 20, 1806. m. 1811 Fevnby Cannon, (m) Julia Rather, b. Jan, 1813, (n) Hulda b. May 15, 1814, (o) Thomas Brown, b. Feb. 24, 1816.

    3 (a) Jane Adams m. Thomas Brown in Knox Co.
    3 (c) John m. Betsy Trice.
    3 (d) William b. 1798, d. 1885 m. Mar. 24, 1829. Lucinda Eblen b. 1811, d. 1904.
    3 (e) Elizabeth m. Daniel Rather.
    3 (g) Patsy Gilmore m. Samuel Grigsby.
    3 (i) James m. Nancy ———.
    3 (j) Nancy m. Samuel Swan, Dec. 21, 1819.
    3 (k) Sally Johnston m. John Mee. (See Mee.)
    3 (l) Polly m. John Matlock.
    3 (m) Julia Rather m. Charles King. (See King.)
    3 (n) Hulda m. 1st. William Wheeler, 2nd. ———- Wheelock.

Children of William and Lucinda: (a) Hugh, (b) William Eblen, (c) Ann Eliza, (d) Martha Jane.

    4 (b) William Eblen b. April 16, 1835 m. Dec. 12, 1867 Martha Jane Brown. Issue Franklin Brown.
    4 (c) Ann Eliza m. George Washington Nixon. (See Nixon.)
    4 (d) Martha Jane m. James T. Shelley. (See Shelley.)
    5 (a) Franklin Brown McElwee m. Corinne Eddy. Issue: (a) Parmelia, (b) Kenneth.

William McElwee b. 1798 was the first white child born in what is now Roane Co.

Thomas B. McElwee, son of James and Nancy b. 1818, m. Martha Matlock. b. 1824. Issue: (a) Frank, b. 1844 m. 1878 Mary, dau. of Gen. John C. Vaughn, b. 1854. Issue: (a) William, (b) James, (c) Hugh, (d) a dau. m. 1st.——— Gilbreath, 2nd. ———Caldwell.

THE HISTORY OF ROANE COUNTY

McEWEN

1. Alexander m. Margaret Houston.
2. John m. Elizabeth Stevenson. Issue.

3 (a) William, son of John and Elizabeth m. Matilda Clark. Issue: 4 (a) William, (b) John, (c) Robert m. Miss Patterson, (d) Mathew, (e) Charles m. Louisa Minor. (f) Susan, (g) Matilda, m. George Netherland, (h) Alice, m. Rev. Houston.

3 (b) John Columbus, son of John and Elizabeth,m. Nancy Mc Clung Patton. 4. Issue: (a) Margaret, (b) Ann Elizabeth, (c) Joanna Columbus.

3 (c) Robert Neilson, son of John and Elizabeth, m. Sally Balfour.

3 (1) Mathew, son of John and Elizabeth, m. Mary Wainwright. Issue:

4 (a) William, (b) Mary, (c) Elizabeth, (d) Alice.

3 (e) Elizabeth, dau. of John and Elizabeth, m. William Mason. Issue:

4 (a) William Taylor, (b) Carrington, (c) Elizabeth Stevenson.

3 (f) Margaret Alice, dau. John and Elizabeth, m. George Lewis Gillespie. Issue:

4 (a) John m. Amelia King, (b) George L. m. Miss McMaster, (c) Anna Neilson m. Arthur Watkins, (d) Elizabeth m. James A. Caaldwell. (See Gillespie).

4 (a) Margaret, dau. of John C. and Nancy Patton McEwen, m. John C. Gillespie. (See Gillespie).

4 (c) Joanna Columbus, dau. of John C. m. Thomas Center. (See Center.

THE HISTORY OF ROANE COUNTY

McPHERSON

1. Henry b. in Virginia 1771 m. 1789 Mary Eaton in Grainger Co. and moved to Roane Co. d. 1816. Issue: (a) John, b. 1809, m. 1830, Ethelinda Mahon b. in Roane Co. Oct. 5, 1813.

THE HISTORY OF ROANE COUNTY

McNUTT

1. James P. McNutt, b. 1822 m. Catherine Horsley and settled at Kingston. Issue: (a) William H., (b) John Fleming, (c) Anna.

2. (a) William H. b. March 22, 1857 m. 1st. Minnie Lowery 1886. Issue: (a) Frank, (b) Anna.

2 (b) John F. b. July 20, 1859 m. 1892 Anna Maud Wester. Issue:

4 (a) John W., (b) Doremus, (c) Margaret Wester.

3 (c) Anna m. Thomas J. Littleton. (See Littleton).

THE HISTORY OF ROANE COUNTY

MEE

1. Joseph b. in Virginia 1773 died in Hawkins Co., in 1851, m. Nancy ─────── Issue:
    2 (a) John b. 1798, (b) Thomas, b. 1800, (c) Joseph, b. 1802, (d) Martha b. 1804, (e) Laird, (f) William, (g) Nancy, (h) Isaac, (i) Jesse.
    2. (a) John m. Feb. 11, 1824 Sally Johnston McElwee b. 1803. Issue:
    3. (a) Rufus F., (b) Columbus Alexander, (c) Joseph F., (d) Rufus McNeal, (e) Margaret Elizabeth, (f) Mary Caroline.
    3. (b) Columbus A. b. 1827 m. Frances Tucker, b. 1842.
    3. (c) Joseph F. b. 1829 m. Louise McDermott. Issue:
    4. (a) Columbus, (b) Paul, (c) Penelope.
    3. (e) Margaret b. 1841, m. Robert Gallop Gross, Issue:
    4. (a) Sally McElwee, (b) Mary Mee, (c) Robert Guelph.
    4. (f) Mary Caroline b. 1843 m. Dr. Samuel Houston Day. Issue: (a) John Isaac, (b) May, (c) Margaret.
    4. (a) Sally McElwee Cross m. George Mason Shelton. Issue:
    5. (a) Clement Clay, 2nd. James Shepherd Hunt. Issue: (b) Margaret Elizabeth, (c) Robert Cross.
    4. (b) Roberta Guelph Cross m. Henry Alva Turner, M. D.
    5. (b) Margaret Elizabeth Hunt m. Lawrence Scales Dowd.

Luke Mee m. Sarah M. dau. of John H. Acuff. Issue:

(a) William Walter, b. 1872, d. 1920, m. 1st 1894 Roberta Nail. 2nd 1914 C. D. Sims.

(b) Hobart Carl b. 1876 m. 1st. Laura Thompson Fisher 1. 1921. m. 1923 2nd. Grace E. Smith.

(c) Claude Rupert b. 1880 m. 1920 Mary Menden Miller.

(a) William Walter Mee m. C. D. Sims. Issue:
(a) William Walter, Jr.

(b) Hobart Carl Mee m. Laura Thompson Fisher. Issue:
(a) Ruth Elizabeth m. 1922 George Rummage.
(b) Edith May m. 1920 John H. Patton, Jr.
(c) James Carl.
(d) William Walter.
(e) Carl Edward.

Claude Rupert Mee m. Mary Menden Miller. Issue:
(a) Thomas Rupert.
(b) Clarence DeWitt.
(c) Mary Claudia.
(d) Roma Dare Mee.
(d) Roberta Claire.

THE HISTORY OF ROANE COUNTY

MILLICAN

William Millican and Samuel Millican and wife came to East Tennessee from Spartanburg District, South Carolina, early in the eighteenth century and settled in the Post Oak Valley, Roane County. Samuel was one of the early members of the County Court, and also Post Master at Post Oak Springs. The children of Samuel Millican and wife were: Moses Scott, m. Narcissus Underwood; Nancy, m. Barney Hill; Elvira. m. ———— Dakin; and one other son, who, with Dakin and his wife removed to Texas during the decade 1830-40.

The children of Moses Scott Millican and wife were: (a) William W., who died in Andersonville Prison during the War Between the States. (b) John Haley, m. Susan Abel, (c) Jaane, m. Harrison Sigman, (d) Moses Franklin, m. Sarah DeLozier, (e) Elvira, m. James Ayers, (f) Lizzie, m. Jefferson Bagwell, (g) Sallie, m. William R. Henderson, (h) Finetta, m. 1st. Thomas Stonecipher, 2nd. Riley Summers, (i) Tennessee, m. James Acuff.

The children of John Haley Millican and wife: William F., m. 1st. Annie Joseph 2nd. Elizabeth Acuff, Annie m. 1st. Samuel East. 2r.d. Gus Greer, J. Robert, m. Mollie Ingram; George W., m. Emma Cooper; John M., m. 1st Katie Greer 2nd. Pearl Isham; Louis D., m. Eliza French; Gideon, m. Louise Collett.

The children of Harrison Sigman and wife were: Ella, m. Joseph T. East.

The children of Moses Franklin Millican and wife were Ida, Emma Elizabeth, m. William H. Joseph; John W., m. 1st. Almeda Owings, 2nd. Lorena Dorton Mobray; Charles F., m. Antonio M. Oyler; Gus G., (died age 37); Mary A., m. J. Florin Regester; Edgar S., m. Lula Russell.

The children of James Ayers and wife were: Calvert and John.

The children of Jefferson Bagwell and his wife were: Addie, m. Thomas W. Day.

The children of Thomas Stonecipher and wife were: Vesta, m. Gus Mayo; Rose, m. Charles R. Green; Carrie m. Anderson Honeycutt. One child, Robert L., was born to the union of Mr. and Mrs. Riley Summers.

THE HISTORY OF ROANE COUNTY

The children of James Acuff and wife were: Fred, John, Bates, Sallie, Anna, Scott and Sydney.

The children of William F., and Annie (Joseph) Millican were: Jennie May, m. John T. Dickson; Emma, m. Ben J. Lamb; Annie, m. Lloyd G. McCluen; Maude, m. Horace Sisson.

The children of William F. and Elizabeth (Acuff) Millican were: Madge, m. W. T. Ferguson; Billie, m. Susan Wyrick; Fred, Margaret and Helen.

One son, John, was born to Gus Geer and wife, Annie (Millican) Greer.

The children of J. Robert Millican and wife were: Annie, Roscoe and Reece.

The children of George W. Millican and wife were: Edith, m. Morton Demoron; Earl, m. Lillie Jefferson; Everett, Elsie.

The children of John M. and Pearl (Isham) Millican, were: Glada, Clifford, Nola, Clyde.

One daughter, Susie, was born to Louis D. and Eliza (French) Millican.

The children of Gideon C. Millican and wife were: Frank, Henry, Louis, Alice, Lizzie.

The children of Joseph T. East and wife were: Addie, m. Eugene E. Sanborn; Samuel, Frank, Ollie, Mollie, m. Herman Qualls; Maude, m. W. Robert Haggard; Fay, m. William T. Martin.

The children of William H. Joseph and wife were: Harry, Alma, Floyd, Irene, Raymond, Edwin, Mary.

The children of John W. and Almeda (Owings) Millican were' Frank, m. Naomi Gray; Thelma, m. Glen McCluen.

The children of Charles F. Millican and wife were: Lawton B., Carita, m. Edwin N. Andrews; Guilford, Delphine.

The children of J. Florin Regester and wife were: Roland, Nell.

The children of Edgar S. Millican and wife were: Catherine, Addie May, Edwin, Floyd, Walter, Charles, James, Lla Ree.

The children of Thomas W. Day and wife were: Mabel, Clifford, Vera, Laura, Thomas.

The children of Charles R. Green and wife were: Carrie Lee, Thomas, Charles, James.

The child of Anderson Honeycutt and wife was: Nathan.

THE HISTORY OF ROANE COUNTY

MONTGOMERY

1. Alexander came from Ireland, settled on Pigeon River in Sevier Co.
 3. (a) John A. m. Mary Winton, dau. of Rev. John and Arabella Cunningham Winton. Issue: (a) William, (b) Alexander, (c) John, (d) Elbert, (e) Margaret, (f) Jane, (g) Mary.
 3. (a) William m. Elizabeth Mitchell. Issue: (a) John, (b) James, (c) Alexander, (d) Mitchell Elbert, (e) Joseph, (f) Creed, (g) Mell, (h) William, (i) Amanda, (j) Sarah, m. James Cole, Dec. 27, 1862.
 3. (b) Alexander m. Frances Parks. Issue, (a) George, (b) John, (c) Joseph, (d) Mary (e) Nancy.
 3. (c) John m. Margaret Jackson. Issue: (a) William, (b) Thomas, (c) Margaret.
 3. (d) Elbert, b. Dec. 23, 1825, m. Caroline Stephens 1851. Issue: (a) William, (b) Mary, (c) Margaret, (d) Laura, (e) Jack.
 3. (e) Margaret m. Sept. 10, 1841 James P. Jackson.
 3. (f) Jane m. Quin Hill. Issue: (a) John.
 3. (g) Mary m. Oct. 21, 1839 John White.

 4. (a) George, son of Alexander and Frances m. Jacqeline Moore.
 4. (b) John m. 1st. Betty Kendrick, 2nd. Nancy Hinds. Issue: (a) Emma, (b) Charles, (c) John, (d) Elizabeth, (e) George.
 4. (c) Joseph, m. Jane Whittenberg, Issue: (a) Lottie, (b) Margaret, (c) Mary, (d) Elizabeth, (e) Henry, (f) Wiley.
 4. (d) Mary m. John Cloud Haley.
 4. (e) Nancy m. 1st. Jack Haley, 2nd. Thomas Marney.
 4. (b) Mary, dau. of Elbert and Caroline, m. Wiley W. Smith. Issue: (a) Elbert Doran, (b) Elizabeth Boyers, (c) James Montgomery, (d) Willie Caroline, (e) Laura Frances, (f) Ezekial Jackson, (g) Robert Ashford, (h) Wiley Corry.
 4 (c) Margaret m. Robert Ashford.
 4. (d) Jack m. Grace Anderson. Issue: (a) Elizabeth, (b) Milton, (c) Margaret.
 4. (e) Laura m. Thomas Avery Corry. Issue: (a) Margaret, (b) Elizabeth.

THE HISTORY OF ROANE COUNTY

5. (a) Margaret m. Norton Zinderstein.

Issue of George and Jacqeline.
(a) James, (b) Katie, (c) Joseph, (d) Sadie, (e) Walter, (f) Bertie.

5. (a) Emma, dau. of John and Nancy m. John Grigsby.

5 (b) Charles m. 1st. Annie Phillips. Issue: (a) Ruby 2nd. wife Nettie Qualls.

5 (c) John m. Alice King.

5. (e) George m. Lela Shallings.

5. (d) Margaret, dau. of Joseph and Jane m. William Grubb.

5. (c) Mary m. Perry Boyd.

5. (d) Elizabeth m. Samuel Treece.

5. (e) Henry m. Mattie Peay.

5. (f) Wiley m. Pearl Holliway.

5. (a) Elizabeth, dau. of Jack and Grace m. Harry Robinson.

5. (c) Margaret, m. Garrett Johnson.

THE HISTORY OF ROANE COUNTY
MORGAN

1. Samuel, of Weathersfield, Conn.
2. Gideon I. m. Rachel Kibbe in Hartford Co., Conn.
3. Gideon II. b. 1751 in Springfield, Mass., m. June 16, 1772 Patience Coggswell b. 1754 Washington, Conn. Issue:
4. (a) Calvin b. 1773 at New Preston m. Jan 10, 1801 Sarah Fackler.
4. (b) Luther b. 1776 at New Preston m. Ann Cameron Dodd, Feb. 1, 1798.
4. (c) Gideon III. b. New Preston 1778 m. Margaret Sevier.
4. (d) Rufus M., b. Feb. 19, 1781 at New Preston m. 1809 Elizabeth Trigg b. Mar. 10, 1791.
4 (e) Mary (Polly) b. 1783 at New Preston m. Asa Hazen.
4. (f) William b. 1786 at Moon Point m. Nancy Sewell.
4. (g) George Washington b. 1788 at Saratoga Springs, N. Y., m. Frances Irby.
4. (h) Elizabeth b. 1792 at Staunton, Va.
4. (i) Henry b. at Staunton, Va.
After the death of Patience, Gideon m. Elizabeth Hardin.

Children of Calvin and Sarah Fackler.
5. (a) Eliza Jane, (b) Franklin Henry b. Dec. 26, 1803, (c) Rufus b. Mar. 12, 1807, (d) Amanda Maria b. Jan 1, 1810, (e) Ellen Patience b. Apr. 14, 1812, (f) John Fackler b. Aug. 19, 1814, (g) Alexander McDermott b. Nov. 14, 1817, (h) Sara Ann, (i) Calvin b. July 6, 1822, (j) Catherine Matilda.

5. (a) Eliza Jane, dau. of Calvin and Sarah b. Feb. 15 1802, d. Aug. 18, 1870, m. Mathew McClung, June 9, 1818, who was b. Oct. 10, 1795, d. Oct. 5, 1844.
5. (b) Franklin Henry m. Mary Jennings.
5. (c) Rufus M., m. Jane Williams.
5. (d) Amanda Maria m. Andrew Park.
5. (e) Ellen Patience m. William L. Christy.
5. (f) John Fackler m. Louisa Porter.
5. (g) Alexander McDermott m. 1st Ann Eliza Hill 2nd. Mary Hurt.
5. (i) Calvin b. July 6, 1822 m. Virginia Hill.

THE HISTORY OF ROANE COUNTY

Children of Eliza Jane and Mathew McClung.
  6. (a) Calvin Morgan b. May 14, 1820 d. Feb 19, 1857, m. June 14,——— Kitty Grosh Morgan, b. July 24, 1834, dau. of Calvin C. Morgan.
  6. (b) Margaret b. Mar. 15, 1822 d. Apr. 6, 1886, m. June 9, 1842 Robert Henry Gardner, b. July 24, 1802, d. Sept. 21, 1883.
  6. (c) Sarah Morgan b. July 3, 1824, d. June 9, 1844.
  6. (d) Charles James b. Aug. 26, 1826, d. Mar. 1907, m. Oct. 16, 1851, Margaret Swan b. Apr. 15, 1832, d. Nov. 17, 1883.
  6. (e) Franklin Henry b. Nov. 23, 1828, d. May 4, 1898, m. May 4, 1854, Eliza Ann Mills, b. June 12, 1833, d. Sept. 4, 1881.
  6. (f) Mathew b. Mar. 11, 1833, d. April 1913. m. Apr. 27, 1858 Julia Frances Anderson. b. June 14, 1837.
  6. (g) Amanda Park, b. Mar. 6, 1835, d. April 29, 1839.
  6. (h) Alexander b. July 5, 1837, d. Feb. 16, 1839.
  6. (i) Hugh Lawson, b. Dec. 24, 1839, d. Feb. 15, 1862 at Ft. Donaldson.
  6. (j) Ellen Christie b. Jan. 30, 1843, m. June 5, 1867, John Marshall.

Children of Charles James and Margaret McClung.
  7. (a) Lucy Swan b. Aug. 7, 1852 m. June 5, 1873 Jacob S. Thomas,
  7. (b) Mathew Grainger b. Sept. 25, 1854 d. Jan. 15, 1888 m. June1, 1876, Bessie Bowen, b. Nov. 12, 1857.
  7. (c) Eliza Morgan b. Sept. 29, 1858 d. June 16, 1860.

Children of Franklin Henry McClung and Eliza Ann McClung.
  7. (a) Calvin Morgan b. May 12, 1855 m. Mar. 3, 1881 Annie McGhee, b. Nov. 7, 1862, d. Sept. 1, 1898, 2nd. Barbara Adair.
  7. (b) Franklin Henry, Jr. b. July 30, 1856.
  7. (c) Essex b. Feb. 19, 1858 d. Apr. 1858.
  7. (d) Matilda Mills b. Nov. 5, 1859, d. Jply 31, 1873.
  1. (e) Eliza Morgan b. July 2, 1861 d. June 1863.
  7. (f) Aurelia Essex b. Oct. 31, 1863 m. Sept. 11, 1888, Rogers Van Gilder, Issue: (a) Frank McClung, (b) John S.

THE HISTORY OF ROANE COUNTY

7. (g) Charles James b. July 12, 1866 m. Jan. 5. 1910 Anna Gay.
7. (h) Robert Gardner b. July 3, 1868.
7. (i) Thomas Lee b. Mar. 26, 1870, d. Dec. 18, 1914.
7. (g) Ellen Marshall b. May 23, 1873, m. Jan. 26, 1879, John Webb Green.

Children of Mathew Grainger and Bessie Bowen McClung
8. (a) Mary Bowen, 8 (b) Margaret Swan, 8 (c) Annie Dee,m. Jan 21, 1904 Frederick W. Chamberlain. Issue: William Porter.
8. (d) Minnie Keith m. 1st. June 8, 1905, Joe McTeer, 2nd. Apr. 8, 1913, J. Harry Price. Issue: (a) Elizabeth Caswell. (b) J. Harry, Jr., (c) Keith McClung.
8. (e) Charles James m. 1st. June 1, 1912, Rebecca Prosser. Issue: (a) Charles James, 2nd. Lelia Woodward. Issue: (b) Betty, (c) Antoinette.

Children of Calvin Morgan and Anna McGhee McClung.
8. (a) Lida M. m. William Cary Ross. Issue: 9. (a) W. Cary, 8. (b) May Lawson, 8 (c) Helen.

Children of Luther and Ann D. Morgan.
5. (a) Calvin Cogswell b. Dec. 16, 1799, (b) Alexander Gatewood, (c) Samuel Dodd.
5 (a) Calvin Cogswell m. Henrietta Hunt. Issue: (a) John Hunt, (b) Calvin, (c) Richard, (d) Charlton, (e) Thomas, (f) Katherine, (g) Henrietta.
5. (b) Alexander Gatewood m. America Higgins, b. Dec. 1, 1799.
5. (c) Samuel Dodd m. Matilda McIntosh, b. Nov. 8, 1798.
6. (a) John Hunt, son of Calvin C. and Henrietta b. June ——— General in Confederate Army, m. 1st. Miss Bruce. 2nd. Miss Reedy. Issue Johnnie, m. Rev. Caldwell, Lebanon, Tennessee.
6. (f) Kitty m. General A. P. Hill, C. S. A.
6 (g) Henrietta m. July 7, 1861 General Basil Duke, C. S. A., b. May 28, 1838 in Scott Co., Ky. Issue: (a) Basil.

7. (b) Thomie m. Judge Ballou. Issue: (a) Barbara.
7. (c) Calvin Morgan m. Jennie Ewing Speed.
7. (d) Currie m. Wilbur Knox Mathews.

7. (e) Henry.
7. (f) Julia Churchill m. Samuel C. Henning.
7. (g) Frances Key m. Charles Richardson Ray.

Children of Calvin Morgan and Jennie Speed Duke (a) Basil, (b) Ewing.

Children of Julia Duke and Samuel C. Henning
8. (a) Julia, (b) Henrietta Hunt, (c) James, (d) John Morgan.

Children of Gideon III and Margaret.
5. (a) Gideon IV, (b) Elizabeth, (c) George Washington, (d) Cherokee America, (e) Peggy Ann, (f) Montesuma, (g) Amanda, (h) Huston M.

(a) Gideon m. Mary L. Payne, (b) Elizabeth m. Hugh McDowell McElrath, (c) George W. m. Martha Mayo, (d) Cherokee A. m. Andrew L. Rogers, (e) Peggy Ann m. ——— Hanks.

Children of Elizabeth Morgan and Hugh M. McElrath.
6. (a) John Edgar m. Eliza Ann Alden.
6. (b) Bertha m. Benjamine Bakewell.

Children of Cherokee A. Morgan and Andrew Lewis Rogers.
6. (a) Andrew Lewis m. Josephine Howard.
6. (b) Connell m. 1st. Florence Nash. Issue (a) Ella Nash, (b) Gertrude Whitman. 2nd. Kate Cunningham. Issue: (c) Marion Sevier, (d) Lewis Byrne, (e) Howard Cunningham, (f) Connell.
6. (c) Hugh Morgan, (d) John Otto, (e) Lucy, (f) Paul, (g) Clifford.

Children of Andrew and Josephine Rogers.
1. (a) Andrew Lewis III, (b) Patricia, (e) Josephine, (d) Kenneth.

Children of Otto McElrath and ———————.
7. (a) Lucy, (b) John Otto

Children of Rufus and Elizabeth.
5. (a) Rachel Kibbe Trigg b. Aug. 19, 1810 m. Nov. 5, 1829 Hugh L. McClung b. May 26, 1810.
5. (b) William King.
5. (c) Eliza P.
5. (d) Sarah Frances b. 1817 m. Marcus Bearden.
5. (e) Rhoda Frances Campbell m. Col. John Williams.
5. (f) Calvin Rufus b. 1823.

THE HISTORY OF ROANE COUNTY

Children of Rachel Morgan and Hugh Lawson McClung
6. (a) Margaret White b. Dec. 3, 1820 m. Rufus Cobb Gov. of Alabama.
(b) Rufus Morgan b. May 31, 1832 m. Rachel F., dau. of Judge Connelly Trigg.
(c) James White, (d) Elizabeth Trigg b. Apr. 20, 1836 m. William Baker.
(d) Mary Frances b. Jan. 16, 1838 m. William B. Francisco.
(e) Rachel Florence b. Sept. 9, 1840 m. Dr. Marcus Lafayette Rogers. ·
(f) Charles Alexander b. Oct. 24, 1842 m. Carrie Miller. Issue: 7 (a) Corrie m. John Davis Kerr. Issue: 8 (a) John Davis, Jr.
7. (b) Mary m. Percival Walker Miller. '
7. (c) Sarah Morgan m. Austin F. Stillman. Issue: 8 (a) Francis Hill.
Rachel Morgan McClung l. Dec. 2, 1842.
Hugh Lawson McClung d. Apr. 11, 1891.

4.. (e) Polly, dau. of Gideon and Patience, m. Asa Hazen, b. in Loudon Co., Conn. 1770. Issue: (a) Franklin b. in Virginia 1802, (b) Sophia Lord, b. in Charlottesville, Va. 1804, (c) William Cogswell b. in Charlottesville, Va. 1806 (d) Mary Lord b. in Knoxville 1808, (e) Gideon Morgan b. in Carthage, Tenn. 1810, (f) Rufus b. in Carthage 1813. Polly after the death of Asa m. Rufus McPherson. 3rd. Rev. White. (g) George Washington, son of Gideon and Patience m. Frances Irby. Issue: (a) Irby, (b) John Tyler Morgan b. June 20, 1824 at Athens, Tenn. General in the Confederate Army and Senator from Alabama, died June 11, 1907. m. ——— Chilton. Irby Morgan m. Cornelia Willis. Issue: . (a) John, (b) Mary, (c) Cornelia, (d) George.
5. (d) Mary Lord, dau. of Polly Morgan and Asa Hazen, m. 1823. Joseph Kimbrough. (See Kimbrough).
5. (e) Gideon Morgan, son of Polly and Asa Hazen, m. Mary Strong, dau. of Dr. Joseph Churchill Strong.
5. (f) Rufus, son of Polly and Asa m. Mary Wallace, dau. of Campbell Wallace.
Children of William and Nancy Sewell Morgan.
(a) Susan, (b) Margaret, (c) Eliza, (d) William.
5. (a) Susan m. J. W. Campbell.
NOTE: Gideon II, served as a Corporal, Capt. Crouch's Co., Colonel Andrew Ward's Reg. of Conn. He enlisted from New Milford, Conn.

MORRISON

1. John b. 1785 in Virginia settled in Roane Co., m. Mary Deatherage. Was a Soldier under General Coffee.

2. Allen Deatherage m. Nancy Sellers.

3. Marcus Lafayette b. 1844 m. Jan. 18, 1877 Katherine Brown. Issue: 4 (a) Charles F., (b) Robert Emmett, (c) Alberta, (d) Marcus, (e) Walter. (f) Ethel, (g) Garnet, (h) Lula, (i) Thomas, (j) Katherine.

4. (c) Alberta m. William Hartley Reynolds. Issue: 5 (a) John Merriam, (b) William Hartley, (c) Marcus Morrison.

4. (f) Ethel m. Sterling Lipscomb. Issue: (a) Katherine, (b) Margaret.

4. (a) Charles F. Morrison m. Rose L. Acuff. Issue:
(a) Robert Acuff.
(b) Charles Francis, Jr.
(c) Catherine Ellen.
d. Rose Brooks.

Marcus Lafayette was Superintendent of Roane Co., Schools for many years and was the publisher of newspapers in Roane and Rhea Counties in pioneer days. He d. Aug 21, 1827.

THE HISTORY OF ROANE COUNTY

NIXON

1. George came from Ireland to Loudon Co., Va. His brothers who came with him were John, who settled in New Jersey, William, who settled in Maryland, Jonah, who settled in Pennsylvania.

2. George, son of George settled at Leesburg, Loudon Co., Va., where he married. One of his daughters married ——— White and they emigrated to Tennessee and settled near Morristown. He had a son, Jonah.

3. Jonah's sons were 4 (a) Jonah, (b) George Washington.

4. (a) Jonah settled at Leesburg, Va.

4. (b) George Washington came to Roane Co. m. Eliza Jane McElwee. Issue 5 (a) William McElwee, (b) George W., (c) Martha Louisa.

5. (a) William McElwee m. Margaret Green, dau. of Jacob Peak.

5. (b) Gtorge Washington m. Elizabeth Knox. Issue: 6 (a) Shelly, (b) Annie, (c) Hugh McElwee. (d) Comer, (e) Lewis Gaines, (f) George Washington.

5. (c) Martha Louisa m. Elbert Robinson. Issue.

6. (a) Carrie, who m. Joseph Baker.

6. Children of William McElwee and Margaret Nixon.

7. (a) Mayme Peak, (b) William Jacob, (c) Charles Wellington.

7. (b) William J. m. Alice Burford Head. Issue: (a) William J. Jr., d. y. (b) Phoebe Shirley, (c) Barbara.

7. (c) Charles W. m. Edith West. Issue: (a) Charles William.

6. (a) Shelley, dau of George W. and Elizabeth m. Ralph Bell. Issue 7. (a) Betty Ann, (b) Marjory, (c) James Timmons.

6. (b) Annie m. Frank Heron.

6. (c) Hugh McElwee m. Rebecca Williams. Issue: 7 (a) Hugh Williams, (b) Paul Knox.

THE HISTORY OF ROANE COUNTY

OWENS (OWINGS)

The first authentic records of the Owings family are found in Burke County, N. C., where Edward Owens married Elizabeth Sumpter, dau. of William Sumpter, a Captain in the Revolution.

Edward Owens b. 1766, d. 1857 in Roane Co. m. 1789 Elizabeth Sumpter. Issue:
    (a) Samuel Sumpter b. 1793, d. 1868 m. 1814 Sarah Randolph b. 1797, d. 1884.
    (b) William Edward m. Abigail Randolph.
    (c) John.
    (d) Alfred m. Polly Long.
    (e) Margaret m. John Pankey.
    (f) Nellie m. William King.
    (g) Judith m. Moses Russell.
    (h) Sarah.
    (i) Elizabeth m. William King.

Samuel Sumpter Owings m. Sarah Randolph. Issue:
    (a) William Jackson b. 1815, d. 1895 m. 1839 Margaret Fauby Kendrick b. 1815. d. 1898.
    (b) Clarinda b. 1818, d. 1903, m. 1838 Julius Hamby b. 1810, d. 1881.
    (c) Martha Susan b. 1820, d. 1893, m. 1838 John Kendrick, b. 1810, d.1888. (See Kendrick)
    (d) Minerva, b. 1822, d. 1851, m. 1843 Levi Jackson Hinds b———— d. 1886. (See Hinds)
    (e) Mary Jane, b. 1823, d. 1893, m. 1850 John A. Acuff, b. 1811, d. 1876.
    (f) Sarah Ann b. 1825, d. 1914, m. 1847 William J. Coleman, b. 1821, d. 1913.
    (g) Rebecca b. 1827, d. 1859, m. 1852 Edward Wattson Robbs, b. 1827, d. 1894.
    (h) Elener b. 1831 m. 1851 John K. Brown.
    (i) Amanda Malvina b. 1833, d. 1909, m. 1851 Levi Jackson Parkins b. 1830 d. 1906.
    (j) Elihu Randolph b. 1835, d. 1875, m. 1859 Eliza Work b. 1837, d. 1893.
    (k) Robert b. 1837.
    (l) Eliza Cornelia b. 1841, m. 1862 Enoch Jackson Kendrick b. 1837, d. 1906.

THE HISTORY OF ROANE COUNTY

(m) Albert Marion b. 1844, d. 1906, m. 1856 Elizabeth Hill b. 1847, d. 1918.

William Jackson Owings, son of Samuel S. and Sarah (Randolph) Owings m. Margaret Fauby Kendrick. Issue:
(a) Mary Elizabeth b. 1840, d. 1918, m. 1863 William Smith b. 1827, d. 1909.
(b) James Campbell b. 1842, d. 1878 m. 1866 Matilda Acuff b. 1847.
(c) John Lock.
(d) William E.
(e) Martha Almeda b. 1848, d. 1891, m. 1867 Thomas J. Brown b. 1839, d. 1922.
(f) Samuel Augustus b. 1850, d. 1899 m. 1876 Martha J. McGregor b. 1858, d. 1921.
(g) Franklin Davis b. 1852, d. 1905 m. 1876 Maggie Ellen Smith b. 1854 d. 1891.
(h) Sarah M.
(i) Nancy Rebecca.

James Campbell Owings, son of William J. and Margaret (Kendrick) Owings m. Matilda Acuff. Issue:
(a) Robert L. b. 1867.
(b) Alice Emily b. 1869 m. 1897 Edward Clinton Wilson b. 1867. Issue: Alice Emily.
(c) Cora Almeda b. 1870 m. 1892 Sam B. Bowers b. 1867.
(d) Mary L. and Margaret L. b. 1872, d. 1872.
(e) Nannie Ethel b. 1873, m. 1895 T. P. Morton b. 1850.
(f) James Campbell m. 1899 Elizabeth Sanborn. Issue: Helen Elizabeth, Esther Matilda.

Samuel Augustus, son of William J. and Margaret (Kendrick) Owings. Issue:
(a) Lennie Leota m. 1894 William S. King.
(b) James Samuel.
(c) Mary Almeda m. 1901 Dorcy Campbell Kindreck.
(d) Samuel Clinton.
(e) Tom Dock m. 1922 Zola Henderson. Issue: Sammie Jene.

Lennie Leota, dau. of Samuel A. and Martha J. (McGregor) Owings. Issue.
(a) Thoma Owings m. 1915 William Thomas Hicks. Issue: (a) Mary Lennie.

THE HISTORY OF ROANE COUNTY

(b) Sammie Augustus m. 1921 E. E. Spann. Issue: (a) E. E., Jr., (b) Betty Jean.
(c) Mollie Dimple m. 1920 Arthur Davis. Issue: (a) James Arthur, (b) Lillian Louise, (c) Mary Frances.
(d) Mattie Katherine.
(e) William Clinton.
(f) Chess Newell
(g) Phyllis Dolores.

Mary Almeda, dau. of Samuel A. and Martha J. (McGregor) Owings m. Dorcy Campbell Kendrick. Issue:
(a) Leota.
(b) James Samuel.
(c) Clarence Augustus.
(d) Phillip Campbell.

Franklin Davis Owings, son of William J. and Margaret (Kendrick) Owings m. Maggie Ellen Smith.
(a) Margaret Luella.
(b) Ollie Almeda m. 1905 Edward A. Roberts. Issue: (a) Jack Wager.
(c) Roscoe C., m. 1906 Annie Laura Leeper. Issue: (a) Franklin Davis, (b) Robert Clayton.

Clarinda, dau. of Samuel S. and Sarah (Randolph) Owings m. Julius Hamby. Issue:
(a) William Jackson.
(b) Sarah Mahala b. 1841 m. 1868 James Polk Underwood.
(c) James Newton b. 1844, l. 1884 m. 1868 Amanda Narramore.
(d) Martha Jane b. 1847 d. 1916, m. 1876 William Henry King. (See King).
(e) Mary Elizabeth b. 1850 m. 1873 George Washington King b. 1852.
(f) Gilbert Randolph b. 1854, d. 1896 m. 1875 Sarah King b. 1854.
(g) Dorinda Cornelia b. 1857 m. 1909 John A. Turner b. 1854.

James Polk Underwood m. Sarah Mahala, dau. of Julius and Clarinda (Owings) Hamby. Issue:
(a) Campbell.
(b) Amanda m. John Bledsoe.
(c) Frederick m. Eva Skeins.
(d) Artelia m. 1st. James Angel. 2nd. ———James.

THE HISTORY OF ROANE COUNTY

(e) Thomas m. Carrie ―――――
(f) William m. ――――― Ammous.
(g) Sarah.
(h) Alice m. Henry Meyers.

James Newton, son of Julius and Clarinda (Owens) Hamby m. Amanda Narramore. Issue:
(a) Charles Allen.
(b) Mary Etta.
(c) William Gilbert m. 1917 Sallie Long, Issue: (a) William Anton, (b) Gilbert Winfrey, (c) Kenneth.
(d) Jimmie Lavenia.

Gilbert, son of Julius and Clarinda (Owings) Hamby m. Sarah King. Issue:
(a) Mary Ella m. 1903 J. P. Hamby.
(b) Eliza Cornelia.
(c) Honora Helen m. 1904 Floyd M. Gamble.
(d) Grace Lillian.
(e) Margaret Richard.

J. P. Hamby m. Mary Ella, dau. of Gilbert R. and Sarah (King) Hamby. Issue:
(a) Lois Magdalene m. 1921 William H. Mahan. Issue: Charles William.
(b) James Gilbert.

Floyd M. Gamble m. Honora Helen, dau. of Gilbert R. and Sarah (King) Hamby. Issue:
(a) Grace Magdalene m. 1922 Ollie Pass.
(b) Floyd Gilbert.
(c) Charles Richard.
(d) Harry Thomas.
(e) Kendell Edwin.

William D., son of John H. and Mary Jane (Owings) Acuff m. Eliza Brooks Smith. Issue:
(a) Ida May m. 1901 J. E. Nelson. Issue: (a) Dorothy May, (b) Lucas.
(b) Rose Lena m. 1909 Charles F. Morrison (See Morrison.)
(c) Min Ellen.
(d) Robert William.
(e) James Charles m. 1915 Reece Ingram. Issue (a) Dorothy Ingram, (b) Catherine Rose, (c) James Polk, (c) William Turner.
(f) Alma Acuff.

THE HISTORY OF ROANE COUNTY

Sarah Ann, dau. of Samuel S. and Sarah (Randolph) Owings m. William J. Coleman. Issue:
(a) Araminta.
(b) Elizabeth m. 1870 Thomas Hasty.
(c) John C. b. 1852 m. 1907 Lula Riggs.
(d) William J. b. 1854, d. 1913, m. 1877 Mary Abigail Smith.
(e) Samuel Houston b. 1857, d. 1910 m. 1879 Alice Clarissa Hangley.
(f) Stephen Douglas.

Elizabeth, dau. of William J. and Sarah (Owings) Coleman m. Thomas J. Hasty. Issue:
(a) Guy Waaldo m. 1892 Olla Grace Bobbitt.
(b) May b. 1880 m. 1901 Frederick E. Wise.

John C., son of William J. anl Sarah Ann (Owings) Coleman m. Lula Riggs. Issue:
(a) John W.
(b) Dorothy M.
(c) Elizabeth K.

William J., son of William J. and Sarah Ann (Owings) Coleman m. Mary Abigail Smith. Issue:
(a) George LeRoy.
(b) Pearl m. 1903 Emil Helff. Issue (a) Bernice, (b) Frances.
(c) Lincoln Lee m. 1910 Eula Hayes.
Issue: (a) Virginia, (b) William, (c) Elizabeth.
(d) Grant Smith m. 1915 Lillian Champ. Issue: (a) Grant C., (b) William J.
(e) Sarah Florence m. 1915 Harry Gray. Issue: (a)
(f) William Houston m. 1919 Edna Smith. Harry, (b) George.
(g) Laura Alice m. 1922 Walter Berg.

Samuel Houston, son of William J. and Sarah Ann (Owens) Coleman m. Alice Clarissa Langley. Issue:
(a) Nellie May m. 1903 Emmet Clark Boyles. Issue: (a) Houston.
(b) Anne Leone m. 1910 Frank H. Licthenwalter. Issue: (a) Coleman R. (b) Eugene R., (c) Frank H.
(c) Elizabeth Coleman m. 1904 Henry H. Russell. Issue: (a) Henry Hawley.

THE HISTORY OF ROANE COUNTY

Rebecca, dau. of Samuel S. and Sarah (Randolph) Owings m. Edward Wattson Robbs. Issue:
   (a) William Alexander m. 1894 Kate Cantrell.
   (b) Sarah Caroline b. 1855, d. 1894 m. 1875 William H. Tarwater b. 1849, d. 1883.
   (c) Margaret Jane.

William Anderson, son of Edward Wattson and Rebecca (Owings) Robbs m. Kate Cantrell. Issue:
   (a) Edgar.
   (b) Margaret.
   (c) Grace.
   (d) Roy.
   (e) Milton.

Sarah Caroline, dau of Edward Wattson and Rebecca (Owings) Robb m. William H. Tarwater. Issue:
   (a) Ida Catherine.
   (b) Edward. A.
   (c) James Fletcher.
   (d) William Frank.

Ida C, dau. of William H. and Sarah Caroline (Robbs) Tarwater m. Charles Bowling. Issue:
   (a) William T. Bowling m. 1922 Loraine Mayberry. Issue: (a) William L. (b) Elizabeth Ann.
   (b) Margaret Edith.
   (c) Virginia Marie m. 1922 Walter Lee Brown. Issue: (a) Dorothy Katherine, (b) Robert Lee (c) Charles William.
   (d) Katherine Robbs.

Elener, dau. of Samuel S. and Sarah (Randolph) Owings m. John K. Brown. Issue:
   (a) Robert Samuel.
   (b) William Jackson m. Ann Roberts.
   (c) Sarah Elizabeth m. John A. Turner.

William Jackson, son of John K. and Elener (Owings) Brown m. Ann Roberts. Issue:
   (a) Edward.
   (b) Robert.
   (c) Ira.
   (d) Nellie.
   (e) Harry.

THE HISTORY OF ROANE COUNTY

Harry, son of William Jackson and Ann (Roberts) Brown m. Maggie Baldwin. Issue:
(a) Robert.
(b) Evelyn.

Sarah Elizabeth, dau. of John K. and Elener (Owings) Brown m. John A. Turner. Issue:
(a) Jackson Clarence m. Lucile Smith. Issue: (a) Jackson Clarence.
(b) Margaret Alice.
(c) Robbie Elener.
(d) Thomas Myer.
(e) Fay Marie b. 1897 m. 1919 George Majors b. 1895. Issue: (a) Sammy Anthony.

Amanda Malvina, dau. of Samuel S. and Sarah (Randolph) Owings m. Levi Jackson Parkins. Issue:
(a) Elmira Tennessee b. 1852 l. 1875.
(b) Lewis Alexander b. 1854, d. 1898 m. Minerva Farmer.
(c) Stephen Augustus b. 1857 m. Mary Hatfield.
(d) Robert Samuel b. 1859, d. 1883 m. Ruth Henson.
(c) Mary Ellen b. 1861, d. 1883.
(d) Eliza Cordelia b. 1863, d. 1883.
(e) Martin Luther b. 1865 m. 1886 Martha Alice Hatfield b. 1837.
(d) Sallie Ethel b. 1868 m. 1895 Henry Dick Franklin.
(e) James Alpheus.
(f) Margaret Louise.
(g) Cora Antha Alice b. 1875 m. 1st ——— Craig. 2nd D. R. Walker.
(h) Willie and Wilbur.

Martin Luther, son of Levi Jackson and Amanda M. (Owings) Parkins m. Martha Alice Hatfield. Issue:
(a) Cora Elizabeth b. 1887 m. 1905 Floyd Anderson Hatfield. Issue: (a) Eula Gladden.
(b) Hallie Etta b. 1889 m. 1909 Elza James Smith. Issue: (a) Betty Jean.
(c) Ada Cleo b. 1891 m. 1914 Arthur James Watkins. Issue: (a) Lewis Parkins.
(d) Lella May b. 1893 m. 1911 Robert Lee Plumber. Issue: (a) Robert Terrell (b) Martha Elizabeth.

THE HISTORY OF ROANE COUNTY

Cora Elizabeth, dau. of Martin Luther and Martha A. (Hatfield) Parkins m. Floyd Anderson Hatfield. Issue:
(a) Eula Gladden.

Sallie Ethel, dau. of Levi Jackson and Amanda M. (Owings) Parkins m. Henry Dick Franklin. Issue:
(a) Henry Clay m. Nellie Phillips.
(b) Lee Curtis.
(c) Blanche m. 1924 Howard Raymond Brooks.
(d) Lynn Kimball.
(e) Levi Parkins.
(f) John Randolph.

Elihu Randolph, son of Samuel S. and Sarah (Randolph) Owings m. 'Eliza Work. Issue:
(a) William Augustine b. 1860, d. 1921 m. 1884 Rebecca Fuller b. 1865, l. 1891.
(b) Mary Geneva b. 1861, d. 1912 m. 1883 William C. Snow, b. 1860 d. 1887.
(c) Luella b. 1867, d. 1899 m. 1886 Thomas Wilkey b. 1857, d. 1913.
(d) John Locke b. 1870 m. 1898 Ruby Pollock b. 1874.
(e) Sarah Henrietta b. 1871 m. 1901 Lucian H. McReynolds b. 1868.
(d) Julia A'delaide b. 1873 m. 1907 William R. Williams.
(e) Daisy Maud.

William Augustine, son of Elihu R. and Eliza (Work) Owings m. Rebecca Fuller. Issue;
(a) William Frederick.
(b) Bertha May m. Lee Burgess.
(c) Minnie.

(1) Margaret m. Chas. E. McConkey. Issue: (a) Charles William, (b) Albert, (c) Margaret.

Mary Geneva, dau. of Elihu R. and Eliza (Work) Owings m. William C. Snow. Issue:
(a) Jesse Clyde.
(b) Willie m. Thomas Richards.

Willie, dau. of William C. and Mary (Owings) Snow m. Thomas Richards. Issue:
(a) Hillard.
(b) Thomas.
(c) Harry.

John Lock, son of Elihu R. and Eliza (Work) Owings m. Ruby Pollock. Issue:
    (a) Hattie.
    (b) Fannie May.
    (c) Garnet.
    (d) John W.
    (e) James Morley.
    (f) Alice.

THE HISTORY OF ROANE COUNTY

PARKS

Robert came from Anderson Co., Tenn. m. Nancy Easley May 26, 1802. Issue:
2 (a) Margaret, (b) Rebecca, (c) Eliza, (d) Polly, (e) Mariah, (f) Joseph, (g) Francis, (h) Ruth.

3 (a) Margaret Parks m. Allison Howard. Issue:
4 (a) Tate, (b) John, (c) Ruth.

3 (b) Rebecca Parks m. George Gordon who built the first Iron Furnace in Tennessee 1828.

3 (c) Eliza Parks m. Wash Short. Issue, 4 (a) Robert, (b) Miller, (c) Buck, (d) George, (e) Alex Christoper, (f) James, (g) Rebecca, (h) Charlotte, (i) Sarah.

3 (d) Polly Parks m. Joseph Smith. Issue: 4 (a) Robert, (b) William, (c) Joseph, (d) Margaret, (e) Alexander, (f) Miller Mary, (g) John, (h) Tressie.

3 (e) Mariah Parks m. ———— Underwood.

3 (f) Joseph Parks m. Sarah Love.

3 (g) Frances Parks m. Alexander Montgomery. (See Montgomery).

3 (h) Ruth, dau. of Robert and Nancy Parks, m. 1st. Thomas Hinds. Issue:

4 (a) Thomas. 2nd. husband, Ned Martin. Issue:
4 (a) Samuel, (b) Robert, (c) William, (d) Mary (e) Eliza, (f) Elizabeth.

4 (d) Mary Martin m. Samuel Blair.

4 (e) Eliza m. Samuel Mathney.

4 (f) Elizabeth m. Gideon Johnson. Issue: (a) Eugene, (b) Samuel, (c) Gideon, (d) Buelah, (e) Casey, (f) James.

4 (b) Miller Parks m. 1st. ———— Van Pelt. Issue:
5. (a) Joseph, (b) Rebecca, 2nd. Sarah Robb. Issue, (a) George, (d) Robert, (e) Frances, (f) Elizabeth, (g) Eliza.

(e) Frances Parks m. ———— Burdoff.

(f) Elizabeth m. Jack Ferguson.

(g) Eliza m. Jesse Hall. Issue, (a) Robert (b) Earnest.

(c) Nannie m. William Trotter.

(d) Mary m. Ebra Frazier.

(e) Jennie m. 1st, Rufus Hood, 2nd. Charlie Sheets.

(f) Carrie m. Harold Cousins.
(g) Byrd m. William Grant.
(h) Arch m. May Holloway.
(a) Robert m. Mary Watson.
(b) Earnest m. Grace Hill.
(i) Frank, (j) John, (k) Stanley.

5 (a) Eugene, son of Elizabeth and Gideon Johnson m. Grace Brown. Issue: (a) Eugene, (b) Jack, (c) Nell (d) Betty
5 (b) Samuel m. Anna Childress.
5 (c) Gideon m. Neal Cleveland.
5 (d) Beulah m John R. Bradley.

THE HISTORY OF ROANE COUNTY

PATTON

1. David b. in Rockbridge Co., Va. Aug. 31, 1789 m. 1809 Elizabeth Purris, b. April 22, 1791 in same country.

2. Issue, (a) Teresa Rebecca, (b) John Purris, (c) Nancy McClung, (b) Jane McDowell, (e) Willia, (f) David (g) Samuel.

(c) Nancy McClung m. John Columbus McEwen, Dec. 11, 1832. (See McEwen).

2. (d) Jane McDowell m. Rev. Thomas Brown. (See Brown).

2 (e) William Steele m. Adelia Martin.
2 (b) John Purris m. Mary Winston.
2 (a) Teresa Rebecca m. Samuel Hall Smith.
2 (f) David Emmerson m. ———
2. (g) Samuel Fisk m.———————.

Children of John Purris and Mary Winston.
3 (a) Purris.
3 (b) Elizabeth m. Major ——— Ellis.
3 (c) John P. m. 1886 Mary Malvina Lea b. 1868.
3. (d) Nannie M. m. Richard Neerguard.
3 (e) James m. 1st. ———————. 2nd. Burns.
3 (f) Theresa m. ——— Newton.
3 (g) Minnie.

Children of Theresa and ——— Newton.
4 (a) John, (b) Richard Y., (c) Mary, (d) Theresa, (e) William, (f) Winston, (g) Ruth.

Children of John P. and Mary Lea.
4 (a) Eugene Byrd b. 1887 m. 1912 Myrtle Marie Tedder. Issue 5 (a) John Morris, (b) Eugene Byrd, Jr., (c) Marie Tedder.

4 (b) Mary Virginia b. 1889 m. 1911 Alfred J. Baker. Issue, 5 (a) May Patton, (b) John Goodwin.

4 (c) Minnie Overton b. 1891 m. Daniel Oscar Harris. Issue, Daniel Overton.

4. (d) George Earnest b. 1892, m. 1914 Virginia Lea. Issue: (a) Virginia, (b) Baxter C.

4 (e) Rose Frances b. 1898 m. Van Stowe Pickel. Issue: (a) Marie, (b) Nancy Stove.

4 (f) Ruth Lea b. 1906.

Children of Nannie Patton and Richard Neerguard.

4 (a) William, (b) John, (c) Frederick, (d) Ralph.

5 (a) William m. Caroline Young. Issue: 5 (a) Richard (b) Carl, (c) Ruth.

4 (b) John m. Miss Abel. Issue: 5 (a) John T., (b) Forest, (c) Lester, (d) Pauline.

4. (c) Frederick m. Miss Runyon.

4. (d) Ralph m. Lillie Pickle. 5. Issue: Mary Winston, (b) Ralph, (c) Grace, (d) Nancy.

THE HISTORY OF ROANE COUNTY

PRATER

1. Benjamine Franklin b. Apr. 30, 1772 m. Nov. 6, 1798 Nancy E. Lane and moved to Roane Co. the same year. Issue:

2 (a) Samuel b. Oct. 14, 1800, (b) Thomas b. 1801, (c) Elizabeth b. Nov. 12, 1805, (d) George b. ——, (e) Letitia b. ——, (f) Clarisa b. ——, (g) William b. July 23, 1811.

2 (b) Thomas, son of Benjamine m. Julia, dau. of John Browder. Issue:

3 (a) Darius, b. July 5, 1822, d. Feb. 26, 1846.
3 (b) Nancy Elizabeth b. 1824.
3 (c) Benjamine b. Oct. 8, 1826.
3 (d) John Jefferson b. Oct. 17, 1828.
3 (e) James Madison b. May 16, 1831.
3 (f) William Alexander b. Apr. 9, 1834, d. Sept. 7, 1863.

3 (b) Nancy Elizabeth, dau. of Thomas and Julia m. 1st Nov. 28, 1844, James Leeper b. Jan. 18, 1818. Issue:

4 (a) Julia Ann Malinda b. Jan. 3, 1846, d. Mar. 14, 1926, m. Feb. 12, 1862, 1st. C. P. Bussell, 2nd. T. C. Foster.

4 (b) Elizabeth dau. of Nancy and James Leeper b. Sept. 29, 1847, m. Feb. 21, 1866, M. B. Carter. Issue, 11 daus. 2 sons

4 (c) James Madison Leeper, b. Aug. 10, 1849, d. Jan. 15, 1919, m. Jan. 3, 1871 Myra Foster, b. Jan. 6, 1846, d. 1908.

2 (a) Elizabeth, dau. of Benjamine and Nancy Eliza m. George Alexander Lisle.

2 (e) Letitia, dau. of Benjamin and Nancy Eliza, m. James Danforth.

2 (f) Clarissa, dau. of Benjamin and Nancy Eliza, m. Josiah Johnson.

2 (g) William, son of Benjamin and Nancy Eliza, m. Mary Blair Leeper.

Issue of Julia Leeper and G. P. Russell.
4. (a) Thomas, (b) Frank.
Issue of Julia Leeper and T. C. Foster.
4 (c) Elizabeth, (d) James Edward, (e) Henry C., (f) Ann Elizabeth.

THE HISTORY OF ROANE COUNTY

Issue of James M. and Myra Leeper.

4 (a) Julia E. Rebecca b. Sept. 14, 1871 m. Dec. 12, 1893 Allison Montcastle, (a) Sarah, (b) Myra, (c) Inez, (d) James L.

4 (b) Lucy Amanda b. Feb. 4, 1873 m. Dec. 12, 1893 W. A. Logan. Issue, 5 (a) James Leeper, (b) Edward, (c) Elizabeth T., (d) Annie M. T., (e) Martha.

4 (c) James Thomas b. July 3, 1877 m. Nov. 11, 1903 Annie Foster, b. May 23, 1879. Issue, 5 (a) James Avery, (b) Randolph Foster.

4 (d) Nancy Myra b. Jan. 8, 1880 m. Nov. 5, 1919 S. I. Yarnell. Issue: Samuel I.

3 (f) William, a son of Thomas and Julia m. Mary Bussell, b. April 27, 1840, d. Nov. 1, 1881. Issue, 4 (a) Cordelia.

3 (c) Benjamin Franklin m. Amanda Pitner. Issue, 4 (a) Willia, (b) Lelia, (c) Elizabeth (Betty), (d) Roy.

3 (d) John Jefferson m. Margaret Simpson.

3 (e) James Madison m. Adelia Carter, Issue, Josephine, who m. W. F. Foute.

4 (a) William, son of Benjamin and Amanda m. ——— Freeman. Issue, Benjamin.

4 (b) Lelia, dau. of Benjamin and Amanda m. John F. Monning. Issue, 5 (a) Louise, (b) Benjamin, (c) John.

4 (c) Elizabeth (Betty) dau. of Benjamin and Amanda m. Mel Chambers. Issue, 5 (a) Maud, (b) Prater, (c) Katherine.

4 (c) Elizabeth, dau. of Julia Leeper and T. C. Foster m. W. N. Lacey. Issue, 5 (a) Linnie, (b) Foster, (c) W. N., Jr., (d) Annie Elizabeth.

4 (d) James Edward, son of Julia and T. C. Foster, m. Beulah Montgomery. Issue, 5 (a) Helen, (b) Julia Margaret. Margaret.

4 (e) Henry C., son of Julia and T. C. Foster m. Mattie Dyer. Issue, 5 (a) Thomas, (b) Mary Lynn, (c) Henry, (d) Martha.

(f) Annie Elizabeth, dau. of Julia and T. C. Foster, m. E. R. Callaway. Issue, 5 (a) Edgar, (b) Foster, (c) Thomas, (d) Hugh.

5 (a) Linnie, dau. of Elizabeth F. and W. N. Lacey m. Martin Moore.

5 (b) Foster son of Elizabeth F., and W. N. Lacey m. Frances Jackson.

5 (c) W. N., son of Elizabeth F. and W. N. Lacey m. Mattie May Falkner.

5 (a) Sarah, dau. of Julia Leeper and Allison Montcastle m. D. K. Young. Issue.

6 (a) Sarah, (b) Woodson, (c) Julia.

5 (b) Myra, dau. of Julia and Allison Montcastle m. Robert T. Griffitts.

5 (c) Inez, dau. of Julia and Allison Montcastle m. Joseph Long.

Children of William and Mary Leeper Prater.

3 (a) James Alexander m. Artie Alexander. Issue.

4 (a) William Berry, (b) Carrie, (c) George W., (d) James Thomas, (e) Edgar P., (f) Joseph Lloyd, (g) Louella, (h) Herbert A., (i) James E.

4 (a) William Berry m. Mary M. Dorton. Issue, Carrie.

4 (d) James Thomas m. ——— ———. Issue.

5 (a) Louella, (b) Eugene.

4 (e) Edgar P. m. Mayme Chapman. Issue, 5 (a) Artie, (b) Myrtle, (c) Winona, (d) Edgar P., (e) Loyd.

4 (f) Joseph Lloyd m. Garley Cox. Issue, 5 (a) Henry Clayton, (b) Pauline m. ——Cox, (c) Mayme.

4 (g) Louella m. John Valley McKnight. Issue, Mary Margaret.

4 (h) Herbert Alexander m. Katherine Cox. Issue, 5 (a) Willie May, (b) Helen Gertrude, (c) Artie Elizabeth.

4 (i) James Eugene m. Effie Mae Wood.

3 (b) Hugh Blair, son of William and Mary Leeper Prater m. Mollie Lee.

3 (c) George William, son of William and Mary L., m. Elizabeth Brooks.

THE HISTORY OF ROANE COUNTY

RANDOLPH

William Randolph was born in Virginia and came to Roane Co. in 1809. He was a Lieutenant in the Revolutionary War. Married Louisa, daughter of Gamaliel Bailey. William Randolph, 5, Grief 4, Henry 3, Henry 2, Henry 1st.) b. 1754 d. 1815 m. 1782 Louisa Bailey. Issue. (a) Robert m.Jemima. ? (b) William m. Dorcas—— (c) Elihu m. Polly Garrett, (d) Hezekiah, (e) Sarah m. Samuel Sumpter Owings, (f) Abigail m. William Edward Owings, (g) Rebecca m. ———— Swann.

William Randolph, son of William and Louisa (Bailey) Randolph, b. 1796 d. 1881 m. Dorcas ——b. 1895 d. 1859 Issue: (a) Mahala b. 1816 m. ——Slaughter, (b) Sarah Dorinda b. 1818, (c) Gilbert A. m. 1838 Sarah Dorinda Myers, d. 1885, (d) Gilmore b. 1822 m. 1837 Mary Brookster b. 1825, d. 1884, (e) Malinda m. Thomas Williams, (f) Gillam C. m. 1858 Hester Modena Washburn, (g) Malissa m. Eli Dixon d. 1859.

ROBINSON

1. Thomas b. in Virginia 1789 m. July 28, 1811 Sarah King, b. in Kentucky in 1788, dau. of Major Robert King, U. S. A. officer. Thomas' two brothers were John W. and James Robinson. Issue of Thomas and Sarah:

2 (a) James R., (b) Fannie, (c) Elizabeth, (d) Susan, (e) Nancy, (f) Mary, (g) Minerva, (h) John W., (i) Robert King.

2 (a) James R. b. 1824 m. Sarah Smith b. 1827. Issue, 3 (a) Robert King b. 1849 m. Texie Hunt. Issue, 4 (a) Auria, (b) Robert, (c) Bertie.

2 (b) Fannie m. Samuel Lane.

2 (c) Susan m. 1st. Mayo. 2nd. Lewis.

2 (e) Nancy m. James C. Haskins.

2 (f) Mary m. E. D. Robinson.

2 (g) Minerva m. William Robinson.

2 (h) John W. b. Jan. 17, 1829 m. 1853 Mary M. Smith.

THE HISTORY OF ROANE COUNTY

SENTER

1. Tandy a Rev. Sol. b. in Virginia 1761 d. Jan. 1865 age 103, 7 mos. m. 1st. Susan Lyon. Issue, 6 children. 2nd. m. Mary Ann Crumbliss. Issue 6 children. He settled near Blue Spring Creek at Cardiff near the old Indian trace. It is said that he m. a Carson for whom Carson-Newman College was named and that Mrs. Carson Senter d. and was buried in what is now Hembree graveyard. Some of his children were William T., one daughter, m. Elliott Graves, one m. William Barnett, Minerva m. Sept. 3, 1840 William Margraves, one m. ———— Rice, Seaborn, Abner. One m. ————Mee.

2. William T. b. in Grainger Co., Tenn. 1800 d. 1847, m. Nancy White b. 1813. Issue (a) Clinton Dewitt, (b) Susan Sarah, (c) Lucinda, (d) Mary Eliza, (e) Rebecca, (f) Nancy, (g) William T.

3 (a) Clinton Dewitt b. Mar. 26, 1830 m. Sept. 1, 1859 Harriett T., dau. of P. M. Senter. He was Gov. of Tenn. 1867-71.

3 (b) Susan Sarah m. Joseph P. Conway. Issue, 4 (a) Sarah Porter, (b) Nancy, (c) William, (d) Charles, (e) Joseph, (f) Dewitt, (g) Edward.

3 (d) Ann Eliza m. George M. Murrell. Issue, 4 (a) Martha, (b) Ada, (c) ———.

3 (e) Rebecca m. George Hodges.

3 (f) Nancy m. John H. Everett. Issue, 4 (a) Wilmer, (b) Robert, (c) Sallie.

3 (g) William T. m. May Mayo. Issue, (a) Dewitt, (b) Nancy, (c) Rebecca, (d) Harriett, (e) William.

2. Seaborn, son of Tandy m. August 28, 1817 Nancy Carson. Issue, 3 (a) Albert N. m. 1st. Katherine L. Meek. Issue, 4 (a) Thomas N., (b) Carrie A. 2nd. Elizabeth Longley. Issue, (c) John, (d) Frances, (e) Marcus.

4 (a) Thomas N. b. Feb. 15, 1858 m. March 30, 1883, Dora Smith b. 1863.

4 (b) Carrie m. William Rape. Issue, William.

4 (c) John F. m. Mary Trevitte.

4 (d) Frances m. Richard Prince.

4 (e) Marcus m. Rosabelle Finzer. 5 (a) Marcus, (b) Nicholas.

Children of Thomas N. and Dora Senter.
5 (a) William Robert m. Marchie Love.
5 (b) Carl Lee.
5 (c) Lester Treadway.
5 (d) Thomas Smith.
5 (e) Leland R. m. Thelma Russell.
5 (f) Anita.

Dose Mee, a grandson of Tandy Senter, was married five times and had between twenty-five and thirty children.

THE HISTORY OF ROANE COUNTY

SEVIER

1. Elbridge Gerry, son of James, son of Gen. John, b. March 19, 1805 m. Nov. 13, Mary Caroline Brown, b. Feb. 27, 1810. Issue.

2 (a) Thomas Brown b. Sept. 16, 1828.

2 (b) Henry Clay b. July 16, 1831 d. at Liberty, Mo., 1918, m. Mary J. Tipton, Dec. 19, 1853. Issue, 3 (a) Elizabeth b. 1856, (b) William James, b. 1858 m. Mary McGuinness. Issue, 4 (a) Herbert Eugene b. 1885, (m. Grace Muriel). Issue, (a) Jean, (b) Alice, (c) Mary, (d) John Woodrow, (e) Mary Elizabeth, (f) Hazel, (g) Madeline, (h) Parker.

4 (b) Roy, b. 1887 (m. Lois Froman), (c) Oscar b. 1877 (m. Vivian Ritter). 4 (a) Ethel b. 1891 (m. Kellar Bell), 4 (e) Stella b. 1872 (m. Frank Jackson), 4 (f) Robert Earl b. 1895 (m. Virginia Kendrick), 4 (g) Anna Bernice, 4 (h) Hazel Madeline.

3 (c) Robert E. b. 1865 (m. May Waddell). Issue, 4 (a) Helen May, (b) Roberta Ann, (c) Charles Sevier b. 1867 (m. Elizabeth Talboy). Issue 4 (a) Charles Henry, (b) Robert Fields.

2 (c) Rowena Jane b. May 14, 1832, m. Henry W. Von Aldehoff. Issue 3 (a) Florence Carolina b. July 2, 1851 (m. Thomas Augustus Hurt). Issue 4 (a) Augusta m. Frederick T. Mosely., (b) John Sevier b. Sept. 2, 1852, (c) Alice Eugenia b. Jan. 13, 1855, (d) John Sevier. 2nd. b. Sept. 14, 1856. (e) Blanch, b. April 10, 1859.

2 (d) James b. August 1, 1835, d. 1908.

2 (e) Elbert Franklin b. Dec. 25, 1843 m. Bettie Taylor. Issue, (a) Taylor, (b) Evelyn (m. Gray Gentry). Issue, Fenton Allen.

2 (f) Samuel Conway b. Nov. 7, 1848, d. 1923.

2 (g) Ann Elizabeth b. Nov. 7, 1848 m. Noah Lybarger.

2 (h) Charles Bascom b. Nov. 12, 1856 m. Alice Zedder. Issue, Mary Katherine m. Thomas F. Reimer.

THE HISTORY OF ROANE COUNTY

SHELLY

1. Jacob D. b. at Guilford C. H., North Carolina 1798, m. Polly, dau. of James Craven, Hawkins Co., Tenn. Issue, (a) James Thomas.

2 (a) James Thomas m. 1850 Martha Jane McElwee, b. Aug. 12, 1832. Issue, (a) Jacob Oscar, (b) William Carlyle b. 1854, (c) George McElwee, b. 1857, (d) Robert Cravens, b. 1860, James Thomas, b. 1868.

3 (c) George McElwee m. Mary Alice Adkinson. Issue, (a) J. Osgood, m. Melissa Hopkins, (b) Robb'e, m. Edward A. Warwick, (c) George M. m. Clara Goodman, (d) Roy C. m. Emma Genereski, (e) Grace D. m. Greenwood B. Davis, (f) Oliver F., (g) Ruby, (h) Jane Ann, m. Charles T. Culbert, (i) Jean, m. Robert A. Schaad.

3 (d) Robert Craven, (b) 1860 m. Mary Lillian Fay. Issue, (a) Fay, (b) Ethel, 4 (a) Fay m. Elmer Rule, Issue (a) Shelly, (b) Fay.

4 (b) Ethel m. William Robert Piatt. Issue, (a) Robert, (b) Sara.

3 (a) Jacob Oscar b. Oct. 11, 1851 m. Minnie Lelia Hyatt, of Macon, Co., N. C. Issue, (a) Jennie Weaver, who m. Edareth Edward Teague, (b) James Hyatt, m. Kathleen Gribble, (c) Martha Elizabeth m. Clarence Bell Hipp, (d) Oscar Barnette m. Wilhelmina Christina Avery, (e) Robert Long m. Gladys Howard, (f) William Bays m. Lucy Ward, (g) Mary Lelia.

3 (b) William Carly'e m. Nannie Roberts. Issue, (a) Carlyle, (b) Larla, (c) Tully m. Hazel ———. Issue, (a) Tully, Jr.

4. Issue of Jennie W. and E. F. Teague.
(a) Edareth, Jr., (b) Shelley, (c) Seth Woodrow.

4. Issue of Martha E. and Clarence B. Hipp.
(a) Elizabeth Shelley, Clarence Bell, Jr.

4. Issue of Robert and Gladys, (a) Robert Tunsford.

THE HISTORY OF ROANE COUNTY

SIENKNECHT

Dr. Frederick Sienknecht, b. Feb. 1st, 1803 Preetz in Holstein, Germany d. July 16th. 1883 Wartburg, Tenn.

Katherine Heik, 1st. wife b. May 10th, 1812 Ploen, Germany d. Oct. 6th. 1853 Wartburg, Tenn.

Children all b. in Preetz.
1. Theodore F. b. Oct. 17th. 1833 d. May 26th. 1915.
2. Augusta Charlotte b. 1835 d. 1891.
3. Henry Christian Ludwig b. March 1st. 1838 d. May 25th. 1916.
4. Wilhelmina Katherine b. Sept. 6th. 1840 d. Dec. 11th. 1914.
5. Christina H. M. b. April 2d. 1845 d. Jan. 3rd. 1900.
6. Charles Christian b. Oct. 18th. 1841 d. Jan. 12th. 1920.

Theodore F. Sienknecht m. 1st Charlotte Oliver Sept. 1860 d. May 24th. 1889. Children: Mary Katherine m. Rev. W. B. Brown, Sarah Augusta, Jackson Oliver, Frederick and Christine (Twins).

Theodore F. Sienknecht m. 2nd. Matilda Adelaide Muecke Dec. 23rd. 1869. Children: Frederica Christine, b. 1870, d. 1916 m. William C. Denton, Joseph Augustus m. Mamie Richards June 9th, 1909, Theodore Adolphus m. Marguerite Albright Dec. 21st, 1903, Hannah, Willie Henrietta Florence m. B. H. Phillips, Oct. 8th, 1907, Louie Christian, Henry Edward, Elmer Charles, m. Mattie Houston Gallaher April 9th., 1911, Adele Elizabeth.

Augusta Charlotte Sienknecht m. Herman A. Kaiser, b. 1820 d. 1907. Children: Minnie, Theodore, Gustave, Henry O., Fred C., Albert, Nannie, Edward.

Dr. Henry Christian Ludwig Sienkhecht m. Oct. 18th., 1868 Barbara Ann Tadlock, b. Jan. 8th. 1849 d. June 25th., 1718. Children:

James Theodore m. Margaret Prater.
Nettie m. Joseph Richards.
Frederick m. Eula Paul.
Daisy m. Dr. J. T. Haynes.

THE HISTORY OF ROANE COUNTY

William Henry m. Nancy Bray.

Lula Jane.

Wilhelmine Katherine Sienknecht b. Sept. 6th. 1840 Preetz, Germany d. Dec. 11th, 1914 Collinsville, Ala. m. Oct. 17th. 1859 Oscar Benno Carl von Steinwehr b. Aug. 22d. 1823 Wesel on the Rhine d. Dec. 1st. 1900. Came to Roane Co. 1848. Children:

1. Charlie Frederick b. July 23, 1860 Kingston m. Grace Rex. Sept. 28, 1900 d. May 13th. 1923 Los Angeles, California.

2. Mary C.

3. Lizzie M., m. Dec. 26th. 1889 Virgil M. Brindley.

4. Oscar.

5. Alice H. m. Sept. 26th. 1893 John D. Avery.

6. Annie C. m May 2d. 1900 Jasper Hazen Wilson.

Dr. Charles Christian Sienknecht b. Oct. 18th. 1841, Preetz, Germany d. Jan. 12th. 1920 m. Dec. 3d. 1885 Amanda Pettyjohn of Va. Children:

Margaret m. Charles A. Lotz, Sept. 25th. 1925.

Mary Lila m. J. H. Riddle March 8th, 1920.

Children of Alice Steinwehr and John Dixie Avery.
1. Wilma (m. Oscar Shelley.)
2. Allen, 3. Nealey, 4. Bess, 5. Mary.

THE HISTORY OF ROANE COUNTY

MERRIWEATHER SMITH

Col. Francis Smith, b. in Essex Co., Va. Va. m. Lucy, dau. of Capt. Francis Merriweather, Clerk of Essex Co. 1692. Issue, (a) Merriweather, (b) Eliza, (c) Mary.

2 (a) Merriweather b. 1730 at Bathurst, Essex Co. m. 1st. 1760 Alice, dau. of Phillips Lee, of Maryland. Issue:

3 (a) George, (b) Merriweather, Jr. b. 1769 in Louisa Co., Va. d. June 27, 1838.

3 (b) Merriweather m. June 9, 1796 Sally, dau. of William and Mary Payne, of Fluvanna Co., Va. b. D c. 19, 1772, d. April 27, 1847.

4 (a) Granville Payne b. June 9, 1797 in Grassy Valley, Knox Co., (b) Wiliam P., b. July 6, 1798 at the same place, d. May 2, 1847, (c) Merriweather, Jr. b. July 6, 1800 at Headquarters of 4th U. S. Reg. Southwest Point., (d) John Young, b. April 30, 1802, (e) George Washington, b. Feb. 22, 1804, (f) Letitia b. March 18, 1806, (g) Samuel Hall and Mary Ann Clark b. Feb. 25, 1807, (h) Thomas Jefferson b. Sept. 5, 1809, (i) Susannah Payne b. Feb. 24, 1812, (j) Sally Josephine.

4 (b) William Payne m. Eliza Jane Wiley. Issue. Mary.

4 (d) John Young m. Leah Lenoir. Issue, (a) Caroline m. 1st. F. G. Correy,, 2nd. John A. Winton, (b) Merriweather, (c) William, (d) John Ashby, (e) El'zabeth (f) Laura Waightstill, (g) Samuel, (h) Maria, (i) George, (j) Thomas, (k) Susan.

4 (g) Samuel Hall m. Teresa Patton. Issue, (a) Mary.

4 (g) Maryann m. Oct. 16, 1828 Alexander Black, b. Oct. 25, 1804, son of Samuel and Mary Gordon Black. Issue.

5 (a) Samuel, (b) John, (c) Susan, (d) Thomas, (e) Mary Louisa. (f) Robert, (g) Alexander, (h) Merriweather.

4 (j) Sallie Josephine m. William Doyle. Issue, William Payne, Jr. who m. Jane Mitchell.

5 (a) Mary, dau. of W. P. and Eliza Jane Smith m. J. H. Vanderson.

5 (a) Mary, dau. of Samuel and Teresa Smith m. James Preston Smartt.

THE HISTORY OF ROANE COUNTY

5 (a) Samuel, son of Alexander and Maryann Clark Smith m. Eliza Latham Rowan.

5 (b) John, son of Alexander m Sophia Greenwood.

5 (c) Thomas, son of Alexander m. Emma Jean Young, (b) Mary Alice, (c) John Y, (d) Sarah Colville, (e) Susan Louise, (f) Emma Y., (g) Thomas Alexander, (h) Clara Josephine, (i) Leah Lee, (j) Georgia Ruth.

5 (d) Robert, son of Alex B. and wife, m. Ida Mandelbaum.

5 (e) Mary Louise Black m. Rena Hall Mason.

5 (f) Alexander, Jr. m. Martha Luck.

6 (e) Susan Louise Black m. Dr. Morris Clayton Leonard, Oct. 25, 1904. Issue, (a) Jean Young, (b) Richard Black, (c) Nancy Emmet.

Note: The Bible records of Merriweather and Sally Smith show that all of their children born in Roane Co. were christened by the Rev. John Winton.

JACOB SMITH

1. Jacob Smith, born in Washington Co., Md., served in Capt. Jacob Saren's Co. War of the Revolution. m. Mollie Dugger, 1766.
2. Ezekiel Lafayette, b. 1789 m. Nancy Doran.
3. Daniel b. 1821 m. Rachel Edmondson.
4. William Wiley b. 1848 m. Mary Montgomery.
5. (a) Elbert Doran, son of William W. m. Nell Fleming. Children ———.
5 (b) Willie Carolyn, dau. of William W. m. Rev. J. L. Mullens.
5 (c) Laura Frances, dau. of William W. m. 1915 Elbert F. Campbell. Children, (a) Frances Parker.
5 (d) Ezekiel Jackson, son of William W. m. Kate Leeper. Issue, Jacqueline.
5 (e) Robert Ashford, son of W. W. m. Willie Dickey. Issue, 6 (a) Martha, (b) Sarah Elizabeth, (c).

THE HISTORY OF ROANE COUNTY

JOHN SMITH

1. John came to Roane Co. from Virginia 1790.
2. Anthony born in Va. came to Roane Co. when a child. m. Anna Bailey, b. in Blount Co. about 1787 who also came to Roane when a child. Issue.
3. William Smith m. 1863 Mary Elizabeth Owings. Issue: (a) James Edward b. 1868, (b) Fedelia b. 1871

James Edward Smith m. Ella Ervin 1898 Issue (a) Ervin James, b. 1901, (b) Mary Edna b. 1902.

THE HISTORY OF ROANE COUNTY

STAPLES

1. John, came from England, was Capt. in Revolutionary War under Gen. Washington. Was promoted to rank of Major 14th Regt., Va. Came to Roane Co. from Virginia in 1810. Issue, (a) William, (b) Thomas, (c) Abner, (d) Benjamin Tolliver, (e) John M., (f) Malinda. All born in Richmond,, Va.

2 (c) Abner m. May 6, 1818 Ellery Toomey.

2 (d) Benjamin T. m. Elizabeth Hall.

2 (e) John M. m. Dec. 10, 1818 Polly Bryant.

3. Samuel, son of Benjamin and Elizabeth b. 1841 m. Mary, dau. of John and Mary (Bowling) Childress. Issue, 4 (a) Samuel, (b) John, (c) William, (d) Thomas.

3. Abner m. Malinda Davis.

3. Malinda m. Charles Davis.

Children of Abner and Malinda Davis.

4 (a) Eliza, (b) John M., (c) Joseph, (d) Mary, (e) William, (f) Susan.

4 (a) Eliza m. John Cagel. Issue, 5 (a) Joseph, (b) Sadie.

4 (b) John M. m. 1st. Ruth Duncan. Issue, 5 (a) Melinda, (b) Joseph, (c) Mary, (d) Ella, (e) Walter. 2nd. ——Morgan. Issue, (f) Katherine, (g) Anna.

4. (b) Sadie, dau. of Eliza and John Cagel m. Robert E. Runger.

4 (d) Mary m. John H. Blake. (See Blake).

5. (a) Malinda, dau. of John M. and Ruth m. Richard Purcell.

5. (f) Katherine, dau. of John m. David Black.

4 (g) Anna, dau. of John M. m Fred Beneger. **Issue,** (a) Orton.

2 (b) Thomas m. ——. Issue.

3 (b) John, son of Samuel 1 m. Mamie Smith.

3. (a) William m. —— Fuller.

3 (c) Annie.

3 (d) Walter.

THE HISTORY OF ROANE COUNTY

TEDDER

The first records of the Tedder family are found in North Carolina, where Thomas Tedder married a Brown, he died and she came to Roane County with her five children.

2. (a) James b. in Greene Co., North Carolina, m. Feb. 1821 Elizabeth Todd in Roane Co.

2. (b) John Brown Tedder b. 1789, d. 1862, m. Feb. 4, Mary Robbinson b. 1796 d.1872. Issue:

3. (a) Minerva b. 1820, d. 1884.
3. (b) Spencer J. b. 1821, d. 1904, m. 1883 Sallie Gillespie b. 1846.
3. (c) John Brown.
3. (d) Martha Jane, b. 1831, d. 1896.
3. (e) Sallie M. b. 1838, d. 1896.

4. (c) John Brown Tedder b. 1828 d. 1913 m. 1861 Sarah Jane Shadden b. 1844 d. 1913. Issue:

(a) Eugene Spencer m. Annie Campbell.
(b) John Vaden.
(c) Joseph Clyde.
(d) William Wiley m. 1898 Cora Waterman.
(e) Charles Thomas m. 1900 Callie Ingram.
(f) Robert Gideon.

Eugene Spencer Tedder, son of John B. and Sarah J. (Shadden) Tedder b. 1862 m. 1884 Annie Campbell b. 1863. Issue:
Robert L.
Nellie Gray.
John Brown.
William Rush.

Robert L. Tedder, son of Eugene S. and Annie (Campbell) Tedder b. 1886 m. Florence Koger. Issue:
Ethna Madge.

Ethna Madge Tedder, dau. of Robert L. and Florence (Koger) Tedder, m. Ed Moore. Issue.
Ewell.
Robert L.

John Brown Tedder, son of Eugene S. and Annie (Campbell) Tedder b. 1896 m. Agnes Roberts. Issue:
Charlotte June.

John Vadden Tedder, son of John B. and Sarah J. (Shadden) Tedder b. 1866, d. 1927, m. 1891 Hester Ingram. Issue:
Addie Florence.
Hazel.
Elisha Ingram.
Hilda Rose.

Joseph Clyde Tedder, son of John B. and Sarah J. (Shadden) Tedder, b. 1866, m. 1893 Nora Hill. Issue:
Thomas C.
Sadie E. m. Fred Lamb.

Thomas C. Tedder, son of Joseph C. and Nora (Hill) Tedder. m. Ruth La Rue. Issue:
Robert La Rue.
Kenneth Allen.
Charles Richard.

Charles Thomas Tedder, son of John B. and Sarah J. (Shadden) Tedder b. 1875 m. 1900 Callie Ingram. Issue:
Clifford.

Robert Gideon Tedder, son of John B. and Sarah J. (Shadden) Tedder m. 1918, Carrie King. Issue:
Sarah Louise.
Veneta.
Robert Gideon.

3. (c) Sarah, dau. of John and Mary m. Joseph A. Shadden. Issue. (a) Mary, (b) Annie (c) Ernest B., (d) Joseph C.

4. (a) Mary m. Joseph E. Clark. Issue, (a) Maud (b) Joseph.

4. (b) Annie m. Isaac Milligan. Issue, (a) Hilda, (b) Helen, (c) Virginia, (d) Ernest, (e) Sarah.

4. (c) Ernest B. m. Lillie E. Black. Issue 5 (a) Ernest B. Jr., m. Dora Alden, (b) William N., (c) Mary E., (d) Vaden C., (e) Joseph J.

THE HISTORY OF ROANE COUNTY

4. (d) Joseph C. m. Alma Hamby. Issue: 5 (a) Spencer, (b) Florence, (c) Alma.
   5. (a) Hilda m. L. Jack Spence.
   5. (c) Virginia m. Charles Erskine.

Maria L. Tedder m. Oct. 20, 1863 Morgan B. Hawkins.

George, son of Pleasant m. Julia Denton. Issue:
- (a) Della m. John R. Cowan. Issue John R., Jr.
- (b) Charles m. Nancy Taylor, Issue: Janice.
- (c) Ralph m. Reece Parker.
- (d) Edith m. J. R. Zigenfuss. Issue: Dorothy.
- (e) Sue m. Harold Whitson.
- (f) George W.
- (g) Ray.
- (h) Bruce.

THE HISTORY OF ROANE COUNTY

VAN DYKE

1. Thomas James b. in Dover Delaware 1777. Studied Medicine in Baltimore,, graduating in 1799. Was appointed an ensign in United States Infantry and later promoted to Captain. Was stationed at South West Point, Roane County where he married Penelope Smith, dau. of Judge David Campbell. Later he lived in Kingston and was one of the first Trustees of Rittenhouse Academy. 1806 was appointed from Roane Co., as Trustee of East Tennessee College Knoxville. His children born in Roane Co., were. (a) Alexander Outlaw, b. Jan. 16, 1800, (b) Jefferson Campbell b. Jan 16, 1801, d. 1862, (c) Thomas Nixon, b. Jan. 22, 1803, (d) Mary Houston, b. 1805, (e) Eliza Rhea b. 1807.

Alexander Outlaw enlisted in the Navy and was lost at sea.

Jefferson Campbell m. Eliza Cook.

Thomas Nixon m. Eliza Ann Deaderick.

Mary Houston m. Gen. William Smith, of Huntington, Penn. Settled at Mineral Point, Wis.

Eliza Rhea, m. ———— Scott, Laurence Co., Ala.

In 1811 Thomas James removed to Washington, Rhea Co., to practice medicine. He was appointed a surgeon in the army under Gen. Daugherty and went on two campaigns, 1813-14, against the Indians. Died in 1814 while in camp at Fort Claiborne, Ala.

THE HISTORY OF ROANE COUNTY

WALLER

1. John b. 1617 of Virginia m. Mary Key Issue: (a) John, (b) William.
2. (a) John m. Dorothy King.
2. (b) William b. in Henry Co., Va. Sept. 24, 1671. Issue: George and others.

(3) George, Issue, (4) George, Jr., b. 1734 m. Anne Winston Carr, b. 1733. Issue: (a) John, (b) Mary, (c) Elizabeth Anne, (d) George, (e) Edmund, (f) William, George, Jr. was given 1000 acres of land (for his services during Revolutionary War) on the Clinch River opposite Paw Paw Ford. He gave it to his son William, who settled on it in 1802.

5. (a) William b. in Henry Co., Va. 1781 m. 1802 Mary Barksdale, b. in same Co. May 6, 1783.

6. Issue, (a) John B. b. Nov. 28, 1803, (b) George b. June 25, 1805, (c) Carr. b. Feb. 22, 1807, (d) William b. Feb. 20, 1809, (e) Sarah, b. Feb. 20, 1811, (f) Anna W., b. Mar. 30, 1813, (g) Mary b. Mar. 2, 1815, (h) Edmond, b. Mar. 1, 1817, (i) Henry b. 1819.

William, Sr. died in 1819, his wife in 1863.

(a) John B. m. Katy Pickel. Issue 6 sons, 7 daughters.

7. (a) P. A. oldest daughter m. William Mounger and settled in Missouri about 1852.

7. (b) Mary Jane m. John H. Davaney.

7. (c) Elizabeth E. m. Abner L. Dickey and moved to Dodd City, Texas.

7. (d) Henry A. m. Sophrona Dickey.

7. (e) J. L. m. Amanda Steele, lives in Roane Co.

7. (f) Sarah K. m. John C. Jones, lives in Roane Co.

7. (g) Carr M. m. Ann Mounger lives in Dodd City, Texas.

7. (h) Martha C. m. William Raybourn, lives in Famir Co., Texas.

7. (i) Eliza W. m. Samuel Talliaferro, lives in Indian Territory.

7. (j) Amanda Savannah m. William Jones, lives in Missouri.

THE HISTORY OF ROANE COUNTY

6. (b) George, second son of William and Mary, m. Mariah Butler. Issue, (a) Jesse M., (b) Manly B., (c) Thomas J., (d) Jacob C., (e) Texas J., (f) Nancy D., (g) Mary K., (h) Martha A., (i) Elizabeth E.

7. (g) Mary K. m. ——— Delaney, (h) Martha m. Simpson. All of this family moved west.

6. (c) Carr m. Keziah Eblen. Issue: (a) William, who married Caroline Amos and moved to the State of Washington, (b) Lewis m. Alpha Goodwin, (c) Hardin m. Eliza Elkins, (d) James, (e) John, (f) George m. Sarah A. Reed, (g) Mary m. Henry Holston, (h) Sarah m. Jack Pickel, (i) Eliza, (j) America m. Peter W. Goodwin, (k) Matilda, m. Gen. Ballew, 2nd. Robert Waller, (l) Margaret m. George P. Waller.

6. (d) William m. Mary Siler and moved to Bay County, Mo., thence to California. Issue, Louis J.

6. (e) Sarah m. Stephen Barksdale and moved to Missouri. Oldest son, William.

3. (f) Annie Winton m. William Ellis.

3. (g) Mary m. William Snow. Issue, (a) George m. Miss Elder, (b) James P., (c) John W. m. Miss Peacock, moved to Lake Co., Tenn., (d) Elizabeth m. Benjamin Carrothers, (e) Sarah m. Jake Tener, (f) Texas, (g) Savannah, (h) Tennessee.

3. (h) Edmond, m. April 11, 1838 Nancy Eblen. Issue, (a) Sarah m. Joseph Hinds, (b) William wounded while in the Confederate Army and died, (c) John P. m. Sarah Sturgis White..

Edmond's 2nd. wife was Jency Ellis. Issue, (a) Louis E. m. Mary Cardwell, (b) S. A. m. Sarah Holston, (c) Robert m. Matilda Balew, (d) Franklin, (e) Jane m. S. L. Eblen.

Louis E. and S. E. Waller are ministers of the Primitive Baptist Church.

3. (i) Henry m. Sarah Pickel. Issue, (a) Columbus m. Miss Hues, lives at Wichita Falls, Tex, (b) George m. 1st. Margaret Waller, 2nd. Louisa Hair. (c) M. B. m. Nancy Brazeale, (d) Mary m. 1st. Joe Cardwell, 2nd. Thomas Eblen.

THE HISTORY OF ROANE COUNTY

WELCKER

1. John Henry b. Dec. 4, 1776 in Darmstadt, Germany, embarked from the city of Bremen Mar. 2, 1797, landed at Baltimore, July 19, 1797, m. Jan. 15, 1805 Elizabeth Inman, of Washington Co. b. Mar. 21, 1790, d. Dec. 24, 1840. John Henry d. Aug. 26, 1838. Issue:

2. (a) William Lewis b. July 6, 1807, d. Feb. 10, 1830 m. Malinda Mitchell.

2. (b) Charles Freeling b. Feb. 3, 1809 d. July 20, 1861, m. Caroline Virginia Mitchell Sept. 2, 1835.

2. (c) George Lewis b. Apr. 6, 1811, d. May 24, 1848.

2. (d) Henry Inman b. Mar. 18, 1813, d. July 25, 1839.

2. (e) Frederick Augustus b. Apr. 5, 1815, d. May 27, 1841.

2. (f) James Monroe b. May 29, 1817, d. Sept. 8, 1858 m. Margaret Parks.   Issue. (a) Elizabeth.

2. (g) Catherine Freeling, b. Mar. 18, 1819, d. Oct. 8, 1889, m. Albert S. Lenoir. (See Lenoir).

2. (h) Benjamin Franklin b. Apr. 5, 1821, d. Aug. 28, 1884.

2. (i) Albert Galatin b. Nov. 25, 1823 d. May 4, 1868 m. Nancy White.

2. (j) Mary Jane McDowell, b. Mar. 11, 1826, d. Sept. 3, 1854.

2. (k) Dewitt Clinton b. Mar. 10, 1829, d. July 23, 1856.

Children of William Lewis and Malinda Welcker:

3. (a) Margaret Elizabeth b. Nov. 10, 1826, d. May 24, 1846.

3. (b) James Henry b. Mar. 21, 1829, d. July 12, 1841.

3. (c) William Thomas, b. June 24, 1830, m. July 23, 1857, Katie Adair.

Children of Charles Freeling and Caroline Virginia:

3. (a) Sarah Catherine b. Jan. 20, 1838, m. 1st. Jan. 25, 1855 William C. Robinson, 2nd. William B. Hope, Apr. 10, 1862.

THE HISTORY OF ROANE COUNTY

3. (b) Elizabeth b. Apr. 10, 1842 m. Aug 15, 1867 Jackson Lackey. She d. Nov. 15, 1871.
3. (c) William Lewis b. Feb. 17, 1849 m. Sept. 17, 1884. Annie Crawford. Issue, Annette. b. Sept. 29, 1889.
3. (d) James Henry b. Aug 27, 1854 m. Feb. 4, 1886 Daisy Welcker, dau. of Benjamin Franklin.
3. (e) Fredericka Texana b. Feb. 10, 1857 d. Aug. 24, 1894 m. Reil Dani. June 5, 1892.
3. (f) Ellen Virginia b. June 22, 1859 m. Nov. 15, 1882 Litton Thomas.

Children of William T. and Katie Adair Welcker.
4. (a) Adair b. May 26, 1858.
4. (b) Mendell b. Apr. 3, 1862.
4. (c) Katherine b. Dec. 8, 1865.
4. (d) Henrietta b. Sept. 6, 1874.

Children of Sarah Catherine and William Robinson:
4. (a) Frank Welcker b. Dec. 6, 1855 m. Dec. 25, 1887, Ella Davis. Issue, (a) Alma, b. Oct. 3, 1890, (b) Frank Welcker.

Children of Albert Galatin and Nancy White:
3. (a) Mary, (b) Katherine, (c) Belle.
4. (b) Katherine m. William J. McNutt. Issue Katherine m. Richard P. Johnston.
4. (c) Belle m. Edward E. McMillan. Issue, 5 (a) Margie Belle m. Hal Mebane. Issue: (a) Hal, (b) Edward.

5. (b) Edward J. m. Mamie Henegar. Issue, (a) Nancy, (b) Helen.
5. (c) Helen m. Lucian Briscoe.

4. (b) William Charles Joseph b. Sept. 2, 1857 m. Mary Brennaman.

Children of Sarah Catherine and William B. Hope:
4. (c) Henry Welcker b. Jan. 24, 1863 m. 1st. 1888 Dorothy C. French. 2nd. Julia Eaton. Issue: (a) Nell, (b) Kate.

(4. (d) Mary Virginia b. Jan. 1, 1865 m. James C. Buchanan Jan. 6, 1886. Issue, (a) Kate, (b) William Andrew, (c) Margaret and Elizabeth.

5. (a) Kate m. Chester Harvey.

THE HISTORY OF ROANE COUNTY

    4. (e) Katie Louise b. Aug. 30, 1872 m. Robert Mabry. Issue, (a) Hope.
    4. (f) Sarah Elizabeth b. Oct. 8, 1874 m. Walter W. Prater. Issue, Mary Kate.
    4. (g) Minnie Caroline b. Apr. 7, 1877 m. J. B. Smith Mar. 17, 1896.
    4. (h) Thomas Frederick b. June 11, 1880 m. Claire McClure. Issue, (a) Evelyn, (b) Caroline.

Children of Elizabeth and Jackson Lackey:
(a) Charles b. May 10, 1862, m. Daisy Gallaher.
(b) William W. b. Oct. 28, 1889.
    2. (h) Benjamin Franklin Welcker m. Hester Ish. Issue, (a) Dixie, (b) Henry, (c) Albert.

    3. (a) Dixie m. James H. Welcker.
    3. (c) Albert m. Lillie Williams.

Children of James Henry and Daisy Welcker.
    4. (a) James Dewitt b. June 10, 1890.
    4. (b) George Lewis b. Feb. 26, 1892.
    4. (c) Frederick William b. April 28, 1894.
    4. (d) Henry Ish, b. Sept. 18, 1897.

THE HISTORY OF ROANE COUNTY

WESTER

1. John Fulgum b. in England 1723, settled near Tarboro, North Carolina.

2. Fulgum b. 1760 in Virginia d. 1822 in Jefferson Co., Tenn. m. 1783 Edith Wolley in Edgcomb Co., North Carolina, (was a Revolutilonary Soldier in Col. Thomas Hunter's Reg., North Carolina Volunteers.) Issue:

3. Daniel b. Dec. 23, 1786 d. Aug. 2, 1857. At the age of fifteen went with Capt. William's Co., to Natchez, Miss. to quell an Indian and Spanish Rebellion. Later was with Gen. William H. Harrison in the Battle of Lake Erie. On May 1, 1804 m. Elizabeth Loyd, b. Dec. 5, 1789, d. Nov. 7, 1845 in Bedford Co., Tenn. Moved to Kingston 1810. Served under Col. Uriah Allison in War of 1812. Issue, (a) John Wesly, b. Jan. 2nd, 1805, d. 1874, (b) William Houston b. Feb. 1, 1807, (c) Edith G. b. June 1, 1809, (d) Rachel Loyd, b. Sept. 22, 1811, (e) George W. b. Mar. 27, 1814, (f) Daniel Loyd b. Nov. 30, 1816, (g) Minerva M. b. June 8, 1819, (h) Carroll B. b. Sept. 24, 1821, (i) Lewis M. m. June 28, 1823, (j) Christopher Columbus b. Jan. 17, 1826, (k) James A. b. Sep. 3, 1828, (l) Elizabeth Jane, b. Oct. 24, 1829. On Feb. 6, 1851 m. Mary A. Breedlove. Issue, (a) Margaret Louisa, b. Feb. 17, 1852, (b) Francis Asbury b. Jan. 20, 1854, (c) Charles W. b. Jan. 16, 1856.

4. (a) John Wesley m. Mar. 26, 1836 1st. Mary Jane Brown, b. 1816, d. 1834. Issue: (a) Sarah Brown. John Wesley in 1844 m. Catherine Jane Allison b. Jan. 1822, d. 1864. Issue, (a) Ephriam Foster, (b) Josephine M., (c) John M., (d) Catherine Ann, (e) Alice, (f) Adelaide V., (g) Edith May, (h) Margaret Hamilton, (i) Annie Maud.

5. (b) Josephine Mariah m. John M. Wester. Issue: (a) John, (b) Elmer, (c) Thomas H., (d) Paul, (e) Marvin, (f) James, (g) Catherine, (h) Grady.

5. (a) Sarah dau. of John Wesley and Mary Brown Wester m. 1878 Wiley W. Love.

5. (d) Catherine Ann m. 1st. Harry Miles, 2nd. John Hathaway. Issue: Maude Miles, Eola Miles, Earl Miles, Carl Miles. 2nd. John Hathaway.

5. (e) Alice m. 1872 Robert Kendrick. Issue, (a) Willie, (b) Charles W., (c) Robbie May. 2nd Henry Crowder. Issue: (a) Katherine, (b) Ford, (c) Tully.

THE HISTORY OF ROANE COUNTY

5. (f) Adelaide Victoria m. 1878 Thomas King. (See King.)

5. (h) Margaret H. m. Nov. 13, 1879. Thomas C. Erwin. Issue, (a) Maud, (b) Robbie May, (c) Thomas C., (d) Margaret H., (e) Josephine.

5. (i) Annie M., m. 1888 John F. McNutt.

4. (b) William Houston m. 1st. Dec. 30, 1827 Keziah Cardwell, b. 1810, d. 1844. Issue, (a) Rachel. 2nd. Minerva Stone.

5. (a) Rachel b. Dec. 5, 1828, m. William McKamey.

4. (c) Edith G. m. Feb. 17, 1826, John Turner. Issue: (a) William b. Dec. 2, 1826, (b) John L. b. Sept. 26, 1828, (c) Elizabeth, b. Oct. 1830, (d) Daniel M. b. Oct. 27, 1831, (e) Nathaniel B. b. Nov. 7, 1833, (f) Margaret S. b. Dec. 13, 1835, (g) Rachel Denny, b. July 4, 1838, (h) Christopher b. Apr. 27, 1840, (i) Thomas b. May 5, 1843, (j) Albert b. Aug. 22, 1845.

4. (d) Rachel Loyd m. Feb. 13, 1834, John Hamilton. Issue: (a) George and Henry, (b) Rachel, (c) Thomas, (d) Sarah, (e) Elizabeth.

5. (a) George, son of Rachel and John m. Elizabeth Luckey.

5. (a) Henry, son of Rachel and John, m. Nannie West.

5. (b) Rachel, dau. of Rachel and John, m. William Green.

4. (e) George Washington, son of Daniel and Elizabeth m Millie Delozier, Apr. 27, 1833. Issue, (a) George W., Jr., (b) James.

4. (f) Daniel Loyd, son of Daniel and Elizabeth m. Sept. 17, 1835, Julinda Claiborn, b. July 5, 1817.

4. (g) Minerva Marion b. Jan. 8, 1819 m. Aug. 4, 1839 John Yandel. Issue, (a) William H., b. Oct. 17, 1839, (b) John W. b. Feb. 7, 1843, (c) Sarah E. b. Oct. 19, 1845.

4. (h) Lewis Marshall. 1st. m. Oct. 24, 1841 Sarah Hamel. Issue: (a) Rachel, b. 1842, (b) John M. b. 1845, (c) Josephine Mariah b. 1848, (d) Sarah, 2nd. wife, Catherine Yost b. 1829. Issue, (a) Mary (b) Katie, (c) Margaret. 3rd. wife was Martha Brown Smith.

4. (j) Christopher Columbus 1st. m. Mar. 30, 1848 Mary A. Johnson b. Jan. 8, 1824. Issue: (a) Samuel Daniel,

THE HISTORY OF ROANE COUNTY

b. Jan 10, 1849, (b) James Marshall, b. July 4, 1850, (c) John W., b. Jaan. 14, 1852, (d) William C., b. Nov. 17, 1854, (e) Lizzie Gates b. Aug. 14, 1855, (f) Mary Kate, (g) Rachel Arabell, (h) John C., (i) Henry J. 2nd wife Elizabeth Roddy, m. Mar. 5, 1878.

4. (l) Elizabeth Jane, dau. of Daniel and Elizabeth m. Feb. 6, 1845 Thomas B. Coleman, Issue, (a) Scott, (b) Margaret, (c) Ida May.

5. Margaret Louisa, dau. of Daniel and Mary Breedlove Wester, m. William Wann.

5. Francis Asbury, son of Daniel and Mary m. Martha —————. Issue: (a) Francis Asbury, (b) James, (c) Lillian, (d) Lucile, (e) Thomas, (f) Charles.

6. (c) Margaret, dau. of Lewis Marshall Wester m. 1874 John Wright. Issue, (a) John, (b) William, (c)

6. (a) Samuel D., son of Christopher Wester m. Lelia A. Rice.

6. (e) Elizabeth Gates, dau. of Christopher m. Ruel McGoughey. Issue, (a) Nellie.

6. (d) William, son of Christopher m. Mary Neil. Issue, Earl, who married Lucille Gerstle.

5. (a) Issue of Daniel L. and Julinda Wester. (a) Loyd.

5. (a) Issue of Lewis M. and Sarah H. Wester (a) Rachel b. 1842 m. 1857, James Sturges, (b) John M., b. 1845 m. Josephine Maria Wester 1865. (c) Cornelia, m. Charles Stegall.

5. (c) Ida May, dau. of Elizabeth Jane and Thomas B. Coleman b. 1850 m. ————— Crickman.

6. (a) Katherine, dau. of Alice and Henry Crowder m. Fred Haggard.

6. (b) Ford, son of Alice and Henry Crowder m. Gladys Thompson.

6. (f) Tully, son of Alice and Henry Crowder m. Clara May Marshall Issue: (a) Henry Thomas, (b) Martha Ann.

6. (a) Maud, dau. of Adelaide and Thomas King m. Frank Robinson.

6. (c) Josephine, dau. of Adelaide and Thomas King m. James Jones.

6. (a) Maud, dau. of Margaret and Thomas Ervin m. George Wrinkleman.
6. (b) Robbie May m. Fletcher Howell.
6. (d) Margaret H. m. Charles M. Ford.
6. (e) Josephine m. Capt. Charles M. Kemp.
6. Issue of George Hamilton and Elizabeth Luckey Hamilton, (a) Jennie, and Elizabeth, (b) Seth, (c) George, (d) Neal, (e) Henry.
6. (a) Elizabeth m. Thomas Hardadge.
6. Issue of Henry and Nannie West Hamilton, (a) Willia, (b) Katherine.
5. (a) Issue of Rachel, dau. of William Houston Wester m. 1848 William McKamey, (a) Albert.
6. (c) William m. Ruby Bullock.
6. (a) Maud, dau. of Catherine Ann and Harry Miles m. ——————— Owens. Issue.
6. (b) Eola Miles m.
Elmer Elsworth m. May Chambers.

THE HISTORY OF ROANE COUNTY

WILKEY

1. Samuel m. Cynthia Hartley June 2, 1840.
1. Roger m. Oct. 29, 1836 Mariah West.
1. Martin m. Jan. 15, 1839 Letitia Yost. Issue, (a) Calvin Vanburen, (b) Delia, (c) Walter, (d) Martha, (d) Mary, (e) Thomas, (f) Sally, (g) James.

    2. (a) Calvin Vanburen m. Elvira Underwood. Issue, (a) Maggie, (b) Evans, (c) Charlie, (d) Mack, (e) Martin, (f) Ella.

    2. (b) Delia m. Jack Marney. Issue, (a) Sally, (b) Walter m. Belle Campbell.

    2. (d) Martha m. Thomas Wright. Issue, (a) Delia, (b) Elizabeth.

    2. (d) Mary, twin sister of Martha m. Pleasant Wilson. Issue, (a) Walter (b) Kate, (c) William.

    2. (e) Thomas m. Lucilla Owings 1886. Issue:

    (a) Frances Dalton b. 1889 m. 1915 William J. Thigpen, b. 1877.

    (b) Letitia.

    (c) Kathryn.

3. William J. Thigpen m. Frances Dalton Wilkey. Issue:

(a) Kathryn b. 1919.

(b) Jane Randolph, b. 1925.

2. (f) Sally m. James Robinson.

Issue of Walter and Belle Wilkey:

3. (a) Clyde Wilkey, m. Frank Wright.

3. (b) Eugene B. m. Katherine Hunter.

3. (c) Hugh m. Geraldine Henderson.

THE HISTORY OF ROANE COUNTY

WINTON

1. John b. Nov. 8, 1761 m. Arabella Cunningham, b. May 18, 1763. They settled near Muddy Creek Station before 1775. Issue, (a) William, (b) James, (c) Stephen, (d) Robert, (e) Nancy (f) Mary, (g) Dollie, (h) Lucretia.
John was a minister of the Methodist Church.

2. (a) William m. Mary Mitchell, dau. of Rev. Morris Mitchell. Issue, George B.

2. (b) James b. 1789 m. Rhoda Mitchell b. 1796. Issue, (a) Wiley B., (b) John A., (c) Frank, (d) Rufe, (e) Albert, (f) Lucretia, (g) Harriet.

2. (d) Robert m. Susie Jackson. Issue, (a) William, (b) James, (c) Robert, (d) Jefferson, (e) Susie (f) Dollie.

3. (b) James m. Jan. 22, 1840 Jane Alford.

2. (e) Nancy m. Samuel Johnson. Issue, (a) William, (b) James, (c) John, (d) Mary.

2. (f) Mary m. John A. Montgomery.

2. (g) Dollie m. John Grant. Issue, (a) Cape, (b) Dollie.

3. (b) John A. b. Feb. 2, 1819, son of James m. Feb. 2, 1843 Susan Baker of Va. 2nd. wife Correy, dau. of John Y. Smith. Issue, (a) John Lenoir, (b) Mary.

3. (e) Albert m. Bettie Gillam.

3. (f) Lucretia m. Elijah Haley Sept. 25, 1839. Issue, (a) John B., (b) Elijah, (c) George, (d) Mary (e).

3. (g) Harriet, dau. of James and Rhoda m. Christopher Kimmer. Issue, James, Susan, Louisa.

John W. b. Aug. 19, 1829 m. Eliza Browder. Issue: Julia C. and others.

Julia, dau of John W. and Eliza m. George W. Hardin July 30, 1861.

Amanda Winton m. Oct.6, 1852 Thomas Jones.

THE HISTORY OF ROANE COUNTY

EARLY RESIDENTS OF ROANE COUNTY

James and Achasa (Ponder) Freeman came from Virginia.
Daniel and Mary (Brashears) Mason.
George and Elizabeth Preston.
James and Charlotte Preston all of Virginia.
Hugh McGill b. Feb. 5, 1802. m. Rebecca Smith b. Dec. 11 1905.
William Hyden and Mary (Baldwin) Hyden.
Major John and Catherine Leftwich from Virginia.
Capt. Samuel Walker b. 1748 in Botetourt Co., Va., m. Susan McDonald. Their daughter, Jane Patterson m. John McKamey.

Col. Joel Hambree b. Mar. 25, 1793 in Spartanburg, South Carolina a soldier of 1812 and War with Mexico. Served three terms in State Legislature and was in the State Senate.

Absalom Fooshee b. Nov. 20, 1797 in North Carolina.
John Fooshee b. Nov. 28, 1817 and his wife Susan (Hinds).

Thomas A. R. Nelson born in Roane Co. was elected Judge of the Supreme Court in 1875.

Thomas C. Lyons b. 1810 in Roane Co. Was a brilliant lawyer and profound Jurist. He served on the Staff of General Wood during the Mexican War with the rank of Major.

John Ross went to school in Kingston, was a clerk in the store of William D. Neilson and began his public career in 1809. He was appointed by Return J. McMinn as agent to the Cherokee Indians.

Samuel Houston was a clerk in the store of John McEwen, when he was a young man.

Thomas Jefferson Mason, 2nd. Lieut. in United States Army assisted in the removal of the Cherokee Indians.

Lieut. Carrick, age 19, while with the 4th Regiment U. S. Cavalry at Post Oak Springs died and is buried in the grave yard as are Captain Samuel Walker, Colonel Abraham McClelland and other Soldiers.

INDEX

-A-

Abeel, Rachel 104
Abel, (Miss) 276
  Susan 252
  Thelma 187
  (Dr.) William L. 186, 187
Abels, Christopher 200, 202
  Elizabeth 200, 202
  George 202
  James 202, 203
  Louisa 202
  Rachel 197
  Robert 202
  Susan 202
  William 202
Absten, Katherine Matilda 195, 196
Acree, Crocomus 27, 31
  James 29
Acuff,_____ 42
  Alma 267
  Anna 253
  Bates 253
  Catherine Rose 267
  Darius M. 222
  Dorothy Ingram 267
  Elizabeth 217, 252
  Emaline 222
  Fred 253
  Harry 217
  Ida May 267
  James 252, 253
  James Blaine 222
  James Charles 208, 267
  James Polk 267
  Joe Donley 218
  John 253
  John A. 264
  John H. 46, 250, 267
  John R. 222
  Lethe M. (Kendrick) 217
  Lillie A. 222
  Margaret A. 222
  Mary Jane (Owings) 287
  Mary M. 141, 217
  Matilda 265
  Min Ellen 267
  Minnie Murray 217
  Nelle 218
  Robert Rilla 217
  Robert William 267
  Rose L. 262
  Rose Lena 267
  Sallie 253
  Samuel 217
  Sarah M. 250
  Scott 253
  Sydney 253
  Tennessee (Millican) 253
  William D. 267
  William J. 217
  William Turner 267
  Willie 222
Adair, Barbara 258
  Katie 299
  William 79
Adams, Dianah 75
  Sally 107
Adcock, Beauregard G. 218, 219
  Bula Maud 218
  Etoile May 218
  Lorelle Cornelia 218, 219
  Mary Lee (Kendrick) 218, 219
  Milburn Kendrick 218
  Tula Claude 218
Adkins, Charles 107
  Fannie 237
Adkinson, Abraham 86
  James 98
  Mary Alice 285
  Sally 86
  Wilkerson P. 22
  William W. 22
Aiken, James 28, 29
Akard, Sarah 48
Albright, Marguerite 286
Alden, Dora 294
  Eliza Ann 260
Alexander,_____ 11
  Artie 279
  William 21
Alford, Elsie 142
  Jane 307
  John 123
  Myra 142
  Paul 142
  Robert 142, 176
  Robert H. 142
Algood, John 28
Alif, Polly 105
Allcorn, Albert 59
Allen, Andrew 137
  Edwin Porter 211
  Elias 80
  Elizabeth 75
  James 28, 29
  John 20, 81
  Kiziah 97
  Richard 15, 28
Allin, Betsy 76
Allison, (Col.) 34
  Albert W. 156
  Annie 133
  Benjamine 134
  Betsy 93
  Catherine Jane 133, 134, 302
  Charles McClean 134
  Charlie 63, 65
  Edna 133
  Elizabeth 134, 172
  Elizabeth Lee 134
  Frank 172
  James 63, 65, 66, 172
  Jane 133
  Jesse 62
  Jesse Byrd 133, 134
  Jinney 81
  John Adair 134
  Joseph Hill 134
  Lida J. 54
  Lou 133
  Lucy A. 54
  Lucy G. 54
  Margaret 133, 209, 210
  Maria 133
  Maria Louise 133
  Mariah 133
  Mary 133
  Mary Jane (Eblen) 172
  Mary Moore 133, 147
  Mathew 42, 171, 172
  Nancy (Byrd) 134
  Nancy Clark Cox 147
  Nancy R. 134
  Robert 13, 16, 28, 62, 99, 133
  Robert M. 54, 133, 134, 156
  Ruff 133
  Samuel 133, 134
  Samuel Henley 134
  Sarah 133
  Susan 133
  Susan (Howard) 134
  Thomas 133, 134, 172
  Uriah 81, 95, 133, 164
  (Capt.) Uriah 32, 33, 54
  (Col.) Uriah 133, 134, 147, 164, 302
  William 133, 172
  William Dickson 134
  Willis W. 54
  Young Ewing 134
Altridge, Oliver Hamilton 186
Ambrose, David 110
Ambuster, Asa 245
Amey, Thomas 20
Ammerman, Stephen 20
Ammous,_____ 267
Amos, Caroline 298
  (Mrs.) Elizabeth 193
Anderson, Adah 204
  Addie 204
  Bessie 204
  Charles E. 166
  Elizabeth McIlwaine 204

Anderson (cont.)
  Emma 204
  Grace 255
  Isaac 95
  (Rev.) Isaac 46, 52, 59
  (Capt.) James O. 133
  John 207
  John Bachman 166
  Joseph 15
  Joseph M. 204
  Julia Frances 258
  Margaret 166, 195
  Margaret (Huff) 204
  (Mrs.) Matilda C. 49
  Michael 106
  Reece 204
  Rhea 204
  Robert R. 204
  (Mrs.) S.H. 193
  Samuel 204
  William 15, 82, 105
  William Dulaney 166
  William W. 165, 166
Andrews, Betty 236
  David 236
  Edwin N. 253
  Garnet 236
  Garnett 236
  Katherine 236
  Samuel 102
Angel, James 266
  John 241
Anthony, Jacob 18
Aplegate, Nathaniel 85
Arbuckle, Catherine 20, 149
  Catherine H. 83
Armstrong, Elizabeth 145, 166
  Frances Lucille 152
  Frank 152
  James B. 152
  Martin 13
  Mary 126
  Richard 13, 22
  Robert 13
  Samuel B. 152
Arnold, George 88, 125
  Helen 181
  Jonas 171
  Michael 14, 17, 99
  (Mrs.) Patsy 48
  William 92
Arp, Ford W. 37
Arrants, Alexandria 186
Arrowood, Howard P. 174
Arsterton, Catey 98
Arthur, Bessie 240
  Flora 240
  John 240
  Johnnie 240
  Lewis 240
  Louis 240
  Mamie 240
Arwood, Loyd 172
Asbury, (Bishop) 11, 44
  D. 62
  James T. 44c
Ashe, Emily 189
Asher, Charles 100
  Leonard 100
Ashford, Robert 255
Ashire, Samuel 18
Ashley, Amanda 48
  Joseph 96
  Noah 57
Ashmore, Joshua 16, 22
Atkins, (Rev.) K. C. 43
  Sarah 170
Ault, Edith 227

George D. 227
George W. 226, 227
Katie Rebecca 227
Rufus W. 227
Ausburn, Dewey 37
Austin, Lou 210
Avery, Allen 287
  Bess 287
  Elizabeth 235
  John Dixie 287
  Keziah 188
  Mary 287
  Nealey 287
  Peter 29
  Waightstill 235
  Wilhelmina Christina 285
  Wilma 287
Ayers, Alexander 148
  Alpha 148
  Eliza 79
  James 252
  Mary Ellen (Brown) 148
  Peggy 86
  Sophia 100, 148
  Sophia Matilda 213
  Susan 212
  William 148
  William B. 61
  Zachariah 57
  Zacheus 9, 10, 15, 118, 147, 148

–B–

Bachman, _____ 135
  Mary 166
Bacon, (Capt.) Allen 32
  Allen S. 32
  Frederick Sayford 209
  Joseph 201
  Mary Overton 158
Bagwell, Addie 262
  Jefferson 252
Bailey, Anna 291
  Daniel 90
  David H. 15, 18
  Eliza 48
  Elizabeth 168
  Gamaliel 280
  Hiram 216
  Isaac 113, 242
  James 82
  John 29
  Leon D. 181
  Louisa 280
  Patsy 113, 117
  Thomas Fritts 181
  William 89, 90
  Worthey 47
Baily, Isaac 18
Baker, (Capt.) 18
  Alfred J. 275
  John Goodwin 275
  Joseph 263
  Mattie Snodgrass 202, 203
  May Patton 275
  Michael 18
  Susan 307
  William 261
Bakewell, Benjamine 260
Bakon, Betsy 90
Balden, Fielding 86
Baldwin, Delia 227
  (Mrs.)Dollie 193
  Ed 37
  Edith 227

Jesse 125
Maggie 270
Rebecca 125
Balew, Matilda 298
Balfour, Sally 247
Ball, Thomas 165
Ballard, Ann 235
  Mary Ann 155
  William 77, 172
Ballew, (Gen.) 298
  Nancy M. 128
Ballou, Barbara 259
  Judge 259
Bane, Arthur 94
Barger, Peter 16
Barkley, Margaret Lucinda 138
Barksdale, Mary 297
  Stephen 298
  William 298
Barnard, Albert 135
  Alexander 135
  Alice 135
  Almarinda/Amarinda 135, 136
  Anna 135
  Arch 135
  Bertha 135
  Caroline T. 136
  Carter 28, 29
  Charles 135
  Claire 136
  Cora 135, 136
  Crowder 135
  Eblen 135
  Elija 135
  Eliza 135
  Elizabeth 135
  Elizabeth Campbell 177
  Fred 136
  George 135
  Hazel Genevieve 136
  Helen Marie 136
  Henry Gibson 136
  Henry Gibson (Jr.) 136
  Hyre 135
  Jack Carson 136
  James 135
  John 135
  (Col.) John A. 177
  John Anderson 135
  John C. 135
  Jonathan 107, 110, 112, 135
  (Col.) Jonathan 34
  Jonathan L. 120
  Jonathan M. 135, 136
  Jonathan Robert Campbell 135, 136
  Laura 135
  Lucinda 135
  Lula May 136
  Lydia 135
  Mack 135
  Margaret 135
  Marjorie 136
  Mary 135
  May 135
  Morgan Clack 136
  Nancy 135
  Newton 135
  Polly 135
  R. T. 64, 66
  Rachel 135
  Rebecca (Weiss) 136
  Reuben 135
  Richard 135
  Robert Arthur 136
  Sallie 135
  Samuel 135
  Samuel T. 136

Barnard (cont.)
  Sarah 135
  Saraphine 177
  Seraphine 135
  Thomas 135
  Walter 135
  William E. 136
  William J. 135
  Zedic 135
Barnes, A. A. 160
  Nichodemus 15
  Wm. 152
Barnet, John 22
  Richard 22
  William 15, 22
Barnett, Cilby 80
  Mary 188
  William 10, 13, 14, 74, 159, 282
Barnwell, Alice 64, 65
  Allen 63, 64
Bartlett, Alex 52
  Elizabeth 164
Bartley, David 15
Barton, Gailbreath 14, 19
  Gillesreath 89
  Hugh 16, 32
  (Mrs.) Margaret 47
  Roger 47
Bashears, ___ 168
  Bazzle 17
  Betsy 81, 167
  Isaac 167
  Philip 15
  Robert 78
  Yaza 78
Baskin, Rosey 76
Bayley, R. P. 42
Beard, ___ 188
  Catherine 180
Bearden, Marcus 260
Beattey, Hugh 29
Beatty, Hugh 9, 14, 15, 31
Beaty, Hugh 19
Beauchamp, Mary Etta 170
Beaujolair, Comte de 11
Beavers, James 97
  William 97
Beddo, P. T. 61
  Phillip 59
Beeler, ___ 183
Bell, Betty Ann 263
  James Timmons 263
  Kellar 284
  Marjory 263
  Ralph 263
  Robert 13
  Thomas 105
Belt, (Rev.) 43
Bender, George 188
Beneger, Fred 292
  Orton 292
Bensete (?), William W. A. 102
Benson, John 216
  Kate 219
  Mary 209
Berdendistle, Theresa 150
Berfit (Buford), John 19
Berford, John 16
Berg, Walter 268
Berk, Robert 17
Bernard, R. T. 65
Berry, (Mrs.) 48
  Annie 172
  Eliza 171
  Elizabeth 172
  Elizabeth Walker 51
  Hiram 171, 172

Hyram 100
Isaac 172
John 172
Keziah 89
Lucy 172
Maud 185
Peter 77
Polly 103
R. Caroline 48
Sarah Meredith 51
Thrusia Ruth Meredith 51
William 95
William W. 48, 51
Betterton, Whitlow 136
Beverly, Jane 114
Billings, Clyde 38
Garrett H. 37
Billingsley, John H. 155, 156
Joseph Byrd 156
Margaret May/Wray 156
Mary Ann 156
Billingsly, ___ 136
J. D. (Sr.) 46
John Reuben 201, 202
Mary Elizabeth 201
Mary Lorraine 202
Minnie 210
Sarah Annie (Hinds) 201, 202
Billingsly/Billingsley, David 201, 202
Bingham, Clara 228
Bird, Caty 77
  Joseph 21
Birdwell, Elizabeth 193
  John 15, 17
  Joshua 17
  Patsy 100
Bishop, Massey 121
Biss, Henry 63, 65, 66
  Henry D. 208
Black, Alexander 111, 288, 289
  Alexander (Jr.) 289
  Clara Josephine 289
  David 292
  Emma Y. 289
  Georgia Ruth 289
  Herbert 189
  John 288, 289
  John Y. 289
  Leah Lee 289
  Lillie E. 294
  Margaret Elizabeth 189
  Mary Alice 289
  Mary Gordon 288
  Mary Louisa/e 288, 289
  Maryann Clark Smith 289
  Merriweather 288
  Robert 288, 289
  Samuel 288, 289
  Sarah Colville 289
  Susan 288
  Susan Louise 289
  Thomas 288, 289
  Thomas Alexander 289
  William 13, 14, 16
Blackburn, Benjamine 16
  John 240
Blackstone, Robert 116
  Thomas 80
Blackwell, Armstead 97
  David 28, 29
  George 102
  Jesse 15, 30
  Raymond 199
Blain, James Holman 184
Blair, ___ 158
  Allen 137
  Anne 156

Arthur 138
Barclay 210
Betsy 137
Callie 138
Callie Alice 138
E. R. 181
Elizabeth 137
Elizabeth Ann 137
Elizabeth Caroline 137
Elizabeth (Johnson) 138
Fannie 138
Finnie 138
Francis 156
Frankie 137
George M. 137
Grace 156
Hugh 137
(Dr.) Hugh Allen 137, 138
Hugh E. F. 138
Isabelle 137
James 13, 16, 18, 137, 138
James M. 138
(Dr.) James Thomas 137, 138
Jane 137
Jane (Gamble) 137
Jennette 138
Jenny 137
Jessie 138
Jimmie Hugh 138
John 29, 32, 123, 137, 138, 156, 212
John Allen 138
John Johnson 137, 138
L. T. 212
Laura 138, 156
Lilliam Olivia 138
Lucy 138
Lula 138
Mahala 137
Margaret 138
Martha 137, 138
Martha Eliza 138
Martha Patsy 137
Mary Belle 205
Mary Dawson 137
Mary Jane 137, 138
Nancy Isabelle 137
Patsy Ann 137
Polly 137
Rachel 137, 138
Ruth 156
Samuel 137, 273
Samuel Douglas 138
Sarah 137
Thomas 137
Tie 156
Vincent 137
Vinson 137
Virginia 181
Walter 138
Wiley 137, 212
Wiley W. 138
William 13, 18, 21, 137, 156
William R. 137, 138
William (Wiley) 137
William Wiley 137, 138
Winn 138
Blake, Anna Laura 139, 140
Benjamine F. 139
Charles 139, 140
Charles C. 139
Charles Edward 139
David 139
Elija 139
Fay 224
George Washington 139
Georgia Fay 139, 140
J. Alvin 139

Blake (cont.)
  James F. 139
  James Morgan 139
  John 139
  John H. 139, 292
  Joseph 139
  Joseph Frederick 139
  Mary 101, 139
  Mary J. 139
  Mary (Staples) 139
  Mary Thelma 139
  Nathan 139
  Robert K. 139
  Ruth 139, 140
  Samuel Monroe 139
  Susan Elizabeth 139, 142
  Thomas 23, 107, 139
  Velia M. 139
  William Anderson 139
  William G. 103, 139
  Willie May 139
Blankenbecker, Mollie 219
Bledsoe, Aaron 34
  John 266
  Joseph 34
  Sidney 197
Blevens, Polly 115
Blevins, Artie 222
  Martha Ann 222
  Mary Ellen 222
Blizzard, Edith 210
Blount, Wilie 15
  (Gov.) William 9
Bobbitt, Olla Grace 268
Boden, Jinny 90
Bogart, Abraham 95
  Ann Eve 48
  Elizabeth 128
  Hiram 204
  Joseph 204
  Lida 204
  Margaret 121
  Mary K. 204
  Nancy 95, 143
  Robert 204
  William 84, 95
  William Huff 204
Boggess, (Col.) A. F. 36
  Abijah 177
  Catha 177
  Dixie 177
  Elisha 177
  Levina Sharp 177
  Sudie 177
Bohannon, James 155
Bolton, Allen 105
Boman, Eliza 121
  Sally 108
Bond, Emily 121
Bonds, Barbara Ann 104
Booth, (Col.) 238a
  Hortense 186
  William 106
Boswell, Lilian 152
Bowen, Bessie 258
Bower, Mathilda 64
Bowers, Alice 141
  Alice Ruth 141
  Benjamine 141
  Betsy 94
  Caledonia 168
  David 142
  David G. 141
  Elmer O. 141
  George 126, 141
  Green 141
  J. D. 141
  James 92, 94
  James J. 141
  Jesse M. 141
  John 85, 94, 100
  John Ed 141
  John W. 83, 141, 217
  Kitty 81
  Mahala 123
  Mary 141
  Mary E. 141, 176
  Mathilda 65
  Matilda 64
  Myrtle 141
  Nelle/ie 141
  Patsy 92
  Raymond S. 141
  Rose 141
  Rufus S. 141
  Sam B. 141, 265
  Sam B. (Jr.) 141
  Samuel 141
  Sarah 141
  Thomas 210
  Thomas L. 141
  Tom R. 141
  Will S. 141
  William 85
  (Rev.) William 43
Bowlin, Lucy 174
Bowling, Charles 269
  Elizabeth Ann 269
  Levinia 124
  Margaret Edith 269
  Mary 50
  Thelma 199
  Virginia Marie 269
  William 38
  William L. 269
  William T. 269
Bowman, _____ 144
  Anna 142
  Anna (Poole) 142
  Bettie 142
  David Franklin 142
  Dixie Lynn 142
  Edward 118
  Eliza 141, 142
  Frank 142
  Frankie (Eblen) 142
  Grace 142
  Helen 142
  James 139, 142
  James H. 139
  James Harper 142
  John 27, 29, 31, 82, 142
  John W. 142
  Lennie 142
  Lewis 106
  Linnie Fay 139
  Mary Frabk (?) 142
  Mildred 142
  Myra 142
  Nancy 82, 142
  Owenby 142
  Ruth 142
  Samuel 142
  Saunders 142
  Thomas Leeper 142
  Thurston 219
  Wendel 139
  William 84, 142, 176
Box, Nancy 96
Boyd, Amelia 236
  Anna Howard 178
  Anne Eugene 196
  Catherine E. 196
  Frank 231
  Hugh 197
  James 196
  Margaret A. 196
  Mary Helen 196
  Michael 21
  Perry 256
  (Judge) Samuel 178
  Susan Mason 178
  Taylor 190
  Thomas 231
  William 28, 29
  William H. 49
Boyles, Emmet Clark 268
  Houston 268
Bozeman, Thomas 74
Brabson, Mary 239
Brackett, Rebecca 124
Brading, Louis Edward 185
Bradley, John R. 274
  Samuel 78
Brady, Edwin 186
  Ernest R. 38
  Harry Hurst 153
  Martha L. 206
  Nell Christie 153
  Thomas 15
  William 153
Brageale, Benjamine F. 18
Bragg, _____ 35
Braham, Polly 121
Braley, Thomas 15
Branam, Mamie 195
Brandon, (Rev.) 43
  Adam 104
  Ann 104
  Malinda 120
Branham, George 94
  Jane 102
  Linsey 122
  Nellie 91
  Thomas 91
  William 119
Brannan, Jesse 38
Brannon, Benjamin 20
Brashears, Isaac 16, 19
  Joseph 116
  Mattis 28
  Robert 16, 19
Brause, Charles F. 12
  Charlie 49
Brawn, Marquis D. L. 201
Bray, Nancy 287
Brazeal, Henry 15, 73
  John 98
  Mary 48
Brazeale, _____ 228
  A. M. 113
  Adaline 143
  Alexander 143
  Amanda 143
  Amanda W. 208
  B. F. 14
  Betsy 48
  Carrick 143
  David R. 143
  Elijah W. 143
  Elizabeth 102, 143
  Henry 12, 78, 99, 111, 143
  Henry Miller 143
  Hortense 143
  Hugh L. 143
  J. H. 143
  J. W. M. 12, 100, 103, 104
  James 75, 143
  Jane 143
  John W. M. 143
  Maraline 208
  Martha 143
  Martha J. 111
  Nancy 298

Brazeale (cont.)
  Nancy (McMullen) 143
  Oscar 143
  Robert 111, 143
  Robert H. 104, 143
  Sally 100
  Samuel Alexander 143
  Sarah 143
  Sarah Woods 143, 208
  Thomas B. 143
  William 143
  Willis 143
  Willis (Jr.) 143
Brazeales, (Mrs.) Betsy 51
  (Mrs.) Betsy Morgan 51
  Columbus 51
  Eliza Jane 51
  Franklin 51
Brazelton, Jacob 13, 16
  John 16, 18
  Nancy 184
  Nellie 83
Breeden, Brien 18
  John 89
  Mary Ann 125
  Nancy (Barnard) 136
  Samuel 136
  William 32, 135, 136
Breeding, Evans 115
  William 85
Breedlove, Mary A. 302
  Sarah 174
Brennaman, Mary 300
Brewer, Solomon 16
Brezeal, Henry 22
Bridges, Ephriam 84
Brigg, (Capt.) Alexander 238a
Briggers, Lola 190
Briggs, James 111
  S. W. 172
Brindley, Virgil M. 287
Briscoe, Lucian 300
Bristow, Kate 209
Brock, Isaac 15
  Reuben 15, 17
  William 119
Brogdon, Whitmill 33
Brooks, Elizabeth 279
  Howard Raymond 271
  (Mrs.) S. M. 194
Brookster, Mary 280
Brouse, C. 52
  Constantine 49, 52
  Eliza 49
  Elizabeth C. 49
  Mary 49
Browder, Alice 145
  Amanda 145
  Betsy 144
  Byrd 155
  Charles D. 145
  Clyde 145
  Darius 16, 18, 32, 245
  David A. 145
  David Newton 145
  Edmund 144
  Eliza 115, 144, 307
  Elizabeth 145
  Ella 188
  Ellen 144, 145
  Fannie 144
  Frank Vaughn 144
  George L. 144
  Ginsie 144
  Horace Lackey 145
  James 144
  James Madison 145
  James Patterson 145

Jane 144
Jeptha 144
John 109, 144, 277
John F. 144
John Jefferson 145
John W. 145
Joseph Crump 144
Joseph G. 144
Joseph Rowan 144
Julia 144, 277
Lucy 145
Lula May 144
Martha J. 144
Mary 144, 145
Maryline 145
Mattie Elizabeth 144
Maud 144
Minerva E. 144
Nancy 145
Nancy (Polly) 144
Nancy Jane 145
Nellie B. 144
Newton 156
Patsy 83
Robert 145
Robert H. 144
Samuel 144, 145
Sarah 145
Sarah J. 144
Theresa 144
Thomas 156
William 32, 144, 145, 156
William D. 145
William H. 144
William J. 144
Willie Rice 144
Brown, _____ 44, 293
  (Miss) 146
  Ada 150
  Agnes Nelson 153
  Albert 151
  Alexander 15, 90
  Amanda 148, 149
  Ann 150
  Ann (Roberts) 270
  Ann (Roddy) 167
  Arthur 37
  Arthur L. 154
  Barton 150
  Bell 150
  Benjamine 146-148, 174
  Bert 199
  Bessie 154
  Beverly 146
  Bevinds 88
  Billie 199
  Caleb 148
  Caroline Gamble 149
  Carrie 68
  Carrie Meadors 148
  Catherine 150
  Catherine Emely 151
  Catherine Jane 148, 226
  Catherine Valle 149
  Cecil 146, 154
  Charles 149
  Charles Betts 154
  Charles C. 150
  Charles Robert 148
  Charles William 269
  Clara Maud 146
  Cora 150
  Cora A. 149, 150
  Curtis L. 154
  Daisy 154
  Daniel 75
  David G. 146
  Dorothy Katherine 269

Duncan 161
Edna 148
Edna (Trowers) 149
Edward 146, 269
Elener (Owings) 269, 270
Elijah 210
Eliza Jane 147, 148, 244
Elizabeth 148, 167
Elizabeth Gillen Waters 147, 151
Elizabeth Trimble 161
Ella 149
Ellen 150
Emely 150
Emma Frances 148
Ernest 148
Eusannah 146
Evariest Ambrose 150
Evelyn 270
Fielding 141
Florence 148, 149
Frances A. 61
Francoise Valle 150
Frank 151, 209, 210
Franklin 43
Genevieve 150
George 63, 148, 149
George Albert 151
George Bartlett 147, 148
George Franklin 148
George Tully 161
Georgia 210
Gilbert L. 154
Gladys 186
Glessner 152
Grace 274
Guardians 20
Gypsie 148
H. Virginia 146
Hadley 146
Harriett 150
Harriett Ethel 152
Harry 269, 270
Harry L. 146
Helen Holton 153
Henry 146, 161
Howard 150
Hugh 134
Huldah 146
Ida 152
Ignatius Cyprian 146
Ira 169
Isaac 96
Isaiah 28, 89
J. W. 61
James 146
James Polk 146
James Trimble 161
Jane 47
Jane Adams (McElwee) 148
Jane S. 146
Jennie 146
Jno. W. (Jack Brown) 43
Joe 199
John 13, 16, 44a, 44b, 57, 75, 83, 100, 146, 147, 151, 154
(Capt.) John 146, 147
(Col.) John 32
(Gen.) John 13, 55, 57, 133, 147, 148, 164
John C. 161
John Ellis 148
John Fenwick 149
John K. 264, 269, 270
John P. 146
John Smith 148
John Smith T. 147, 149, 154

Brown (cont.)
John W. 61
John Winston 147, 148
John Winton 152
Julia 150
July Mary 151
Katherine 239, 262
Katherine Robbs 269
Laura 146, 150
Lena 152
Leona M. 154
Leslie 152
Lois Amanda 146
Louis Franklin 150
Lucille 152
Lucinda 62
Lunn 210
Mabel 153, 221
Margaret (Ingram) 210
Margaret Roddye 152
Martha Jane 246
Mary 60, 61, 146, 150, 151
Mary C. 108
Mary Caroline 147-149, 284
Mary E. 146, 151
Mary Ella 165, 166
Mary Ellen 146-149, 154
Mary Jane 147, 148, 302
Mary Louise 153
Mary M. Allison 147
Mary Roddye 149
Mary Tarver 147
Matilda 148, 149
Myra Letitia 161
Nancy 146
(Mrs.) Nancy 48
Nancy Cox Allison 147, 148
Neil 161
Neil S. 161
Nellie 151, 269
Nellie May 154
Peyton 187
Polk 148, 149, 167
Rachel Jackson 147, 148
Rebecca 146-148
Robert 15, 16, 64-67, 146, 148, 269, 270
Robert Allison 147, 151
Robert Allison III 153
Robert F. 64, 66
Robert Hugh 151
Robert Lee 269
Robert Samuel 269
Robert T. 150
Robert Tarver 146, 147, 149, 150
Rowena 146
Roxanna 51
Sallie 64, 65, 67, 68
Sallie B. 66
Samuel 23, 44a, 146
Samuel Eskridge 147, 152
Sarah 62, 148, 149, 188, 214, 216
Sarah Elizabeth 269, 270
Sarah Tarver 147
Susan 150
Susan Elizabeth 151
Susan Howard 147, 148
Susan Louisa 161
Susan Jennie 154
Thomas 10, 14, 15, 42, 53, 57, 59, 92, 95, 116, 146-148, 151, 154, 246
(Gen.) Thomas 55
(Maj.) Thomas 147-149
(Rev.) Thomas 51, 52, 275
Thomas Albert 147, 149

Thomas J. 148, 265
Thomas Jefferson 148
Thomas Joseph 150
Thomas T. 62
Thomas W. 148
Thos. A. 42, 62
Thos. B. 62
Trimble 161
Valle 150
Vassie 149
Victoria 148, 149, 184
Virginia 146
(Rev.) W. B. 286
W. F. (Frank) 42
W. L. 42
Walter 150
Walter Lee 269
Walter Roddye 147, 152, 153
Wilbert Otho 148
Wilbur 148
William 13, 15, 23, 32, 59, 60, 75, 85, 108, 111, 112, 116, 118, 119, 146-149, 151
William A. 150
William Franklin 147, 148
William Gillen Waters 147, 151
William Jackson 148, 269, 270
William L. 146-149, 183
William Leonidas 51
William Lytle 161
Zeno 150
Zollicoffer 149
Browne, Anne Pride 156
Brownie 156
Evelyn Ruth 156
Jane Leatherwood 156
Marguerite Blanch 156
Mary Louise 156
Theron 156
Bruce, (Miss) 259
Green M. 92
Margaret Jane 50
Nancy 47
(Mrs.) Nancy 50
Bryant, James A. 37
Joseph 32, 93, 104, 109, 112, 192
Little B. 21
Patsy 179
Polly 292
Walter L. 164
Buchanan, (Mrs.) 48, 51
Eliza Claris 51
Eliza Jane 51
Elizabeth 300
Horeulas 34
James 96
James C. 300
Jeminia 80
Jeremiah 14, 34
John Whiteside 51
Kate 300
Lafayette 51
Margaret 300
Mary 91
Mary Ann 51
Moses 34
Rebecca 77
Sarah 99
Sterling 51
William Anderson 51
William Andrew 300
Buck, David M. 46
Buckingham, Irma Jones 153
Nathaniel B. 15, 29

T. N. 153
Bucklen, Joanna 90
Bullar, Isaac 82
Bullard, H. L. 22
J. M. 22
John 22
Samuel 22
Bullock, Ruby 305
Bunn, Martha Helen 180
Burch, Phillip 77
Burdett, Avery 238
Eliza Lenoir 237
(Dr.) George M. 237
Isabella 237
James 237
Margaret 237
Burdoff,_____ 273
Burford, Susan 220
Burgees, Catherine 150
Charity 150
Elizabeth 150
Henry 150
James 150
Joe 150
Mattie 150
Valle 150
Zeno 150
Burgess, Lee 271
Buries, George 215
Burk, Charlie 82, 142
George L. 12
Milton 113
Robert 15
Susan 110
Burke, Geo. L. 44d
James Donahue 240
Richard 240
Robert 28
Burkett, John 126
Parmelia 126
Burnes, Mary 73
Burnett, David 118
James 180
Maria 115
Mary 208
Moses 84
Patience 49
Patsy 118
Samuel 96
Stacey 84
Burnette, Tennessee 66
Tennie 68
Burns,_____ 275
Jinsy 89
John W. 15
Laird 28, 29
Patrick 15
William H. 115
Burnside, (Gen.) 35
Burris, Elizabeth 127
Henry 13
Isaac 109
Lewis 13
Burrus, Patrick 10
Burselly, James 104
Burton, Roberta 152
Bush, Enoch 28
Bussell, C. P. 277
Butler, Clarence F. 38
J. M. 127
Mariah 298
Phebe 107
Valentine 15
Buttram, Jane Geneva 174
Byrd, (Mrs.) 48
Abraham 12, 31, 157
(Mrs.) Ann 47
Ann Pride 54

Byrd (cont.)
Ben Augustus 156
Charles 156
Eliza 155
Emma 145, 155, 156
Ernest 157
Ethel May 156
(Dr.) Eugene Hamilton 155
Flora Nelissa 156
Francis 156
Frank 156
George Gillespie 155
James Standifer 54, 155, 156
Jesse 15, 54, 57, 74, 77, 95, 155, 156
John 59
John Hamilton 155, 156
John L. 155, 156
Joseph 92, 155
(Col.) Jospeh 13, 32, 54
Joseph (Jr.) 54, 155
Joseph Rush 156
Lou 155
Maria H. King 54
Mariah King 155
Mary 156
Mary Ann (Ballard) 156
Mary Ellen 54, 155
Mary L. 44c
Mary Lea 54, 156
Mary Louise 156
Mary (McDuffie) 156
Nancy 99, 133, 156
Narcissa (McMillan) 156
Nena Terressa 156
Newton 157
Oscar 156
Robert 155-157
Robert K. 49, 234
Robert King 54, 155
(Capt.) Robert King 22, 34, 35, 44c
Rose 157
Sam Lee 156
Samuel 157
Samuel Jackson 54, 155
Sarah 155, 156
Sarah Ruth 54, 155, 156
Savannah (Margraves) 155
Shannon 156
Thomas Brown 54, 155
Vada 155, 156
William 15
William Hardin 155

-C-

Cady, ___ 226
Cagel, John 292
Sadie 292
Cagnee, Eleanor 106
Cain, James 17
Caldwell, ___ 246
(Rev.) 259
Addie Ellen 236
Allen 236
Catherine 236
Elsie 185, 186
Gideon 236
Hardwick 186
James 16
James A. 185, 186, 247
James Harvey 236
Laura 209
Louisa 236
Mary Elizabeth 236

Percy 185
Rhobie 185, 186
Robert 14
Callaway, E. R. 278
Edgar 278
Foster 278
Hugh 278
Thomas 278
Campbell, ___ 45
Annie 293
Belle 306
Bessie 238
David 11, 16, 29, 296
Elbert F. 290
Eliza 135
Frances Parker 290
J. W. 261
James 29, 30
Jefferson 13
William 10, 15, 20
Campfield, Fred L. 156
Candance, ___ 175
Cane, Dicey 106
William 106
Cannon, Bartlett 18
Fevnby 246
William 16
Cantrell, Kate 269
Stephen (Jr.) 44b
Caphers, Abraham 114
Capps, Gideon 124
Mark C. 124
Caps, Moses 106
Capshaw, Thomas 15
Car, Catherine E. 109
Card, Richard 93
Carden, A. 23
Sallie 91
Cardwell, Joe 298
Keziah 303
Mary 298
R. L. 50
(Tyler) R. L. 44c
Richard Livingston 238a
Susan Ann 238a
Carick, Hugh Lawson White 51
Carmichael, Alexander 9, 10
Daniel 18
Jane 137
John 16
Carmicheal, John 212
Carnes, Thomas 16
Carot, (Mrs.) 236
Carr, Anna 135
Anne Winston 297
Carrick, (Lieut.) 31, 308
Addison 47, 50-53, 103
Betsy M. 60, 61
Elizabeth 61
(Mrs.) Rebecca 47
Rebecca McDowell 50
Sam Davis 51
Sidney Gamble 50
Carroll, Hiram 120
Jane 102
Susannah 95
William 28, 101
Carrothers, Benjamin 298
Carson, ___ 282
Adam 22
Nancy 88, 282
Carswell, William 185
Cartamount, Elizabeth 241
Carter, Adelia 278
Ann 73
Bonna Rozine 238a
Elvira 124
Hal Dismukes 238a

Jesse 101, 113
John 119
M. B. 277
Margaret 190
Micaja 15, 73
Moses 118
Paul Dillard 238a
Rachael 80
Rachel 114
Susannah 92
Thomas Walter 238a
Carthcart, Elizabeth 211
Cartwright, M. Lucian 220
Caruthers, Hannah 137
Casey, ___ 153
Alexander 86, 88
Ambler 83
Anthony 85
Barbara 85
Jesse 89
Joshua 112
Cash, (Rev.) James L. 43
Cassell, Margaret Bryan 196
Robert Bryan 196
Cassey, Adeline 153
Annie 202
Castil, Mary 89
Casy, Jesse 19
Cates, Benjamine 111
Catron, John 10
Caudle, Thomas Washington 174
Cave, John 128
Cavet, Richard 74
Cavett, Moses 84
Richard 15
Sally 74
Cavit, Richard 17
Cavy, William 97
Cawood, (Dr.) Campbell 42
Cazey, Alexander 15
Center (see also Senter)
___ 44
Anna 158
Byrd 159
Caroline 158
Charles McEwen 158
Eliza 158
Elizabeth 158, 238a
Evelyn 159
Felix 66, 68, 158
Frank 158
Frank Keener 158
George G. 158
George W. 159
George Washington 158, 159
Georgia 158
Gladys McEwen 159
Hugh Martin 158
Ira 158
James 159
James Gallaher 158
Joanna 159
Johanna (McEwen) 159
Katherine 158
Levina 158, 159
Margaret 158
Martha 158, 159
Martin 96
Mary (Bacon) 159
Mary Gallaher 158, 159
Milton 16, 18, 22, 30, 158, 159, 238a
Nancy 158
Nancy Jane 158, 159
Nancy (Kesner) 159, 238a
Nannie 63, 65
Perrin 158
Sarah Elizabeth 158, 244

Center (cont.)
  Seaborn 88
  Stephen 159
  Thomas 158, 159, 247
  Thomas C. 158
  Thomas Clark 158
  Thos. 62
  Thos. C. 44c
  Virginia 158
  W. S. 60
  William Stephens 158, 159
  Willis 158, 159
  Willis Stephens 158
Chamberlain, Frederick W. 259
  (Capt.) H. S. 13
  William Porter 259
Chambers, Henry 236
  Joseph 236
  Katherine 278
  Kelly M. 174
  Maud 278
  May 305
  Mel 278
  Prater 278
Champ, Lillian 268
Chandler, John D. 169
Chapman, (Col.) 242
  Benjamin 28, 29
  F. A. 216
  Hugh Banks 226
  Mayme 279
Childers, Nancy 87
Childress,____ 242
  A. J. 54
  Alma (Ingram) 211
  Anna 274
  James 211
  James L. 210, 211
  John 292
  Martha 62
  Mary 54, 292
  Mary (Bowling) 292
  Sam 62
  Samuel L. 12
  Samuel T. 125
  Thomas 13, 14
  Thos. 62, 63
Childs, Elizabeth 84
  Emma 228
  Rowland 98
Chiles (Capt.) John 32
Christan, (Capt.) William 32
Christenbury, Joshua 17, 21
Christian, Frances 119
  Matilda 122
Christopher, Logan 210
Christy, William L. 257
Churchwell, Aquilla 33
Cisco, Senders 21
Cissil,____ 150
  Carrie 150
  Robert 150
Clack, John Morgan 222
  John Morgan (Jr.) 222
  Walter 190
Claiborn, Julinda 303
Clair, Henry 170
Clanter, John 33
Clark, Addie 162
  Adelaide 162, 163
  Adelaide Frances 162, 163
  Albert 162
  Alice McCorry 162, 163
  Annie May 161
  Anny 126
  B. M. 22
  Barbara 162
  Beatrice 163
  Benjamin 29
  Benjamin Parker 162
  Carlos Smith 162
  Charles 162
  Charles Spurgeon 163
  Charlie 55, 68
  Edward 162
  Elizabeth 55, 160
  Elizabeth Payne 163
  Estelle 162
  Eugene 68, 158, 160, 161
  Fannie 162, 163
  Florence 163
  Frances 162
  Frank 162
  George Shall 162, 163
  Grady 163
  Harry Terrill 163
  Helen 161
  Henry Terrill 163
  Henry Wood McCorry 162
  Isaac C. 37
  James 30, 160, 182
  James C. 51. 55
  James Payne (Payse) 160, 162, 163
  James Trimble 162
  Jennie 163
  John 32, 96, 121, 160
  John G. 117
  John H. 51
  Joseph 294
  Joseph E. 294
  Joseph M. 101
  Kate 228
  Letitia 78, 160
  Louie 55
  Louisa 160
  Louise 162
  M. A. E. 55
  Margaret 163, 164
  Margaret McAlister 163
  Marina 162
  Mary 160, 162, 182, 189
  Mary A. E. 49
  Mary Elizabeth 163
  Mary Florence 162
  Matilda 160, 161, 247
  Maud 294
  Nancy 160
  O. C. 63, 65
  Patsy Paine 162
  Polly 99, 119
  Richard 113
  Robert 163
  Robert B. 22
  S. C. 12
  Sallie Parker 162
  Sally Payne 160
  Sam 65, 68
  Sam C. 64, 65
  Samuel 160, 161
  Samuel S. 51
  Sarah 95, 121
  Sarah P. 114
  Sheffield 163
  Susan 48, 160
  Susan McCorry 162, 163
  Susan P. 51, 104
  Susan Payne 55
  Thomas 88, 160, 162
  Thomas III 160
  Thomas Morris (Jr.) 55
  Thomas N. 9, 11, 12, 14, 15, 17, 48, 49, 51, 52, 57, 162
  Thomas N. (Jr.) 55
  Thomas N. (Sr.) 55, 59
  Thomas Norris 11, 160-163
  Thomas Sheffield 163
  Thos. N. 47
  W. B. 119
  William 160
  William B. 51, 55, 58, 59, 111, 123, 124
  William Henry 162, 163
  Willie 55
  Willis 162
Cleage, Sarah C. 184
Clemmons, Jacob 15
  Reyna 101
Clenny, Jonathan 16, 80
Cleveland, Hulda 145
  Neal 274
Click, Anna 78
Clift, Polly 100
  William 102, 214
Cloud, Letitia 189
  Mary 141
Clough, Robert 21
Clowers, George F. 38
  James 37
Clowney, Mary 160, 161
Cluck, Henry 109
  William 109
Coatney, Elizabeth 83
  Silas 20
Cobb, Aileen 199
  Ann Lou 199
  Asa 10, 16, 19, 87
  Asa (Esq.) 20
  Billie 199
  Cathryn 199
  George Robert 199
  J. W. 199
  Jacob 16
  Jesse 21
  Luretha 199
  Mary Lizzie 199
  Maud 199
  Minnie (Doughty) 199
  Perry 199
  Raymond 199
  Robert 199
  Roy 199
  Roy Fred 199
  Rufus 261
  William 21, 197, 199
Cockrill, Billy 152
  Coates S. 152
  Joe Brown 152
  Woodson 152
Codey, Charles 81
Cody, Arthur 88
  Charles 82
  Nancy 82
  Rachel 77
  William 38
Coe, Patsy 89
Cofer, James 113
  Nancy 103
Coffee, (Gen.) 262
  Charles 166
Coffer, Thomas 126
Coffman, (Col.) D. M. 12
Coggswell, Patience 257
Coker, Jane 181
Coldwell, William 15
Cole, Abigail 110
  Elizabeth 120
  James 255
Coleman, Addie 148, 154
  Anne Leone 268
  Araminta 268
  Betty 216
  Dorothy M. 268

Coleman (cont.)
  Elizabeth 268
  Elizabeth K. 268
  Ella 148, 154
  (Rev.) G. W. 12
  George LeRoy 268
  Grant C. 268
  Grant Smith 268
  Ida May 304
  James 148
  James P. 37
  John C. 268
  John H. 148, 154
  John W. 268
  Laura Alice 268
  Lincoln Lee 268
  Maggie 66-68
  Mamie 148, 154
  Margaret 148, 154, 304
  Nellie May 268
  Pearl 268
  Rachel Brown 154
  Samuel Houston 268
  Sarah Ann (Owings) 268
  Sarah Florence 268
  Scott 304
  Stephen Douglas 268
  Thomas B. 304
  Virginia 268
  William 268
  William Houston 268
  William J. 264, 268
Collett, Charles 209
  Howard 209
  John 208, 209
  John William 209
  Louise 252
  Margaret 209
  Margaret Martin 208
  Mary Catherine 209
  Ralph 209
  Raymond 209
  Robert 209
  William 208
Collier, John 117
Collins, Littie/Lottie 220
  Neal 38
  Solomon 98
Collock, (Mrs.) James 193
Colt, Alonzo 50, 63, 64
  Amelia 49
  Freddie 64, 65
  J. D. 49
  James D. 63, 65
  Jennie 49
  Lena 64, 65
  Pascal 63-65
  Paschal 50
Colter, James 18
Combs, Louis 85
Condit-Smith, Grace 235
Conizer, Adelaide 236
  Albert 236
  James 236
  James A. 236
  Katherine 236
  Paul 236
  Sarah 236
Conk, Mahaly M. 97
Connely, Corinne 152
Conway, Charles 282
  Dewitt 282
  Edward 282
  Joseph 282
  Joseph P. 282
  Nancy 282
  Sarah Porter 282

William 282
Cook,_____ 212
  Claude 38
  Dora 156
  Eliza 296
  George 18, 22, 125
  Jacob 16, 20
  John 125
  Lucy 205
  Michel 125
  Nancy 125
  Rachel 186
Cooley, Betsy 122
Cooper, Emma 252
  Henry D. 33
  James 85
  James H. 85
  Ruth 203
  Sally 118
Copage/Coppage, Thomas 93
Cope, Baracias 20
  Mary 156
Copeland, Ambrose 20
  James 16, 19
  Lydia 75
  William 13
Corbin, Jesse 21
  Thomas 21
Corey, Mary 83
Corn, Pearl 239
Cornealison, William 93
Correy, F. G. 288
Corry, Elizabeth 255
  J. A. 237
  Margaret 255, 256
  Thomas 237
  Thomas Avery 255
Cory, Harry L. 244
  Hugh Martin 244
  Jean 244
  Julia Reese 244
Cosby, Elizabeth 62
Cosey, Pleasant 116
Cotter, John 15
Cottingham, Sarah 239
Couch,_____ 192
  James 19
  Peter 16, 19
Coulson, John 92
Coulter, Alexander (Jr.) 16
  James 21
  (Capt.) Thomas 9, 16, 30
Council, John 133
Cousins, Harold 274
Cove, John 109
Covington, John 113
Cowan, Jane 212
  John R. 295
  John R. (Jr.) 295
Coward, Nellie Louise 153
Cowden, Bess 151
Cowen, Nora 202
Cox,_____ 14, 279
  Abner Jackson 164
  Alice Letitia 164
  Alma Lee 164
  Anne E. 151
  Bartlett 164
  Carrie Myra 164
  Catherine 164
  Charles W. 164
  Emma 164
  Garley 279
  George W. 151
  Ida 150
  Ida M. 151
  Isham 10, 13, 16, 164

Isham (Sr.) 94
  J. Barton 151
  James 91, 164
  John 28, 29, 62, 119, 164
  Joshua 23, 164
  Katherine 279
  Lafayette Bryson 164
  Leander Monroe 164
  Louisa Catherine 151
  Mary 95, 134, 164
  Mary Ann 120
  Nancy 164
  Nancy Clark 133
  Newton Hamilton 164
  Phillip Shaw 151
  Robert 232
  Thomas 89, 100, 164
  Thomas Samuel 164
  William B. 151
Crabtree,_____ 136
  Cathryn Reece 199
  Edward 199
  William Edward 199
  Woodrow 199
Crafton, John 15
Craig,_____ 270
  J. J. 160
  James 133
  Thomas 79
Craighead, Charles C. 133
  Gillespie 133
  Jack 133
  James R. 133
  Libbie Kate 133
  William 133
  William Alexander 133
Cravat, John 21
Craven, James 285
  Polly 285
Cravens, Ann E. 165, 166
  Charles 166
  Dorothea 165
  Eliza 165
  George L. 166
  Hannah 165
  Hattie 166
  Henry Lyle 166
  James 165, 166
  James R. 166
  James Reagan 166
  (Dr.) James Reagan 165, 166
  Jane Harriet 166
  Jesse 149
  Jesse P. 166
  Jesse Roddye 165, 166
  John 165
  Joseph 166
  Katherine 166
  Lucy 166
  Lydia Love 165, 166
  McMillin 166
  Margaret 165
  Marvin 166
  Mary 165, 166
  Mary E. 166
  Mary L(yle) 166
  Nancy J. 166
  Patsye 166
  Robert 13, 165, 166
  Robert Spencer 166
  Robt. 43
  Roy 166
  Ruth L. 166
  Sallie 165
  Tarver 166
Crawford, Algey/Algie B. 210, 211

Crawford (cont.)
  Anna Dale 152
  Annie 300
  Charles Owen 152
  Charles Owen (Jr.) 152
  Elizabeth Waite 152
  Lindsay 211
  Mary Louise 152
  Norman 152
  Norman (Jr.) 152
  Pearl (Ingram) 211
  Tyler 133
  Wm. Vonnah 152
Crenshaw, John 28
Crevat, Moses 113
Crevet, Betsy 97
Crew, James 102
  Robert 27
Crickman,_____ 304
Crise, John 21
Crisp, Iona Audrey 201
Critchell, Maud 145
Cross, George 10
  Mary Mee 250
  Robert Gallup 250
  Robert Guelph 250
  Sally McElwee 250
Crouch, (Capt.) 261
Crow, Ana 119
  Benjamine 101
  C. C. 22
  Delia 188
  Edward 89
  George 20
  James R. 22
  John 101
  Nancy 111
  Polly 94
  Sarah 158
  Willes 92
  William 92, 98
Crowder, Alice (Wester) 304
  Cardine 135
  Ford 302, 304
  Henry 302, 304
  Henry Thomas 304
  (Mrs.) J. M. 193
  J. W. 64-66
  Kate 223
  Katherine 302, 304
  Martha Ann 304
  Tully 302, 304
  (Mrs.) William 193
Crsery, John 75
Crumbliss, Alice 167
  Caroline 167
  Florence M. 167
  George Muse 167
  George Washington 167
  H. 44d
  Henry 167
  Hugh 81, 167
  Hugh Polk 167
  J. G. 44c
  James 149, 167
  James B. 167
  James Griffin 167
  Lucile 167
  Margaret 167
  Mary 167
  Mary Ann 282
  Penelope 167
  Raleigh 167
  Rosa 167
  Roy 167
  Thomas 30-32, 167
  Vera Trimby 167
  Virginia 167

Crump, Jane 144
Crutchfield, Thomas 59
Culbert, Charles T. 285
Culp, Peggy 81
Cummings, Ruth 136
Cunningham, Arabella 307
  Caroline 165
  Eleanor White 217
  James 17
  Kate 260
  Paul 12, 31
  Rhoda 95
  Rosalie 166
  Valentine 27
Curden, William 16
Curry, William 33

-D-

Dakin,_____ 252
Dallom, Fannie 238
Dalton, Elizabeth 115
  James 110
  Sally 87
  Thomas 176
Dancliffe, Anna 190
Danforth, James 277
  Josiah 117
Dani, Reil 300
Daniel,_____ 151
  Charles Hardin 151
  Elizabeth 152
  Frances 152
  Grace 152
  H. C. III 152
  H. Clay 151
  Jess 37
  Louise Merrill 152
  Mary Brown 152
  Naomi 151
  Pearl Hall 151
  Robert Brown 152
  Robert Edwin 152
  Ruth 151
  Tobias 37
  V. H. Clay (Jr.) 152
  William Gillenwaters 152
D'Armond, John G. 168
  S. J. 168
Darnell, Virginia A. 234
Darwin, Adelia 186
  Alexandria (Arrants) 187
  Alice 186
  Arrant 187
  Audrey 186
  Bertha 186, 187
  Cyrus 186
  Darius 186
  Eleanor 186
  Elizabeth 186
  Ella 186
  Ellen 186
  Frank Sharp 186
  Frederick Perry 186, 187
  Gordon Gillespie 186
  Hannah 186
  James Kenneth 186
  James Robert 186
  Jennie 186, 187
  Margaret Elizabeth 186
  Margaret (Sharp) 186
  Nell 186
  Sidney 187
  Thomas Albert 186
  William Perry 186
  William Peyton 186

Daugherty, (Gen.) 296
Dauret, John 83
Dauthel, Samuel 103
Davaney, John H. 297
Davenport, David 20
  Joseph H. 185
  Margaret McEwen 185
David, Azariah 15
  David 15
  Jenkins 15
  Owen 15
Davidson, Henry 108, 242
  William 16, 30
Davies, Margaret 166
Davis, (Dr.) 43
  (Pres.) 35
  Allen Russell 196
  Ann 127
  Arthur 266
  (Dr.) B. F. 42
  Bazzle 19
  (Dr.) Benjamine F. 148, 153
  Brazzel 16
  Britian 19
  Britton 16
  Charles 292
  Dorothy Randall 196
  Edmond 102
  Edward 16, 19
  Ella 300
  Evan 215
  George 87
  Greenwood B. 285
  Jacob 22
  James 20
  James Arthur 266
  Jennie Medora 148, 153
  John 16-18, 20, 43, 106, 148, 153
  Jonathan 20
  Julia 116
  Lillian Louise 266
  Malinda 292
  Mary Ann 215
  Mary Frances 266
  Matilda 215
  Ora Belle 231
  Pauline 215
  Rebecca 101
  Ruth Tyler 196
  Sally 96
  Samuel 107
  Samuel H. 121
  Sarah 152
  Susan Brown 153
  William 16, 19, 73, 122
  Zilpha H. 154
Dawson,_____ 14
  Darling 170
  Elizabeth 115
  Hallie 170
  Jonathan Smith 170
Day, Addie (Bagwell) 254
  Clifford 254
  John Isaac 250
  Laura 254
  Mabel 254
  Margaret 250
  May 250
  (Dr.) Samuel Houston 250
  Thomas 254
  Thomas W. 252, 254
  Vera 254
  William 107
Deacon, Andrew Gordon 153
  Elizabeth S. 153
  Helen Davis 153
  Mary Belle 153

Deacon (cont.)
Robt. Richardson 153
  William Cory 153
Deaderick, Eliza Ann 296
Deakins, Townley 73, 74
Dealy, Margaret 219
Dean, David 76
Dearmond/DeArmond
  Anna Ruth 168
  Annie Laurie 168
  Archie 169
  Calhoun 50, 168
  David 118
  Drucilla 168
  Elizabeth 168
  Ella 63, 65, 68
  Esther 50, 168
  Fred 168
  G. B. 168
  Grace 168
  Grizzie 168
  Grizzy 50
  Grizzy B. 121
  Jack 169
  Jackson 168
  James 13, 19, 21, 66, 68, 73, 81, 168
  Jane 168
  John 168
  Lester 168
  Lewis 168
  Lula 168, 169
  Mahala 50, 168
  Margaret 168
  Mary 168
  Matilda 168
  Matilda Drusilla 50
  Merrill 169
  Peggy 50
  Polly Elizabeth 50
  Richard 168, 169
  Samuel 60, 121
  Samuel Jackson 168
  Spurdgram 168
  Susan 168
  (Mrs.) Susan 48, 50
  Susan Hannah 168
  Thomas 168
  Wade 169
  Wylie 168
Deatherage, Abner 101, 124
  Browder Kendrick 224
  Ella 224
  Emma (Denton) 224
  Lucinda 124
  Margaret Kendrick 224
  Mary 262
  Mary Sue 224
  Paul 224
  Robert Allen 224
  Sarah 145
  Sexon A. 224
  Virginia 224
Deatherage/Detheridge, Alice 224
Deatheridge, Nancy 128
  Samuel 14, 115
Decker, George 102
Defani, Bernard 150
  Cassie 150
  Esther 150
  James 150
Deitz, Carl 68
  Charles 63
  Charlie 65, 66
  Lillie 64-68
  Margaret 244
  William 244

William Helicus 244
Delaney/DeLaney 298
Byrd 102
Hobart 38
James 142
Paralee 139
Sarah 87
Delmon, Jacob 124
deLossus (see Lossus)
Delozier/DeLozier
  Charles E. 141
  Claude B. 141
  Edward W. 141
  George 79
  Helen 141
  Jesse 62
  Millie 303
  Nellie 90
  Paul 141
  Sarah 252
  Susan 143
Demoron, Morton 253
Denny, David C. 29
Denton,_____ 186
  Emma 224
  J. H. 46
  Julia 295
  Margaret 183
  William C. 286
Depew, (Miss) Nannie 42
Dereux, Eva 211
Derick, George 77
  Henry 77
  John 77
Derosset, Daniel 16
  Louis 93
Derr, Blanch 220
Derrick, Newton 23
Derrit, William 21
Detherel, Samuel 109
Detheridge, Allen 217, 224
  Elizabeth 220
  Polly 112
Devaney, John F. 190
DeYoung, Mina 209
Dial, Beulah 174
Dickens, Richard 91
Dickey, Abner L. 297
  Andrew J. 145
  Ann 183
  Anthony 93
  Dewitt 156
  (Rev.) J. W. 43
  John H. 22
  Mary 116
  Rachel 145
  Sophrona 297
  Willie 290
Dickson, John T. 253
  Margaret 134
  Nancy 125
  Polly 79
Dietz, Elizabeth C. 49
  (Mrs.) Mary 49
  (Capt.) W. H. 44d
  William H. 49, 53
Diggs, Benjamine W. 38
Dildine, Jonathan 89
Dirgin, John 80
Dixon, Absolum 77
  Eli 280
  Mary Dorcas 195, 196
  Osy 90
Doak, (Miss) 161
Dobbins, Major M. 125
Dodd, Ann Cameron 257
Dodson, E. F. 227

Samille Amanda 219
  Tabitha 92
Doherty, George 13
Dolozier, Jesse 14
Dolton, William 21
Donaldson, Mathew 79
  Polly 118
  (Capt.) Vinet 161
Donelly, Janice 232
  Pauline 232
  Richard 232
Donnell, George 112
Donnely, John 15
Donohoo, Thomas 109
Doran, Nancy 290
Dore, Elizabeth 105
Dorton, Mary M. 279
Doss, Georgia 133
  John 83, 133
  Margaret 133
  Mary (Allison) 133
  Mary Kate 133
Doughty, Bailey 198
  Carl 197, 198
  Celia (East) 198
  Charles Franklin 197
  Clarence 198
  Dorothy 198
  Edna 198
  Ella Mae 198
  Floyd 198
  James 197
  James Isaac 197
  John 198
  John Williams 197
  Kate 198
  Kathleen 198
  Lewis 197, 198
  Louise 198
  Lousinda C. 197
  Margaret E. 197
  Mary E. (Hinds) 199
  Mary Eauline 197
  Mattie Pearl 197
  May 199
  Minnie C. 197, 199
  Nell 198
  Paul 198
  Pearl 197
  Raymond 198
  Reuben 198
  Ruben C. 37
  Ruth 198
  Sam 197, 198
  Sarah 215
  Sarah Ann 197
  Sewell 198
  Sherman 38, 198
  Sherman C. 43
  Sidney Caroline 197
  Thomas J. 197
  Velma 198
  Willard 198
  Wiley/Willey 197, 199
Douglas, Arthur 38
Douglass, Mattie 210
Dougthit, W. R. 144
Dover, Joshua 85
Dowd, Lawrence Scales 250
Dowler, John 14
Doyle, Nancy 190
  William 288
  William Payne (Jr.) 288
Draper, Benjamine 20
  Benton 97
  William 21
Drips, David 203
Driver, Harry Preistly 178

Driver, Mary Elizabeth 178
Dryskill, William Y. 125
Dudley, John 15
  Samuel 76
Duff, Addie 210
  Clara 210
  Frank 209, 210
  Margaret 210
  Raymond 210
  Robert 210
  Stella 210
  Sue (Ingram) 210
  William 210
Duffy, Roland 188
Dugger, Daniel R. 241
  Jeptha 84
  Mary A. 222
  Mollie 290
  Samuel 23
Duke, Basil 259, 260
  (Gen.) Basil 259
  Calvin Morgan 260
  Ewing 260
  Frances Key 260
  Henry 260
  Jennie Speed 260
  Julia Churchill 260
  Thomie 259
Duncan,_____ 143, 238a
  Agnes 84
  Frances 106
  R. D. 62
  Robert 13, 15, 17
  Ruth 292
  Stephen 20
Dunken/Duncan, Robert 21
Dunkin, Benjamine 103
  John 33
Dunlap, Benjamine 170
  Bethenia 170
  Clinton 170
  Devereaux 170
  Eady 80, 170
  Evelyn 170
  Hugh 30, 57, 80, 170
  Hugh W. 170
  James Trimble 170
  John 170
  John H. 170
  Marie 170
  Martha 170
  Mignomie 170
  Nancy 170
  Porter 170
  Richard 32, 170
  Richard G. 170
  Ripley 170
  Susan 170
  Susan Gilliam 170
  W. C. 108
  William 170
  William C. 170
Dunnaway, Frances 179
  J. D. 179
  Maurine 179
  Ruth 179
  Waldo 179
Dunning, (Mrs.) Myrtilla 50
Dunwold, Charlotte 120
Duren, Nancy 241
Durne, Daniel 74
Durrell, Harry L. 244
Durret, John H. 21
  Marton 21
  Willes 21
Durrett, John W. 94
  Martin 91
  William 23

Dutton, (Mrs.) Callie 193
Dwire/Dyer, Judith 76
Dyer, Margaret Hiatt 165
  Mattie 278
  Nellie 144

-E-

Eagleton, Elijah McKee 48
  Elvira Hamilton 50
  Isaac Anderson 50
  Margaret 50
  (Mrs.) Margaret 47
  Samuel Ewing 50
  William 14, 93, 103-105, 114
  (Rev.) William 50, 52
Eakin, Absolum 80
Earp, Richard 119
Easley, John 17
  Juda 97
East, Addie 253
  Celia 197
  Ella (Sigman) 253
  Fay 253
  Frank 253
  Joseph T. 252, 253
  Maude 253
  Mollie 253
  Ollie 253
  Samuel 252, 253
Eastabrooke, Angeline M. 49
Easter, Alice 230
  Clifford H. 37
  Polly 123
Eastley, Nancy 273
Eastman, William 163
Easton, John 119
Eatain, Jane 108
Eaton, Elijah 20
  James 20
  John 20
  Julia 300
  Mary 248
  (Mrs.) R. P. 194
Eberling, Carl 186
  (Dr.) Carl 186
Eblen,_____ 142
  (Mrs.) 49
  Anna 171, 172
  Belle 172
  Blanch 173
  Charlie 66
  Dixie 176
  Edward 80, 171
  Effie 172
  Elijah 173
  Eliza 172
  Elizabeth 171
  Elmer Lewis 172
  Frankie 142
  George 173
  Glen 172
  Hiram 172
  Isaac 42, 120, 143, 171
  Isaac Newton 172
  Isham 172
  Isreal 171
  James 172
  James Buren 173
  James Gamble 172
  Jane 172
  John 14, 17, 171, 172
  John (Jr.) 172
  John Lewis 172
  Joseph 172
  Keziah 171, 298

  Lelia 172
  Lillie 49
  Lucinda 171, 246
  M. S. 172
  Mack 172
  Mae 172
  Margaret (Gamble) 172
  Martha 172
  Mary 171
  Mary Jane 171
  Matilda 49
  Mattie 172
  Nancy 100, 171, 298
  Nancy Jane 239
  Nettie 172, 173
  Newton Colvin 172
  Olney Arthur 173
  Pauline Elizabeth 173
  Pearl Grady 173
  Polly 77, 172
  S. L. 298
  Sallie 172, 173
  Samuel 15, 62, 171-173
  Sarah 171, 172
  Sarah McGowan 172
  Sarah (McGowan) 173
  Susan 172
  Terra Franklin 173
  Thomas 298
  Thomas Byron 173
  Walker 172
  Wilkey Al 173
  William 23, 86, 91, 92, 111, 116, 171
  William Carr 171, 172, 183
  Wilma 173
  Wm. C. 42, 43
  Y. B. 172, 173
Eblin, R. J. 64
  W. 65
  Willie 63, 64
Echard, (Mrs.) Sarah 48
Eddington,_____ 144
Eddy, Corrine 246
Edgeman, James 38
Edgman, William 28
Edington, Samuel 112
Edminston, John 96
  Thomas 96
Edmonds, Levisy 84
  Mathew 84
Edmondson, Rachel 290
Edwards, John 122
  Levisy 142
  Lona 237
  Mary 137
  Williams 99
Egleton, (Rev.) William 57
Eichbaum, (Mr.) 46
Eidson, Charles Dean 152
Elben,_____ 44
Elder, (Miss) 298
Eldridge,_____ 144
  Benjamine 93
  (Mrs.) Charles 193
  Jane 122
  Jesse 15, 18, 75
  John 122
  Nancy 105
  Nathan 16, 18
  Peggy 83
  Polly 86, 93
  Samuel 14
  Simeon 16, 18, 28
  Simpson 75
  Thomas 16
Elkins, Eliza 298
  Lydia 100

Ellender, Jane 75
Elliott, Floyd 37, 38
  Josiah 16
Ellis, (Maj.) 275
  Aimee Parthenia 174
  Benjamine 174
  C. J. 174
  Caleb 174
  Charles 119
  Chrissie Winnie 174
  Essie 87
  Foster Kendrick 174
  Francis 174
  Frank 174, 217
  Jency 298
  John 174
  Kate Isabel 174
  Mary Bessie 174
  Maud Elizabeth 174
  Minnie Samantha 174
  Monroe 174
  Rebecca 174, 226
  Samuel Franklin 174
  Sarah 174
  Sarah M. 148
  Sudie 196
  Thomas 174
  Uriah Samuel 174
  Vera Ethel 174
  William 174, 298
  William Elbert 174
  William G. 125
  William M. 174
Ellison, Elizabeth 83
  Frances 172
  Robert 18
Elsworth, Elmer 305
Emery, Jane 214
  Joseph 21
Emmons, Lida 205
Emory, William 214
England, Annie 210
  Dabney 175
  Isaac 88, 175
  John 175
  Lucinda 83, 175
  Pauline 175
  Prudence 104, 175
  St. Claire 175
  Thomas 88, 175
  William 175
Ensley, Enock 161
Ernest, Barbara 171
  Martha 228
Erskine, Charles 295
Ervin, Alma 224
  Effie 152
  Ella 291
  James A. 224
  William 20
Ervin/Erwin
  Josephine 303, 305
  Margaret H. 303, 305
  Margaret (Wester) 305
  Maud 303, 305
  Robbie May 303, 305
  Thomas C. 303, 305
Erwin, Frances 85
  Francis 17, 20
  Margaret 89
  Samuel 99, 208
  William 18, 90
Eskridge, Samuel 23, 57
  (Mrs.) Sophia 48
Essary, Annie 98
  John 98
Estes, Stella 239
Estill, Katherine 239

Etheridge, Charity 102
  Michael 96
  Nancy 98
Etter, Elbert C. 37
Evan, (Capt.) 12
Evans, Abby 176
  Albert Newton 215
  Alcy 176
  Alice 142, 176
  Andrew Jackson 214
  Anna (Bowman) 142
  Ardin 28, 81
  Arthur L. 215
  Benjamine 16
  Bessie M. 215
  Carl Samuel 215
  David H. 176
  Elijah 78
  Elizabeth C. 121
  Ervin 20
  Hannah 127
  Harry Robert 215
  Henry Clay 215
  Hugh Campbell 215
  Jack Frederick 215
  Joe 36, 38
  John 197
  John C. 176
  John Evan 215
  Joseph F. 38
  Joseph S. 215
  Julia 215
  Keziah 176
  Lucretia (Kendrick) 215
  Luther 37
  Martha Susan 215
  Mary E. 176, 214
  Mary Elizabeth 215
  Nancy 81, 112
  Nancy Ann 215
  Nancy Jean 215
  Nehemiah 176
  Oscar 142
  Patrick 142
  Patrick Henry 176
  Patrick W. 141, 176
  Polly 176
  Reuben 105
  Rupert 142
  Ruth Catherine 215
  Samuel 27, 29, 107, 176
  Samuel P. 176
  Sarah L. (Rayder) 215
  Thomas 142
  Thomas H. 176
  Thomas Oscar 176
  Thomas Witherspoon 215
  William 15, 30, 142, 214, 215
  William Fred 215
  William S. 176
  Willis 102, 109
Evens, Aden 19
  William 17
Everett, Crawford Duncan 151
  John H. 282
  Merrill 151
  Robert 282
  Sallie 282
  Wilmer 282
Evins, Betsy 73
Ewing, Annie 111
  Arthur 135
  Arthur C. 177
  Bonnie 211
  Elijah 177
  Elijah B. 177
  Jacob 177

  James 177
  James A. 177
  John M. 177
  Lulini Leati 177
  Martha J. 177
  Mary 177
  Nellie 177
  Samuel 57
  Sarah 114
  Sarah M. 177
  William A. 177
Ezell, Dahlia 179
  Lou 161

-F-

Fackler, Sarah 257
Fain, Margaret 116
  (Col.) R. G. 36
Faina, Joseph 150
Fairies, Richard 85
Falkner, Mattie May 279
Falton, Martha 108
Farman, Thomas 100
Farmer, Elijah 86
  Elizabeth 102
  John 38
  Minerva 270
  Farnum,___ 142
  Farnwalt, John 14
Farr, Joe 37
Fauby, Margaret 214
Faucette, James 236
Fay, Mary Lillian 285
Feils, Jeremiah 21
Fell, James 114
Fendley, Mary 75
Ferguson, Billy Tom 218
  Charles Fred 218
  Jack 273
  Rose 218
  Tom 218
  W. T. 44c, 253
  Willie 66, 68
Ficke, Harry H. 37
Fickey, Charles E. 37
Fiedler, Jeremiah 83
Fields, Jeney 88
Fike, Nathan 33
Fillmore, (Pres.) 161
Finley, John 16, 123
Finzer, Rosabelle 282
Fisher,___ 160
  A. O. 60
  Laura Thompson 250, 251
  William H. 203
Flat, Benjamine 16
  John 16, 18, 21
Flat(t), James 86
Fleiner, Betsy 106
  Richard 106
  Sally 106
Fleming, Andrew Foster 178
  Charles Rhoton 178
  David 62, 178
  James 178
  James Clarke 178
  John 60
  John Miller 178
  Martha 178
  Martha Elizabeth 178
  Mary Miller 178
  Nell 290
  R. D. 62
  Samuel 178
  Wilbur Fisk 178

Flemming, Andrew Foster 55
　Charles Rhoton 55
　David 14
　(Rev.) David 43, 55
　Mary Burem 55
　William 12
Flennigan, William 31
Flinn, Carrie 175
　Corena 175
　Roxanna 175
　William G. 22
　William Groffith 175
Flucker, Owen 168
Foosbee, John 200
Fooshee, Ab 202
　Absalom 308
　John 19, 202, 308
　Jonas 202
　Mary 202
　Susan (Hinds) 308
Ford, Charles M. 305
　Edmond 107
　Janie 149
Formatt, Adam 17
　John (Jr.) 17
Formwalt, John 14
Forrester, Alex 101
　Alexander 179
　Belinda 179
　Benjamine 179
　Benjamine Franklin 179
　Bettie 179
　Caroline 179
　Deborah 179
　Edna 179
　Eliza 179
　Emma 179
　Ethel 179
　Eva 179
　Frank 179
　George 179
　Isham G. 179
　James 179
　Jane 179
　Joseph Bryant 179
　Josephine 179
　Larkin 101, 179
　Louella 179
　M. Hazeltine 179
　Marcus 179
　Maria 179
　Marie S. 179
　Marshall H. 179
　Martha 179
　Menerva 179
　Mildred 179
　Nancy 179
　Polly 179
　Polly Ann 179
　Rachel 179
　Robert 179
　Rufus 179
　Solomon 95, 179, 242
　Thomas 179, 242
　Tuton 179
　Wiley 179
　William 179
Fortner, Frankie 181
Fortsen, Stephen 109
Foster,____ 189
　Annie 278
　Ann(ie) Elizabeth 277, 278
　Annie Myra 245
　Charles E. 37
　Eliza 118
　Elizabeth 277, 278
　Ernest 242
　Helen 278

　Henry 278
　Henry C. 277, 278
　James Edward 277, 278
　Julia (Leeper) 278
　Julia Margaret 278
　Martha 278
　Mary Lynn 278
　Myra 277
　Sarah 228
　Snow A. 245
　T. C. 277, 278
　Thomas 278
　W. Edward 245
Fouche, Nancy 78
Foust, Molly 217, 219
Fout, Julian 95
Foute, W. F. 278
France, (Capt.) Hugh 15
Frances, Hugh 77
Francis, Hugh 9, 15, 30
　Joseph 15, 30
　Woodson 15
Francisco, William B. 261
Franklin, Blanche 271
　Henry Clay 271
　Henry Dick 270, 271
　John Randolph 271
　Lee Curtis 271
　Levi Parkins 271
　Lynn Kimball 270
Frazier, Ebra 273
　Emma 184
　Jane 105
　Victoria 189
Freeman,____ 278
　Achasa (Ponder) 308
　Chastain 126
　James 34, 99, 114, 308
　John 18
　(Mrs.) Polk 193
French, Belle 66-68
　Dorothy C. 300
　Eliza 252
Fritts, Albert 180
　Annie Mary 181
　Benjamin 181
　Benjamin Franklin 180, 181
　Christiana 180
　David 180
　Dock 180
　Elizabeth 134
　Frank 66, 68
　Fred A. Weil 181
　George Washington 180
　Henry 180
　Isaac 181
　Isom G. 180, 181
　Jacob 90, 134, 180, 181
　James 180
　Jerry 181
　Jesse R. 180
　John 90, 180, 181
　John W. 180
　Joseph 180
　Kate 180
　Katie 180
　King 181
　Lena 181
　Martin 180
　Mary 180, 181
　Mary Ann 180
　Mathilda 64-68
　Matilda 180, 181
　Mitchell 180
　Peter 106, 115, 180
　Phillip 115, 180
　Ransom 181
　Robert 180

　Thomas 180
　Thomas Wilson 181
　William 180, 181
　William J. 181
　William M. 180
　William N. 180
　Wylie H. 180, 181
Frizzell, Arch 218
Froman, Lois 284
Frost, Nancy 89
　Paul 168
Fry, George 128
Fryar, Cynthia P. 228
Fulcher, Frances 76
　Francis 15
Fulks, Matsy 201
Fuller,____ 292
　Abraham 119
　George 27, 29, 182
　James 182
　Joshua 182
　Rebecca 271
Fulton, John 15, 18
　Rebecca 95
Funderburk, Catherine 111
Fundley, John 62
Funk, Jacob 117

-G-

Gaines, (Col.) Edmund P. 33, 133
Galbraith, Alexander 48
　Alexander (Sr.) 48
　Amanda 49
　Eliza 48
　Wm. 61
Galbreath, Alexander 82
　Betsy 48
Gallaher, Abiah K. 49
　Allen G. 57
　Charles 62
　Daisy 301
　David 16
　Eliza 158
　Emily C. 49
　George B. 244
　James 73, 82, 127, 158
　Jane 158
　(Mrs.) Jane 49
　Jas. 21
　Lucy 204
　Mattie Houston 286
　Nancy 79
　Nancy Ames 244
　Polly 82
　Robert O. 161
　Rose 185
　Sarah 144
　Sarah Elizabeth 244
　Thomas 13, 16, 21, 101, 127
　W. L. 144
　William Thomas 244
　Wyatt 87
Galliher, James 17
　Thomas 17
Gallion, Charlie 38
　Elmer 37
　Isaac 107
Galloway, Ann 113
　Betsy 97
　Charles 14, 103, 105, 108
　Ginney 74
　James 15, 74
　Jeames 21
　Nancy 47, 98

Galyon, George W. 242
Gambal, Robert 18
Gambell, A. H. 61
  John 73
  Polly 116
  W. P. 61
Gambill, R. W. 44d
Gamble, Adolphus A. 50
  Alexander 15, 30
  Betsy Green 50
  Caroline 148, 183
  Charles Richard 267
  Floyd Gilbert 267
  Floyd M. 267
  George 107
  Grace Magdalene 267
  Harry Thomas 267
  James 183
  Jane 137
  Jane McDowell 50
  John M. 50
  Kendell Edwin 267
  Margaret 171, 183
  Nancy 47
  (Mrs.) Polly 47
  Rebecca 53
  Robert 99
  Robert L. 183
  Samuel 183
  Victoria 183
  William M. 183
  William Purris 50
Gambrill, James 114
Game, Nathan 87
Gammon, William 212
Gannon, Annie 238
Garabrant, John 127
Gardenhire, Adam 85
  Jacob 17, 18, 30
  Margaret 105
  William 15, 17, 21
  Williom 88
Gardiner, John 20
Gardner, Barbara 91, 164
  James 91
  Nancy 95
  Robert Henry 258
  Thomas 113
  William H. 113
Garner, James 15, 20
Garrett, Cynthea 88
  Nancy 89
  Polly 280
  Sally 110
  Sarah 213
Gaspen, Miars 17
Gass, Jacob M. 186
Gattis, Lewis Price 154
Gay, Anna 259
Geass, Martha E. 49
Geese, Eliza M. 51
  Ida Matilda 61
  Martha 51
  Mary Alice 51
  William Henry 51
  William L. 51
Genereski, Emma 285
Gennings, John 108
Gent, Joshia 22
Gentry, Fenton Allen 284
  Gray 284
  Owing 111, 143
George, Barbara 245
Geren, Amanda 49
  Lidia 117
  Sally 82
  Solomon 16, 22, 28, 29, 31, 57, 96, 122

Gerstle, Lucille 304
Gibbons, Elizabeth 120
Gibbs, Mary 68
Gibson, Hattie 208
  James 16
  Madie 156
  Thomas 134
Giddings, J. R. 144
Gideon, Mary W. 121
  Roger 20
Gilbert, Alexander 110
  Benjamine 120
  William 119
Gilbreath,_____ 246
  Alexander 110
  Amanda 60
  Arthur 13
  Joseph 18
  Thomas 21
  William 13, 97
Gilder, Frank McClung 258
  John S. 258
  Rogers Van 258
Gillam, Bettie 307
Gillenwaters, Mary Jane 147
Gillespie, Adelia 184, 186
  Alice 184
  Amelia (King) 186
  Anna Dent 185
  Anna Neilson 184, 185, 247
  Anna Penelope 184
  Annie Dent 184
  Archibald D. 184
  Booth 186
  Charles 184
  Elbert Dave 184
  Elizabeth 184-186, 247
  Etta 184
  Florence 184
  Gay 184
  George 62, 149, 184
  George L. 247
  George Lewis 51, 184, 185, 247
  George Thomas 184
  Hortense 186
  Hugh Swan 184, 185
  (Col.) J. W. 35
  James Anderson 184, 185
  James W. 184
  James Wendel 184
  James Whiteside 184, 185
  Jane Harriet 184
  Jean Neilson 184, 185
  John 79, 247
  John C. 44c, 247
  John Cessna 184, 185
  John King 185, 186
  John King II 186
  John M. 184-186
  Joseph 185
  Joseph Anderson 184, 185
  Joseph McEwen 185
  Joseph Strong 184, 185
  Kyle 185
  Lewis 184
  Lewis G. 185
  Luther L. 184
  (Mrs.) Margaret 51
  Margaret Alice 185
  Margaret Alice (McEwen) 185
  Margaret J. 49
  Mary Blain 184, 185
  Nancy Elizabeth 184, 185, 226
  Neilson 185
  Nellie 184, 185
  Penelope Whiteside 184, 185

Robert N. 184, 186
  Sallie 293
  Thomas 184
  Thomas J. 184
  Thomas Jefferson 184
  Virginia (Swan) 185
  William 184
  William N. 184
Gilliam, Susannah Harding 170
Gilliland, James 17
  Margaret 47
  (Mrs.) Margaret 50
  Mary 60
  Mary Bashears 50
  Robert 13, 57, 58
  Robert S. 92, 158
  (Mrs.) William 194
Ginn, E. R. 154
Gipton, Mollie 66
  Thomas 64, 65
Givens, John 10, 15, 17
  Nancy 74
Gives, Delmas (Jr.) 151
Glasgow, James 16
Gleaves, James C. 163
  Mary T. 163
  Susan Clark 163
  William A. 163
Glenn, Elizabeth 151
Glover, Elizabeth 188
  James 214
Godby, Emma 176
Goddard, Ann 167
  Elizabeth Campbell 237
  Eva Rose 231
  Frank 215
  Frank Lewis 215
  Joseph Paul 215
  Kathleen Bayless 231
  Marvin Wiley 231
  Mary Elizabeth 231
  Nathan 112
  Olive 231
  Ora Frances 231
  Sam 231
  William 112
Golston, Dorothy 140
  Frank 140
  John 140
Gomly, Grover 245
  John 245
  Marcella 245
  Marcellus 245
  Nellie 245
Good, George 117
  James 106
  Zilpe 98
Goodman, Clara 285
Goodner, Mary Rebecca 190
  Sidney Frances 190
  Thomas C. 190
Goodrich, William 77
Goodson, Jennie 201
Goodwin, Ada Frank 211
  Alpha 298
  Catherine 211
  Gilbert 211
  Joe E. 211
  John Barxtol 211
  Kate 211
  Luther 211
  Overton 121
  Peter W. 298
Gorden, James 17
Gordon, Evelyn 166
  George 13, 41, 165, 273
  Jeames 22
  Joshua 121

Goss, Ben 199
Bennie 199
Gossett, Evaline 118
Keziah 123
Gouth, Fred C. 36, 37
Gower, Mathew 18
Goweros, Mathew 22
Graham, George 211
  Joseph 86, 127
  Laura 211
  Margaret 212
  Mathew 33
  William 34
Grammer, James 110
  Polly 121
Granme, Nancy 211
Grant, Cape 307
  Dollie 307
  J. C. 154
  John 307
  William 274
Grasham, Nehemiah 99
Grason, Stacey 75
Grass, (Miss) 149
Grassham, Anderson 214
Graves, Elliott 282
  Eugenia 169
  George 75
Gray, George 268
  Harry 268
  Naomi 253
Grayson, Benjamin 22
Greasland, S. A. 22
Green, A. L. 62
  Andrew 23
  Austin 63, 65, 238a
  Austin A. 145
  Austin Avery 188
  Austin L. 12, 126, 188
  Austin Letheridge 188
  Avery 188
  Blanch 188
  Bluford 188
  Calisty 188
  Carrie Lee 254
  Charles 254
  Charles R. 252, 254
  Charles W. 188
  Ernest 188
  Frances 179
  George 188
  Harold 188
  Henry Pierce 188
  James 80, 101, 254
  Jane 188
  Jennie 188
  John 188
  John B. 63, 65 188
  John Webb 259
  Joseph 30
  Josephine 68
  Katherine 62, 188
  Lella 174
  Leonodas 188
  Mary 188
  Maston 42
  Mattie 188
  Maud 188
  Minnie 188
  Obey 188
  Peter 14
  Rebecca 188
  Rose (Stonecipher) 254
  Surry 188
  Theodric 188
  Thomas 188, 254
  William 13, 93, 97, 303
  William C. 188

Green, Willis Center
Greenwood, Minnie 220
  Sophia 289
Greer, _____ 154
  Annie (Millican) 253
  C. D. M. 170
  Gus 252, 253
  Jane 122
  John 253
  Katie 252
  Solomon 16
Gregoire, August 151
  Francoise 151
Gregory, Eugene Hamilton 155
  (Dr.) Paul 155
Gregsby, George 88
  L. 117
Greib, Daniel 20
Greyson, Benjamine 15
Gribble, Kathleen 285
Griffen, William 126
Griffin, Nellie Penelope 167
Griffis, John 212
Griffith, (Capt.) 242
  Isaac 118
  William 20
Griffitts, Robert T. 279
Griffy, Polly 112
Grigsby, John 256
  Lutherate 117
  Samuel 246
Grinsley, Kiziah 120
Grisley, Samuel 91
Gross, see Cross
Grub, Daniel 17
Grubb, Samuel 116
  William 256
  William M. 122
Crunant, John 108
Guenther, Charlotte 64, 65
  Fannie 244
  G. A. 13
  Gusavus 49
  Gusta A. 244
  Julia Reese 244
  Margaret 244
  Mary 49
Guffy, Nancy 113
Gullick, Reece 16
Gunter, Gustavus A. 53
Gunther, Charlotte 49
Gurley, Alma 209
Gurscot, William 60
Guthrie, _____ 228

-H-

Hacker, Julias 15, 17
  Julius 80
Hackett, John 30
  John (Sr.) 15
Hackney, Fred 210
  James 119
Hager, (Mrs.) Mabel 152
Hagerty, Sarah 80
Hagewood, Benjamine 88
Haggard, Allen Hale 224
  Allen Halen 140
  Claude (Jerry) 223
  Frank 223
  Fred 304
  Frederick 140, 224
  Frederick G. 223
  Harriett 116
  Hobart 223
  Hood 12

  Jerry 223
  John H. 223
  Nancy Jane 224
  Rue 224
  Rue H. 140
  Sattira 125
  Sussanah 85
  W. Robert 253
  William 128
Haggart, James 82
  John 82
Hagler, Sarah 118
Hahins, Susanah 75
Haile, Anna 112
Hailey, John 19
Haines, Josiah 23
  (Rev.) L. K. 144
Hair, Louisa 298
Hale, Hannah 179
  John M. 101
Haley, _____ 44, 227
  Alexander 190
  Allen 103, 189
  Charles 42, 189
  Charles B. 190
  Charles Smith 189
  Charles W. 208
  Clara 189
  David 14, 30-32, 106
  (Maj.) David 189-191
  Elijah 189, 307
  Elizabeth 189, 190
  Eugene 190
  Frances 190
  Frank 190
  George 190, 307
  Henry 189
  Jack 165, 255
  Jackson 190
  James 189
  John 189, 190
  John B. 307
  John Cloud 32, 189, 190, 255
  John Henry 190
  Joseph 190
  Kenneth 189
  Leathy 189
  Margaret 189, 190
  Marion 190
  Martha 189
  Mary 307
  Milton 190
  Milton J. 190
  Nellie 190
  Pearl 190
  Raymond Carter 190
  Robert 106, 189, 190
  Rosco 189
  Sally 231
  Sally T. 190
  Sarah 189
  Sydney (Smith) 190
  Ward 189
  William 42
  William B. 189, 190
Hall, _____ 146
  Adeline 209
  Arch 274
  Billie 196
  Byrd 274
  Carrie 274
  Catherine 196
  Dickinson 15
  Earnest 273, 274
  Elizabeth 196, 292
  Ernest W. 196
  Frank 274
  Fred 210

Hall (cont.)
  Jennie 273
  Jesse 273
  John 137, 274
  Mary 273
  (Mrs.) Maud 193
  May 153
  Nannie 273
  Robert 273, 274
  Samuel C. 19
  Stanley 274
  William 99
Halley, Almerine 34
Halton, Lou 151
Hambree, (Col.) Joel 308
Hamby, Alma 295
  Caroline Hinds 200
  Charles Allen 267
  Clarinda (Owens) 267
  Clarinda (Owings) 266
  Dorinda Cornelia 266
  Eleanor 200
  Eliza Cornelia 267
  Evelyn May 200
  Fannie 226
  Gilbert Randolph 230, 266, 267
  Gilbert Winfrey 267
  Grace Lillian 267
  Honora Helen 267
  J. P. 267
  James Arthur 200
  James Newton 266, 267
  Jimmie Lavenia 267
  John Leslie 200
  Julius 264, 266, 267
  Kenneth 267
  Lois Magdalene 267
  Margaret Richard 267
  Martha Jane 230, 266
  Mary Elizabeth 230, 266
  Mary Ella 267
  Mary Etta 267
  Sarah (King) 267
  Sarah Mahala 266
  Theodore Ewing 200
  Theodore Ewing (Jr.) 200
  William Anton 267
  William Gilbert 267
  William Jackson 266
Hamel, Sarah 303
Hamilton, Elizabeth 303, 305
  Elizabeth Luckey 305
  George 303, 305
  Henry 303, 305
  James 87
  Jas. 62
  Jennie 305
  John 104, 303
  Katherine 305
  Malinda T. 106
  Nannie West 305
  Neal 305
  Polly 113
  Rachel 303
  Sarah 303
  Seth 305
  Thomas 303
  Willia 305
Hamlet, Ruth 146
Hammond, James 22
  Jessey 22
  John 22
Hampton,_____ 179
  Hilton Screven 178
  Oscar 38, 43
Hanapan, Betsy 47
Hancock,_____ 179

Hancock, Stephen 28
Handley, Arthur 17
Hangley (see Langley)
Hankens, Joseph 15
Hankins, James 15, 18, 73, 78, 95, 113
  John 15, 22
  Joseph 17, 76, 99
  Polly 117
  Sallie 78
  Susan 200
Hanks,_____ 260
Hannagan, Anna 229
Hannah, Drucilla 90
  Jane 103
Hapler, William 123
Harbert, John D. 115
Harcourt, Johnetta 170
  Martha 170
  (Dr.) W. 170
Hardadge, Thomas 305
Hardin, Benjamin 17
  Elizabeth 257
  George W. 307
  James 236
  Joseph 14
  (Rev.) Rob 52
  Thomas 156
Hardwick, Virginia 213
Hare, Daniel 15, 75
Harelson, Paul 9, 10, 15
Harmon,_____ 136
  Henry 16
  Phillip 95
Harner, Margaret Delaney 200, 203
  Susan M. 201
Harriett, Jessie 151
Harris, Adeline 211
  Daniel Oscar 275
  Daniel Overton 275
  John 21
  Lizzie 66, 67
  Marian 109
  Ornson 112
  Samuel 93
  Sussanah 115
Harrison, A. S. 61
  Achilla L. 119
  Achilles Leonidas 50
  Archilles 60, 61
  Archilles M. 61
  Archilles S. 61
  (Mrs.) Betsy 50
  Eliza Jane 50
  Ellender 79
  Erasmus Darwin 50
  Hester 165
  James 103
  Jane 60
  John 95
  John Koontz 50
  Mary 165
  Thomas 19
  (Gen.) William H. 302
  (Gen.) William Henry 133
  William McEwen 50
Harskins, Morgan 22
Hart, Amanda 192
  Deborah 192
  Ely 192
  George 192
  Henry 91, 192
  Henry (Jr.) 192
  Henry (Sr.) 192
  John 87
  John J. 240
  John Jay 192

  John Sawyer 192, 242
  Martha 192
  Nancy 98
  Patsy 93
  Samuel 192
  Samuel Henry 192
  Sarah 192
  William 192
Hartley, Cynthia 306
  Henry 17
  Hugh L. 176
Hartman, Joseph 209
Hartsooh, Albert 211
Harvey, Albert 193
  Burton 194
  Charles 193, 194
  Charles B. 194
  Chester 300
  Clyde 194
  Cynthia 194
  Dicie 193
  Dortis 194
  Edgar N. 194
  Eliza Jane 193
  Elkanah 193, 194
  Elmer 194
  Eloise 194
  Ernest 193
  Esper 194
  Frank 193, 194
  Fred 194
  Fred O. 194
  Freeland 193
  George 193
  Harriet 211
  Henry 193
  Hobart 194
  Hope 193
  Hugh 194
  Isaac 194
  Jackson 193
  James 193
  James Monroe 193
  James N. 194
  James R. 193
  James W. 193
  Jane 209
  John 110, 193, 194
  John (Jr.) 193
  John F. 193, 194
  John R. 193
  John W. 194
  Jonathan 97
  Joseph 193, 194
  Josephine 193
  Joshua 194
  Joshua B. 193, 194
  Lee 194
  Lewis W. 194
  Martin 194
  Matilda 114
  Minnie 193
  Nancy 193
  Oliver 193
  Oney 193
  Oney (Jr.) 193
  Oney J. 193
  Ralph 194
  Robert J. 193
  Rufus 193, 194
  Rufus (Jr.) 194
  Sally 88
  Samuel 109, 193, 194
  (Dr.) Samuel 193, 194
  Sanford 193
  Sarah 193
  Smith 193, 194
  Stella Lane 194

Harvey (cont.)
  Susan 194
  Susannah 193
  Thomas 80, 193, 194
  Tressie 193
  Ulys 194
  W. R. 144
  Walker A. 193, 194
  Wallace 193
  Wesley 194
  William 28, 105, 193, 194
  Wilson 193, 194
Harvie, Sallie 179
Harwell, Alexander 188
  Alice 188
  Austin 188
  Charles 188
  Herbert 188
  Jennie 188
  Pierce 188
  Samuel 14, 100
  (Rev.) Samuel 148
  Sarah 150, 188
  Susan 188
  William 188
Hasinger, Canis Blanch 155
Haskins, Betsy 103
  James 73
  James C. 281
  Nancy 73, 107, 108
Hasler,_____ 159, 167
  Simeon 22
Haster, John 105
Hastler, Daniel 83
  Emily 117
Hasty, May 268
  Guy Waaldo 268
  Thomas 268
Hatfield, Eula Gladden 270
  Floyd Anderson 270, 271
  (Mrs.) Maggie 194
  Martha Alice 270
  Mary 270
Hathaway, John 302
Hatley, Phebe 113
Hawkins, George 49
  Morgan B. 295
  Susannah 203
Hawks, Elizabeth 113
Hayes, Eula 268
Haygood, Benjamine 93
Haynes, Henry 77
  (Dr.) J. T. 286
  James P. 107
  Spencer 17
Hays, Jesse 126, [129]
  John 18
  Samuel 10
Hayter, Katherine 178
Hazen, Asa 257, 261
  Franklin 261
  Gideon Morgan 261
  Mary Lord 226, 261
  Rufus 261
  Sophia Lord 261
  William Cogswell 261
Head, Alice Burford 263
Headrick, William 93
Hedgcloth, H. M. 66
Hedgecloth, Henry 63, 65, 68
Hegley, John 21
Heidt,_____ 154
  Marion 154
Heik, Katherine 286
Heiskell, J. N. 145
Helff, Bernice 268
  Emil 268
  Frances 268

Hellums, William 75
Hembree, (Col.) 43
  Charles C. 49
  Eli 128
  Isaac 101, 139
  (Capt.) Joel 19, 32, 34
Henderson, Albert 113
  Charles 143
  Geo. W. 44c
  Geraldine 306
  John 34
  Joseph 15
  Meshack 28
  Sally 101, 104
  Walter 63, 64, 66, 67
  William R. 252
  Zola 265
Hendrick, John 99
Henegar, Mamie 300
Henley, John S. 114
  Samuel O. 204
  William 159
Henly, David 15
Henning, Henrietta Hunt 260
  James 260
  John Morgan 260
  Julia 260
  Samuel C. 260
Henry, Edward H. 164
  Frances 164
  Gladys 187
  Joseph 99
  Marie/Maria 164
  Mary 211
  Reita 164
  Roy C. 38
  William 15
  William W. 186, 187
Henshaw, Benjamine 15
  George 15, 210
  Jesse 15
Hensley, Benjamine 107
Henson, Allen 16
  G. W. Green 18
  Ruth 170
Hentley, (Mrs.) Louisa 50
  William Jasper 50
Herbert, Annie 245
  Scyrethea 99
Heron, Frank 263
Hewett, Nathaniel 48
  (Mrs.) Nathaniel 48
  Robert 82
Hibberts, Thomas 33
Hickey, Anna Elizabeth 202
  Carter 200, 202
  Charles 83, 175
  Edward H. 38
  Elizabeth 202
  Henry 202
  Jane 202
  John 17
  Joseph 202
  Mary 202
  Press 215
  Sarah A. 197
  Susan 202
  Thomas 202
  Thomas C. 201
Hickman, Tempe 195
Hicks, Absolom 107
  Bert 37
  Betsy 86
  Ella 230
  Emma Jean 224
  James Russell 224
  Linda 224
  Mamie Sue 224

Mary 244
Mary Lennie 265
Reba Kendrick 224
Robert 224, 231
William Martin 203
William Thomas 265
Hiden, Elizabeth 110
Higgins, America 259
Highton, Mary Ann 120
Hightower, Patsy 102
Hill, (Gen.) A. P. 259
  Absalom F. 195
  Allen 88
  Ann Eliza 257
  Anne C. 196
  Barney 195, 196, 252
  Barney B. 196
  Bernada 209
  Cap Kendrick 196
  Charles L. 196
  Daisy Dorinda 196
  Eliza Ann 134
  Elizabeth 195, 265
  Elizabeth (Lane) 195
  Ellis Dixon 196
  Frank 195
  Gilbert Isaac 196
  Grace 274
  Grace Dixon 196
  Helen 196
  Isaac A. 195, 221
  Isaac Alexander 195
  Ivy 196
  Jacob 195
  James B. 195
  James Moses 195, 196
  James Rupert 196
  John 86, 207, 255
  John A. 196
  John Nelson 195, 196
  John Paul 196
  Liddy M. 195
  Louise 232
  Margaret Kendrick 196
  Mary 196, 237
  Mary Elizabeth 196
  Mary Margaret 195
  Mary Walker 196
  May 195, 196, 232
  Myrtle 195
  Nancy D. 195
  Nancy (Millican) 196
  Nancy Pearl 196
  Nannie Ellen 196
  Nora 294
  Nora E. 195
  Pauline 196
  Pearl 196
  Quin 255
  Robert Kendrick 196
  Robert L. 195
  Roy C. 196
  Roy R. 196
  Russell 196
  Ruth Irene 196
  Samuel R. 195
  Vara Kendrick 196
  Virgil Albert 196
  Virginia 257
  (Dr.) W. W. 195, 196
  Walter E. 195
  Wesley 196
  Wiley H. 195
  William C. 217
  William Columbus 195
  William Edward 196
  William Leslie 196
  William Walter 196

326

Hill, William Rayborn Massey 196
Hindman, Thomas 42
Hinds (see also Hines)
Hinds, ___ 200
  A. Pearl 203
  Abigail 115
  Albert N. 201
  Almeda M. 201
  Annie 200, 202
  Annie C. 201
  Billy 201
  Bruce S. 200
  Clarence 201
  Clay H. 201
  Clifford C. 201
  Dorsey W. 37
  Eliza May 203
  Elizabeth (Abels) 202
  Ella May 200
  Ewell 200
  Frances 203
  George 200, 202
  George C. 200
  George Washington 203
  Harry 201
  Henry Clay 203
  Henry P. W. 200, 203
  Holman Blaine 202, 203
  Holman Blaine (Jr.) 203
  Homer H. 201
  Ida D. 201
  James 38
  James C. 197
  James Carter 197, 200, 201
  James Lewis 200
  Jane (Long) 201
  John 30, 197, 200
  John (Jr.) 197
  John Reuben (Jr.) 202
  Joseph 197, 200-203, 298
  Kathleen 203
  Katie Kimbrough 200
  Levi Jackson 200, 201, 264
  Lou 197
  M. Malissa 201
  Martha Elizabeth 200
  Martin C. 201
  Mary E. 197
  Minerva (Owings) 201
  Nancy 202, 255
  Otis A. 201
  Pearl 202
  Rilla Catherine 200
  Roscoe C. 37
  Ruth 201
  Ruth Caroline 203
  Rutha Caroline 197, 200, 201
  Sam B. 231
  Samuel Burgess 200
  Sarah 112, 118, 200, 202
  Sarah Annie 201, 317
  Simeon 197
  Susan 200, 202
  Susan (Hankins) 200, 202, 203
  Sylvanus 32, 197, 200
  Taylor 37
  Thomas 273
  Virginia 203
  W. Jack 201
  William Crawford 200
Hines, James R. 104
  John I. 203
  Joseph 203
  Rilla Catherine 208
  Sylvanus 19
Hinson, Allen 18
Hipp, Clarence Bell 285
  Clarence Bell (Jr.) 285
  Elizabeth Shelley 285
Hitchcock, Daniel 12, 31
Hix, Elijah 16
Hodge, Priscilla 230
Hodges, Allen 54
  George 282
Hogan, William 16
Hogg, Sir Douglas McGarel 161
  Mary Caroline 236
Holden, Mary E. 150
Holland, Elizabeth 210
  G. Allison 185
  William 17, 78
Holliway, Pearl 256
Holloway, Christopher C. 38
  May 274
Holly, Sally 80
Holmes, Alberta 156
Holston, Henry 298
  Sarah 298
Holt, Joel 18, 76
  John 33
Honey, Stephen 117
Honeycutt, Anderson 252, 254
  Carrie (Stonecipher) 254
  Nathan 254
Hood, Annie 157
  Bryson 120
  Joel 107, 108
  John 17, 29, 31, 64-66, 180
  John W. 64
  Kate 65
  Martha 63, 65
  Mary 63
  Mary K. 65
  Mathilda 65-67
  Matilda 63
  Rufus 273
  Sydney 146
  Thomas 17
Hook, (Mr.) John 58
  John A. 116
Hooke, Carl 184
  John 184
  John Anderson 184
  Julia 184
  Margaret 184
  Mary Porter 184
Hooper, (Rev.) R. 110
  Robert 14
Hope, Caroline 301
  Elizabeth 127
  Evelyn 301
  HenryWelcker 300
  James 12, 17, 18, 85
  John 106
  Kate 300
  Katie Louise 301
  Mary Virginia 300
  Minnie Caroline 301
  Nell 300
  Samuel 84
  Sarah Catherine (Welcker) 300
  Sarah Elizabeth 301
  Thomas Frederick 301
  William B. 299, 300
Hopkins, Melissa 285
  Polly 84
Horler, Michael 19
Horn, Charity 96
  Ida 151
Hornsby, (Mrs.) Charles 194
  Ellen 206
  James 206
  James W. 206
  Laura 206
  Lemaster U. 118
  Margaret 206
  Martha 206
  Mary 206
  Susan 206
  William 206
  William J. 49
Horsley, Catherine 249
Horton, Feby 73
  Joseph 15
  W. K. 145
Hostler, Michael 21
Hotchkiss, C. M. 207
  Elizabeth 121
  Gabriella M. 123
  Hezekiah 109
  Isabella 207
  Jared 17, 18, 28, 207
  Louisa 207
  Margaret Louisa 241
  Sallie 207
  Samuel 123
House, Mary 185
Houston, (Capt.) 19
  (Rev.) 247
  Adam 98
  (Mrs.) Elizabeth 52
  John 115
  Margaret 247
  Robert 15, 30
  (Gov.) Sam 9
  Samuel 34, 308
  William 19, 22
Howard, Abraham 127
  Albert 124
  Alexander 16, 17, 20
  Alexander (Jr.) 20
  Allison 273
  Arch 37
  Asa 20
  Ava 223
  Bell 150
  Benjamine 97
  Catherine 118
  Charles S. 141
  Cornelia Kendrick 222
  George S. 222
  Gladys 285
  John 273
  Josephine 260
  Margaret Ellen 222
  Martha Christine 222
  Ruth 273
  Sewell 222
  Tate 273
Howell, ___ 192
  Fletcher 305
Howerwell, S. B. 109
Hoyle, ___ 154
Hoyt, Darius 14, 117
Huck, Peter 151
Huddleston, (Dr.) W. C. 188
Hudson, Samantha 163
Hues, (Miss) 298
Hueston, William 16
Huff, Bessie 204
  Eliza Rebecca 204
  Elizabeth 204, 205
  Emely 204
  Emily Jane 204
  Florence Elizabeth 205
  Hannah 117, 204, 205
  Hannah Hues/Hughes 205, 212
  Hugh McCrosky 205
  Isabelle Rhea 205

Huff (cont.)
  James Anderson 189, 204, 205
  James David 205
  James Gallaher 205
  James H. 204
  James Hewey 205
  James R. 205
  James Ransom 205
  James White 204
  John 204, 205
  John Ira 205
  Joseph M. 205
  Lenna 204
  Lucy (Gallaher) 205
  Mabel (Wilson) 205
  Mable Claire 205
  Mamie 204, 240
  Margaret Ann 205
  Margaret Katherine 204
  Mary 204, 205
  Mary Angeline 204
  Phillip 102
  Polly 107, 204
  Prudence 204
  Sallie 204
  Sarah Ellen Augusta 204
  William 114
  William C. 205
  William E. 212
  William Ebenezer 204, 205
  William Ebenezer (Jr.) 204
  William Yates 204, 205
  Woods Wilson 205
Huffine, _____ 172
  Benjamine 157
  Ephriam 122, 208
  Mamie 242
Huffman, Addie 196
Hugenor, Martha 212
Huggins, Zilphia Amanda 153
Hughes, Lane 154
Hughs, William 114
Hugins, John 15
Hume, Eliza 237
  Isabella Jane 237
Humphries, James 94
Hunnicut, Martha 180
Hunt, Henrietta 259
  James 83
  James Shepherd 250
  Margaret Elizabeth 250
  Nina L. 153
  Robert Cross 250
  Texie 281
  Thomas 193
  William 127
Hunter, Katherine 306
  Polly 101
  (Col.) Thomas 302
Hurst, Flora 136
  Mabel 151
Hurt, Albert 110
  Alice Eugenia 284
  Augusta 284
  Blanch 284
  Elizabeth 119
  John Sevier 284
  John Sevier 2nd 284
  Mary 257
  Thomas Augustas 284
Husett, Jinny 80
Husk, John 77
Hutcheson, Samuel C. 236
Hutson, William 116
Hyatt, Alice 245
  Minnie Lelia 285
Hyde, Julia 197
Hyden, Alexander 108

Hyden, Mary (Baldwin) 308
  William 28, 29 308
Hymon, Susan 245
Hynson, Jeremiah 77
Hyten, Anderson 115
  Mary Ann 115

-I-

Ingram, Adeline Hall 209
  Albert Ernest 208
  Alice 209
  Alma 210
  Amanda Brazeale 209
  Amanda Clementine 208
  Amanda W. 209
  Annie Vann 210
  Bonnie Jean 208
  Callie 293, 294
  Callie Lucile 208
  Charles 209, 210
  David 208
  David Carson 208
  Dora 210
  Edith (Blizzard) 211
  Elisha 208
  Elisha Turner 200, 208, 209
  Elisha W. 209, 210
  Elizabeth 240
  Elizabeth Ann 208
  Ella May 208
  Elwin 211
  Floyd 210, 211
  Frank 209
  Fred 210, 211
  Garland 208
  George 211
  (Capt.) George 9, 13, 16
  Goldie Martin 210
  Hannah 239
  Hannah G. 208
  Hanover 122, 208
  Hattie Gibson 209
  Henry 209, 210
  Herbert 209
  Hester 294
  Ida 210
  Ida Bann 210
  Jack 208-210
  James 209, 210
  James Melton 210
  Jane Harvey 210
  Jefferson 208, 211
  John 209, 211
  (Mrs.) John 193
  John J. 37
  Julia 209, 210
  Larkin 208
  Larry 209
  Laura 211
  Laura Caldwell 210
  Lela Emma 208
  Lenice Wood 209
  Lillie 209
  Lou Austin 211
  Louella 210
  Lucinda 209
  Lucinda Catherine 208
  Mabel 211
  Mae 210
  Marcus 210
  Margaret 209, 242
  Margaret Lee 209
  Martin 210, 211
  Mary 141, 208, 210, 240
  Mary Robert 211

  Maud 230
  Maud Blanch 208
  Mollie 210, 252
  Moses 143
  Moses E. 209
  Moses L. 208, 209
  Murray 211
  Nancy Adeline 208
  Oscar 210, 211
  Pearl 210
  Raymond 209
  Reece 208, 267
  Rena 211
  Rilla Catherine 209
  Rilla Hines 208
  Robbie 210
  Robert 209-211
  Rosa Sparks 208
  Sallie Smith 211
  Sally 99, 208
  Samuel 208, 211
  Samuel Houston 208
  Sanford 30, 208
  Sanford Harrison 208, 209
  Sarah 208
  Spencer 211
  Stacia 190
  Stacia Maraline 208
  Stephen 143, 209, 240
  Stephen Harrison 208
  Sue 209
  Susan Smith 210
  Teresa 210
  Thomas F. 210
  Thomas Franklin 209, 210
  Thomas Reed 209
  Tom 210
  Vann 210
  Wagly Dove 210
Inman, Elizabeth 299
Irby, Frances 257, 261
Ireland, Jenny 97
Irvine, Benjamin V. 59, 60
Isbell, John M. 22
Ish, Hester 301
Isham, Fred 188
  Katie 109
  Pearl 252
Ives, Thomas 29
Ivey, James 21

-J-

Jack, Andrew 61
  George 14
Jackson, Andrew 11, 147, 191
  Annie 209
  Frances 279
  Frank 284
  James P. 255
  John 94
  Josiah 144
  Levi 122
  Margaret 255
  Polly 87
  Samuel 134
  Susie 307
Jaco, Roscoe 174
James, _____ 266
  Cory A. 109
  J. A. 116
  James 74
  Malinda 120
  William 121
Jarrett, Eliza 147
Jerome 147, 153

Jarrett (cont.)
John 147
John B. 153
John Brown 153
Leon 164
Louise 153
M. R. 114
Mary 153
Mary Cornelia 147, 152
Nathaniel R. 147
Robert 147, 153
Sarah 153
Susan 147, 153
Jefferson, Lillie 253
Jenkine, Florence 159
Jenkins, (Mrs.) Bessie 194
  Thomas 15
Jennings, Mary 257
Jenson, Joseph 33
Jent, Josiah 16, 19
  William 94
Jett, Thomas R. 38
Jewett, Abbie Fay 196
Johnson,_____ 35, 135, 207
  Abagail 48
  Albert M. 156
  Annie 180
  Betty 274
  Beulah (Buelah) 274
  Calvin 21, 81
  Casey 273
  Elizabeth 137
  Elizabeth (Martin) 274
  Eugene 273, 274
  Garrett 256
  Gideon 273, 274
  Jack 274
  James 212, 273, 307
  James H. 22
  Jeremiah 212
  John 75, 307
  Josiah 277
  Lody 102
  Martha E. 127
  Mary 74, 307
  Mary A. 303
  Nancy 107
  Nell 274
  (Mrs.) Newton 193
  Oxley 91
  Peter 89, 171
  (Mrs.) Peter 193
  Robert Newton 172
  Samuel 273, 274, 307
  William 307
Johnston, Andrew H. 212
  Anne/Annie J. 212
  Dorothy 211
  Ebenezer 117, 205, 212
  Elizabeth 212
  Frances 212
  Francis 15, 212
  Frank 211
  Grace 211
  Hannah Elizabeth 212
  Harriet G. 122
  Hettie 212
  Hugh 16, 212
  Ida (Ingram) 211
  Isaac 210, 211
  Jack 211
  James 18, 96, 97, 99, 101, 102, 212
  James Harrison 212
  James Hervey 205
  James L. 138, 211
  James M. 212
  Jane 212

Jerome 212
John 210, 211
John Yates 212
Joseph 212
Joseph A. 212
Joseph Marshall 212
Josiah 212
Josie 212
Lennie Bell 212
Littledery 123
Louella (Ingram) 211
Margaret 212
Martha 125, 212
Martha F. 138
Mary Jane 212
Mary M. 212
Melisa Clementine 212
Milton Graham 212
Nancy 245
Nannie E. 212
Pelma 205
Rachel 204
Rachel A. 212
Rachel Louise 212
Richard P. 300
Robert 117, 205, 212
Robert Franklin 212
Robert M. 212
Ruth 211
Samuel 212
Sarah 212
Susan 144
Thomas J. 122
Wagly Dove (Ingram) 211
William 74, 212
(Dr.) William D. 138
William F. 212
William McEwen 212
Joiner, Gracey 76
  Winniam 76
Jolly, Henry 100
  John 112
  Lucinda 182
  Nancy 182
  Sarah 135
  William 98, 100, 182
Jones, Amanda 60
  Amy 74
  Anderson 124
  Anna 213
  Betsy 48
  Elizabeth 208
  Elmer 37
  Frankie 157
  Harriett 49
  Hazel 146
  Irma Lee 153
  Jacob 10, 15, 57
  James 13, 21, 304
  Jeremiah 33
  John 17, 76
  John C. 297
  John Paul 156
  Lula 153
  (Mrs.) Margaret 48
  Thomas 16, 116, 307
  Thomas Bass 153
  William 21, 106, 297
  Winney 117
Jordan, Douglass Elma 213
  Ida Alice 213
  John 60
  John Yancy 213
  (Dr.) L. W. 51, 55
  Lewis 57, 213
  (Dr.) Lewis 34, 48, 52
  Lewis W. 52, 213
  (Dr.) Lewis W. 213

Mary 55
Mary Molett 213
Matilda 150
(Mrs.) Matilda 48
Matilda G. 55
Sarah Saphina 213
Saraphina Almyra 51
Sophia 213
Thomas Grayson 213
William Pope 213
Joseph, Alma 253
  Annie 252
  Edwin 253
  Emma Elizabeth (Millican) 253
  Floyd 253
  Harry 253
  Irene 253
  Mary 253
  Raymond 253
  Raymond F. 37
  William H. 37, 252, 253
Juet, Sinthy 110
Julan, John 106
Julian, John C. 106
  William C. 126
Jump, (Dr.) J. R. 204

-K-

Kaiser, Albert 286
  Edward 286
  Fred C. 286
  Gustave 286
  Henry O. 286
  Herman A. 286
  Minnie 286
  Nannie 286
  Theodore 286
Kane, William 102
Keaner, Viney 99
Keefe, Margaret 228
Keelaugh, Margaret 124
Keeling, Welding 110
Keener, Nancy 158
Keeney, Guy 179
  John 179
  John Calvin 179
  Marie K. 179
Keith, Eveline 126, [129]
  William J. 59
Kellar, Ernest R. 233
  Ethel 233
  Howard R. 233
  Lena 233
  Mary M. 233
  Maud 233
  Rosa L. 233
  Thomas W. 233
Keller, Avery 245
  Frank 245
  Margaret 245
  Mary 245
  May 245
  Robert 245
  Ted 245
  William 245
Kelley, William 84
Kellogg,_____ 153
Kelly, Alexander 88
  Doris C. 38
  Jenny 81
Kelso, Hugh 20
Kelton, Carl H. 37
Kemp, (Capt.) Charles M. 305
  Sterling 18

Kendrick, Absalom 214
  Adelaid 163
  Alice Jean 220
  Alice (Wester) 222
  Alma Rose 221
  Benjamin 219
  Bertie Lee 219, 221
  Beth Oleta 221
  Betty 255
  Callie (Norman) 216
  Carlysle 221
  Charles 219
  Charles W. 302
  Charles Winthrope 222
  Clarence Augustus 266
  Clifford Jennings 220, 221
  Clifford Lee 216
  Clovie 219
  Columbia Eleanor 218
  Corrie Lou 216
  Cynthia 222
  Diana 214, 217
  Doyle 216
  Edom 214
  Eliza 216
  Eliza Cornelia (Owings) 219
  Elizabeth 214, 216
  Enoch 216
  Enoch Jackson 217-219, 264
  Frank 219
  George 219
  Glen 221
  Goldie 220
  Henrietta 163
  Henry 97, 214, 216
  Henry B. 220
  Horace 220
  Horace Keith 220
  Ida 219
  Ida Alice 219
  Ira E. 219
  Iva 220, 221
  Jacob F. 217
  Jacob Fauby 214, 216
  James Carlysle 219, 221
  James Polk 221, 222
  James Richard 217, 219-221
  James Samuel 266
  John 214, 216, 221, 222, 224, 264
  John Henry 216
  John W. 217
  Joseph 214, 216
  Joseph Burton 216
  June 220
  Lena 216
  Leona Iris 216
  Leota 266
  Lethe M. 217
  Lethe Maud 218
  Lewis 220
  Louallen 216
  Louisa 216
  Lucretia 214
  Malissa Caroline 219
  Margaret 214, 222-224
  Margaret Amanda 195, 221
  Margaret Fauby 214, 216, 217, 264, 265
  Marshall 220
  Martha Alice 218, 219
  Martha (Owings) 222-224
  Martha Susan 217, 224
  Mary 214
  Mary Elizabeth 217
  Mary Ellen 221, 222
  Mary Frances 220
  Mary Lee 218
  Mary Margaret 219
  Mary (Rector) 217-220
  Melcenia 214
  Melissa Cornelia 221, 224
  Mollie 214
  Nancy 214, 216
  Nancy Araminta 218
  Nancy Jane 221, 223
  Nancy (Smith) 216
  Nellie Fritts 216
  Parthenia 174, 217
  Pauline 220
  Phillip Campbell 266
  Rebecca 216
  Rebecca Ann 221, 223
  Richard 220
  Robbie May 222, 302
  Robert 302
  Robert Otis 220, 221
  Robert Samuel 221, 222
  Ruby Rae 220
  Rufus F. 217, 219
  Ruth 220
  Sam Collins 220
  Sam Tilden 220
  Samantha (Whitlock) 220, 221
  Samuel 30, 31, 42, 214, 216-221, 224
  Samuel M. 219
  Sarah 221
  Sarah Almeda 218, 219
  Stonewall Jackson 220
  Susan (Burford) 220
  Thomas 163
  Thomas A. 217, 219
  Thomas Allen 219, 220
  Virginia 284
  Wallace 220
  Walter 216
  Wanda Marie 221
  William 214, 216, 219
  William Charles 216
  William Edom 214, 221
  William Edward 219
  Willie 302
  Willie T. 222
Kendrick (Kindreck), Dorcy Campbell 265, 266
Kennan, James 90
Kennedy, Casandree 116
  John 80
Kenner, Eskridge 17
  Margaret 48
Kerr, John Davis 261
  John Davis (Jr.) 261
Ketching, Sallie 92
Key, Albert 235
  Albert Lenoir (Jr.) 235
  David 235
  David M. 235
  Elizabeth 235, 236
  Emma 235
  Henry Lenoir 235
  John S. 235
  Kate 235
  Margaret 235
  Mary 297
  Sarah Avery 235, 236
Keys, Isaac 81
  Samuel 78
  Samuel (Sr.) 78
Kibbe, Rachel 257
Killingsmith, Stephen 98
Kim, Peterson 109
Kimball, Peterson 18
Kimbrell, Benjamine 109
  Jennie 98
Kimbro, Robert 62
Kimbrough, _____ 44
  (Esq.) 42
  Asa Hazen 226
  Bessie 227
  Calvin Morgan 226
  Catherine Brown 226
  George Washington 226
  Gideon H. 226
  James O'Neal 224
  Joseph 226, 261
  Kate 68
  Katherine 227
  Martha (Mattie) 226
  Mary 226, 227
  Mary Elizabeth 189, 227
  Mattie 226, 227
  Nancy Jane 224
  Robert 148, 226
  Rufus Franklin 227
  Rufus M. 226
  Sarah 147
  Sarah Ann 226
  William 174, 226
Kimbull, Jenny 98
Kimmer, Christopher 307
  James 307
  Louisa 307
  Susan 307
Kincaid, _____ 135
  Bessie 152
Kindreck, Nancy 175
Kindred, Nina 195
Kindrick, Jacob F. 103
  Polly 79
  William R. 37
King, _____ 14, 139
  Addie 190
  Addie (Wester) 232
  Adelaide 231
  Adelaide (Wester) 304
  Alice 231, 256
  Allen George 231
  Allene 228
  Amanda 228
  Amelia 185, 247
  Ann 228
  Annette 228
  Annie 228
  Anny 126
  Austin 228
  Austin Augustus 228, 229
  Austin Augustus (Jr.) 228
  Austin Augustus III 229
  Benjamine 228, 231
  Beulah 190
  Boyd 231
  Campbell 231
  Carrie 294
  Carrie Zorilda 230
  Charles 190, 230, 231, 246
  Charles Franklin 230
  Charles W. 228
  Chess Newell 266
  Clarence 228
  Dorothy 297
  Ed George 231
  Ed George (Jr.) 231
  Edgar 231
  Edith 190
  Edward 228
  Edward Livingston 228
  Eliza Lisle 228
  Elizabeth 190, 229
  Ella 229
  Ellen 231
  Eula Lee 190
  Evelyn 230
  Fannie 228

King (cont.)
 Feruby 231
 Frances 228
 George Washington 230, 231, 266
 Harry Gilbert 230
 Harry Gilbert (Jr.) 230
 Henry 205
 Inez 181
 Inez Gilbert 231
 Iola 190, 231
 James 208, 231
 James B. 230
 James Burns 231
 James Burns (Jr.) 231
 James William 230
 Jane 228
 Jennie Lisle 229
 Jerome 190, 231
 Jesse 113
 Joe Sam 231
 Joe W. 230
 John Sevier 228
 Joseph Malcolm 230
 Josephine 304
 Julia 231
 Julius Jerome 230
 Lutie Ruth 230
 Major 230
 Margaret 190
 Margaretta 229
 Maria 47
 Martha 228
 Martha Carita 230
 Martha D. 92
 Martin 48
 Mary Belle 229
 Mary (Hamby) 231
 Mary Jane 231
 Mary Juanita 230
 Matilda (Mattie) Woodson 229
 Mattie Katherine 266
 Mattie Viola 231
 Maud 231, 232, 304
 Mollie Dimple 266
 Myra Genevieve 230
 Nancy 229
 (Mrs.) Nancy 48
 Nancy Sevier 228
 Neal 190
 Nellie Clarinda 231
 Newton 231
 Ora Lynn 231
 Penelope 231
 Peter 15
 Phyllis Dolores 266
 Rhoda 231
 Rilla Almeda 230
 (Maj.) Robert 9, 30, 139, 281
 Rufus F. 92
 Ruth 230
 Sammie Augustus 266
 Sarah 230, 266, 267, 281
 Sarah Dorinda 200, 231
 Sidney 190, 231
 Thoma Owings 265
 Thomas 13, 228, 231, 232, 303, 304
 Thomas Edward 231
 Tom Owings 230
 Viola 231
 Virgil Allen 230
 Virgil Leon 230
 Walter 14, 23, 47, 228, 229
 Walter H. 13, 228
 William 190, 228, 230, 231, 264

William Clinton 266
William Henry 230, 266
William S. 265
Wilma Margaret 230
Kingsley, Alpha 79
Kingston,_____ 23
Kinnan, Claborn 94
Kirk, John 15
Kirkland, Thomas R. 37
Kirkpatrick,_____ 161
 Robert 10, 16
 Sarah 62
 Wm. A. 62
Kitchen, Thomas 121
 William 15
Kizer, Flora 233
Kizziah, James A. 37
Klark, Julias 15
Kline, Mary 212
 Sallie 204
Knidred, Letitia 118
Knight, Betsy 207
 Lucy 82
 Thomas 159
 Thomas William 174
Knox, Elizabeth 263
 Joseph 89
Koger, Florence 293
Kowsey, Lucy Ann 48
Kyle, Annie 181
 Samuel E. 37

-L-

Labb, James 20
Lacefield, Peggy 81
Lacey, Annie Elizabeth 278
 Elizabeth (Foster) 279
 Foster 278, 279
 Joseph 87, 127
 Linnie 278, 279
 Titas 106
 W. N. 278, 279
 W. N. (Jr.) 278, 279
 William 120
Lackey,_____ 229
 Annie 233
 Charles 301
 Elizabeth 144
 Elizabeth (Welcker) 301
 Hugh 20, 33
 Jackson 233, 300, 301
 James 32, 91, 103, 144, 233, 245
 Jane 233
 John 233
 John K. 233
 John R. 233
 Laura 233
 Melinda 233
 Samuel 233
 William 233
 William W. 301
Ladd, Nelson 96
 Samuel 175
 William B. 209
 Williamson 34
Lain/Lane, (Sgt.) Charles 28
Lamb, Ben J. 253
 Betsy 99
 Fred 294
 Jerry 43
 Sally 113
Lambkin, Jane Moore 133
Lampkins, William 17, 18

Lancaster, Elizabeth 196
 Howard 196
 Howard M. 196
Landers, Henry 16
Landrum, Thomas 29
Lane, Elias 121, 123
 Elsie 195
 Isabel 93
 Joseph 28, 125
 Nancy Eliza 277
 Samuel 103, 281
 Thomas 101
 Viney 93
 Virry 86
 Wilson 231
Laney, Jenny 114
Professor 188
Langley/Hangley, Alice Clarissa 268
Lanston, Benton 103
 Nancy 88
Lappington, James 79
Larrimore, James 92
LaRue, Ruth 294
Lauderdale,_____ 207
Lauders, Henry 17
Lauston, Rebecca 105
Law, Vida 169
Lawer, Andrew 18
Lawrence, Henry B. 151
Lawson, Andrew 38
 Anna 102
 Arty 107
 Bartley 89
 Betsy 89
 Jennie Mae 198
Laye, Thomas 75
Lea, Albert Eugene 234
 Albert T. M. D. 234
 Aurelia Jane 234
 Francis 10
 Henry 55, 234
 Herndon, 234
 Isaac D. 234
 (Dr.) J. W. 55
 (Dr.) James W. 62, 234
 Levinia 55
 Mary 55, 155
 Mary L. 234
 Mary Malvina 234, 275
 Myrtilla A. 234
 Pleasant 165
 Robert L. 234
 Virginia 55, 234, 275
 Virginia L. 234
 William 12, 121
Leadsinger, John 90
Lee, (Gen.) 35, 36
 Alice 288
 Clarice 240
 David 74, 76
 David Campbell 218
 Francis 15, 20
 Lucy Randolph 218
 Mary 240
 Mollie 279
 Phillips 288
Leeper, Annie Laura 266
 Elizabeth 277
 Inez 278
 James 277
 James Avery 278
 James L. 278
 James Madison 277,278
 James Thomas 278
 Julia Ann Malinda 277
 Julia E. Rebecca 278

Leeper (cont.)
  Kate 290
  Lucy Amanda 278
  Mary Blair 277
  Myra 278
  Myra (Foster) 278
  Nancy Myra 278
  Randolph Foster 278
  Sarah 278
Leftwich, (Mrs.) Ann 48, 50
  Catherine 308
  (Mrs.) Catherine 48
  John 23, 89
  (Maj.) John 48, 308
  William 94
  William John 50
Lehman, Cornell 221
  Edna Rose 221
  Erma 221
  Henry 221
  Norma May 221
Lemons, John 19
Lenoir, A. S. 124
  Albert 236
  Albert S. 34, 299
  Albert Sobieskie 235
  Benjamin B. 238
  Benjamin Ballard 235, 238
  Catherine Welcker 236
  Charles Barton 238
  Eliza Martha 235, 238
  Elizabeth 235
  Frank 238
  Frederick 236
  Henry Lee 238
  Henry Ramsey 238
  Isaac Pickens 235
  Isaac Thomas 235, 236
  James Ramsey 238
  John Albert 237
  John Siler 238
  Julia 236
  Julia Joyce 235
  Kate 236
  Laura 236
  Leah 288
  Leah Adeline 235, 236
  Louisa 238
  Louisa Caroline 235, 236
  Margaret 235, 236
  Mary 236
  Mary Elizabeth 238
  Myra Ann 235, 237
  Myra Florence 238
  Rose 238
  Thornton Pickens 237
  W. F. 238
  Waightstill Avery 235, 237
  Walter Franklin 235, 237
  Walter Thomas 237
  William 32, 235
  (Gen.) William 235
  William B. 23
  William Ballard 235, 236, 238
  William Goddard 237
Lentz, John 219
Leonard, Jean Young 289
  (Dr.) Morris Clayton 289
  Nancy Emmet 289
  Richard Black 289
Letsinger, Allen 120
Lewallen, Frances 124
Lewallin, Tempy 108
Lewellen, (Capt.) 17
Lewen, (Capt.) Chas. 32
Lewis,___ 281
  Anna 139

J. C. 239
James M. 13
Mary Katherine 239
Mary L. 217
Moses 112
William 20, 30
William L. 13
Licking, John G. 51
Licthenwalter, Coleman R. 268
  Eugene R. 268
  Frank H. 268
Liggett, H. 62
  Henry 9, 34, 44c, 44d, 55, 57, 102, 108, 122, 126
  Henry (Jr.) 44c, 62
  Henry (Sr.) 54
  Willie 68
Liggitt, Caroline M. 238a
  Emily 188
  Emily R. 238a
  Henry 238a
  Henry (Jr.) 238a
  Nancy Keener 238a
  Perrin 238a
  Sarah Elizabeth 238a
  William 60
  William Milton 238a
Light, George 16
Liking, (Mrs.) 48
  John G. 48
Likins, L. J. 59
Liles, David 28
  Robert 29
Lillard, (Col.) John M. 36
Lilman, William 21
Linbury, August 65-67
Lincoln,___ 43, 44
  James Hamilton 51
  Jesse 49, 51
  Nancy 49
Lindbury, August 63
  Christine 63, 65
Lindsley, Adrian Van C. 161
Lingford, Menson 21
Link, (Dr.) M. E. 163
Lipscomb, Katherine 262
  Margaret 262
  Sterling 262
Lisle, Dorothea Elizabeth 228
  Eliza Jane 228
  George Alexander 277
  Margaret 152
Litbull, Eliza 106
Little, Daniel 78
Littleton, Addie 239, 240
  Addie Lou 239
  Albert 239
  Albert F. 239
  Albert M. 239
  Amanda 240
  Amelia 239, 240
  Augustine 239
  Benjamin H. 239, 240
  Bessie M. 239, 240
  Bettye Grey 239
  Burton 239
  Carlyle 239
  Charles 239
  Charles C. 239
  Cora 239
  Dock 208, 239, 240
  Douglas 239
  Eliza Jane 239, 240
  Elizabeth 239, 240
  Emma 239
  Ester 239
  Florence 240
  Frank 240

George P. 239
Hannah 239
Henry 240
Hester 239
Irene 239
J. D. 172
Jack 239
James 239, 240
James F. 44a, 204
James Franklin 240
James J. 239
Jane 240
Jennie 240
Jesse M. 239
Jessica 239
Joe 239
John 208, 240
John J. 12, 240
John Jackson 239
Kate 240
(Mrs.) Laura 193
Lee 240
Lincoln 239
Lucinda 208
Lula 240
Mabel Huff 240
Martin 239
Martin L. 239
Martin W. 239
Mary 239, 240
Mary Katherine 239
Maud 239
Minnie 239
Minnie A. 239, 240
Morton 239, 240
Moses L. 239
Penelope 208
Pleasant 208
Pleasant Green 239, 240
Rachel E. 239, 240
Reece 239
Robert A. 239, 240
Sallie 239
Samuel 208
Sanford Nelson 239
Thomas 18, 239
Thomas J. 249
Thomas J. II 239
Thomas J. III 239
Thomas Jefferson 208, 239
Tom Wilk 239
Virginia 239
William 239, 240
William Frances 239
Lockett, Frances R. 122
Logan, Annie M. T. 278
  Edward 278
  Elizabeth T. 278
  James Leeper 278
  Martha 278
  W. A. 278
Lonacre, Ben J. 108
London, Marjory 232
  Robert P. 232
  Robert P. (Jr.) 232
Long, (Rev.) Carroll 43
  Joseph 279
  M. Jane 201
  Polly 96, 264
  Sallie 267
  Sarah 146
  Stephen 201
  William 17, 92
Longacre, B. 115, 117, 118
  Rachel 206
Longbottom, Elijah 114
Longean,___ 119
Longley, Elizabeth 282

Looney, Jane 47
  Joseph 15, 21
  Mary 48
  Michael 47
  Moses 15, 21, 87
  William 16
Lorance, Joseph 115
Lossus, Mary de 150
Lotspeich, Elizabeth 145
Lotz, Charles A. 287
Love, Amanda 49
  Ann 165
  Carrie May 241
  Elizabeth 241
  ELizabeth Avery 237
  Hallie Frank 237
  Hannah Mary 241
  Hannah Price 241
  Herbert Hezekiah 241
  Hesekiah 29, 31
  Hezekiah 122, 241
  James 241
  (Col.) James R. 237
  James Reagen 237
  Jennie 241
  Jesse 241
  Jesse Richard 241
  Jessie Louise 241
  Joel 241
  John 14, 19, 241
  John C. 241
  John M. 241
  Joseph N. 22
  Josiah T. 241
  Josie Elizabeth 241
  Julia Burgwin 237
  Katherine Ethel 241
  Lura W. 241
  Marchie 283
  Margaret 241
  Margaret Bell 237
  Martha Matilda 241
  Mary 241
  Mary Brown 241
  Melissa 241
  Myra Lenoir 237
  Richard H. 78
  Robert 241
  Robert John 237
  Robert Wiley 241
  Samuel 241
  Sarah 241, 273
  Thomas 165, 241
  Viola 241
  Walter 241
  Wiley 241
  Wiley B. 241
  Wiley W. 302
  William 241
  William Lee 241
Lovelace, Polly 124
Loveless, William 108, 112
  Zadak 100
Lovely, William 9
  William L. 77
Low, Dolph 245
  Isaac 245
  Jesse M. 118
  S. D. W. 245
Lowe, David 145
  Estel 145
  James 145
  Jesse 104, 175
  Josephine 145
  Lee 145
  Samuel 145
  William 145
Lower, Andrew 15

Lowery, (Rev.) 43
  Jacob 123
  James Robert 237
  James W. 237
  Joseph Walker 237
  Julia Love 237
  Martha J. 54
  Minnie 249
  Nancy Brown 54
  Susan 54
  William (Jr.) 54
  (Rev.) William P. 54
Loyd, Elizabeth 242, 302
  John 14, 32, 93, 95, 107, 242
  Rachel 61
  Thomas 30, 242
  William 242
  William G. 60
Luck, Alexander 22
  Martha 289
Luckey, Elizabeth 303
Luckjon, Milo 107
Luety, Hannah 184
Lung, (Mrs.) 51
  Absolum 51
  Joseph Luallen 51
  Mary Jane 51
  Rebecca 49
Luster, James 16, 74
  John 16, 74
  William 16
Luten, Wiley 105
Lutey, Sidney Ann 184
Luttrell, Cordelia 167
  George 118
  Katherine 109
  Louisa 143
  Mary Ann 180
  Polly (Turnley) 167
  Richard 167
  Silas 84
Lybarger, Noah 284
Lyle, George W. 166
  George Washington 165, 166
  Jenny 83
  Katherine 166
  Mary D. 165, 166
  Robert 83
  Thomas 166
Lyles, Fannie 77
  Henry 114
  Joseph 103
  Rebecca 119
  Robert 77
  Samuel 14, 118
Lynn, James 125
Lyon, (Capt.) 48
  Louisa 160
  Mary 160
  Susan 282
  Susan Clark 160
  Thomas 160
  (Maj.) Thomas C. 34
  Thomas L. 160
  Washington 160
  William 160
Lyons, Adelaide 235
  Frederick 235
  George F. 37
  James A. 235
  Julia 235
  Kate 235
  Laura 235
  Mary 235
  Thomas C. 308
  William 78
Lytle, Luke 89

-Mc-

McAdams, Peggy 48
McAllister, Hilliard H. 220
  Hugh H. 220
  June 220
  Ruby 220
  Sidney 220
  Wanda 220
McBath, _____ 123
  Mary 123
McBroom, Betty Lou 221
  Christine 221
  Eugene 221
  Ira Nelle 221
  Louis 221
  Richard 221
  Thomas 221
McCabe, Patsy 98
McCain, John 15
McCaleb, Archibald 34
  Lucinda 184
McCall, Candance Ann 175
  Eliza 48
  Henry Puris 175
  Samuel 13-15, 80, 175
  Sarah 175
  Susan 175
  Tolbert 175
  William 32
  William Wade 175
McCallie, Samuel 20
McCally, William 111
McCamey, Isabella 90
  Jane 47
  Margaret 47
  William 79, 81
  (Mrs.) William 51
  William Cooper 51
  Wm. C. 47
McCampbell, Andrew 12, 60, 61, 160
  Ann E. 49
  J. A. 61
  J. T. 61
  James 12, 49, 160
  (Mrs.) James 51
  Jane 49
  John 12, 51
  John Andrew 50
  Louisa 160, 161, 236
  Mary Eliza 51
  Mary Louisa 50
  (Mrs.) Nancy 48, 50
  Susan Ann 51
  Susan J. 49
  Thomas 160
  Thomas Clark 50
  William 60
  William E. 49
  William Payne 57
McCamy, (Capt.) James 32
  William 19
McCannon, Robert 15
McCarroll, Cynthia 118
McCidy, Eleanor 206
McClanehan, James 15
McClellan, (Lieut.) 12
  Abraham 16, 91, 93, 94
  (Capt.) Abraham 19, 23, 30, 31, 47
  Catherine B. 47
  David 30
  Eliza 50
  (Mrs.) Eliza 47

McClellan (cont.)
  John 32, 47
  (Col.) John 31, 80
  Martha Eliza 47
  Mary Ann 47
  Ruth A. 47
  Samuel 30
  William 23, 80
  William R. 47
McClelland, (Lieut.) 157
  Abraham 10
  (Col.) Abraham 308
  David 19, 31
  John 19
  Joseph 91
  Samuel 31
McClerestian, (Mrs.) Mary 49
McClesky, Mary 231
McCluen, Glen 253
  Lloyd G. 253
McClung, (Miss) 160
  Alexander 258
  Amanda Park 258
  Anna McGhee 259
  Annie Dee 259
  Antoinette 259
  Aurelia Essex 258
  Bessie Bowen 259
  Betty 259
  Calvin Morgan 258, 259
  Charles 14, 16
  Charles Alexander 261
  Charles J. 120
  Charles James 258, 259
  Corrie 261
  Eliza Ann (Mills) 258
  Eliza Jane (Morgan) 258
  Eliza Morgan 258
  Elizabeth Trigg 261
  Ellen Christie 258
  Ellen Marshall 259
  Essex 258
  Franklin Henry 258
  Franklin Henry (Jr.) 258
  Hugh Lawson 258, 260, 261
  James White 261
  Lida M. 259
  Lucy Swan 258
  Margaret 258
  Margaret (Swan) 258
  Margaret Swan 259
  Margaret White 261
  Mary 261
  Mary Bowen 259
  Mary Frances 261
  Mathew 257, 258
  Mathew Grainger 258, 259
  Matilda Mills 258
  Minnie Keith 259
  Rachel Florence 261
  Rachel Morgan 260
  Robert Gardner 259
  Rufus Morgan 261
  Sarah Morgan 258, 261
  Thomas Lee 259
McClure, Claire 301
McComb, Polly 97
McConkey, Albert 271
  Charles William 271
  Chas. E. 271
  Margaret 271
McConnell, Angeline 49
  Betsy 51
  (Mrs.) Catherine 48
  Peggy McAdams 51
  Thomas 13, 48, 51, 52
  William 93
McCord, John 73

McCorkle, (Capt.) 17
  Robert 15
McCormick, Roy Justin 164
McCorry, Susan Hunt 162
McCowl, Eliza 104
McCoy, Isaac 143
  John 31
McCrery, Barbary 106
McCroskey, Ada 204
McCube, Nancy 92
McCuen, Eliza 47
McCulley, Andrew 43
  (Mrs.) Elvira 50
  Flora 67
  Susan 110
McCullock, Alexander 93
  Andress 120
  Andrew 123
McCullough, Charles B. 37
  Ed 38
  John F. 37
McCullum, Polly 100
McCully, _____ 216
  Flora 63, 65-67
  Wesley 216
McDaniel, Caleb 92
  Charity 95
  David 91, 92
  Paul 37
McDermott, Louise 250
McDonald, Bertha 230
  Susan 308
McDonnel, Betsy 48
  Betty 51
  Charlotte 51
  Frederick 51
  James Jackson 51
  William McDonnell 51
McDonough, Albert 236
  Andrew 33
  James 33
  (Dr.) James S. 236
  Katherine 236
  Mary 236
McDowell, (Col.) Joseph 245
  William 15
McDuffee, Angeline 62
  George 60
  R. N. 63
  Robert N. 62
McDuffer, Edward 121
McDuffie, Mary 155
  Rhoda C. 181
McDuffy, Ed. 13
McElrath, Bertha 260
  Cherokee Morgan 171
  Hugh McDowell 260
  John Edgar 260
  John Otto 260
  Lucy 260
  Otto 260
McElwee, _____ 44
  (Capt.) 41
  (Mrs.) 48
  Ann Eliza 246
  Eliza Jane 263
  Elizabeth 246
  Frank 246
  Franklin Brown 246
  Hugh 246
  Hulda 246
  James 17, 18, 30, 31, 245
  Jane 55
  Jane Adams 147, 246
  John 246
  John C. 48
  Julia Rather 231, 246
  Kenneth 246

(Mrs.) Lucinda 43
Margaret 246
Martha Jane 246, 285
Mary 246
Nancy 93, 246
Parmelia 246
Patsy Gilmore 246
Polly 48, 246
Polly Gilmore 246
Sally Johnston 246, 250
Sarah 103
Thomas B. 246
Thomas Brown 246
William 42, 43, 148, 171, 246
William II 246
William Eblen 246
McEwan, John 47
McEwen, (Mrs.) 51
  Alexander 247
  Alice 247
  (Miss) Alice 50
  Ann Elizabeth 247
  Charles 50, 51, 247
  Edminston 50
  (Mrs.) Eliza 48, 50
  Eliza M. E. 105
  Eliza Mary 50
  Elizabeth 184, 247
  Joana Columbia 51
  Joanna Columbus 247
  Johanna 158
  John 13, 14, 75, 93, 184, 247, 308
  John Columbus 50, 184, 247, 275
  John L. 51
  M. J. 49
  M. P. 61
  Margaret 48, 247
  Margaret Alice 184, 247
  Margaret Ellis 50
  Marguerita 161
  Mary 247
  Mary A. 51
  Mathew 50, 61, 247
  Mathew P. 50, 51
  Matilda 247
  (Mrs.) Nancy 51
  Nancy P. 184
  Nancy Patton 247
  Robert 247
  Robert E. 51
  Robert Neilson 247
  Robert Newton 50
  Susan 247
  Susan E. 51
  W. M. 62
  W. S. 59, 62
  William 58, 161, 247
  William J. 51
  William L. 49, 51
  William S. 57
  William Stephenson 50
McFaddin, Edward 17
McFarland, Arthur 109
  Margaret 167
McGaughey, Margaret 205
McGee, David 16
  Silas 112
McGhee, Annie 258
McGill, Hugh 308
  James 18
  John 18
  Peter T. 37
McGinness, Ella Hastings 146
McGoughey, Nellie 304
  Ruel 304

334

McGowan, Sarah 172
McGregor, Martha J. 265
McGruder, Mary 185
McGuffey, Barbara 139
  Sarah 128
  Sarah E. 139
McGuinness, Mary 284
McHenry, Robert 102
McIntire, Elizabeth 112
  Hugh 16
  James 16
McIntosh, Matilda 259
McKamey, Albert 305
  Anna 143
  John 308
  M. C. 89
  Margaret 125
  Nancy 81
  W. C. 13
  William 86, 89, 97, 98, 303, 305
  William C. 94, 99, 101
  William N. 125
McKamy, Anna 104
McKane, John 115
McKenney, William E. 97
McKinney, (Mrs.) Henry 193
  Jesse 114
  John 10, 15
  Roland 15
  Syntha 143
  Syntha Ann 111
McKinnie, Reuben 83
McKinny, John 18
  Rawling 18
McKnight, John Valley 279
  Mary Margaret 279
McLester, (Mrs.) Metcalf 244
McMahan,_____ 226
McMaster, (Miss) 247
McMasters, (Miss) 185
McMeans, (Mrs.) 48
  John S. 42
McMillan, Edward E. 300
  Flora 119
  Margie Belle 300
  Narcissa Tennessee 155
  Rector 19
McMillen/McMillin
  Ann(a) Craven 165, 166
  David Caldwell 165, 166
  Douglas N. 166
  Edwin W. 166
  James P. 165, 166
  Jonathan P. 165, 166
  Nancy Jane (Cravens) 166
McMillin, Laura 166
  Robert 166
McMinn, Margaret T. 107
  Return J. 308
McMullen,_____ 171
  James 18, 22, 96, 98, 99, 102, 106
  Nancy 143
  Thomas 15, 18, 30
  (Capt.) Thomas 42
McMullens, Beckey 126
McMurray, Ralph 242
  William 145
McNabb, (Mrs.) Alice 194
  Andrew 119
  George 123
  James 240
  John 240
  Nathaniel 240
  Sam 240
  Sarah 87
  Thomas 99

McNatt, John 94
McNealy, Robert 21
McNeel, James 16
McNeeley, Robert 18
McNight, Polly 105
McNutt, Anna 54, 63-67, 239, 249
  Anna E. 54
  Annie Elizabeth 49
  Catey 78
  Doremus 249
  Frank 249
  J. W. 13, 44c
  James 13, 54, 60, 63
  James (Jr.) 54
  James P. 249
  Joel 33
  John 29, 66-68
  John F. 303
  John Fleming 249
  John W. 249
  Katherine 300
  M. L. 54
  Margaret Wester 249
  Nannie 67
  Robert 105
  Robert B. 54
  Sarah Agnes 54
  Sarah M. 49
  Thomas 105
  W. 65, 67
  (Dr.) W. H. 54
  W. M. 66-68
  William 13, 64, 105
  William H. 50, 249
  William J. 300
McPhail, Daniel 17
McPherson,_____ 216
  Corrie 197, 198
  Elener 94
  George 10, 16
  Henry 10, 19, 248
  Hugh L. 61
  James 57
  Jesse 14
  Jinny 96
  John 248
  Joseph 16, 89
  Margaret 103, 214
  Polly 216
  Rufus 261
McReynolds, David W. 201
  David W. (Jr.) 202
  Dorothy 201
  Elinore 201
  Evelyn 202
  Lucian H. 271
McSpaddin, Samuel 17
McTeer, Joe 259
McVey, Peggy 93
McWilliams,_____ 192
  David 179
  Thomas 179

-M-

Mabry, Hope 301
  Robert 301
Machamer, Roy 232
Maddox, Glenn 153
  Louise 153
Maddux, Ledora 219
  Robert Lee 219
Maddy, Sarah 123
Madison, Dolly Payne 160
  (Pres.) James 34

Madrin, Robert 96
Magill, John G. 124
  William 14, 106, 115
Maguffee, James 22
Magus, Abner 19
Mahaffee, John 120
Mahan, Alexander 18
  Charles William 267
  James Gilbert 267
  William H. 267
Mahon, Ethelinda 248
Mahoney, Charlie 188
  Cora 188
  Edger 188
  Emma 188
  Guy 188
  James 188, 204
  John T. 188
  Nell 188
  O. E. 204
  Ray 188
  Wilbur 188
Maiden, Mignonie 170
Mains, (Capt.) Jesse G. 32
Majoribank, Archibald J. 161
Majors, Abner 77
  George 270
  Ira 37
  Sammy Anthony 270
Malinda, Julia 172
Malone, (Mrs.) Effie 194
Man, Robert 18
Mandelbaum, Ida 289
Manifold, George 47, 50
  Mary 47
  Mary B. 47
  Sarah H. 47
  William Fleming Calverey 47
Mann, Nancy 111
  Rebecca 91
Manning, Mary 104
  Peter 102, 104
Mansfield, Nicholas 16, 88, 91, 92
Mantin, Olsey 102
Mapee, Anna 92
Mapes, John 96
March, Roe 245
Margraves, Betsy 47, 87, 103, 143
  George Thomas 136
  Harry Eugene 136
  James Barnard 136
  Robert Ervin 136
  Savannah 155
  Thomas 32, 33
  W. 66-68
  William 282
  William Thomas 136
Maricle, James 37
Marko,_____ 162
  Thomas Clark 162
Marney, Amos 15, 18, 29, 31, 242
  Betsy 242
  David 242
  Elizabeth Spence 242
  Jack 306
  Letitia 192, 242
  Malinda 242
  Margaret 242
  Margaret (Peggy) 179
  Mary 242
  Patsy 108, 242
  Pheby 242
  Polly 242
  Rebecca 242
  Robert 13, 114, 119, 242

Marney (cont.)
  Sally 306
  Samantha 242
  Samuel 94, 242
  Sarah 95, 179
  Susan 128
  Thomas 255
  Walter 306
  Wiley 211
Marr, Betsy 242
Marrell, Eldridge 136
  Hester 136
  Susan Allison 136
Marshall, Clara May,304
  Humphrey 35
  John 258
  Martin,_____ 44, 237
  Ada (Winston) 238
  Adelia 275
  Alice 186
  Anna Neilson 185
  Charles 64, 66
  Charles Nelson 50
  Charlie 67, 68
  Eliza 244, 273
  Elizabeth 238, 273
  (Mrs.) Emily C. 50
  Ernest 185
  Fannie (Dallom) 238
  Fannie Inman 238
  Felix Zollicoffer 189
  George 112
  Goldie 209
  Grace Elizabeth 244
  Herbert Dallom 238
  Hugh 49, 158, 238, 244
  J. B. 52
  Jack 244
  James 60, 118, 244
  James B. 52
  James Edward 213
  James Edward (Jr.) 213
  James R. 50
  James Reagen 238
  James Reese 244
  Jane 126
  Jean 244
  John 238
  (Col.) John 238
  John C. 185
  John G. 186
  Johnny 231
  Joseph 49, 244
  Joseph Brown 34
  Julia Reece 49
  Lida 244
  Mabel 244
  Margaret 244
  Margaret Alice (Gillespie) 186
  Margaret F. 49
  Mary 49, 244, 273
  Myra 209
  Nancy 244
  Nancy (Gallaher) 244
  Nancy McIlwaine 244
  Ned 273
  Olive 244
  Rachel 212
  Rachel Winston 238
  Robert 273
  (Miss) Sallie 50
  Sallie Russell 238
  Sally Roberts 49
  Samuel 14, 57, 244, 273
  Samuel C. 50
  Scott 63, 65
  Walter L. 213
  William 148, 186, 208, 273
  William A. 185
  William McGruder 185
  William P. 244
  William Porter 244
  William T. 253
  Zollicoffer 244
Mason, Carrington 247
  Daniel 15, 32, 308
  Elizabeth Stevenson 247
  John B. 110
  Mary (Brashears) 308
  Nathaniel 15
  Rena Hall 289
  Thomas Jefferson 32, 308
  William 94, 247
  William Taylor 247
Massengail, James 21
Mathaney, Anna 177
  (Mrs.) C. W. 179
  Elijah 177
  John A. 124
Mathew, Evelyn 166
Mathews, Britton 83
  Jennie 88
  Maria 134
  Wilbur Knox 259
Mathis, Archalas 17
  Britain 17
Mathney, Samuel 273
Matlock, (Miss) 144
  Abbie 245
  Absolom 245
  Amanda 245
  Ann 245
  Avery Lenoir 245
  Beulah 245
  Elizabeth 189
  Eveline 245
  Isaac 103
  James 82, 245
  James (Jr.) 86
  Jane 103, 233, 245
  Jane Lackey 245
  Jason 16, 17, 245
  John 14, 16, 17, 22, 245, 246
  Lena 245
  Lottie 245
  Louisa 245
  Malinda 245
  Martha 246
  Martin 42, 62
  Mary 239, 245
  Maude 245
  Minerva 109, 144
  (Mrs.) Minnie 194
  Moore 82, 245
  Richard 245
  Robert 245
  Ruth Russell 245
  S. M. 62
  Sally 82
  Sarah 148
  T. B. 62
  William 16, 45, 73, 92, 245
  William (Jr.) 18
Maughan, Alexander 15
Maxey, Mary 204
May, James 84
Mayberry, Loraine 269
  Sarah Elizabeth 159
Mayo,_____ 281
  Gus 252
  Martha 260
  May 282
Mays, (Miss) 208
  Lois 239
Mazer, Solomon 16
Mead, William 27
Meadows, Guy S. 37
  Mary 211
Means, James 16
  John 16
Mear, Hugh 73
  John 73
Mebane, Edward J. 300
  Hal 300
  Helen 300
  Nancy 300
Medlock, Nathaniel 20
Mee,_____ 282
  Carl 203
  Carl Edward 251
  Clarence Dewitt 251
  Claude Rupert 250, 251
  Columbus 250
  Columbus Alexander 250
  Dose 283
  Edith May 251
  Hobart Carl 250, 251
  Isaac 250
  James Carl 251
  Jesse 250
  John 103, 246, 250
  Joseph 45, 250
  Joseph F. 250
  Laird 250
  Luke 250
  Margaret Elizabeth 250
  Martha 250
  Mary Caroline 250
  Mary Claudia 251
  Nancy 250
  Paul 250
  Penelope 250
  Roberta Claire 251
  Roma Dare 251
  Rufus F. 250
  Rufus McNeal 250
  Ruth Elizabeth 251
  Thomas 250
  Thomas Rupert 251
  William 250
  William Walter 250, 251
  William Walter (Jr.) 250
Meek, John Fleming 178
  John Lamar 178
  Katherine L. 282
Megill, John 21
Mehlhorn, Emma 216
Melentick, James 21
Melton, Edna 208
  Esther 86
  (Col.) J. M. 44d
  James 118
  John 21
Melvin, Thomas 122
Menord, Agnes 150
  Catherine 150
  Edward 150
  Henrietta 150
  Jasper 150
  Lucille 150
  Nora 150
  Rochford 150
  Rose 150
  Stella 150
Meredith, Richard 13, 18, 22
Meriot, John 21
Merrill, Austin H. 151
  Austin H. (Jr.) 151
  Elizabeth Brown 151
  Patricia Ann 151
Merritt, Edward 91
Merriweather, (Capt.) Francis 288

Merriweather, Lucy 288
Mesamore, Jacob 119
Meucke, Adelaide M. 49
 (Mrs.) Frederica 49
Meyers, Henry 267
Middleton, Wesley 123
Milbanks, Charles 14
Miles, Annie 228
 Carl 302
 Catherine Ann (Wester) 305
 Earl 302
 Eola 302, 305
 Harry 302, 305
 Jacob 21
 Maud/e 302, 305
 Robert R. 38
Millard, Samuel H. 46
 Susie 202
Miller, Abraham 96
 Adam 19, 29
 Alex 74
 Alexander 16
 Ammy 74
 Carrie 261
 Cynthia 178
 David 9
 Dunlap 170
 Eliza 103
 Ephriam 240
 Epriam 125
 Evaline F. 125
 Evelyn 170
 Frances 75
 Henry 16, 30, 34
 Ida 165, 166
 James 15, 16, 75
 Jane 104
 John 16, 172, 178
 Lee 211
 Mary 245
 Mary Buren 178
 Mary Menden 250, 251
 Nancy 87
 Noah 114
 Peggy 75, 143
 Percival Walker 261
 Robert 13, 16, 32
 Robert (Jr.) 16
 Samuel 9, 15, 18, 21, 22
 Susanna 170
 Thomas Austin 170
 W. P. 240
 William 15, 16
Millican, Addie May 253
 Alice 253
 Almeda (Owings) 253
 Annie 211, 252, 253
 Annie (Joseph) 253
 Antonio (Oyler) 253
 Billie 253
 Calvert 252
 Carita 253
 Catherine 253
 Charles 253
 Charles F. 252, 253
 Clifford 253
 Clyde 253
 Delphine 253
 Earl 253
 Edgar S. 252, 253
 Edith 253
 Edwin 253
 Eliza (French) 253
 Elizabeth (Acuff) 218, 253
 Elsie 253
 Elvira 252
 Emma 253
 Emma (Cooper) 253

 Emma Elizabeth 252
 Everett 253
 Finetta 252
 Floyd 253
 Frank 253
 Fred 253
 George W. 252, 253
 Gideon C. 252, 253
 Glada 253
 Guilford 253
 Gus G. 252
 Helen 253
 J. Robert 252, 253
 James 253
 Jane 252
 Jenny May 253
 John 202, 252
 John Haley 252
 John M. 252, 253
 John W. 252, 253
 Ida 252
 Lawton B. 253
 Lizzie 252, 253
 Lla Ree 253
 Louis 253
 Louis D. 252, 253
 Louise (Collett) 253
 Lula (Russell) 253
 Mabel Frances 218
 Madge 218, 253
 Margaret 253
 Mary 48, 195
 Mary A. 252
 Maude 253
 Mollie (Ingram) 211, 253
 Moses Franklin 252
 Moses Scott 252
 Nancy 252
 Nancy Green 195
 Nola 253
 Pearl (Isham) 253
 Reece 211, 253
 Robert 210, 211
 Roscoe 211, 253
 Sallie 252
 Samuel 252
 Tennessee 252
 Thelma 253
 W. F. 217, 218
 W. F. (Jr.) 218
 W. W. 42
 Walter 253
 William 195, 252
 William F. 252, 253
 William W. 252
Milligan, Ernest 294
 Helen 294
 Hilda 294, 295
 Isaac 294
 Sarah 294
 Virginia 294, 295
Mills, Charles 149
 Eliza Ann 258
 Elizabeth 149
 (Mrs.) Ida 194
 Ruth 149
Milsap, Jane 141
Milton, Mattie S. 149
Mimms, C. W. 154
Minor, Louisa 247
Minton, Polly 112
Mitchell, Charles 85
 Elizabeth 255
 Caroline Virginia 299
 George 114
 James 14, 16, 111, 112
 Jane 288
 Malinda 299

 Margaret 185
 Mary 307
 Morris 111
 (Rev.) Morris 307
 Rhoda 307
 William 19
Mizell, Daniel 105
Mobray, Lorena Dorton 252
Molting, Cretora 107
Mond, James 97
Monger, Henry 155
Monnger, Joseph J. 109
Monning, Benjamin 278
 James 278
 John F. 278
 Louise 278
Monroe, James 34
Montcastle, Allison 278, 279
 Inez 278, 279
 Julia (Leeper) 279
 Myra 278, 279
 Sarah 278, 279
Montgomery, _____ 44
 Alex 43
 Alexander 255, 273
 Allen 140
 Amanda 255
 Andrew C. 233
 Bertie 256
 Beulah 278
 Beulah M. 233
 Charles 255, 256
 Creed 255
 Elbert 255
 Elbert C. 43
 Elizabeth 255, 256
 Ellen Fay 140
 Emma 255, 256
 George 255, 256
 Grace (Anderson) 256
 Henry 255, 256
 Jack 255, 256
 Jacqueline (Moore) 256
 James 255
 Jane 255
 Jane (Whittenberg) 256
 John 202, 217, 255, 256
 (Capt.) John 245
 John A. 255, 307
 John C. 233
 Joseph 255, 256
 Josiah 21
 Katie 256
 Laura 150, 255
 Lottie 255
 Luke H. 218, 219
 Luke Hamilton 219
 Margaret 255, 256
 Margaret P. 233
 Mary 255, 256, 290
 Mary Jane 190
 Mell 255
 Milton 255
 Mitchell Elbert 255
 Nancy 190, 255
 Nancy (Hinds) 256
 Rita Cornelia 219
 Robbie Randolph 219
 Ruby 256
 Sadie 256
 Sarah 255
 Thelma Maud 219
 Thomas 255
 Walter 256
 Wiley 255, 256
 William 255
Montpensier, (Comte de) 11
Moon, Jonas 106

Moon, Lydia 106
Moore,_____ 229
  (Capt.) 19
  (Dr.) 162
  (Mrs.) 48
  Adelaide 102
  Alexander 20, 133
  Ann Eve 48
  Anthony Wayne 50
  Austin Merrill 152
  Benjamine 47, 50
  Ed 293
  Eliza 51
  Eliza Ann 51
  Ewell 293
  George 16, 18, 22
  Helen Lane 152
  Jacob 49, 60, 61
  Jacqueline 255
  James 16, 17, 52, 88, 90, 96
  (Rev.) James 182
  Jas. 61
  Jenny 91
  Jno. N. 42
  John 48, 51, 52, 61, 95
  John N. 49
  John Trotwood 152
  Joseph 18
  Joshua 41, 120
  Martin 279
  Mary 94
  Mary Daniel 152
  Mary Ruth 50
  Morris 76
  Polly 79
  Robert L. 293
  Rowena (Brown) 146
  Roxie Cowan 133
  Samuel 48
  Samuel Perry 50
  Samuel Pride 50
  (Sgt.) Solomon 33
  Susan 146
  (Mrs.) Susan 48, 50
  Thomas 17, 49, 76, 79
  Thomas J. 146
  Thomas J. (Jr.) 146
  Thomas Jefferson 51
  William 29
  William Adolphus 50
Moorman, Rudolph 91, 96
  Ruth Genoa 229
Morehead, Richard 103
Morgan,_____ 292
  (Gen.) 35
  Alexander Gatewood 259
  Alexander McDermott 257
  Amanda 260
  Amanda Maria 257
  Ann (Dodd) 259
  Betsy 99, 143
  (Mrs.) Betsy 48
  Calvin 257, 259
  Calvin C. 258
  Calvin Cogswell 259
  Calvin Rufus 260
  Catherine Matilda 257
  Charlton 259
  Cherokee America 260
  Clifford J. 37
  Cornelia 261
  Currie 259
  Dorothy 166
  Edgar 37
  Eliza 261
  Eliza Jane 257
  Eliza P. 260
  Elizabeth 55, 142, 257, 260
  Elizabeth (Trigg) 260
  Ellen Patience 257
  Frankie 47
  Franklin Henry 257
  George 48, 261
  George Washington 257, 260, 261
  Gideon 14, 30, 31, 44b, 48, 55, 99
  Gideon I 257
  Gideon II 257, 261
  Gideon III 257, 260
  Gideon IV 260
  Gideon (Jr.) 32
  Gideon (Sr.) 44a, 55
  Henrietta 162, 259
  Henry 257
  Huston M. 260
  Irby 261
  (Sen.) J. T. 60
  John 21, 120, 261
  John Fackler 257
  John Hunt 259
  John Tyler 261
  Johnnie Hunt 259
  Katherine 259
  Kitty Grosh 258
  Luther 257, 259
  Margaret 261
  Margaret (Sevier) 260
  Mary 261
  Mary (Polly) 257
  Montesuma 260
  Nancy 100
  Nancy Sewell 261
  Patience (Coggswell) 261
  Pauline 186
  Peggy Ann 260
  Polly 261
  Rachel Kibbe Trigg 260
  Rhoda Frances Campbell 260
  Richard 259
  Rufus 55, 260
  Rufus M. 257
  Samuel 257
  Samuel Dodd 259
  Sara Ann 257
  Sarah Frances 260
  Susan 261
  Thomas 259
  William 257, 261
  William King 260
Moross, Elizabeth Dwight 164
  Frances Dwight 164
  Wm. P. D. 164
Morris, Edith Margaret 222
  George 23
  Ida 151
  Isaac 18, 23
  James 16, 18
  Jinny 92
Morrison, Alberta 262
  Allen Deatherage 262
  Andrew 52
  Catherine Ellen 262
  Charles F. 262, 267
  Charles Francis (Jr.) 262
  Edward 20
  Ethel 262
  Garnet 262
  John 262
  Katherine 262
  Lula 262
  Marcus 262
  Marcus Lafayette 262
  Robert Acuff 262
  Robert Emma 262
  Rose Brooks 262
  Thomas 262
  Thomas B. 208
  Walter 262
Morrow,_____ 154
  James 17
  Ruthvin 49
Morton, A. T. E. 170
  T. P. 265
Mosely, Frederick T. 284
Moses, Martha 181
Motes, Columbus 181
Moton, John 81
Mounger, Ann 297
  Edward 172
  (Rev.) Joseph 113
  William 297
Mounts, Providence 245
Mtredith, Richard 14
Mueche, Edward 50
Muecke, (Mrs.) 51
  Gustavus A. 51
  Joseph A. 49
  Matilda Adelaide 286
Mulkey, Issac 46
Mullens, (Rev.) J. L. 290
Mullins, Ann 125
  B. L. 108
  Thomas 23
Munds, Nelson 126
Munger, Susan 143
Muns, Alyse 102
Munsey, (Rev.) T. K. 43
Muriel, Grace 284
Murphy, (Maj.) 160
  Alice 160
  Annie Belle 161
  Benjamine 177
  Coleste 150
  Florence 160
  Mary 232
  Nancy 177
  Nell 161
  William 13
Murray,_____ 181
  E. D. 61
Murrell, Ada 282
  George M. 282
  Martha 282
Murrey, Rachel 100
Muse, Mabel 167
Musgrove, Edward 90
  Wm. 61
Mutney, Samuel 22
Myers, (Lieut.) Clarence G. 37
  Sarah Dorinda 280
Mynders, Elizabeth 181
Myres, Barbary E. 49

-N-

Nail, Acquila 20
  Alexander 118
  Andrew 88, 95
  James 76
  John 18, 21, 107
  Joseph 21, 17, 89
  Mathew 21
  Miriam 107
  Nancy 88
  Nicholas 15, 18, 21, 30, 31
  Nicholson 10
  Roberta 250
  William 19
Nance, Charles D. 37

Nance, Patsy 96
Napier, Thomas 126
Narramore, Amanda 266, 267
　Emma 202
　Julia 143
　Polly Tenn___ 124
　Wade 124
Nash, Florence 260
Neal, Amanda B. 149
　Evans 37
　George F. 149
　John 15, 79
　John R. 60, 149
　(Col.) John R. 42, 63
　Lucinda 77
　Mary P. 149
　Nora K. 149
　Ruth 210
　Serena 192
Neergartte, Richard W. 50
Neerguard, Bud J. 68
　Carl 276
　Forest 276
　Frederick 276
　Grace 276
　John 276
　John T. 276
　Lester 276
　Mary Winston 276
　Nancy 276
　Nannie Patton 276
　Pauline 276
　Ralph 211, 276
　Richard J. 66
　Ruth 276
　Theo. 64, 66, 67
　William 276
Neerguard/Nearguard
　Paul J. 63, 65
　Richard 63-65, 67, 275, 276
Neighbors, Sarah Armor 226
　William S. 226
Neil, Mary 304
Neilson, Anne 184
　William D. 32, 84, 308
Nelson,_____ 14
　(Dr.) Charles 244
　Dorothy May 267
　Hugh 9, 10
　J. E. 267
　Julia Reese 244
　Lucas 267
　Mathew 9, 14, 17, 57, 76
　Polly 141
　Sallie 65
　Thomas 105
　Thomas A. R. 308
　William 244
　William D. 17
Nesmith, Alexander 23, 71, 86, 89, 95
Netherland, George 247
Newberry, Caroline 128
　Nellie White 232
　Wagner 232
　William W. 232
Newman, Henry 100, 143
　Minnie B. 166
　Nimrod 124
　Viola 225
Newton,_____ 275
　John 275
　Mary 275
　Richard Y. 275
　Ruth 275
　Theresa 275
　William 275
　Winston 275

Nichols, Jennie 161
　John 14, 20, 63, 65, 101,
　Josiah 14
　William B. 168
Nicholson, Anna 181
　Annie 134, 263
　Elizabeth 134
　George 133
　Henry 134
　Hugh 134
　John 134
　Lizzie 68
　Mary 62, 134
Nickand, William 102
Nickard, William 143
Night, Lewis K. 23
Nimsco, Alonia 71
Niper, Caswell Allen 126
Nipp, Samuel 82
Nipper, James 92
Nixon, Barbara 263
　Charles Wellington 263
　Charles William 263
　Comer 263
　George 263
　George W. 64, 263
　George Washington 246, 263
　Hugh McElwee 263
　Hugh Williams 263
　John 263
　Jonah 263
　Lewis Gaines 263
　Margaret (Peak) 263
　Martha Louisa 263
　Mayme Peak 263
　Paul Knox 263
　Phoebe Shirley 263
　Shelly/Shelley 263
　William 263
　William Jacob 263
　William Jacob (Jr.) 263
　William McElwee 263
Noal, James 20
Nobles, Robert 75
Noel, Ann S. 150
　Nancy 83
　Polly 97
Norman, Callie 214, 216
　(Mrs.) John 194
Norton, Sallie 180
Norvel, M. 44b
Nowlan, David 18
Nummert, Dora 228

-O-

O'Bryn,_____ 216
Ochsears, Samuel 20
Oden, Thomas 87
Odin, John 82
Odum, Abraham 101, 104
Ogden, Thomas 10
Ogle, Elsie 176
O'Grady, Cooper 164
Oliver, Charlotte 286
　Eli 87
　James 117
　Joel 86
　John 106
　(Capt.) Lunesford 32
　Mary 89
　Mary Ann 89
　Richard 75
　(Capt.) Richard 9, 15
　Verne 168
　William 81

Ollis, C. C. 22
Olliver, Thomas 73
Olmstead, Roland 186
O'Neal, John 15
Orr,_____ 179
Osborne,_____ 245
　Alice 237
　Hattie 238
　Lucy George 138
Osbourn, Nathaniel 29
Osburn, Mary 138
Otter, John 16
Outlaw, Alexander 13, 30
Overton, Joseph 29, 115
　Robert 29
Owen, Edward 16
Owens,_____ 305
　Wince 38
Owens (Owings), Albert Marion 265
　Alfred 264
　Alice 272
　Alice Emily 265
　Amanda Malvina 270
　Bertha May 271
　Clarinda 264, 266
　Cora Almeda 265
　Daisy Maud 271
　Edward 264
　Elener 264, 269
　Elihu Randolph 264, 271, 272
　Eliza Cornelia 264
　Eliza (Work) 271
　Elizabeth 264
　Esther Matilda 265
　Fannie May 272
　Franklin Davis 265, 266
　Garnet 272
　Hattie 271
　Helen Elizabeth 265
　James Campbell 265
　James Morley 272
　James Samuel 265
　John 264
　John Lock 265
　John Lock(e) 271, 272
　John W. 272
　Judith 264
　Julia Adelaide 271
　Lennie Leota 265
　Luella 271
　Malvina 264
　Margaret 264, 271
　Margaret (Kendrick) 266
　Margaret L. 265
　Margaret Luella 266
　Martha Almeda 265
　Martha J. (McGregor) 265, 266
　Martha Susan 264
　Mary Almeda 265, 266
　Mary Elizabeth 265
　Mary Geneva 271
　Mary Jane 264
　Mary L. 265
　Minerva 264
　Minnie 271
　Nancy Rebecca 265
　Nannie Ethel 265
　Nellie 264
　Ollie Almeda 266
　Rebecca 264, 269
　Robert 264
　Robert Clayton 266
　Robert L. 265
　Roscoe C. 266
　Sammie Jene 265

Owens (Owings), Samuel Augustus 265, 266
  Samuel Clinton 265
  Samuel Sumpter 264-266, 268-271
  Sarah 264
  Sarah Ann 264, 268
  Sarah Henrietta 271
  Sarah M. 265
  Sarah (Randolph) 265, 266, 268-271
  Tom Dock 265
  William Augustine 271
  William E. 265
  William Edward 264
  William Frederick 271
  William Jackson 264-266
Owings (see also Owens) 208
  Albert Marion 195
  Alfred 96
  Almeda 252
  Cora 141
  Edward 19, 42
  Eliza Cornelia 217, 218
  Jesse 124
  Lou Ann 230
  Louisa Bailey 217
  Lucilla 306
  Martha Almeda 148
  Martha Susan 214, 221
  Mary Elizabeth 291
  Minerva 200, 201
  Samuel 32
  Samuel Sumpter 280
  W. J. 46
  W. T. 45
  William 115
  William Edward 280
  William Jackson 214
  Zorilda 173
Oxshear, Samuel 16
Oyler, Antonio M. 252

-P-

Padgett, Frank 176
Page, Audrey 215
Paget, Nathan 97
Paine, Polly 77
Pankey, John 264
Pardee,_____ 14
Pardue, Mary 211
Parham, Creed 37
Park, Andrew 257
Parker, Flo 242
  Ida 231
  J. S. 44c, 44d
  John 16, 22
  Joseph 108
  Reece 295
  William 80
Parkings, D. 119
Parkins, Ada Cleo 270
  Amanda M. (Owings) 270, 271
  Cora Antha Alice 270
  Cora Elizabeth 270, 271
  Eliza Cordelia 270
  Elmira Tennessee 270
  Hallie Etta 270
  James Alpheus 270
  Lella May 270
  Levi Jackson 264, 270, 271
  Lewis Alexander 270
  Margaret Louise 270
  Martha A. (Hatfield) 270
  Martin Luther 270
  Mary Ellen 270
  Robert Samuel 270
  Sallie Ethel 270, 271
  Stephen Augustus 270
  Wilbur 270
  Willie 270
Parks, Abner 93
  Eliza 273
  Frances 255, 273
  Francis 273
  Joseph 34, 116, 273
  Margaret 273, 299
  Mariah 273
  Nancy (Eastley) 273
  Polly 99, 273
  Rebecca 176, 273
  Robert 273
  Ruth 273
Parr, John 27
Parry, John 29
Parsons, Margaret 154
Pass, Ollie 267
Pate, Jeremiah 16
Patten, Cartter 236
  Z. C. 236
Patterson, (Miss) 247
  A. M. 179
  Andrew 37
  Anna Cora 51
  Clark 163
  Cora 236
  (Mrs.) E. F. 49
  Edward 236
  James L. 163
  Letitia 145
  N. A. 12, 51
  Newton 60
  Newton A. 236
  Oscar M. 37
  Robert Mead 163
  Robert Meade 163
  William Gleaves 163
Patton,_____ 50
  (Mrs.) Addia 50
  Baxter C. 275
  Betsy 47
  (Mrs.) Betsy Purris 50, 51
  D. 62
  David 17, 22, 47, 48, 51, 52, 61, 64, 65, 80, 117, 146, 275
  (Mrs.) David 48
  David E. 49
  David Emmerson 275
  David William 50
  Elizabeth 63, 146, 275
  Eugene Byrd 275
  Eugene Byrd (Jr.) 275
  Florence 149
  Frank 149
  George Earnest 275
  Henry 149
  J. P. 52, 61
  James 275
  James G. 49
  James Gamble 51
  Jane 53, 60
  Jane M. 48
  Jane McDowell 50, 275
  Jane N. 146
  John 68
  John A. 13
  John H. (Jr.) 251
  John Morris 275
  John Newton 51
  John O. 63, 65
  John P. 48, 52, 61, 275
  John Purris 50, 234, 275
  Marie Tedder 275
  Mary E. 49
  Mary H. 49
  (Mrs.) Mary Overton 50
  Mary Virginia 275
  Minnie 275
  Minnie Overton 275
  Nancy 60, 61
  (Miss) Nancy 61
  Nancy M. 48
  Nancy McClung 50, 247, 275
  Nannie 68
  Nannie M. 275
  Neal 149
  P. 61
  Purris 275
  Rose 211
  Rose Frances 275
  Ruth Lea 275
  Samuel Fisk 51, 275
  Teresa 68, 288
  Teresa Rebecca 48, 50, 275
  Theresa 275
  Thomas David 51
  Virginia 275
  W. S. 49, 52
  Willia 275
  William S. 244
  William Steele 51, 275
Patty, (Rev.) 43
  Josiah 121
  Vanilia 116
Paul, Eula 286
Paulus, Marie 244
Payne, James 54
  Lester Lavins 219
  Mary 288
  Mary L. 260
  Neil S. Brown 219
  Otis Kendrick 219
  Robert Carney 219
  Sally 288
  Susan 160
  Vera Maud 219
  William 288
Peacock, (Miss) 298
Peak, Jacob 263
  Margaret Green 263
  Standifer 133
  Walter 133
Pearson, Ellis 162
  William 123
Peay, Mattie 256
Peaycord, (Mrs.) 242
Peck, Jacob 14
Pelfrey, Ernest 38
  Samuel J. 37
Pelfry, Betsy 96
Pellum, Jesse 81
Pembleton, John 15
Penland, Mary 102
Pennick, Susan 104
Perkepile, Catherine 123
Perriman, Framina 85
Perry, Josiah 108
  Peter 104
  Sarah 120
  William 224
Peters, Benjamine 19
  Laura 184
  William 15, 21
Petty, (Mrs.) Mary 50
Pettyjohn, Amanda 287
Phifer, George 38
Phillips, A. 52
  Annie 256

Phillips (cont.)
  B. H. 286
  Betsy 85
  (Mrs.) C. A. 193
  Clemmens 83
  Clemmons 16
  Clemons 19
  (Mrs.) Guy C. 179
  Jacob 104
  John 23
  Lewis 22
  Mary/May 215
  Nellie 271
  Patience 85
  Polly 76
  Rebecca 82
  Reuben 81
  (Rev.) Sewell 43
  Susan Clark 55
  William 160
  William D. 104
Phillpot, Barton 111
Piatt, Robert 285
  Sara 285
  William Robert 285
Pickel, Charlie 211
  Gilbert 211
  Jack 298
  James E. 211
  Jessie 211
  Joe 211
  John H. 145
  Katy 297
  Lillie 211
  Marie 276
  Matilda 180
  Maud 157
  Nancy Stove 276
  Sarah 298
  Tom 211
  Vann 211
  Van Stowe 276
  (Mrs.) William 193
Pickle, George 85
  John 17
  Lillie 276
  Pearl L. 239
  Polly 84
Piddy, Franklin 22
Pike, S. 59
Pimerlore, William 83
Pitcher, Joseph Warren 229
  Margaret Lisle 229
  Robert Warren 229
Pitner, Amanda 278
Plemons, Effie Lee 224
Plumber, Martha Elizabeth 270
  Robert Lee 270
  Robert Terrell 270
Plumlee, J. C. 62
Podester, Mary 153
Poindexter, Catherine 111
  Jane 186
  John 186
  John S. 186
  Mary Lee 186
Poland, John E. 37
Pollock, Ruby 271, 272
Polston, Bonnie May 215
  Clarence Franklin 215
  Fred Lewis 215
  Joseph Daniel 215
  Lucille Elizabeth 215
  William Henry 215
Ponder,____ 135
  Axey 99
Pool, Gilbert 78, 79, 81
Poole, Anna 142

Poor, Betsy 99
Pope, Dallas A. 37
  John 14
  Mary McNutt 176
  William 14
Porter, Benjamine 90
  Charles 170
  Dudley 170
  John Davis 170
  Louisa 257
  Susannah 170
  Thomas Kennedy 170
Post, Mary Florence 172
Potter, Absolum 20
  Jeffrey 16
  John 93
  Solomon 86
Powell, Alexander 83
  Asa A. 139
  Houston E. 37
  Ida 216
  John 73
  Joseph 139
  Josie May 139
  Lester F. 37
  Matilda 98
Power, Jesse 90
Prater,____ 137
  Amanda (Pitner) 278
  Artie 279
  Artie Elizabeth 279
  Benjamin(e) 17, 277
  Benjamin(e) Franklin 277, 278
  Carrie 279
  Clarisa/Clarissa 277
  Cordelia 278
  Darius 277
  Edgar P. 279
  Elizabeth 277
  Elizabeth (Betty) 278
  Eugene 279
  George 277
  George W. 279
  George William 279
  Helen Gertrude 279
  Henry Clayton 279
  Herbert Alexander 279
  Hugh Blair 279
  J. W. 148
  James Alexander 279
  James Eugene 279
  James Madison 277, 278
  James Thomas 279
  John 74
  John Jefferson 277, 278
  Joseph Lloyd 279
  Josephine 278
  Julia (Browder) 277, 278
  Lelia 278
  Letitia 117, 277
  Louella 279
  Loyd 279
  Margaret 233, 286
  Mary Kate 301
  Mary Leeper 279
  Mayme 279
  Myrtle 279
  Nancy Elizabeth 277
  Oscar B. 233
  Pauline 279
  Roy 278
  Samuel 277
  Thomas 144, 277, 278
  Walter L. 233
  Walter W. 301
  Willia[m] 278
  William 277, 279

  William Alexander 277, 278
  William Berry 279
  William W. 233
  Willie May 279
  Winona 279
Prestedge, Frances Davis 152
  Robert 152
Preston, Carl 211
  Charlotte 308
  Elizabeth 20, 128, 308
  Elizabeth Gertrude 151
  George 9, 16, 20, 308
  Hester Elizabeth 151
  Hetha Hill 151
  James 10, 17, 19, 81, 84, 308
  (Capt.) James 32
  Jane 86
  Jenny 84
  Jesse 95
  John H. 151
  Moses 133
  Polly 95
  Thomas Benjamine 151
  Walter Roddye 151
  William Brady 151
Prettyman, Arthur S. 151
  Thomas Brown 151
Prewet, William 16
Prewett, Drusilla 83
Price, Elizabeth Caswell 259
  Hurd 33
  J. Harry 259
  J. Harry (Jr.) 259
  Keith McClung 259
  (Rev.) P. N. 43
  Richard 14, 17, 30
Priddy, Martin 23
  William 23
Pride, Ann 92, 155
  (Mrs.) Patsy 48
  Ruth 47
  Samuel 48
  Sarah A. 49
Prigmore, Ruth 84
  Sally 88
Prim, Garland 172
Prince, Richard 282
Pritchet, Thomas 22
Pritchett, E. 79
  Edward 104
  Ephriam 20
  Patsy 106
  Phillip 99
  Thomas 75
  William 99
Prititch, Phillip 102
Probasco, Scott Livingston 186
Prosser, Rebecca 259
Pruet, Elijah 33
  Elisha 30
Pruitt, Andrew 79
  William 74
Pryor, Edmund 125
  Mathew 19, 30
  Mathew (Jr.) 20
  Mathew (Sr.) 20
  William 20
Pulliam, Rosa B. 166
Punt, William 17
Purcell, Richard 292
Purcey, Thomos 125
Puree, Mary Ann 135
Purifoy, (Dr.) 154
Puris, Betsy 78
  John 23, 87
  William 23
Purris, Betsy 80

Purris, Elizabeth 275
Esther A. 49
H. S. 48, 61
John 46, 47, 52, 57, 80, 87
Sarah 47
Purser, Robert 174
Pursley, James 110
Pybas, Adelaide 162
  Clark 162
  Francis 162
Pyott,_____ 44
  J. W. 62
  John 42, 43
  Joseph 231
  Sam'l 62, 63

-Q-

Qualls, Elbert 208
  Ethel 195
  Herman 253
  Jack 208
  James 111
  Nettie 256
  William B. 208
Queen, William 34
Queener, Margaret 112
Quick, Hezekiah 94

-R-

Ragel, Catherine 214
Ragsdale, Edward Brown 152
  Edward Woodson 152
Ragsdon, Vinnie 201
Raines, Belle 195
Rainfrow, Agness 74
Rains, (Mrs.) Elizabeth 49
Ralston, Anna 112
  Lou 143
Ramsey,_____ 27
  (Dr.) A. B. 138
  Annie 236
  Elizabeth 236
  F. A. 241
  Henrietta Rutlelge 238
  (Dr.) J. G. M. 238
  Jennie 236
  Julia Ann Campbell 236
  Lula 236
  Reynolds A. 236
  Samuel 95
  Thomas 236
  Thomas Isaac 236
  Waightstill 236
  Waightstill Avery 236
  William 16, 21
  (Col.) William 161
  William Lenoir 236
Randle, Nell 185
Randolph, (Mr.) 46
  Abigail 115, 264, 280
  Dorcas 280
  Elihu 280
  Elisah 19
  Gilbert A. 280
  Gillam C. 280
  Gilmore 280
  Grief 280
  Henry 280
  Hezekiah 280
  Jemima 280
  John 19
  Louisa (Bailey) 280

Mahala 280
Malinda 280
Malissa 280
Rebecca 280
Robert 19, 280
Sarah 264, 280
Sarah Dorinda 280
William 30, 280
Rankin, John Carter 238a
  (Dr.) Nelson Henry 238a
Ransom, William 205
Rape, William 282
Rashears, Isaac 81
Rather, (Capt.) 18
  Daniel 17, 246
  Jesse 18, 21
  John 21, 88
  Nancy 79, 103
  Polly 111
Rathers, John 111
Rawlings, Moses 14
Ray, John 33
Rayborn, Jack 38
Raybourn, William 297
Rayburn, Joseph 242
  Lucroso 94
  Thomas 10, 94
Rayder, Sarah L. 215
Raymon, Benoni 19
Read, Samuel R. 235
Reagan, Columbus 64-68
Reagen, Frank H. 237
  (Gen.) James A. 237
  James Avery 237
  John Martin 237
  Julia 237
  William Ballard Lenoir 237
Reaves, (Mrs.) J. L. 193
Rebourn, Thomas 17
Rector, Absalom 201, 217
  Cumberland 16, 18, 31
  Elijah 111
  Eliza 94
  Enoch 214
  Frankie 217
  John 10, 82
  Landon 18
  London 117
  Mary 214, 217
  Nancy 112
  Nancy S. 195
  Nancy Short 216
  Polly 82
  Rebecca 88, 175
  Richard 214, 217
  Sally 80
  Uriah 28, 31
Reddle, Henry 17
Redferrin,_____ 197
Reece, Isaac 19
  Thomas 15
Reed, Frank Trimble 161
  John 161
  Sarah A. 298
  Thomas 18, 21
  William 121-123
Reeder, Elizabeth 125
Reedy, (Miss) 259
Reel, John 150
Rees, Arthur Wilbur 153
  Marshall Stroud 153
  William Marshall 153
Reese, Adelia 244
  Charles Nelson 244
  Flue 212
  Hazel 221
  Julia 244
  Margaret 244

May 204
Samuel 204, 244
Sarah 244
Scott 244
Sue 185
Regester, J. Florin 252, 253
  Mary (Millican) 253
  Nell 253
  Roland 253
Reid, Emma Florence 49
Reimer, Thomas F. 284
Rend, Robert 50
Renfro, Jane 121
  John 114, 127
  Joshua 16
  Lewis 48, 113
  Martha 63
  Stephen 12, 31
Renfroe, Columbus 63-66
  Mark 75
  Martha 65
Reno, Ida May 63, 65
Renolds, George 90
  James 90
Rentfroe, Joseph 42
Repeto, William 30
Reves, Jessey 22
  Richard 103
Rex, Grace 287
Reyborn, Frankie 90
Reyburn, Betsy 83
  Peggy 111
Reynolds, Alfred 33
  Ethel 262
  James 144
  John Merriam 262
  Marcus Morrison 262
  S. D. 212
  William Hartley 262
Rhail, Amanda 49
Rhea, John 14, 16, 30, 44b
  John W. 124
Rhem, Henry 150
Rhoel, Anna 68
  Annah 66
  Belle 66, 68
  Frank 68
Rice,_____ 189
  Betsy 79, 189
  Isaac 45, 46
  James 84
  John 86, 92
  John B. 78
  Lelia A. 304
  Lucy 84
  Miller 189
  Passy 85
  Polly 78
  Rebecca 86
  Stephen 15
Rich, George 59
  Jeremiah 121
  (Mrs.) Lurana 49
  Pheobe 49
  (Miss) Pheobe 59
Richards, Gabriel 86
  Gambal 18
  George 18
  Harry 271
  Hillard 271
  John 200
  Joseph 286
  Mamie 286
  Patience 126
  Richard 86, 94, 98, 100,
    120, 126, [129]
  (Dr.) Richard 59, 147
  Talliaferro 20

Richards (cont.)
Thomas 271
William 76
Richardson, (Miss) 144
Allen P. 228
Allen P. (Jr.) 228
Allen Preston 228
Allene 228
Matilda 62
Preston 228
Robert 228
Thomas 83
Walter 228
Walter E. 219
William 228
Richbery,_____ 229
Richbery (?), Elsie 229
Fannie 229
Roland 229
Richey, Andrew 17
Richmond, Ruth 226
Riddle, J. H. 287
John 97
Margaret 115
Riggs, Emma 189
Lula 268
Matilda 183
Riley, Elizabeth 81, 82
John 77, 79
Polly 78
Samuel 20, 78, 79
Rinkell, Abraham 110
Rinkle, Jacob 105
Ritter, Vivian 284
William C. 22
Roach, Sarah 116
Roane, Archibald 11
Roath, William 100
Robb, Kesiah 110
Sarah 273
Robbins, Della 216
Robbinson, Mary 293
Robbs, Edgar 269
Edward Wattson 264, 269
Frankie 202
Grace 269
Margaret 269
Margaret Jane 269
Milton 269
Rebecca (Owings) 269
Roy 269
Sarah Caroline 269
Wattson 202
William Alexander 269
Roberson, Alexander Lawrence 167
Hugh 167
Isaac 85
Mariana 167
Nell 167
Ruth 167
Roberts,_____ 165
Agnes 294
Ann 269
Bashears 105, 110
Betsy 73
Caty 77
David 113, 117
David M. 18
Edward 100
Edward A. 266
Elias 15
Jack Wager 266
James 76
John 211, 216
Lewis M. 123
Little B. 103
(Mrs.) Mary H. J. 49

Nancy 228
Nancy Ann 149
Nannie 63, 65, 66, 285
(Rev.) Nelson 42
Phebe 101
Rite 15
(Rev.) Samuel 60
Susan 115
Thomas 149
(Rev.) Thomas 52
Thomas E. 181
Weight 17
Yerb 211
Zacheus 15
Robertson, (Rev.) J. W. 237
James K. 122
Joseph 19
Patsy 81
Robins, Bartlett 20, 78
Camille 154
Robinson,_____ 153
Alma 300
Ann 76
Auria 281
Bertie 281
Billie 168, 169
Blanch 168, 169
Carrie 263
Charles B. 168, 169
Christopher 80
Drury 113
E. D. 281
Elbert 263
Elizabeth 281
Eva 168
Fannie 281
Frank 232, 304
Frank Welcker 300
Harry 256
Jacob (or James) 10
James 16, 19, 81, 82, 281, 306
James R. 281
Jessie 153
John 168, 169
(Mrs.) John 193
John W. 281
Joseph 16, 119, 122
Judy 101
Lewis 80, 87
Lucy 93
Mary 94, 281
Milly 103
Minerva 281
Nancy 281
Nathan 16
Paul 153
Polly 93
Robert 281
Robert King 281
Samuel 98
Sarah Catherine (Welcker) 300
Susan 281
Susan H. 169
Thomas 15, 281
William 281
William C. 299, 300
Zada 152
Rockford, Mary J. 150
Rockwood, (Maj.) W. A. 13
Roddy, Elizabeth 304
Mary 189
Roddye,_____ 226
Catherine 165
Jennie Mahaffa 165
Jesse 165
Mary 148

Rodgers, Rufus M. 37
Rody, Jesse 19
Roe, Frank 193
Roebuck, Benjamin 14
Roger, (Capt.) 19
Rogers, (Dr.) 51
Addie 138
Andrew Lewis 260
Andrew Lewis III 260
Anna D. 92
Annie Clark 160
Archibald 160
Archibald C. 114
Catey 91
Clifford 260
Connell 260
Dewitt 160
Ella Nash 260
Eustace 160
Frank 160
George 19
George D. 144
Gertrude Whitman 260
Harriet Newell 165, 166
Howard Cunningham 260
Hugh Morgan 260
James 16, 82, 160
(Capt.) James 32, 133
James B. 17
James Edgar 160
James R. 19
Jeames 21
Jenny 96
(Capt.) John A. 33
John Brown 160
John Otto 260
John Thomas 160
Josephine 260
Josephine (Howard) 260
Josephine Virginia 160
Kenneth 260
Lelie 160
Lewis Byrne 260
Lucy 260
Malinda 49
(Dr.) Marcus LaFayette 261
Marion Sevier 260
Mary Louisa 160
Matty 74
Patricia 260
Paul 260
Thomas 160
Virginia 51
William 160
(Dr.) William 49
William Thomas 160
Rollins, Aaron 61
Roof, Mary 185
William W. 185
Rooker,_____ 216
Rorex, William 15
Rose, Anna 200
Carl 219
Charles M. 242
Clarice 240
Donald 242
Edward 240
Elizabeth 128
Ellen 240
Emma 242
Francis 240
Frank 240
Hal. 242
Hal M. 209
Helen 242
Hugh 242
J. D. 240
John 209

Rose (cont.)
  Mary Ruth 242
  Oscar 142
  Rachel 242
  Robert 240
  Roscoe 242
  Susan 242
  William 240
Ross, Helen 259
  John 308
  Mary Lawson 259
  Nanny 85
  W. Cary 259
  William Cary 259
Roth, John 67
Rothe, Annie 67
  John 63, 65
  Samuel 66
Rothi, John 66
Rouder, Perina 79
Rouff, James F. 49
Row, Elijah 110
  Solomon 118
Rowan, Eliza Latham 289
Rowden, Abraham 104
  Ekale 80
  Mishac 87
  Susan 80
Rowlette, Robert A. 211
Rozier, Frank 150
  Sylvester 150
Rule, Elmer 285
  Fay 285
  Shelly 285
Rummage, George 251
Runger, Robert L. 292
Runym, (Miss) 276
Rushing,_____ 135
Russell, Alexander 79
  Elendor 105
  Frank 277
  G. P. 277
  Hamilton 245
  Henry H. 268
  Henry Hawley 268
  James 105
  John L. 233
  Lula 252
  Margaret 233, 245
  Mathew D. 120
  Moses 264
  Rosanna Gillespie 233
  Savilla H. 125
  Thelma 283
  Thomas 277

-S-

Saffell, (Col.) R. M. 36
Saffold, (Judge) B. F. 154
  Burney 154
  Ida 154
  Marion 154
  Ray J. 154
  Roy 154
St. John, Frank 237
  Frank Love 237
  George W. 138
  Julia Love 237
  Louise Avery 237
Sanborn, Elizabeth 265
  Eugene E. 253
Sappington, Jonah 150
Saren, (Capt.) Jacob 290
Saunders, Pansy 134
Sauterland,_____ 192

Sawords, William 104
Sawrie, Idella 163
Sawyer,_____ 192
  Eleanor 211
  Larkin 84
  Robert Cravens 166
  William J. 166
Scales, Elizabeth 137
  Mary Ann 50
Scarborough, James 127
  Prudence 122
Scarbrough, Eliza 123
Scarbury, John 22
  Robert 23
Schaad, Robert A. 285
Schaff, Carl 150
  Caroline 150
  Cecelia 150
  Edward 150, 151
  Louis 150
  Mary 150
  Walter 150
Schard, Clarisa 50
  John 51
  (Mrs.) Sarah 50, 51
Schrimper, Fate 240
Scott,_____ 296
  Alexander 15
  Fletcher F. 37
  James 21
  Jane 93
  Julian 62
  Nancy 119
  William 21, 109
  Wilma E. 172
  (Gen.) Wingfield 176
Seaver, Fannie 139
  William 139
  William F. 139
Seilay, Victor 245
Seinknecht, Christina M. 49
Seinknicht, Robert 66
Selbe, John 95
Self, Daniel 76
  Henry 76
  Levi 76
Sellers, Isaac 100
  Micah 99, 100
  Micaja 14
  Micale H. 125
  Michael 95
  Nancy 262
Seltz, Anna 117
Selvey, Susan 109
  Thomas 23
Selvidge, Jane 103
  M. K. 114
Senknicht, Catherine 63, 65
Senter (see also Center)
Senter, Abner 33, 282
  Albert N. 282
  Anita 283
  Ann Eliza 282
  Carl Lee 283
  Carrie A. 282
  (Mrs.) Carson 282
  Clinton Dewitt 282
  Dewitt 282
  Dora (Smith) 283
  Frances 282
  Harriett 282
  Harriett T. 282
  John F. 282
  Leland R. 283
  Lester Treadway 283
  Lucinda 282
  Marcus 282
  Mary Eliza 282

Milton 31
Minerva 282
Nancy 282
Nicholas 282
P. M. 282
Rebecca 282
Rice 282
Seaborn 282
Susan Sarah 282
Tandy 29, 31, 32, 158, 282
Thomas N. 282, 283
Thomas Smith 283
W. S. 62
William 282
William Robert 282
William T. 282
Serrill, Bessie 196
Sevier, Alice 284
  Ann Elizabeth 284
  Anna Bernice 284
  Annie E. 49
  Charles 50, 64, 284
  Charles Bascom 284
  Charles Henry 284
  Charlie 66, 67
  Elbert Franklin 284
  Elbert G. 191
  Elbridge Gerry 149, 284
  Eldbridge G. 42
  Eldridge G. 108
  Elizabeth 284
  Ethel 284
  Evelyn 284
  H. C. 62
  Hazel 284
  Hazel Madeline 284
  Helen May 284
  Henry 62
  Henry Clay 284
  Herbert Eugene 284
  James 12, 23, 44c, 44d, 50, 284
  Jean 284
  John 228
  (Gen.) John 9, 11, 284
  John Woodrow 284
  Madeline 284
  Margaret 257
  Mary 284
  Mary C. 49
  Mary Elizabeth 284
  Mary Katherine 284
  Nancy 228
  Oscar 284
  Parker 284
  Robert E. 284
  Robert Earl 284
  Robert Fields 284
  Roberta Ann 284
  Rowena Jane 284
  Roy 284
  Samuel Conway 284
  Stella 284
  Taylor 284
  Thomas 49
  Thomas Brown 284
  Thos. B. 62
  William James 284
Seward, Henry 14
Sewell, Maud 148
  Nancy 257
Sexton, Sally 90, 180
  William 104
Shackelford, William 125
  Zachariah 120
Shadden, Alma 295
  Annie 294
  Ernest B. 294

Shadden (cont.)
  Ernest B. (Jr.) 294
  Florence 295
  Joseph A. 294
  Joseph C. 294, 295
  Joseph J. 294
  Mary 294
  Mary E. 294
  Sarah Jane 293
  Spencer 295
  Susan 168
  Vaden C. 294
  William N. 294
Shaddon, Robert 16
  Suckey 73
Shadwick, Joseph 109
  Rebecca 102
Shaefer, A. K. 80
  Abraham 80
Shafer, Abraham 77
Shahan, Patty 107
Shaifer, Abner G. 78
Shallings, Lela 256
Shamhart, Edison 37
  Wilmer H. 217
Shanks, Henry 152
  Margaret 152
Shannon, Maria 179
Sharkey, Betsy 73
Sharp, Alice Neilson 185, 186
  Beamy 108
  E. Frank 186
  Elizabeth 185, 186
  Ellen 185, 186
  J. P. 186
  John 30
  John A. 124
  John Cessna 185, 186
  L. Japheth 185
  Margaret 96, 185, 186
  Margaret Jaspheth 186
  Nellie Gillespie 186
  Polly 90
Shaw, David 91
  John Sherman 167
  (Mrs.) Mollie 193
  Omy 122
Sheets, Charlie 273
Shell, Lucinda 112
Shelley, Jacob 32, 165
  James T. 12, 246
  (Maj.) James T. 35
  Oscar 287
  Thomas 20
  Will 44d
Shelly, Carlyle 285
  Ethel 285
  Fay 285
  George M. 285
  George McElwee 285
  Grace D. 285
  Hazel 285
  J. Osgood 285
  Jacob D. 285
  Jacob Oscar 285
  James Hyatt 285
  James Thomas 285
  Jane Ann 285
  Jean 285
  Jennie Weaver 285
  Larla 285
  Martha Elizabeth 285
  Mary Lelia 285
  Oliver F. 285
  Oscar Barnette 285
  Robbie 285
  Robert Craven(s) 285
  Robert Long 285
  Robert Tunsford 285
  Roy C. 285
  Ruby 285
  Thomas 13
  Tully 285
  Tully (Jr.) 285
  William Bays 285
  William Carlyle 285
Shelton, Clement Clay 250
  George Mason 250
  Roberta Guelph Cross 250
Shepherd, Louisa 73
Sherald, William 17
Sherard, Jesse 76
  Martha 76
Sherky, John 15
Sherold, William 22
Sherrel, Adam 16
Sherrill, Elizabeth 109
  Raymond 37
Shields, Anna 174
  Arnold 20
  Benjamin 84
  J. Harrison 174
  John 90, 123
  Milton 231
  Robert 20
Shillings, George 195
Shinn, Levine 151
Shnall, Isaac 15
Shoemaker, Clinton 164
  Elizabeth 164
  Evan 16
  M. H. 164
  Richarl 164
  Robert 164
  William 16
Short, Alex Christopher 273
  Buck 273
  Charlotte 273
  Diana 216
  Edom 216
  Elias 216
  Eliza 273
  Elizabeth 273
  Frances 273
  Franklin 216
  George 273
  Jackson 216
  James 273
  Jasper 216
  John 216
  Joseph 273
  Julius 216
  Laura 216
  Margaret 216
  Matilda 93
  Melthenia 216
  Miller 273
  Miller Parks 273
  Patty 78
  Ralph 38
  Rebecca 273
  Robert 273
  Samuel 216
  Sarah 273
  Standifer 216
  Wash 273
  William 216
  Willis 214, 216
Shorts, ___ 43
Shoy, Thomas 16
Shualt, Isaac 77
Shye, Thomas 15
Side, Samuel 97
Sienknecht, Adele Elizabeth 286
  Augusta Charlotte 286
(Dr.) Charles Christian 286, 287
Christina H. 286
Christine 286
Daisy 286
Elmer Charles 286
Florence 286
Frederica Christine 286
Frederick 286
(Dr.) Frederick 286
Hannah 286
(Dr.) Henry Christian Ludwig 286
Henry Edward 286
Jackson Oliver 286
James Theodore 286
Joseph Augustus 286
Louie Christian 286
Lula Jane 287
Margaret 287
Mary Katherine 286
Mary Lila 287
Nettie 286
Sarah Augusta 286
Theodore Adolphus 286
Theodore F. 286
Wilhelmin/e Katherine 286, 287
William Henry 287
Willie Henrietta 286
Siezer, J. B. 146
Sigman, Ella 252
  Harrison 252
Siler, Edgar 140
  Edgar Allen 140
  Edwina 140
  Florence 238
  Margaret Virginia 238
  Mary 298
Silvey, Laura 196
  Rial 115
  Samuel 21
  William 21, 121
Simmonds, Sarah 137
Simmons, Fannie 75
  Reuben 16
Simpson, ___ 298
  Campbell 121
  Margaret 278
  Richard 127
  Roy 213
Sims, C. D. 250
  George 107
  (Capt.) Gray 9, 16
  Littlepage 78
  Mathem 22
Sisco, R. T. 195
Sisson, Horace 253
Skeens, Edward 38
Skeins, Eva 266
Slaughter, ___ 280
  Clarence 190
  Rosalie 166
Sloane, William 94
Small, Alma Ray 225
  Chloe Rector 224
  Clarence 225
  Effie Lee (Plemons) 225
  Ella Jane 225
  George Washington 50
  James Thomas 225
  Lora Louise 225
  Mary 47, 50
  (Mrs.) Mary 50
  Mary Kendrick 224
  Patsy 47
  Pearl Ada 224
  Samuel 224

Small (cont.)
Samuel H. 225
Thomas Edward 225
Thomas H. 224
Viola (Newman) 225
Wilma Sue 225
Smalley, Samuel 62
Smallman, Frederick 186
Smartt, James Preston 288
Smith,_____ 14, 193
  Alexander 273
  Alice 178
  Alma 223
  Amanda 48
  Ann 113
  Anthony 32, 291
  Arthur 68
  Benjamin(e) F. 59, 204
  Betty Jean 270
  Caroline 288
  Caroline P. 62, 237
  Correy 307
  Curtis 38
  Curtis E. 36, 37
  Daniel 290
  Dora 282
  Edna 268
  Edward 19
  Elbert Doran 255, 290
  Eliza Brooks 267
  Elizabeth 85, 156, 237, 288
  Elizabeth Boyers 255
  Elza James 270
  Ervin James 291
  Eva 239
  Ezekial Jackson 255, 290
  Ezekiel Lafayette 290
  Fedelia 291
  (Col.) Francis 288
  George 288
  George W. 120
  George Washington 288
  Grace E. 250
  Granville Payne 288
  (Mrs.) H. B. 49
  Henry 62
  Hezekiah 112
  Hugh Craig 185
  Isaac 119
  J. B. 301
  J. T. 61
  J. Y. 12
  Jacob 30, 31, 290
  Jacqueline 290
  James Coleman 203
  James Edward 291
  James Montgomery 255
  James P. 37
  Jane 107
  (Rev.) Jno. Y. 43
  John 15, 82, 116, 217, 237, 273, 291
  (Maj.) John 42, 45
  John Ashby 288
  John E. 38
  John Y. 60, 62, 307
  (Rev.) John Y. 236
  John Young 288
  Joseph 273
  Joshiah 59
  Kate Prudence 152
  Laura 237
  Laura Frances 255, 290
  Laura Waightstill 288
  Letitia 288
  Lucile 270
  Lucretia 86, 171
  Lula 240

Lydia B. 49
M. 57
M. P. 62
Maggie Ellen 265, 266
Mamie 292
Margaret 189, 273
Maria 288
Martha 290
Martha Brown 303
Mary 93, 288
Mary Abigail 268
Mary Ann Clark 288
Mary Edna 291
Mary Susan 208
Mary M. 281
Meriwether 9, 15, 17, 23, 54, 57
Merriweather 288, 289
Merriweather (Jr.) 288
Merriwether P. 236, 237
Miller Mary 273
Nancy 97, 214
Penelope 296
Polly 189
Rachel 90
Ralph 120
Rebecca 308
Robert 273
Robert Ashford 255, 290
Rubin 15
Sallie 208
Sallie/y Josephine 288
Sally (Payne) 289
Samuel 288
Samuel H. 49, 61
Samuel Hall 275, 288
Sarah 75, 82, 193, 281
Sarah Ann 111
Sarah Elizabeth 290
Sarah P. 49, 62
Stephen 33
Susan 288
Susannah Payne 288
Sydney R. 189
Thomas 288
Thomas Basil 185
Thomas Jefferson 288
Tressie 273
Virginia Louise 185
Waightstill Avery 237
Wiley Corry 255
Wiley W. 255
William 265, 273, 288, 291
(Gen.) William 296
William E. 62
William Lenoir 236
William Payne 288
William Wiley 290
Willie Caroline 255, 290
Wm. L. 62
Smith T., John 9, 10, 13, 14
Smithy, John 117
Sneed, Allen 15
Snodgrass, Peggy 110
Snow, Dudley 116
  Ebenezer 29
  Eliza 111
  Elizabeth 298
  George 298
  James P. 298
  Jesse Clyde 271
  John W. 298
  Louise 139
  Mary (Owings) 271
  Polly 91, 114, 192
  Rachel 139
  Sarah 298
  Savannah 298

Tennessee 298
Texas 298
William 298
William C. 271
Willie 271
Solomon, Agnes 105
  Jessey 22
  Joel 22
  Nancy 121
Sorrell, Mattie 232
  Ruth 232
Souke, Amanda 48
Soward, Henry 106, 113
Spaggins,_____ 230
Spann, Betty Jean 266
  E. E. 266
  E. E. (Jr.) 266
Spark, Samuel P. 159
Sparks, Rachel 135
  Rosa Arabella 208
Spears, Grace Kendrick 223
Speed, Jennie Ewing 259
Spence, Elizabeth 94, 242
  L. Jack 295
  Thomas 96, 110, 118
Spencer, Elizabeth Wallis 51
  Jacob 51
Spind, Polly 108
Spivey, George B. 153
Spoon, Sarah 180
Spooner, (Mrs.) 48
  Jacob 58, 59
  Jacob K. 48, 59
Stafford, Thomas 16, 76
Stallcup, Lorena Elizabeth 180
Stanchell,_____ 216
Standfield, S. D. 13
Standifer, (Capt.) James 32
  William 16
Stanfield,_____ 159
Stansberry, Andrew 102
Staple,_____ 42
Staples, Abner 91, 292
  Anna 292
  Annie 292
  Benjamin Tolliver 292
  Eliza 292
  Ella 292
  John 30, 292
  John M. 62, 91, 292
  Joseph 292
  Katherine 292
  Kitty 139
  Malinda 292
  Malinda Davis 292
  Mary 139, 292
  Melinda 292
  Samuel 292
  Susan 292
  Thomas 292
  Walter 292
  William 292
  Wm. 62
Starks, Betsy 87
Starnes, Nicholas 17
Staton, Polly 100
Staunton, Lula Maud 151
Stean, Nancy 86
Stearns, Mary Ann 242
Steele, (Mrs.) 49
  Amanda 297
  James 20
  (Mr.) William 51
  (Mrs.) William 51
  William M. 49
  William Richard 51
Steels, Lucy 110
Steens, Nicholas 18

346

Stegall, Charles 304
Clifford 38
Steinwehr, Charlie 66
Steinwher, Charles 63, 65
Mary 63, 65, 66
Stennett, Mahaley Jane 126
Stephens, Caroline 255
George 79, 89
Mary Agnes 151
Philip 88
Phillip 89
(Rev.) Rufus 43
Sally 162
Stephenson, (Mrs.) 47
Alice 48
Ariel 166
James 111
Jas. 62
John 49
Sterling, John 14, 15
Sterns, George 19
Stevens,_____ 189
Meshea 20
Stevenson, Anna 242
Elizabeth 247
Steward, Pauling Shriver 186
Stewart, Alexander 19
C. W. 213
Charlie 170
David 18
Mary Eleanor 123
Sandal 170
Stigler, R. A. 184
Stiles, Ethel Gordon 167
George Gordon 167
Penelope Elise 167
Stillman, Austin F. 261
Francis Hill 261
Stocker,_____ 150
Charles 150
Stockton, Davis 15
Thomas 97, 100, 103, 105, 107, 108, 112
Willis 17
Stokes, Amanda 195
Stone, Barton W. 45
Elizabeth 145
James 145
John 9, 14, 15
Malinda 145
Minerva 303
Sarah 74
Stonecipher, Carrie 252
Peggy 79
Rose 252
Thomas 252
Vesta 252
Stoner, Jefferson 116
Stose, John 13
Stout, Abner 14
Abraham 85
Frederick 186
George W. 122
Joseph 19
Moses 98
Nancy 90
Robert 95, 115
Ruth 81
Samuel 80, 87
Stow, Elizabeth 143
Solomon 112
Stowe, Catherine 211
Elizabeth 211
Lucinda (Ingram) 211
Savannah 211
Van Nann 208, 211
Stowers, Egbert B. 169
Helen B. 169

Strang, Frances Thornton 186
John Cessna 186
Samuel Bartow 186
Strange, Joseph 128
Street, Anthony 14, 15
Elizabeth 142
Strickfuss, Florence 172
Strickland, Joseph B. 23
Stripling, Walter B. 38
Strong,_____ 188
Augustus 73
(Dr.) Joseph 261
Mary 261
Maston 21
Stuart, David 17
Stubbs,_____ 95
Jesse 17, 22
John 107
Stubs, Jesse 16
Sturges, E. C. 65, 66
J. M. 66
James 304
John M. 63
Wentley 106
Sturgess, James 12
Sturgis, John M. 65
Sublette, Zoe 239
Sudath, Evelyn 159
Frank S. 159
John 159
Margaret 159
Milton Graves 159
Nancy 159
Stephen B. 159
Suddath, Charles 190
Frank 190
J. L. 145
S. L. 62
William 190
Suddeath, Melton 22
S. B. 23
Suddoth, Benjamin 29
Sullens, Josiah 118
Nathan 16
Sullins, Josiah 20
Joseph 19, 20
Nathan 30
Sullivan, Mathew 59
Sulte, Katherine 186
Summers, Betsy 139
Leona 196
Riley 252
Robert L. 252
Sumter, A. T. 22
Elizabeth 264
Louis M. 117
William 264
Suttle, Mary Ann 117
Sutton, Betsy 101, 113
Jane 80
John 17
Louis 113
William 101
Swafford, Jesse Brown 186
Jesse Lucille 186
Samuel Perry 186
Swalm, Helen 146
Swan, Margaret 258
Samuel 93, 165, 246
Virginia 184
Swann,_____ 280
Swiger, Richard 19

-T-

Tadloçk, Barbara Ann 286
Tait, Mary 154
Talbot, Nancy 85
Vance 181
Talboy, Elizabeth 284
Talbut, Eli 14
Taliferro, Betsy 117
Tallent, William 172
Talliafero, C. D. 62
Samuel 297
Tankersley, Henry C. 37
Tannehill, Wilkins 44a, 44b
Tarver, Elizabeth 149
Mary Little 146
Tarwater, Bardon Absalom 223
Cora Ellen 223
Dorothy 223
Dorothy Spearman 223
Edward A. 269
Ida Catherine 269
James F. 223
James Fletcher 269
James Lawrence 223
James Polk 223
John Kendrick 223
Madge 189
Madge Cornelia 223
Martha 223
Maud Catherine 223
Mildred Rebecca 223
Nellie Jane 223
Penelope Maud 223
Polk 223
Reba Ann 223
Rebecca Josephine 223
Rebecca (Kendrick) 223
Sarah Caroline (Robbs) 269
Thomas William 223
Thomas William (Jr.) 223
William Frank 269
William H. 269
William Polk 223
Tate, Rebecca 114
Tauchton, Hazel 220
Tausher, Dora 197, 198
Taylor,_____ 100
Allen Davis 152
Arthur Jarrett 152
Arthur Jarrett (Jr.) 152
Arthur Robert 153
Bettie 145, 284
Christopher C. 37
Clasky 149
D. G. 62
Elise 152
Elizabeth 178
Emily 152
Etheldred 149
Ethelridge 99
Ethereld 83
Evelyn 184
Frances Eva 152
Franklin 178
Fred A. 37
(Rev.) Grimsfield 178
James 111
James Fleming 178
Jane 106
Jean 178
Jincy 149
John 113, 149
John H. 13
Joseph 178

Taylor (cont.)
  Kinchen 149
  (Mrs.) Lena 193
  Leonard Henderson 152
  Lois 152
  Martha Henderson 152
  Mary Elizabeth 178
  Mary Emmet 153
  Mary Frances 153
  Nancy 178, 295
  Nancy Susanna 178
  Nathaniel 30
  Nena 153
  Peggy 78
  Polly 149
  Rebecca 149
  Rebecca Brown 149
  Robert 147, 149
  Sarah 149
  Starnes Treadwell 153
  Virginia 178
  William 149
  William Vonnah 5th 152
  (Dr.) Wm. Vonnah 2nd 152
  Wm. Vonnah 3rd 152
  Wm. Vonnah 4th 152
Teague, Edareth (Jr.) 285
  Edareth Edward 285
  Seth Woodrow 285
  Shelley 285
Tedder,_____ 44
  Addie Florence 294
  Alonzo 195
  Annie (Campbell) 293, 294
  B. A. 168
  Bessie 168
  Bruce 295
  Charles 295
  Charles Richard 294
  Charles Thomas 208, 293, 294
  Charlotte June 294
  Clifford 294
  Della 295
  Edith 295
  Elisha Ingram 294
  Elizabeth 195
  Ella Blain 168
  Ethna Madge 293
  Eugene Spencer 293, 294
  Florence (Koger) 293
  George 295
  George W. 295
  Hazel 294
  Hilda Rose 294
  James 98, 293
  James P. 22
  Janice 295
  John 42, 43, 94, 114, 168, 294
  John Brown 293, 294
  John Vaden/Vadden 208, 293, 294
  Joseph 195
  Joseph Clyde 293, 294
  Kenneth Allen 294
  Maria L. 295
  Martha Jane 293
  Mary 294
  Minerva 293
  Myrtle Marie 275
  Nancy 92
  Nellie Gray 293
  Nora (Hill) 294
  Pleasant 295
  Ralph 295
  Ray 295
  Robert Gideon 230, 293, 294

Robert L. 293
Robert LaRue 294
Rush W. 37
Sadie E. 294
Sallie M. 293
Sarah 294
Sarah J. (Shadden) 293, 294
Sarah Louise 294
Spencer J. 293
Sue 295
Thomas 293
Thomas C. 294
Veneta 294
Will 168
William A. 22
William Rush 293
William Wiley 293
Tener, Jake 298
Terrill, Elizabeth 163
Terry, John C. 122
  Martha 241
Thacker, Benjamin 29
  John 83
Thalkill, Betsy 108
Tharkill, James 22
Thigpen, Jane Randolph 306
  Kathryn 306
  Sally 306
  William J. 306
Thomas, David 20, 83
  Hugh M. 212
  Jacob S. 258
  James 15, 17
  John 16, 85, 92
  John Martin 238
  Joseph D. 238
  Kitty 92
  (Mrs.) L. L. 194
  Litton 300
  William 79
Thomasson, Elizabeth 166
  Elma 226
  Ema 226
  Eugene 185
  Eugene Barnard 226
  Eugene Morgan 226
  Joseph 226
  (Maj.) L. L. 42, 43
  Lemuel 226
  Leona 226
  Margaret 226
  Mary Kimbrough 226
  William K. 226
Thomison, Clara 187
  Maud 187
  Walter Agnew 187
  (Dr.) Walter F. 186, 187
Thompson, Alfred 116
  Atwell 165
  Dyke 203
  Elsie 142
  Gladys 304
  James 77
  John 20
  Joseph 84
  Joseph E. 204
  Laura 203
  Lillie May 203
  Margaret Minerva 203
  Nancy 77
  (Lieut.) Robert H. 37
  Robert William 203
  Samuel 125
  Waddy 100, 111
  William A. 120
Thornton, Robert 118
Thorpe, (Mrs.) Jane Blount 170
Thouston, C. M. 78

Thrailkill, Elizabeth 127
  Kezziah 127
  Polly 127
Thrasher, Jacob 20
Tifton, Thomas Jefferson 213
Tillery, Parmelia 183
  Robert H. 142
Tindell, Tilla 230
Tiner, Lewis 13, 15
Tippet, Absey 85
Tipton, Mary J. 284
  Mollie 63, 65
Todd, A. Lafayette 151, 153
  Agnes Loretta 153
  Elizabeth 98, 153, 293
  Howard Allison 153
  James 10, 17
  John Silas 153
  Lafayette 153
  Nancy 100
  Samuel 128
  William Brady 153
Tolbert, Sarah 119
Tomlinson,_____ 161
Tommason,_____ 44
Toomey, Ambrose 91
  Elery 91
  Ellery 292
Toomy, William 16
Tooten, Beatrice 209
Tootle, Harry 229
  Lillian 229
  Mary 229
  Milton 229
Tower, Jacob 121
  (Rev.) William 43
Towers, Dellia 124
  George 124
Tracy, Mabel 223
Treadwell, Timmons Lewis 153
Treece, Samuel 256
Trevitte, Mary 282
Trice, Betsy 246
Trigg, (Judge) Connelly 261
  Elizabeth 257
  Rachel F. 261
Trimble, Andrew 160
  Eliza 160, 161
  James 10, 12, 29, 78, 160, 161
  John 160, 161
  (Capt.) John 32
  Letitia C. 161
  Louisa 160, 161
  Mary Ann 160, 161
  Susan 160, 161
  Thomas 160, 161
Trimby, Vera 167
Trotter, William 273
Troutt, (Mr.) 46
Trowers, Edna 147
Tucker, (Mrs.) 50
  Adonifale 50
  (Mrs.) Ann 47, 50
  Easter 47
  Esther 47
  Fannie 47
  Frances 250
  James Sloan 47
  Jane 47
  Mary Ellender 47
  Otis 47
  Rebecca 47
  Samuel 47, 88
Tunnel, Emeline 205
  William 204, 205
Tunnell, Keziah 114, 204, 205

Tunnell, Lettice 119
Tunmins, Polly 78
　Samuel 78
Turnbull, Ann 180
Turner, Albert 303
　Christopher 303
　Daniel M. 303
　Elisha 14, 107, 121, 124, 126
　Elizabeth 303
　Ervin B. 38
　Fay Marie 270
　(Dr.) Henry Alva 250
　Jackson Clarence 270
　John 303
　John A. 266, 269, 270
　John L. 303
　Loyd 211
　Margaret Alice 211
　Margaret S. 303
　Nathan 96
　Nathaniel B. 303
　Rachel Denny 303
　Robbie Elener 270
　Thomas 303
　Thomas Myer 270
　Vicey 119
　William 303
Turpin, David 126
Tuten, Sarah 101
　Susan 127
　Wiley 77, 82, 115
Tuton, Wiley 128
Tutterow, Balser 173
　Frank 172
　(Mrs.) Lissie 194
Tuttle, Absolom 124
　Wyley 60
Tyler, Peter 107
　Sally 100
Tyrtll, William 13
Tyson, Jones 154

-U-

Umphris, John 126
Underwood,＿＿＿ 273
　Alice 267
　Amanda 266
　Artelia 266
　Campbell 266
　Carrie 267
　Elvira 120, 306
　Ernest 38
　Ethalenda 126
　Frederick 266
　James Polk 266
　Jonathan 100
　Narcissus 252
　Nimrod 23
　Sarah 267
　Thomas 267
　William 123, 267
Underwool, Betsy 188
Upshaw, Della 139
　Etheleen 149
　Peter 88
Upton, Thomas 75
Usury, Phillip 16
　Thomas 16
Utley, Jacob 110

-V-

Valance, William 17
Valle, Catherine 147
Vance, Patrick 38
　Samuel 97
　(Gen.) Samuel 242
　Sarah 242
Vanderbilt, Cornelius (Jr.) 240
Vanderson, J. H. 288
Vanderverr, Rachel 242
Van Dyke, Alexander Outlaw 296
　Eliza Rhea 296
　Jefferson Campbell 296
　Mary Houston 296
　(Dr.) Thomas J. 13, 31, 57
　Thomas James 296
　Thomas Nixon 296
Van Leer, Carlos Clark 163
　John 163
　Samuel 163
Vann, Annie 209
　Dennis 122
　George 209, 210
　Ida 209
　John 122, 210
　(Mrs.) Kate 194
　Lucinda (Ingram) 210
Van Pelt,＿＿＿ 273
Vaughn, Celia 86
　Hugh 246
　James 246
　(Gen.) John C. 246
　Mary 246
　Nancy 89, 164
　William 246
Vaugn, George 77
Vermillion, (Mr.) 46
Vickey, Chryleena 91
Vincent, John 92
Voigt, Laura 185
Voiles, Levi 122
Von Aldehoff, Florence Carolina 284
Von Alderhoff, Henry W. 60, 284
Von Steinwehr (see also Steinwehr)
　Alice H. 287
　Annie C. 287
　Charlie Frederick 287
　Lizzie M. 287
　Mary C. 287
　Oscar 287
　Oscar Benno Carl 287
Vorhees, Frank 236
　Frederick 236
　James 236

-W-

Waddel, Mary 245
Waddell, May 284
Waddy, Samuel 14, 78
Wadkins, Abraham 33
Wadly, John 17
Wagner, Adelaide/Adeline 231, 232
　Caroline 231, 232
　Charles 231, 232
　Edith 232
　Hugh 231
　James 231, 232
　Julia 231, 232
　Kathleen 232
　King 231, 232
　Martha King 232
　Noah J. 231
　Paul 232
　Richard 232
Wagoner, T. H. 166
Wainwright, Mary 247
Wakefield,＿＿＿ 174
Walker,＿＿＿ 97, 167
　(Mr.) 48
　Audley P. 97
　B. F. 54
　Barbara 47
　Betsy 47
　Buckner 113
　Catherine 47
　Catherine O. 47
　D. R. 270
　Eama 74
　Edly P. 47
　Elizabeth 47
　Elizabeth C. 196
　Elizabeth M. 47
　Ephriam 16, 73
　(Capt.) James 15
　James B. 47
　James C. 47
　Jane 47
　Jane Patterson 308
　John 46, 47, 74
　(Capt.) John 9, 15, 16, 20, 28
　John Blackburn 47
　John M. 47
　(Mrs.) Margaret 47
　Margaret L. 47
　Mary 47
　Nancy R. Aberthrot 47
　Nettie 146
　Sally 73
　Samuel 46, 47
　(Capt.) Samuel 28, 31, 42, 308
　Samuel R. 47
　Suckie 79
　Susan 47
　Theopheles 47
　Thomas 16, 18, 73
　Wesley 16
　Wiley 81
　William 10, 73
　Zachariah J. 47
Wallace, Amanda 197
　Campbell 160, 261
　John 48, 104
　Mary 261
　Oliver 48, 50
　Olliver 47
　(Mrs.) Olliver 47
　(Miss) Pollie 48
　Ruth 47
　Sally 48
　(Mrs.) Thankful 48
　Washington Wade 50
Waller, Amanda Savannah 297
　America 298
　Anna W. 297
　Annie Winton 298
　Carr 297, 298
　Carr M. 297
　Columbus 298
　Edmond 298
　Edmund 297

349

Waller (cont.)
Edward 13, 74
Eliza 298
Eliza W. 297
Elizabeth Anne 297
Elizabeth E. 297, 298
Franklin 298
George 13, 297, 298
George (Jr.) 297
George P. 298
Hardin 298
Henry 297, 298
Henry A. 297
J. L. 297
Jacob C. 298
James 298
Jane 298
Jesse M. 298
John 297, 298
John B. 297
John P. 298
Lewis 298
Louis E. 298
Louis J. 298
M. B. 298
Manly B. 298
Margaret 298
Martha A. 298
Martha C. 297
Mary 297, 298
Mary (Barksdale) 298
Mary Jane 297
Mary K. 298
Matilda 298
Nancy D. 298
P. A. 297
Robert 298
S. A. 298
S. E. 298
Sarah 297, 298
Sarah K. 297
Texas J. 298
Thomas J. 298
William 22, 17, 297, 298
Wallis, (Capt.) 17
John 51
William 51
Walters, Noel S. 186
Walton, Susan 161
(Capt.) William 41
Wann, William 304
Ward, (Col.) Andrew 261
Jane 107
John D. 38
Lucy 285
Nicholas 112
Samuel 19
Warner, Florence 189
Warrell, Lillian Dee 237
Warren, Edward 86, 93, 95
Jacob 10, 100
James 81
John 17
(Gen.) Joseph E. 228
Warwick, Edward A. 285
Washburn, Hester Modena 280
Joshua 15
Washington, (Gen.) 292
Wasson, Martha Burkett 206
Waten, Jesse 94
Water, Christopher Columbus 50
(Mrs.) Polly 50
Waterfield, Charles 219
Waterhouse, Caroline 186
James 169
James Franklin 169
Waterman, Cora 293

Waters, Abner 83
Beren 236
Julia 151
(Mrs.) Polly 48
Richard 151
Watkins, Arthur 185, 247
Arthur James 270
Lewis Parkins 270
Watson, A. H. 245
Jacob 20
Laura 168
Leander 117
Mary 274
Nathan 110
Watt, James M. 75
Richard 126
Watts, William 227
Wear, Deborah S. 234
John 13, 15
Malvina 234
Robert 234
Samuel 234
Weatherford, Walter Clyde 203
Webb, Levisy 105
Lucy 116
Webber, John 33
Weber, Ada 150
Alvin 209, 210
Catherine 210
John 150
Joseph 150
Julia (Ingram) 210
Nellie 150
Sarah 150
Weece, Abraham 121
Wees, Peter 29
Weese, Nancy 117
Polly 108
Samuel 124
William 106, 117, 124
William S. 117
Weir, Andrew 85
Mary 85
William Lee 218
Weiss, Rebecca 135
Sarah 105
Welch, (Dr.) 139
Welcher/Welcker, (Dr.) 62
Wm. 62
Welcker, Adair 300
Albert 301
Albert Galatin 299, 300
Annette 300
Belle 300
Benjamin Franklin 299-301
Caroline Virginia (Mitchell) 299
Catherine Freeling 235, 299
Charles Freeling 299
D. 62
Daisy 300, 301
Dewitt 62
Dewitt Clinton 299
Dixie 301
Elizabeth 299, 300
Ellen Virginia 300
Frederick Augustus 299
Frederick William 301
Fredericka Texana 300
George Lewis 299, 301
Henrietta 300
Henry 301
Henry Inman 299
Henry Ish 301
James Dewitt 301
James H. 301
James Henry 299, 300, 301
James Monroe 299

John Henry 299
Katherine 300
Katie Adair 300
Malinda (Mitchell) 299
Margaret Elizabeth 299
Mary 300
Mary Jane McDowell 299
Mendell 300
Nancy White 300
Sarah Caroline 299
W. L. 44d
William Charles Joseph 300
William Lewis 299, 300
William Thomas 299, 300
Welhite, Isaac 115
Wells, Elizabeth 143
Lucile 199
Ludy 109
Margaret 199
Margaret Middleton 139
Pearl 199
Roy 198
West, Buena V. 146
Edith 263
Elizabeth 219
George R. 166
Jane 122
Jesse 95
John 87, 122
Katherine Jane 223
Lyle B. 166
Mariah 124, 306
Nancy 113
Nannie 303
Nicholas 87
Patsy 96
Peggy 109
Polly 94
Westbrook, Amanda 114
Wester, Addie 231
Adelaide Victoria 302, 303
Alice 222, 302
Amanda J. 124
Anna 66, 68
Anna Maud 249
Annie Maud 302, 303
Carroll B. 302
Catherine 302
Catherine Ann 302
Charles 304
Charles W. 302
Christopher Columbus 302-304
Cornelia 304
Daniel 32, 34, 242, 302-304
Daniel Loyd 302-304
Earl 304
Edith G. 302, 303
Edith May 302
Elizabeth/Lizzie Gates 304
Elizabeth Jane 302, 304
Elizabeth (Loyd) 303, 304
Elmer 302
Ephriam Foster 302
Francis Asbury 302, 304
Fulgum 302
George W. (Jr.) 303
George Washington 302, 303
Grady 302
Henry J. 304
James 302-304
James A. 302
James M. 222
James Marshall 304
John 34, 302
John C. 304
John Fulgum 302
John M. 302-304
John W. 304

350

Wester (cont.)
  (Dr.) John W. 11, 134
  John Wesly/Wesley 302
  (Dr.) John Wesley 148
  Josephine Maria 304
  Josephine Mariah 302
  Julinda (Claiborn) 304
  Katie 303
  Lewis Marshall 34, 302-304
  Lillian 304
  Loyd 304
  Lucile 304
  Maggie 63, 65, 66, 68
  Margaret 303, 304
  Margaret Hamilton 302, 303
  Margaret Louisa 302, 304
  Martha 304
  Marvin 302
  Mary 303
  Mary Breedlove 304
  Mary (Brown) 302
  Mary Josephine 222
  Mary Kate 304
  May 63-66, 68
  Minerva Marion 302, 303
  Paul 302
  Rachel 62, 303-305
  Rachel Arabell 304
  Rachel Loyd 302, 303
  Samuel Daniel 303, 304
  Sarah 241, 303
  Sarah Brown 302
  Sarah (Hamel) 304
  Thomas 304
  Thomas H. 302
  William C. 304
  William Houston 302, 303, 305
Westmorland, Ruth 97
Wheat, John 103
  Lear 109
  Levi 93, 103
Wheeler, William 246
Wheelock, _____ 246
  John S. 149
  William 149
  William Neal 149
Whitaker, Elizabeth 232
  Maud 221
White, _____ 14, 43, 44, 263
  (Rev.) 261
  Albina Mensco 89
  (Miss) Alonia Nimsco 71
  Benjamine 23
  Betsy 84
  Elizabeth 49, 109
  George 20
  Hugh 74
  I. 62
  James 241
  Jesse 10, 21
  John 16, 18, 62, 235
  Jonathan 21
  Julia A. 168
  (Miss) Kate 203, 211
  Luther 89, 109
  Moses 21
  Nancy 160, 282, 299
  Rebecca 91
  Robert 13, 19
  Samuel 16, 18
  Sarah Sturgis 298
  Thomas 33
  William 9, 28, 30, 90
  William (Jr.) 16, 18, 21
  William (Sr.) 16, 18, 20
  (Capt.) William 20, 32
Whiteside, Jenkins 20

Whiteside, Penelope 184
Whith, Eany 88
Whitlock, Samantha E. 217
  Samantha Elizabeth 217, 219
Whitson, Harold 295
  Harvey Thurman 218
  James 16
  Jean 218
  Jere B. 218
  Mary Frances 218
Whittenberg, Jane 255
Whittle, Lucy 180
Widener, Lewis 78
Wilder, (Gen.) J. T. 13
Wiley, Alexander 19
  Andrew C. 62
  Eliza J. 49
  Eliza Jane 288
  H. H. 12, 13, 61
  John 20
  Mary 49
  (Mrs.) Mary B. 49
  Thomas 21
Wilkerson, Francis H. 151
  Samuel 143
  (Lt. Col.) W. H. 36
  William 143
Wilkey, _____ 179
  Belle (Campbell) 306
  Calvin Vanburen 306
  Charlie 306
  Clyde 306
  Delia 306
  Ella 306
  Eugene B. 306
  Evans 306
  Frances Dalton 306
  Henry 19
  Hugh 306
  Kathryn 306
  Letitia 306
  Mack 306
  Maggie 306
  Martha 306
  Martin 306
  Mary 306
  Roger 124, 306
  Ruth 186
  Sally 306
  Samuel 306
  Thomas 271, 306
  Walter 306
Wilkinson, James 84
Wilkison, William 100
Willet, James 13, 75
  Sarah 75
Willett, Enoch H. 125
Willey, Alexander (Jr.) 20
  Alexander (Sr.) 20
William, (Capt.) 302
  John 20
  Thomas 20
Williams, _____ 192, 244
  (Capt.) 183
  Amelia 101
  Arthur L. 37
  Asa 63, 65, 68
  Asa Coleman 244
  Asa Coleman (Jr.) 244
  Coleman 244
  Eleanor 186
  Elisha 82
  Elizabeth 127
  Frances Jane 115, 180
  Hugh Martin 244
  James G. 91
  Jane 257

  John 126
  (Col.) John 260
  John F. 22
  Julia Martin 244
  Leola 219
  Lillie 301
  Lucinda 97
  Margaret Cornelia 186
  Margaret Lydia 136
  Martin 126
  Nancy 110
  (Mrs.) Nancy 49
  Parmelia 106, 180
  Penelope 161
  Polly 97, 118, 180
  Rebecca 263
  Richard 180
  Robert 18, 88, 116, 120
  Robert H. 186
  Robert Patten 186
  Samuel 73
  Sarah Elizabeth 244
  Thomas 280
  Tibitha 122
  Timothy Clarence 244
  William R. 271
Williamson, Elijah 91
Willis, Ann 205
  Cornelia 261
  Frances 114
Wilmot, James 115
Wilshire, Lilie 184
Wilson, _____ 144, 197
  Alice Emily 265
  C. L. 198
  Caroline 149, 186
  Charles 189
  Claud 189
  Daniel 20
  Edward Clinton 265
  Elizabeth 164, 171, 189
  Emmey 75
  Florence Woods 189
  Frances 198
  George Edward 189, 223
  Helen 156
  Henry Haley 189
  Isabelle 189
  J. W. (Sr.) 44b
  James 198
  James Charles 189, 190
  James Woods 189
  Jasper Hazen 287
  Jennie B. 156
  John 156, 189, 242
  John M. 92
  Joseph 128
  Kate 306
  Katherine 190
  Mabel 189, 204
  Mabel Claire 189, 190
  Mamie 149
  Margaret 190
  Margaret Lyon 189
  Mary 156, 189
  Mary Edna 198
  Mary Elizabeth (Kimbrough) 190
  Maud 239
  Mildred 198
  Pleasant 306
  Richard T. 212
  Robert 22, 123, 149, 156, 189, 190, 227
  Samuel 156, 164
  Violet 198, 241
  Walter 306

Wilson (cont.)
  Warren 190
  Willard Warner 189
  William 59, 98, 306
  (Dr.) William 149
  Woodrow 198
Winchester, (Brig. Gen.) James 133
Wingener, Peter 78
Winston, Ada S. 238
  Mary 275
  Nannie 50
Winter, Jacob 105
Winters, Moses 19
Winton, ___ 44
  Albert 307
  Amanda 307
  Arabella Cunningham 255
  Dollie 307
  Eliza (Browder) 307
  Frank 307
  George B. 307
  Harriet 307
  James 307
  Jefferson 307
  John 14, 17, 19, 307
  (Rev.) John 255, 289
  John A. 43, 288, 307
  John Lenoir 307
  John W. 115, 237, 307
  John Wesley 144
  Julia C. 307
  Letitia 189
  Lucretia 307
  Mary 255, 307
  Nancy 307
  Rhoda (Mitchell) 307
  Robert 307
  Rufe 307
  Stephen 307
  Susie 307
  Wiley B. 307
  William 307
Wise, Frederick E. 268
Wiseman, James 108
Witt, ___ 202
Wolf, Alexander 188
  Daniel C. 37
Wolley, Edith 302
Womack, Andrew 151
  Dorothy 151
Womble, Mollie 213
Wood, Effie Mae 279
  John 29, 74, 75
  Mathew 19, 81
  Peggy 74
Woodburn, Thomas 112
Woodridge, Sarah 205
Woods, Delilah 76
Woodson, Mattie 228
Woodward, Lelia 259
Woody, Brice 116
  Hannah 88
  Jenny 96
  John 29, 102
  Julia 116
  Rebecca 48
  Samuel 88, 99
Woolwine, Eugene G. 226
Work, Eliza 264, 271
  Fleming 62
  Jacob 75
  Jacob A. 42
  Joseph 15
  Mariah 99
  Sophia 94, 172
  William 13
Wray, John 20

Wren, Bessie 230
Wright, Clarence S. 38
  Delia 306
  Elizabeth 306
  Frank 306
  Hansel 116
  James 38
  Joel 114
  John 304
  John H. 122
  Marjory 235
  Mary 66-68
  Matilda B. 116
  Stephen 80
  Thomas 306
  (Capt.) Timothy A. 37
  Timothy Asbury 223
  Timothy Asbury (Jr.) 222, 223
  William 304
  Willie 66, 67
Wrinkle, John 101
  Margaret 108
Wrinkleman, George 305
Wroe, Catherine 48
  (Mrs.) Sarah 48
Wyatt, Dillia 126
  (Rev.) E. W. 52
  (Rev.) E. W. P. 52, 53
  Edward 29
  Hugh 210
Wyley, Sallie Ann 207
Wyrick, Susan 218, 253

-Y-

Yancy, Sarah 213
Yandall, James 118
Yandel, John 303
  John W. 303
  Sarah E. 303
  William H. 303
Yanf, Nancy S. 109
Yarnell, S. I. 278
  Samuel I. 278
Yates, Mary 204
  William 106
York, Patty 87
  Thomas 86
Yost, Adelaide 158
  Allen 62
  Allen H. 54
  Alma 158
  Catherine 303
  E. A. 44c
  Eldridge 158
  Geo. W. 44c
  George 13, 60
  (Rev.) George 54
  George Center 158
  James 158
  James C. 54
  Katherine 158
  Letitia 306
  Manson S. 54
  Margaret 54
  Sarah Elizabeth 158
Young, Caroline 276
  D. K. 279
  E. E. 12, 44c, 44d
  Elizabeth 123
  Emma Jean 289
  Frances 231
  Freemoten 60
  Isham 29
  James 64, 65

Jane 143
John 21
Julia 279
Martha 171
Patsy 242
Sarah 279
Thomas 76
William 105
Woodson 279

-Z-

Zedder, Alice 284
Zein, (Mrs.) Julia 49
Zigenfuss, Dorothy 295
J. R. 295
Zimmerman, Mattie 153
Zinderstein, Norton 256

ADDITIONS

Thompson, Absalom Pinkeny 203
Walker, Barbary M. 47
Wilkey, James 306
Wright, James Tarwater 223

www.ingramcontent.com/pod-product-compliance
Lightning Source LLC
Chambersburg PA
CBHW070011010526
44117CB00011B/1509